KB044459

English Grammar *for* **Matriductive Learners**

엄마표 영어로 인풋이 안정된 친구들을 위한 영문법

We would like to thank Editage(www.editage.co.kr) for English language editing.

이 책의 내용 전문은 원어민 감수 전문기관 Editage에 감수를 의뢰하였고, 교정된 내용을 모두 반영하였음을 알려드립니다.

엄마표 영어로 인풋이 안정된 친구들을 위한 영문법

English Grammar
Grammar
for
Matriductive
Learners

AJ(안재환) 지음

seosawon

Foreword

Stop studying English and start acquiring it!

영문법, 어디까지 해야 하나? 영문법을 꼼꼼히 배워야만 영어습득이 완성되는 것일까?

2018년 2월에 출간된 『엄마표 영어 이제 시작합니다』는 초등학교 1학년에 처음 영어를 만난 아이가 **그림책부터 고전까지 8년간의 원서읽기를 통해 영어습득 완성을 확인한 경험을 풀어놓은 책이다.** 이 책에 영문법에 대한 언급은 이 두 문장이 전부다. 언급할 무엇이 없었기 때문이다. 원서를 읽고 원음의 영상을 즐겨보는 것 이외 이렇다 할 학습 경험이 없었다. 영문법까지도 깊이 만나지 못하고 영어를 모국어로 쓰는 나라의 대학에 입학하게 되었다. 그런데 끊임없이 글을 써서 제출해야 했던 에세이나 리포트, 프레젠테이션에서 문법적 오류를 지적 받는 일은 거의 없었다. 유학 1년 차 어느 즈음부터는 막연함이 아니라 정확한 오류의 이유까지도 문법적으로 설명 가능했다. 신기하지 않은가? 모든 시간을 지켜봤던 엄마는 신기했다.

엄마표 영어교육 8년 동안 '과연 이것이 옳은 방법일까?' 의심하게 되는 **일반적이지 않은** 선택들이 많았다. 일반적이지 않다는 것은 시대적 트렌드로 자리잡은 방향이나 경향들과 달랐다는 의미다. 흔들리면서도 부러지지 않고 영어 완성의 끝을 보고 나니 '옳은 선택이었다!' 확인된 것들, 그 또한 적지 않다는 것이 흥미롭다. Phonics가 그랬고 Sight Words가 그랬고 연따나 음독이 그랬고 기타 등등이 그랬다. 실천 방법에 있어 그 무엇도 정답이 있어 맞다 틀리다 이분법으로 나눌 수 없다. 각자의 선택에 확신을 갖고 최선을 다한다면 내 아이에게 맞는 적절한 '해답'이었구나 그런 느낌표는 만나진다. 그래서 '제대로' 엄마표 영어는 쉽지 않지만 근사하고 매력 있는 길이다.

기타 등등의 하나에 영문법이 있다. 여기에서 영문법은 중고등학교 내신 또는 여타 다른 시험의 문제 출제를 위한 영문법을 말하는 것이 아니다. 혼자만의 느낌표였다면 위험하거나 무모한 선동이겠지만 오랜 소통은 긍정적 데이터를 넘어 또 하나의 확신으로 이어졌다. **엄마표 영어를 하는 친구들에게 최고의 약점으로 보이기도 하지만 최고의 강점이 영문법이다.** 좋은 책에 담긴 좋은 문장을 또래의 사고에 맞게 꾸준히 읽으며 초등학교 고학년에 이른 친구들이라면 별도로 떼어서 학습하지 않아도 자연스럽게 체득되는 것이 문법이기 때문이다. 수년간 매일매일 원서를 읽고 원음의 영상을 즐기다 보면 그 속에서 보고, 듣고, 읽어왔던 문장들 안에서 반복해서 만나지는 문법적 요소들에 자연스럽게 익숙해진다. 의식하지 않아도 **오류에 대한 부자연스러움을 눈치채고 피할 수 있게 된다.**

"문법적 설명은 불가능해도 문법에 오류가 있는 문장은 쉽게 알아차린다." 엄마표 영어로 앞서간 선배들이 전

해주었던 이 문장을 공감을 넘어 경험으로 확인했다. 같은 경험으로 같은 확인을 하고 있는 친구들이 늘어가고 있다. '좋은 책(원서)'을 강조하는 이유는 무엇 때문일까? 되는대로 아무 책이나 영어로 쓰여진 책이면 되는 일은 아니기 때문이다. '초등학교 고학년에 리더스북이나 초급 챕터북을 읽을 수 있다.' 이 정도 수준에서는 **바라기 힘든 눈치다.**

아이의 영어교육이 좋은 성적을 위한 '학습'이 목표가 아니어야 했다. **영어로부터 완벽한 자유를 위한 '습득'이** 목표였다. 가르치기보다는 더디더라도 아이 스스로 익혀 나가는 길을 선택했다. 하지만 그럴 수 있는 방법을 공교육에서도 사교육에서도 찾을 수 없었다. 그래서 선택한 것이 엄마표 영어였다. 과정은 모국어에 익숙해지는 것과 다르지 않았다. 이런 익히는 시간의 꾸준함을 놓치지 않는다면 우리말로 말을 하고 글을 쓸 때 문법적 어색함을 스스로 눈치채듯이 그런 어색함을 피할 바탕을 다질 수 있다 믿었다.

연령만큼 영어 자체 사고력 향상을 위해 **'해마다 또래에 맞게 리딩레벨을 업그레이드'하는** 진행이었다. 아이의 흥미와 사고에 맞는 영어책 이해가 우리말 책과 다름없이 편안해지기까지 만 3년이 걸렸다. 4학년에 북레벨 4점대 이상의 단행본 소설을 읽기 시작하며 아이가 읽을 책을 고르는데 각별히 마음을 썼다. 좋은 어휘, 좋은 문장, 좋은 주제를 담은 책과 함께한다면 문법적 요소가 잘 녹아져 있는 정확하고 좋은 문장들, 그리고 그 구조들에 익숙해질 수 있을 거라는 기대에서였다. 5학년 이후 '문학성'을 선정의 핵심 요건으로 삼는 Newbery 수상작에 집중했던 이유이기도 하다.

가르치려 하면 할수록 습득하기 어려운 것이 언어이며, 문법은 문법책으로 이해하기가 가장 어렵다는 것을 우리 세대는 뼈아프게 경험했다. 원서 학습서가 되었든 우리말로 된 학습서가 되었든 서둘러 영문법을 '공부'하는 것을 권하지 않는다. 모국어와 마찬가지로 영어 또한 꾸준히 책을 읽는다면 기본적인 문법들은 자연스럽게 체득된다. 하지만 그 자연스러운 체득으로는 한계가 있다. "자연스럽지 않은 것이 틀린 문장이더라." 이 막연함이 통하는 것은 가벼운 소통에서다. 만일 가벼운 의사소통 정도가 아이 영어 교육의 최종 목표였다면 굳이 영문법을 고민하지는 않았을 것 같다.

언어 습득이 완성에 가까워 자신의 의사를 설득력 있게 말이나 글로 표현해야 하는 시기, 그때는 체득된 문법에 더해 어기지 말아야 규칙, 그 규칙의 살짝 벗어남으로 인한 파워 있는 전달력까지 보다 분명하게 알아야 할 것들을 알고 있어야 한다. 그러니 문법을 공부하지 않아도 되는 것은 아니다. 때가 되면 공부해야 하는 것이 문법이다. 하지만 그때가 언어를 배우고 익히는 시기는 아니다. 해당 언어를 소통의 '도구'로 써먹을 수 있는 시작 어디쯤, 그때가 적기라 생각했다.

이 정도의 바탕을 먼저 두텁게 해놓고 좋은 어휘와 구조, 정확한 문법 등으로 아름다운 문장을 엮어 나간 깊이 있는 **책들을 꾸준히 읽고**, 더불어 **생각을 쏟아내는 글 또한 꾸준히 쓰다** 보면 모국어처럼 편해진 언어에 대한 문법 또한 안정되지 않을까? 그럴 수 있다 생각했는데 그럴 수 있구나 확인된 것이다.

영어, 잘하고 싶다면 읽어라!

우리의 경험을 나누는 소통 8년 차가 되었다. 여타의 외부 도움 없이 『엄마표 영어 이제 시작합니다』 책 한 권을 붙들고 오로지 이 길에서 원하는 목표를 달성하고 '엄마표 영어 졸업'을 선언한 친구가 등장할 정도의 시간이 흘렀다. 그 졸업의 소회가 남달랐던 한 친구는 습득된 영어로 **모든 학습적 경험의 '주언어'가 영어가 되었다.** 영어를 영어답게 써먹는 중이다. 그것도 국내에서. 원어민 수업? 영어캠프? 1~2년 조기유학? 이런저런 잠깐의 경험이 아니다. 앞으로 지속적으로 이어 나갈 모든 학습적 경험에 주언어가 영어가 될 수 있기까지, 즉 **지식을 습득하고 사고를 확장해 나가는 '도구'**로 평생을 곁에 두고 편히 써먹을 수 있는 언어로 모국어 이외 영어가 더해지기까지 얼마나 걸렸을까? 이 길에서 '초등 6년의 전력질주', 어정쩡하게 흘려보낼 수 없는 그 시기에 대한 공감이 컸던 엄마이고 아이였다.

코로나로 인해 세계적으로 온라인 강연이 활발해지면서 영어가 편한 친구들은, 선생님도 함께 수업하는 친구들도 모두 원어민으로 글로벌하게 만날 수 있는 온라인 교육 프로그램들이 폭발적으로 늘었다. 아이들 **교육에 있어서는 세계가 하나 된 세상이** 이미 우리 일상에 깊이 들어와 있다. 경계도 한계도 없이 지식 습득과 사고 확장을 영어로도 마음껏 누릴 수 있게 되었다. 정상적인 자연스러운 변화로 도래된 것인지 세계적으로 전염병이 대유행하는 Pandemic 상황으로 인해 그 속도를 가속화시킨 것인지 그건 중요하지 않다. 그런 세상이 낯설지 않고 그런 변화된 세상을 마음껏 누리기 위해 내 아이가 든든하게 무장하고 있어야 하는 것이 무엇이어야 하는지 중요한 것은 그것이다.

영어교육의 방향을 학습이 아니라 습득으로 잡고 이 길에서 애쓰고 있는 친구들이 많아졌다는 것은 반가운 일이다. 수년 동안의 꾸준한 원서읽기로 **영어라는 언어를 '도구'로 사용할 수 있겠다 기대될 정도의** 친구들이 늘어가고 있다. 그렇게 터를 잘 다져 나가고 있는 친구들을 만나는 행운은 Newbery Book Club(NBC)을 진행하면서였다. NBC 기획은 오랜 독자들의 하소연이 시작이었다. 수년간 채워진 인풋으로 고학년에 들어서며 굳이 의도하지 않아도 새어 나오는 아웃풋 조짐이 반가웠지만 채워진 만큼을 Speaking과 Writing으로 적절히 발현시키고 다져줄 수 있는 외부 도움을 찾기 어렵다 했다. 의외였다. 대형 어학원부터 사설학원, 공부방, 개인 과외까지 영어 습득을 돕는 외부 도움이 차고 넘치는 세상인데?

원하는 방향은 분명했다. 그런데 도움받을 수 있는 선생님을 가까이에서 찾을 수 없었고 함께하면 시너지가 높을 비슷한 또래의 비슷한 실력을 가진 친구들은 더 찾기 어렵다는 하소연은 이해도 되고 공감도 되었다. **원하는 방향은 기존 사교육 시장에서 흔히 볼 수 있는 모습이 아니었다.** 새로운 커리큘럼을 준비해야 한다. 선생님 입장에서는 만만치 않은 시간 투자가 필요하다. 하지만 잘 만들어 놓은 커리큘럼이라 하더라도 가까이에서 이 정도 수준의 수업을 함께할 친구들을 그룹화하기가 쉽지 않다. 선생님이 실력이 없어서가 아니다. 굳이 그럴 필요가 없어서 하지 않는 수업이니, 찾기 힘든 수업인 거다.

코로나로 인한 대면강연 불가로 Zoom 소통이 활발해지며 유사한 고민을 하고 있는 이웃들에게 도움될 수 있는 기획이 떠올랐다. 이동 부담이 없다면 수업을 이끌어줄 안성맞춤 선생님도 생각났다. 전국 단위 모집이 가능하니 비슷한 또래, 비슷한 수준의 그룹화가 용이할 것 같았다. 커리큘럼을 완성하고 참가 희망자를 모집했다. 수업에 대해 자세히 설명하고 아이의 동의를 받는 것이 우선이라 못박았다. 그럼에도 불구하고 엄마의 욕심이 전부인 신청도 일부 있었다. 그런 신청을 제외한다 해도 아웃풋 발현이 기대되는 탄탄한 인풋을 채워 놓은 친구들이 많다는 것을 확인하며 놀랍고 반가웠다. 대전을 비롯해서 서울 경기 쪽은 물론이고 부산, 거제, 포항, 경주, 김해, 광주, 속초 등등. 그야말로 전국구 신청에 일부 바다 건너 타국에 계신 분들도 보였다. 온라인 수업의 장점이었다. 기수가 이어질수록 참가 희망 경쟁은 치열해졌다.

일주일에 한번 아이들과 90분은 특별했다. 단순 질문에 단순한 답을 채워 나가며 무언가를 기억하기 위한 시간이 아니었다. 같은 책을 읽은 또래들과 함께 책을 읽고 갖게 된 각자의 생각을 말로 풀어놓는데 선생님은 교통정리만 해주면 되었다. 우리말로 하라 해도 쉽지 않은 수업인데 우리말 못하는 English Only Class다. **억지로라도 집어넣을 수 있는 인풋 수업이 아니다. 채워진 만큼 끄집어 내는 아웃풋 발현 유도 수업이다.** 사고력이 바탕이 되지 않는 아웃풋은 금방 바닥이 드러나게 되어 있는데 선정한 책들은 북레벨도 주제도 만만치 않은 뉴베리 수상작들이다. 일주일에 한 권씩, 한 기수에 24권을 함께한다.

이리 멋진 이야기가 담긴 책들을 학습을 위한 교재로 사용하고 싶지 않았다. 한 권의 책을 소화하는데 여러 날이 필요한 친구들이 아니었다. 모국어가 아닌 언어로 쓰여진, 좋은 책으로 공식 인정받은, 상당한 난이도의 책을 **'원문 그대로' 글쓴이가 전하고자 하는 것을 받아들이고 이해하고 공감할 수 있는 친구들이다.** 그래서 매주 새로운 책으로 함께하는 것이 가능했던 것이다.

NBC 1기 수료증

영어 수준은 이미 엄마를 능가했으니 답지도 없는 Before Class 준비도 After Class 과제도 오로지 혼자 힘으로 해결해야 하는데 수업 형식도 과제도 피드백도 낯설기만 한 쉽지 않은 수업이었다. 그런데 힘들어도 놓고 싶지 않은 이 수업의 매력이 무엇이었을까? 말을 물가로 끌고 갈 수는 있어도 물을 억지로 마시게 할 수는 없고, 놀아보라 멍석을 깔아주어도 멍석 위에서 주인공이 되어 놀 것인지 멍석 주위에서 구경꾼이 될 것인지 누구도 등 떠밀 수 없다는데 어디에 맑은 물이 있는지 알려주면 뚜벅뚜벅 자기 걸음으로 걸어가 시원하게 들이킬 준비가 된 아이들이 NBC 친구들이었다.

NBC를 기획하며 아웃풋 발현도 이 방법이 옳다는 확인을 하게 된다면 이 길에서 확인하고 싶은 마지막 파트 English Grammar_English Only Class를 욕심 부려보겠다 했었다. 어머님들 또한 영어 습득의 마지막 단계라 할 수 있는 문법에 대한 고민은 깊었다. 특히나 중학교에 진학을 했거나 진학을 앞두고 있는 고학년들이니 학교 교육에 맞는 영문법 준비를 가벼이 여길 수 없는 시기였다. 때가 되면 시험을 위한 영문법 학습도 필요한 교육제도이니까. 그렇다고 **지난 노력과의 괴리감이 너무 큰 접근을** 그저 타협하고 받아들이는 것도 쉽지 않았다. 가지고 있는 영어 실력이 그러기에는 아쉬움이 많은 친구들이었다.

고민을 나누고 의견을 수렴하고 몇 개월을 리서치하며 NBC 친구들을 위한 마무리, 문법 수업 방향을 잡아봤다. 완성된 커리큘럼은 처음에 내가 생각했던 것과 많이 달랐다. 그저 '영문법을 영어로'라는 생각만 했지 이 정도 내공의 친구들에게 진짜 필요한 영문법이 무엇인지 감도 잡지 못했던 것이다. 생각에 발전이 없는 옛날 사람임을 반성했다. 장기간 아이들과 직접 함께했던 NBC 선생님은 나누는 대화에서, 제출 받은 Writing 과제에서 문법에 대해 공부해본 적 없는 친구들이지만 영문법 기본 규칙들이 올바르게 쓰여지고 있음이 확인되었다 한다. 본인도 영문법을 누구에게 배워본 기억이나 스스로 깊이 학습해본 적 없지만 **원문의 글을 많이 읽고 많이 쓰면서 자연스럽게 체득된 것이 문법이라** 생각했는데 그런 모습이 NBC 친구들에게 보였던 것이다.

이런 친구들에게 필요한 영문법은 어떤 것일까 고민해봤다. 시험문제에서 틀린 영문법을 골라내기 위해 배우는 문법은 아니었다. 그런 도움을 위한 영문법 학습서는 원서도 한국어 버전도 단계별로 너무 많이 나와 있다. 유튜브 강연도 넘쳐난다. 인터넷은 그 모든 것을 품고 있다. 언제든 검색하면 원하는 데이터를 참고할 수 있다. 그래서 수업 방향은 영어로 좋은 글을 쓰기 위해 반드시 알아야 하는 문법들 다져놓기였다.

다양한 타깃으로 영문법 책이 나오고 관련 웹페이지들은 넘쳐나는데 **책**을 읽으며 영어 실력을 성장시켜온 친구들에게 도움이 될 만한 **정리된 원문의 텍스트가** 보이지 않았다. 상당히 많은 문법책을 살펴보았지만 NBC 친구들의 문법수업에 적절한 책을 찾기 어려웠다. 결국 교재 없이 수업이 진행되었고 3개월 과정으로 마무리되었다. 한번의 수업으로 영문법이 정리되는 것은 아니라는 것을 알았지만 터무니없이 짧은 시간이었다. 매주 수업을 녹화해서 복습 가능하도록 제공했지만 두고두고 참고할 수 있는 주요 내용이 정리된 텍스트가 없다는 것이 못내 아쉬웠다. NBC 선생님께 수업 내용 모두를 텍스트로 정리해줄 것을 요청했다. 이 책의 시작이다.

글을 잘 쓰고 싶다면 먼저 좋은 글을 많이 읽어야 한다. 꾸준한 원서 읽기는 영어 습득을 위한 방법으로 대세를 넘어 가장 빠르고 옳은 길이라는 것이 입증되고 있다. 뉴베리 수상 작품이 원서로도 편안한 친구들은 더 높은 수준의 영어 완성을 위해 **힘있는 글을 쓸 수 있을 정도의 좋은 터를 다져 놓았다 할 수 있다.** 기본적인 영문법 또한 이미 숙달되어 있다. 이제는 많은 글을 써볼 때가 되었다. 자신이 쓰는 글에 부자연스러움을 줄이고 보다 힘있는 글을 쓰기 위한 연습이다. 진짜 문법 공부가 필요한 때가 된 것이다. 좋은 글이 되기 위해 지켜야 하는 규칙들, 어기지 말아야 할 주의사항, 전달력 좋은 함축적 어휘 활용 등 보다 멋진 글을 쓸 수 있는데 도움 되는 것들을 **한 권의 이야기 책을 읽듯이** 편하게 만나주었으면 하는 기대로 이 책을 엮게 되었다.

미리 밝혀둔다. 이 책은 영문법을 누구에게 배워본 경험도 없고, 학습서를 가지고 스스로 깊이 있게 공부해본 경험도 없는 사람이 정리한 글이다. 더 유의해야 하는 것은 시험을 위한 문법 교육이 주를 이루는 대한민국의 중고등학교 학교 교육에 속했던 경험도 없는 사람이다. 뿐만 아니라 영어를 포함해서 다른 학과목에서도 일반적인 사교육과 거리가 많이 멀었던 학창 시절이었고 NBC 시작 전까지 누군가를 가르치는 일도 낯설었던 사람이다. 해서 학교 문법시험을 위해 도움되기를 원한다면 피해야 하는 책이다. **원문의 텍스트가 편안할 친구들에게 말을 걸듯 구어체로 쓰였지만** 일정 수준, 적어도 북레벨 5점대 원서 읽기가 편안하지 않다면 전문이 원문으로 쓰여진 것 또한 부담일 수 있다.

지금 이 책이 필요하고 도움되는 친구들은 대한민국에서 영어 습득을 위해 일반적이지 않은 선택을 한 소수일지도 모른다. 하지만 머지않아 이 책이 도움되는 친구들은 점점 늘어갈 것이다. 영어 습득에 있어 "Why?"라는 질문의 답으로 "The limits of my language mean the limits of my world." 이 문장에 대한 공감이 깊은 이들은 그 **한계를 무너뜨리기 위한 방법, "How?"**가 무엇인지 모르지 않으니까.

2004년에 출간된 스티븐 크라센(Stephen D. Krashen)의 저서 『The Power of Reading: Insights from the Research』가 2013년 『크라센의 읽기 혁명』이라는 번역서로 국내에 등장하며 제목답게 부모들에게 혁명에 가까운 파장을 불러왔다. 읽기는 언어를 배우는 최상의 방법이며 **읽기 외에 언어를 배우는 다른 방법은 거의 효과가 없다**는 결론을 분명히 하는 저자는 영문법에 대해 이렇게 언급했다.

"The study of complex grammatical constructions does not help reading (or writing); rather, mastery of complex grammar is a result of reading. With enough reading, good grammar, good spelling, and good style will be part of them, absorbed or acquired effortlessly."
(복잡한 문법 구조에 대한 학습은 읽기나 쓰기에 도움이 되지 않는다. 오히려 복잡한 문법을 숙달하는 것은 읽기를 통해 가능하다. 충분한 독서로 문법, 철자법, 문체를 노력하지 않고도 습득할 수 있다).

크라센의 연구 결과가 세상에 등장하기도 전이었던 2002년 행운처럼 영어 습득을 위한 옳은 길이 무엇인지 알게 되었다. 그리고 8년의 노력으로 그 길이 진짜 옳은 길임을 경험으로 확인했다. 이웃 아이들의 성장에서 20년이 지난 지금도 옳은 길임이 증명되고 있다. 읽기 이외 언어를 습득하는 더 좋은 방법이 등장할 수 있다. 읽기 이외 영문법에 익숙해지는 더 효과적인 방법이 등장할 수도 있다. 그런 것들이 대다수의 동의를 얻고 많은 이들의 경험으로 확인되기까지 얼마나 걸릴까? **지금 곁에 있는 내 아이를 위해 기다려도 좋을 시간인지 헤아려보자.**

소통의 창구를 활짝 열어 놓은 지 8년이 되었다. 아이의 영어 첫 시작이 **[누리보듬식] 엄마표 영어였다고** 전해 주는 독자들에게 무거운 책임을 느낀다. 주시는 어떤 글에도 같이 고민하고 도움이 되었으면 하는 생각을 전하는 것을 소홀히 하지 않는 이유다. 7세 또는 8세에 한 페이지 한 줄 문장의 동화 보기로 영어를 처음 시작한 친구들이 고학년이 되었고 세계적으로 인정받은 소설들을 원문 그대로 읽으며 감동받고 있다. 이제 이 친구들은 지식을 습득하고 사고를 확장해 나가는 언어로 모국어뿐만 아니라 영어도 도구로 사용할 수 있게 되었다. **그 도구가 날카로운 쓰임이 될 수 있도록 잘 다듬어 가는 마지막 단계가 영문법이다.** 이 책이 그런 연마에 작게라도 도움이 되기를 바란다.

마지막으로 이 길을 선택함에 많이 불안했을 시작, 그리고 수많은 시행착오에 마음 흔들렸을 초기 단계를 현명히 넘기며 아이들 영어 성장에 있어 안정을 넘어 완성의 단계까지 리드했을 엄마들에게 경의를 표하고 위로와 축하도 함께 전하고 싶다.

2022년 5월
누리보듬

Preface

Benjamin Franklin once said, "Diligence is the mother of good luck." What he probably meant was to work hard and eventually luck will find its way. However, the exact opposite happens more often in life—good luck comes to you first, and *then* you realize you have been preparing for it your entire life.

If someone had told me a few years back that I'd be running one of the most desired English classes in Korea, I'd have probably laughed it off. Even now, to have students line up and take interviews to join my class feels unreal. And, to be requested to teach English grammar when I've never had proper grammar education myself—I mean, that's ridiculous, isn't it? But now, having taught English for over a year, I realize that I've *always* been preparing for this—this is the *fruit* of my journey through the English language.

Back when I was in elementary school, the plague of private English education was blossoming in Korea. With the continuing reign of English as the *lingua franca* since the 18th century, English had already become a mandatory subject in Korean schools long before I entered one. However, there was one problem: English (and any other language, for that matter) is too broad of a topic to master at school. Therefore, as I entered elementary school, private institutes offering supplementary English education began appearing left and right. By the time I progressed to second grade, most of my classmates were already enrolled in these private institutes. However, my mother did not approve of their teaching methods—these institutes only focused on perfecting their students' ability to provide the correct answer to English exam questions. My mother regarded this type of education absolutely unacceptable for the acquisition of *any* language. Hence, she decided to employ her own plans to help me conquer English. And now, almost fifteen years later, I am the product of my mother's pioneering research and application of what's called, the "*Matriductive*[1] *Way*" of learning English: an approach of acquiring English at home wherein *the mother* is heavily involved in the planning, the acting, and the instructing of the child.

The crux of the *Matriductive Way* is to expose the child to luscious English literature and speech. Even as a little child, a plethora of ostensibly appealing starter tools for English was available in Korea (e.g., workbooks about phonetics and phonology). However, my mother had a strong disapproval toward these materials—she considered them too technical and unnecessarily complicated. She instead handed me *English books* and *videos*. At the age of eight, I picked up my first English book, and throughout my later elementary school years, I ploughed through countless English children's novels (mostly Newbery-awarded and -nominated books). After I graduated elementary school, I found myself enjoying more sophisticated "classic" English novels, such as *Brave New World, 1984, The Invisible Man,* and *A Tale of Two cities.* At the same time, my go-to leisure activity was watching English shows and movies on the Disney Channel and Nickelodeon.

An astral crossing of lucks sent me to Australia and placed me in an undergraduate course at the

---

1 A word that I've created and used in this book to refer to the particular method of learning English explained in text. *Matri-* = mother; *-duc-* = to lead

age of sixteen. Let me repeat: I got admitted into a university in an English-speaking country at sixteen. Moreover, my performance there was exceptional—enough to earn me a seat in the Vice Chancellor's Merit List. All this gave my mother enough confidence to spare her knowledge of the *Matriductive Way* in the form of a book. A surprising number of Korean parents were inspired by it, and they decided to apply the strategy on their children. Several years later, I came to the pleasant realization that countless Korean children were following the same process whereby I learned English.

Then, just about a year ago, I was offered to lead some of these children in a book club—I was given a chance to discuss Newbery books with Korean students who have been following the *Matriductive Way*. The premise was this: children who've practiced the *Matriductive Way* have never had a chance to *speak* in English. Furthermore, they've never had a chance to test their English skills within a *class setting*. And what better class to run with these children than a *book club*? (Recall that the core of the *Matriductive Way* is to expose children to various forms of English media, including *books*.)

The only problem was this: I had neither taught nor had been taught English before. However, my worry soon disappeared when I was handed the Newbery books the parents wanted me to discuss. They were the exact books I read while growing up—I was delighted to see them again! In hindsight, of course they would be the same books. The Newbery Medal has been being annually awarded to the "most distinguished contribution to American literature for children" by the American Library Association for *over a hundred years*. Even after decades, the Newbery-awarded books would remain as great picks for children. Books never change; only the reader does.

Reading the books again, I realized that I *did change*. Unlike when I was a kid, I could comprehend the books more thoroughly—I could understand their lessons; I could read between the lines. The more I read the books, the better idea I got on how to run the class. And the more I read the books, the more I wanted to discuss their messages.

In the end, I decided to set the focus of my class on those *messages* the books were trying to send. In other words, I decided to place more emphasis on the *ideas* the books contained, rather than their respective plots. I didn't want to turn my class into a memory game of remembering little details from the story. Instead, I wanted to guide the students to the lessons the books were trying to give, the ideas they were trying to convey, and the messages they were trying to deliver. After I had a clear idea of what I wanted to do, I accepted the offer and started preparing for the class.

Thus, the "Newbery Book Club" was born—one book a class, one class a week, twenty-four books in total (i.e., six months total). Having marked its first anniversary not too long ago, I've already had the honor to lead countless students within the book club. And now, students line up to take interviews just to have a chance at entering my class—how profound! Every class was memorable, every student improved their English substantially, and most importantly, we formed a strong bond. To see the students mature in their thoughts under my instruction flooded me with unique emotions that I *know* I won't be able to experience in any other way.

The students' advancements in their English skills and their thoughts were clearly witnessed through their *writing homework*—for each book, I presented the students with a question closely related to the main theme of the book. When I received their homework, I was surprised by two things: the level of their thought and the level of their writing. Especially, I was taken away by their *exceptional grammar*. Remember: these were the children who had been studying English like me—they had never had any proper grammar education before. For them to bear such high levels of grammar was truly eccentric.

This got me thinking. How do they have such good grammar? How do *I* have good grammar? Then I realized: reading numerous great writings automatically *grants* you grammatical skills! Repeated exposure to great examples of English writing unconsciously instills you with a respectable level of grammar. However, my students still needed help—they were still novice English users, and they made countless grammatical errors in their writings. And while I improved on grammar by fixing mistakes on my own, I didn't want them to go through the same painful process.

Therefore, I started to think about how I could help them with their grammar. Unfortunately, the English grammar classes Korean public schools and private institutes offered were *not* good starting places. Their lessons were merely aimed at perfecting the students' ability to select the correct (or the incorrect) grammar in exam question settings. This is *not* what I wanted to teach my students. This kind of information is already widely available on the internet—whenever my students are confused with a piece of grammar, they can always consult Google. I wanted to teach them how to *upgrade* their writings; how to make them *more opulent*; how to make them *more powerful*.

After careful consideration, I decided to teach my students the English grammar techniques required to *write excellence*; I decided to teach them the techniques required to *communicate brilliance*. To do so, one must first encounter numerous other excellent writings and observe countless other brilliant communications (my students already have this part covered, as you can tell by now). Next, one must know how to use sophisticated grammatical techniques. These are not the kind of techniques provided in the books that teach you how to pick the correct option in English tests. These are the techniques that allow you to *persuade*, to *entertain*, and to *enchant* others with your writing.

This book holds lots of those divine grammatical techniques. This book will not only teach you the basics of English grammar but will also guide you on how to create powerful, immersive writings. I've dissolved all my sixteen years of English experience plus the knowledge from various materials into this single book. Regardless of your personal English experience, I am confident that you'll find parts of this book (if not the entirety) eye-opening and entertaining.

Yet, I consider the biggest selling point of this book as my approach of introducing and explaining each topic. In catering this book to my students (and to make grammar at least a little interesting), I decided to tell you a *story* of why each piece of grammar is important. For each topic, I present a *tale* that sheds light on *why* you need to learn the topic and *where* you can apply it in real life. The entire book is written like this *Preface*! I hope you can enjoy this book just like a novel. Imagine as if you're reading a long story about English grammar. I bet you'll find this book more fun and informative than a lot of the other grammar books out there.

- AJ

Contents

The Journey Begins

grammar: the rules by which words change their form and are combined into sentences

1.1 Words of Greetings

Hello to everybody who's decided to open this book! My name is AJ, and this is my sincerest attempt at making English grammar at least a bit palatable. As an unchained soul myself, one of my greatest fears is learning to follow a new set of rules. And it particularly irritates me if the set of rules involved is a stupid one. Unfortunately, I can say with confidence that English grammar is indeed stupid. And I hate it for that.

What makes me say that English grammar is stupid? Let me break it down. As I said, English grammar is a set of rules. More specifically, this set of rules is a how-to guide for arranging and modifying words based on their usage. Now, let's take a step back and think about "rules" in general. What distinguishes a good set of rules from a not so good set? When it comes to sets of rules, quality is determined by degree of completeness. In turn, completeness is determined by the number of exceptions included in the set; the more exceptions a set of rules has, the less complete it is and the lower its quality. And I can guarantee that you'll be bombarded with exceptions while learning English grammar.

By now, you'll probably have two questions in mind: 1) "Why do I have to learn English grammar if it's so stupid?" and 2) "Why does English grammar have so many exceptions?" First question first. What's another set of rules that you are already following in your life? Something that you may not even realize that you're already following? Why, of course, your national constitution! What would happen if we didn't have a constitution to follow? Well, we would likely be living in complete chaos! The constitution is what keeps the people (us) in line, what directs us to behave properly. Without it, some people would act however they wanted to, which could result in absolute anarchy. Now let's get back to English grammar. First of all, English is a language, which means that it is a form of communication. What would happen if everybody spoke English however they wanted to? Communication would be nearly impossible! We need a set of rules or instructions on how to use English so that two people (who know those rules) can speak English harmoniously with one another.

Okay, time to address the second question: Why does English grammar have so many exceptions? Well, to understand that, we must discuss the history of the English language.

1.2 The History of English (in Brief)

Have you ever thought about how the English language came to be? It has gone through lots of changes since its first appearance. As with most languages, there's no clear-cut moment that English began. But it is believed that the language first surfaced when the Germanic tribes invaded Britain in the 5th century AD. The Germanic tribes, consisting of the Angles, the Saxons, the Jutes, and the Frisians, had migrated from places we now call northwest Germany, southern Denmark, and the Netherlands. They spoke what we now call "Old English." Even though Old English looks and sounds very different from the English we use now, our Modern English takes about half of its words from Old English, including "be," "strong," and "water."

In come the Normans. In 1066, England was invaded by William the Conqueror, the Duke of Normandy. William, then ruler of the Duchy of Normandy (now northwestern France), led an army of Normans to England, and seized victory over the Anglo-Saxon inhabitants. With their migration to England, the Normans imported the roots of Modern French. Following this conquest, Old English started receiving French words and grammar. As the Normans took over Britain, French became the language of the Royal Court, as well as the language of the ruling classes. There was also a moment of linguistic class division throughout this time, during which the upper class spoke French, and the lower class spoke English. Nevertheless, as Britain entered the 14th century, English remerged as the dominant language.

We now move on to the 16th century, wherein two important events happen: 1) the start of the British Empire and 2) the start of the Renaissance Era. The British Empire marks its beginning in 1497, the year John Cabot discovered Newfoundland, a large island off of the east coast of what is now the United States. Over the next five centuries, the British sailed around the world, taking colonies and extending their territory. The British Empire reached the height of its power in 1920, when it took up some 24% of the Earth's total land area and had over 400 million people under its reign. It became so large that at one point there was at least one British colony in every continent, including Antarctica. Naturally, words and grammar from various other languages—from the languages of colonized lands—were accepted into the English language during this era. Meanwhile, with the British Empire growing so big, by the start of 20th century, English had become the international language. Interestingly, English remained the *lingua franca* even after the fall of the British Empire.

Coincidentally, in Europe, the Renaissance had bloomed during this period. In particular, the English Renaissance began in the 16th century, led by great writers and architects such as William Shakespeare, Edmund Spenser, and Inigo Jones. Out of these, you probably know Shakespeare the best, as he left behind many superb pieces of literature that are still widely read today (e.g., *Hamlet, Romeo and Juliet, Macbeth*). What you perhaps didn't know (until now), however, is that Shakespeare invented over 1,700 English words that are still in use today. Wait, is it possible for an individual to make up that many words and have them included in the dictionary? Well, probably not anymore. But English was still very much evolving throughout the 16th century, and during that time, inventing your own words and using them in your writings was accepted as artistic freedom. As such, even within England, English underwent major changes during the 16th century. We refer to the English used in that period (1500-1700) as "Early Modern English," by the way.

Finally, we return to the present. The "Late Modern English" that we use today emerged around the 18th century. By that time, English had already been influenced by all kinds of different languages. However, yet another important event ends up altering the language even further and introducing more new words: the Industrial Revolution, which took place from the mid-1700s to the mid-1800s, demanded new English vocabulary and grammar to describe the new industrial processes.

And that is the basic evolution of English up to this point. That said, English is still evolving, just like any other language in the world. Especially, with the rapid development of the internet in recent ages, new words to describe this new digital world are continuously being added to the dictionary (e.g., email, website, webpage). Isn't it amazing how much history a single language can encompass? Unfortunately, what's not so amazing is that because English has received so many words and grammar rules from so many different languages throughout this evolution, it's now a hazy mash-up. And, while having more words is always awesome, having more grammar rules is not always so awesome. Accepting grammar from different languages has led to countless conflicts among grammar rules—that's why English grammar includes so many exceptions. This is, why English grammar is, again, in my honest and humble opinion, stupid!

Have you ever been to IKEA? Yes, I'm talking about the home furnishings department store. When you go to an IKEA, what do you see? That's right—you see all those nicely arranged, fully built pieces of furniture. But what do you get when you order a piece of furniture from IKEA? Is the furniture delivered to your house pre-built and ready to use? No. You usually get the <u>individual parts</u> that you put together to make a complete piece of furniture, and you get an <u>instruction manual</u>. It's your job to assemble the furniture.

If you think about it, English is very similar to IKEA. Whenever someone speaks or writes in English, what do they use? <u>Sentences</u>. A sentence is the most fundamental unit of communication in any language. In other words, when you first encounter <u>English</u> (= <u>IKEA</u>) what you see are nicely written <u>sentences</u> (= fully built pieces of <u>furniture</u>). However, English doesn't just place these fully assembled sentences at your disposal. Instead, English gives you <u>words</u> (= <u>furniture parts</u>) and <u>grammar</u> (= the <u>instruction manual</u>). You yourself must then use grammar to assemble the words in order to form sentences.

Here's the thing about IKEA instruction manuals though—some "rebels" (like me) often <u>ignore</u> these manuals because they think the furniture assembly process is self-explanatory. And truthfully, it often is. Let's say that you order a dining table from IKEA. Most likely, the pieces you'll get will include one large rectangular flat top, four legs of identical length, and a variety of bolts and nuts to hold everything together. Using nothing but common sense, you can probably figure out that one of the four table legs included must be attached to each corner of the rectangular tabletop. Using only that common sense, without any help from the instruction manual, you can probably assemble the dining table just fine. Okay, but can you apply this process to speaking and writing English? Can you skip grammar and go straight into forming sentences? Well, kind of, but that might not be the best idea. Let's discuss this a little further.

Let's take a step back and think about <u>where that "common sense" comes from</u>. How did you know that you needed to attach one of the four table legs to each corner of the rectangular table top to form a dining table? Well, it's because you've <u>already seen many dining tables</u> in your life. You know exactly what they look like, and you also know how they function. Therefore, you were able to build that dining table without using the instruction manual. Applying the same logic to English, if you've seen enough <u>sentences</u> (= <u>dining tables</u>), you can probably skip <u>grammar</u> (= the <u>instruction manual</u>) and try building your own sentence with the <u>words</u> (= the <u>parts</u>) you have. What could go wrong? Well, actually, several things.

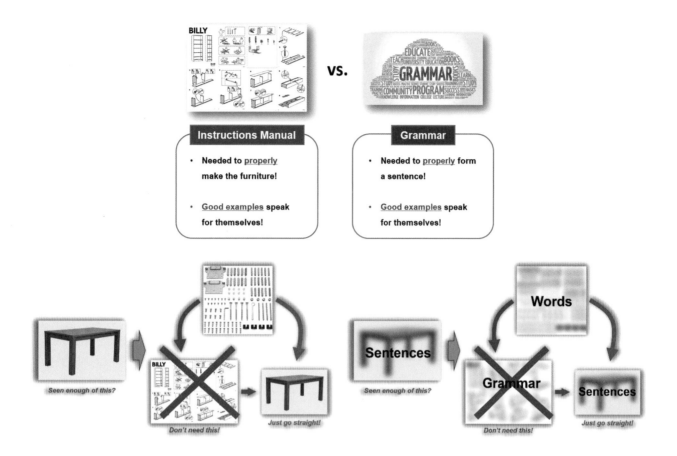

The thing is, based on the fact that you're reading this book, you're probably <u>not yet an expert</u> at making your own sentences in English. Okay, so who then are these "experts," and what do they have that we don't have? Experts are people who learn or study one particular area so that their skills and knowledge in that area are unmatched. Since their focus is so specific, they rarely make mistakes in their area of expertise, and even if they do make a mistake, they can fix it in no time. So, who are the furniture building experts? The professional carpenters specializing in making furniture. Okay, and who are the English sentences experts? The English linguists, scholars, historians, and grammarians. If you were already an English grammarian, you probably wouldn't be reading this book (and if do happen to be an English grammarian, please go easy on me; I know I don't have perfect grammar myself).

Okay, so what could happen if a non-professional furniture builder tries to assemble a piece of furniture without referring to the instruction manual? Well, for one thing, their likelihood of <u>making a mistake</u> would be high. Let's reconsider the dining table example. If a non-expert attempts to assemble the table without consulting the instruction manual, they could end up with something like the picture in the diagram below.

You might think this is ridiculous, but it could easily happen to an amateur. If a non-professional tries to do a professional job without consulting the manual, the non-professional will be <u>prone to error</u>. But do you know what's worse than a non-professional making a mistake? A non-professional <u>not knowing how to fix</u> their mistake. And do you know what's even worse than that? A non-professional <u>not even realizing</u> that they've made a mistake.

Now back to English. Like the non-professional furniture assembler, if you, a non-professional, try to assemble sentences without consulting those rules, you are <u>bound to make mistakes</u>. And as I suggested, you might <u>not even realize</u> it when you've made one. Thus, we arrive at an important conclusion: you, as a not-yet professional, should consult the rules of English grammar in order to make spotless sentences.

The reading of all good books
is like conversation
with the finest men of past centuries.

- René Descartes (1596-1650) -

CHAPTER 02

Parts of Speech

categories of words distinguished by usage, such as noun, verb, and adjective

2.1 The Furniture Pieces

Before I start detailing the English sentence <u>instruction manual</u> (<u>grammar</u>), it'll help if I go through the <u>individual pieces</u> (<u>types of words</u>) that English offers you; with these pieces, you can build your own <u>furniture</u> (<u>sentences</u>). One thing about these building blocks is that, unlike our furniture pieces, how they fit together is not so self-explanatory. In other words, it is crucial that you deeply explore all the pieces before you think about building your own furniture out of them. But, worry not, as I will guide you; I will explain how to use each piece, step by step.

English offers you <u>nine</u> main varieties of words, and they are at your disposal for making sentences. Collectively, these <u>nine</u> parts are referred to as the ***parts of speech***. The table below outlines all <u>nine</u> of them.

Parts of speech	Definition/Purpose	Examples
Noun	A "thing"—a name, object, concept, or person	cat, house, water, happiness
Pronoun	Replaces a noun to avoid repetition	he, she, it, we, they
Adjective	Describes a noun or a pronoun	tall, clever, beautiful, green
Verb	Describes an action	eat, run, sing, play, ride
Adverb	Describes verbs, adjectives, or other adverbs	easily, loudly, quite, very
Preposition	Describes the relationship between different nouns in a sentence	in, at, on, of, for
Conjunction	Joins words, phrases, or clauses	and, because, but, while
Interjection	Expresses a thought or feeling, usually in the form of an exclamation or remark; usually followed by "!"	Ah! Hey! Hi! Wow!
Determiner	Introduces & identifies a noun; puts a noun in context ☆☆ **<u>Articles: a, an, the</u>**	this, that, your, his, some, many, two, eleven

Consider the following short piece of writing.

- **The old man was sitting under a tree, patiently, but worriedly waiting for his granddaughter to arrive. She was very late for dinner. Meanwhile, the little girl was running toward home, thinking, "Oh dear! I am late for dinner!"**

This passage contains <u>all nine</u> *parts of speech*. Can you identify them all? Here's the answer.

The old man was sitting **under** a tree, patiently, **but** worriedly waiting **for** his granddaughter **to** arrive. She was very late **for** dinner. Meanwhile, **the** little girl was running toward home, thinking, **"Oh dear! I am late for dinner!"**

➤	Nouns	man, tree, granddaughter, dinner, girl, home
➤	Pronouns	she, I
➤	Adjectives	old, late, little
➤	Verbs	was, sitting, waiting, arrive, running, thinking, am
➤	Adverbs	patiently, worriedly, very, meanwhile
➤	Prepositions	under, for, to, toward
➤	Conjunctions	but
➤	Interjections	oh dear
➤	Determiners	the, a, his

Got them all? Maybe not? It's okay. This is probably your first time breaking down a sentence into its individual pieces like this. And if so, it's understandable if you find it very confusing. As I said, we'll explore each part in great detail in the upcoming chapters. I'm certain that by the end of this book you'll have a very good idea about what all the *parts of speech* entail.

2.2 Additional Context

Before we move on to actually studying the *parts of speech*, please keep the following points in mind.

- **<u>Where most critical mistakes happen</u>**: *Nouns, Pronouns, & Verbs*
  Often, if you make a grammatical error with your *nouns*, *pronouns*, or *verbs*, your <u>entire sentence ends up not making any sense</u>.

- **<u>Where mistakes happen most frequently</u>**: *Prepositions, Conjunctions, & Determiners*
  Even native speakers make <u>frequent mistakes</u> with these. Since mistakes in these areas often don't critically impact the entire sentence, they are often overlooked. However, that <u>doesn't</u> mean you should treat them carelessly.

- **<u>What you need to become a great writer</u>**: *Adjectives & Adverbs*
  These are what you need to become a <u>powerful writer</u>. However, what's even more important than usage (i.e., grammar) is <u>vocabulary</u>. You should aim to continuously add new *adjectives* and *adverbs* to your vocabulary.

Parts of Speech Exercise 01

✓ **Identify each bold word as one of the 9 parts of speech:**

1) They **attended** the concert last weekend.
2) Several cats ran **into** Bob's garage.
3) The truck driver delivered the packages **quickly**.
4) **Fast** runners won all the awards at the track meet.
5) My friends and I walked home **after** school.
6) I wanted a peanut butter **and** jelly sandwich for lunch yesterday.
7) **She** was counting the ballots during social studies class.
8) **Hey**! That's my seat!
9) Will **they** finish the test on time?
10) The **diagram** was pretty complicated for us.

Parts of Speech Exercise 02

✓ **Sort the words in the following paragraph by which part of speech they belong to:**

The world is very different now. For man holds in his mortal hands the power to abolish all forms of human poverty and all forms of human life. And yet the same revolutionary beliefs for which our forebears fought are still at issue around the globe—the belief that the rights of man come not from the generosity of the state, but from the hand of God.
(Taken from John F. Kennedy's famous "Presidential Inauguration Address.")

Today a reader, tomorrow a leader.

- Margaret Fuller (1810-1850) -

Phrases, Clauses, and Sentences

phrase: a group of words that holds a unique meaning of its own and acts as a single part of speech.

clause: a group of words that contains a subject and a verb, but which is usually only part of a sentence.

sentence: a group of words that has a subject and a verb and expresses a complete thought or asks a question. Sentences written in English begin with a capital letter and end with a period, a question mark, or an exclamation point.

3.1 Sentence = Chest of Drawers   3.3 Clauses

3.2 Phrases   3.4 Sentences

3.1   Sentence = Chest of Drawers

*(※ Note: The terms, "**phrase**," "**clause**," and "**sentence**" are highlighted <u>only in this chapter</u>, as <u>they're such common words</u>, and because <u>most of the time, the words do not stand for the grammatical unit</u>.)*

Imagine that your house simply cannot handle how much of a fashionista you are! What you need is an extra chest of drawers, also known as a dresser. So, you ordered one from IKEA and have just received it. You open the delivery box and are immediately shocked! What you see inside is a bunch of wooden planks, bolts, nuts, and hinges. Looks like this might take some time, yeah? Glad that this is your day off, you reluctantly grab an electric drill and start building the furniture.

After an hour or so, you have the body of the dresser put together, and after another fifteen minutes or so, you have built one drawer that fits into one of the spaces in the body. Where am I going with this? Well, in just a moment, you will see. The <u>single drawer</u> that you built ate up several wooden boards and some bolts, nuts, and hinges. However, it's still <u>not a whole dresser</u>; it's only <u>a part of a dresser</u>. In terms of English grammar, we can think of the wooden boards, bolts, nuts, and hinges as <u>words</u> (and <u>punctuation marks</u>). We also know that the entire dresser, once built, will be a single, complete <u>sentence</u>. What then is the <u>drawer</u>? What does it represent in our analogy to English grammar? The drawer, my friends, is to the dresser similar to what **phrases** and **clauses** are to the sentence. Read on for all the juicy details.

3.2.1 What are Phrases?

Both **phrases** and **clauses** are <u>units of a sentence</u>, and they both comprise <u>two or more words</u>. Just like that drawer, **phrases** and **clauses** are made of multiple parts but are not complete pieces of furniture; they are just parts of a whole. Let's start by looking at **phrases**.

A **phrase** is defined as a group of words that together act like one of the nine **parts of speech**. As we saw in the previous chapter, words that belong to different **parts of speech** are used to form sentences. As such, a **phrase** is one of a sentence's <u>basic building blocks</u>. A **phrase** though is made up of <u>several words</u>, not just one, and it's important to realize that a **phrase** can never stand alone as a sentence. It can only ever be a <u>part</u> of a sentence.

So, can **phrases** act like all nine **parts of speech**? Well, technically yes, but not really. **Phrases** usually act like <u>six</u> (of the nine) **parts of speech**—**nouns**, **verbs**, **adjectives**, **adverbs**, **conjunctions**, and **prepositions**. There are actually <u>eight</u> types of **phrases**—three of the types act like **nouns**, and the other five types act like the other **parts of speech** listed above.

Types of Phrases	Acts Like	Example
Noun phrase	a noun	a tiny mouse
Verb phrase	a verb	was reading
Adjective phrase	an adjective	very tall
Adverb phrase	an adverb	only occasionally
Principal phrase	a conjunction or an adverb	saddened by tragedy
Prepositional phrase	a preposition	on the table
Gerund phrase	a noun	eating shellfish quickly
Infinitive phrase	a noun	to swim in dangerous waters

Consider the following sentence.

1. **My brother Tom, who is very handsome, has been running every day for the past eight years to stay fit.**

Look at this sentence. There are <u>five</u> different types of **phrases** in there. Can you identify them all? Here's the answer.

For each *phrase* type, there's a "main word" that corresponds to the ***part of speech*** that the *phrase* <u>acts like</u>. For example, in the ***noun phrase*** "**my brother Tom,**" above, the main word is "**Tom,**" which is actually a ***noun*** in and of itself. "**Tom**" is the person we're talking about, and "**my brother**" is an <u>explanation of Tom</u> that contextualizes him. Here's another example: the main word in the ***prepositional phrase*** "**for the past eight years**" is "**for,**" which is, again, an actual ***preposition*** in and of itself.

3.2.2 When to Use Phrases

So, why do you think we use ***phrases***? When would a ***phrase*** do a better job than a word? We use ***phrases*** to <u>provide more information</u> about the main word in the ***phrase***. Let's take #1 again. The main word in the ***noun phrase*** "**my brother Tom**" is "**Tom.**" The extra words that make up the ***phrase*** "**my brother**" contextualize "**Tom.**" Without that information, your reader or listener could be confused as to which "**Tom**" you're talking about. Take another example: in the ***adjective phrase*** "**very handsome,**" "**handsome**" (which is an ***adjective***) is the main word, while "**very**" is an extra word that modifies the strength of the main word. Without "**very,**" the tone would be different—a "**very handsome**" man is clearly different than man who is just "**handsome**".

So, should we use ***phrases*** whenever we can? It's definitely a nice idea to write informative sentences, but, as with everything in life, <u>there can be "too much of a good thing."</u> A sentence with too many ***phrases*** can be <u>clunky</u> and <u>hard to read</u>. A good rule of thumb in any situation is to ask yourself, "<u>is this really necessary?</u>" For example, without "**my brother,**" your listener might not know which "**Tom**" you're talking about. However, you probably don't need to say that he's "**very handsome.**" Saying that Tom is "**handsome**" is probably enough to make your listener's heart beat a little faster.

 Clauses

3.3.1 The Subject and the Predicate

A ***clause*** is another <u>group of words</u>. However, ***clauses*** are often a bit <u>bigger</u> than ***phrases***. Imagine the drawer you built. Now imagine that you have attached a <u>handle</u> to it. You can think of ***phrases*** as <u>drawers without handles</u> and ***clauses*** as <u>drawers with handles</u>.

Given that, what exactly are ***clauses*** and how are they different from ***phrases***? First of all, a ***clause*** is defined as <u>a group of words with a **subject** and a **predicate**</u>. Okay then, what's a "***subject***" and what's a "***predicate***"? Simply put, the ***subject*** <u>performs the action</u>, and the ***predicate*** is the <u>action itself</u>. However, be mindful that not all ***clauses*** are required to include an action; a ***clause*** can also <u>describe the state</u> of the ***subject***. In more general terms, the ***subject*** is <u>the **noun** in focus</u>, and the ***predicate*** is <u>the rest of the **clause**</u>. In terms of their placement, the ***subject*** is usually the word that <u>comes first</u> in the ***clause***, and the ***predicate*** is <u>the rest of the **clause**</u>. Also, note that a ***predicate*** usually <u>starts with a **verb**</u>. Consider the following examples.

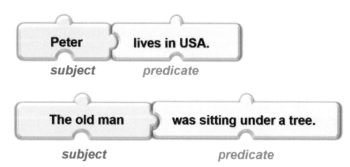

3.3.2 The Independent Clause and the Subordinate Clause

There are two types of *clauses*: *independent clauses* and *subordinate clauses*. An *independent clause* is a complete thought; in other words, it can stand alone as a sentence. The following are both *independent clauses*.

1. He runs.

2. The car has skidded to a stop in front of the barricade.

Conversely, a *subordinate clause* is not a complete thought. Therefore, it cannot stand alone as a sentence. *Subordinate clauses* often start with a *relative pronoun* (e.g., **that**, **which**, **who**, **whom**, **whose**), but they don't have to. The following are examples of *subordinate clauses*.

3. who is tall

4. which is unexpected

Let's return to the sentence about Tom from the previous section. That sentence has both an *independent clause* and a *subordinate clause*.

- *independent clause*

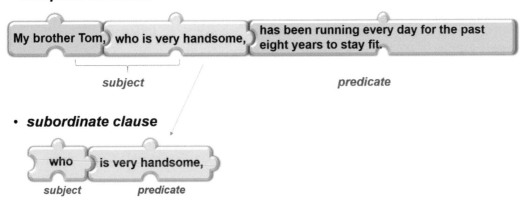

- *subordinate clause*

*(The **subordinate clause** is a description of a **subject**, and hence can be seen as a part of the **subject**.)*

Phrases, Clauses, and Sentences Exercise 01

✓ Write "C" if it's a clause. Write "P" if it's a phrase.

1) _____ feeling good about it
2) _____ he went up the mountain
3) _____ killed all the rats
4) _____ they were here
5) _____ we met some important people
6) _____ traversing through the river
7) _____ through difficult times
8) _____ clever and intelligent dog
9) _____ the girl had a dream
10) _____ there is little hope

Phrases, Clauses, and Sentences Exercise 02

✓ **The following sentences are formed by a combination of one independent clause and one dependent clause. Underline the independent clause.**

1) Because he ran, he was able to get on the train.
2) Until the sun rises, I will stay with you.
3) As the lights dim, we say good-bye.
4) Wherever he should go, I will follow him.
5) As long as it's possible, I will be waiting for you.
6) Before the food gets cold, you should eat it.

3.4 Sentences

3.4.1 What are Sentences?

In the preceding section about *clauses*, I said that an *independent clause* can stand alone as a *sentence*. If you flip that, you get the definition of a "*sentence*"—a *sentence* is equal to an *independent clause*. More specifically, a *sentence* is a group of words with a *subject* and a *predicate* that expresses a complete thought.

3.4.2 Four Types of Sentences

Sentences are distinguished into four different categories according to their purpose and tones: *declarative sentences*, *interrogative sentences*, *imperative sentences*, and *exclamatory sentences*. The table below explains each one.

Types of Sentences	Purpose & Punctuation	Example
Declarative Sentence	To state something Ends with a *period* (".").	I have a blue dress.
Interrogative Sentence	To ask something Ends with a *question mark* ("?").	When are we eating?
Imperative Sentence	To give an order Ends with a *period* (".").	Clean your room.
Exclamatory Sentence	To show strong feeling Ends with an *exclamation point* ("!").	The dog has fleas!

Phrases, Clauses, and Sentences Exercise 03

✓ **Read each sentence and add the correct punctuation mark (".", "?" or "!").**
Then, label it imperative, declarative, interrogative, or exclamatory

1) How was school today ____
2) Do your assignments on time ____
3) I'm so ecstatic I aced the test ____
4) Crossing that road is so dangerous____
5) Who will be on the stage tonight ____
6) You need to read up on the rules ____
7) He is the leader of the group ____
8) What is your favorite song ____
9) Congratulations on winning the prize ____
10) That was a difficult game ____

3.4.3 Five Basic Sentence Patterns

One English sentences topic that we must cover is the <u>five</u> **basic sentence patterns**. In English, all basic sentences start out with a **subject** followed by a **verb**. That basic structure can be modified for a variety of purposes, as you shall see.

Before we talk about the **basic sentence patterns**, I'll summarize some important grammatical terms relating to **sentences**. All these terms will appear frequently in upcoming sections, so you should familiarize yourself with them here.

A. **Subject:**
The person or thing that <u>performs the act</u> or <u>is described</u> in the sentence; is either a **noun**, **noun phrase**, or **pronoun** and (usually) appears <u>at the start of the sentence</u>.

B. **Predicate:**
In a sentence, the **predicate** is <u>everything other than the **subject**</u>; it usually <u>starts with a **verb**</u>.

C. **Verb:**
A word that describes an <u>action</u> or a <u>state</u>. There are <u>two</u> main types of **verbs**—**action verbs** and **linking verbs**.
Action verbs describe <u>actions</u> (e.g., run, jump, kick). They can be further divided into **transitive verbs** and **intransitive verbs**. **Transitive verbs** (e.g., address, borrow, bring) take an **object**; **intransitive verbs** (e.g., laugh, sit, increase) do not take an **object**.
Linking verbs describe <u>states of being</u> (e.g., appear, become, feel).
(See Chapter 4)

D. **Object:**
The person or thing that the **subject** <u>acts upon</u> or that <u>receives the action</u>.
A **direct object** is who or what the **subject** <u>acts upon</u> (who or what is <u>affected by the action</u>); an **indirect object** is who or what <u>receives the action</u> (who or what <u>benefits from the action</u>).
A **transitive verb** requires a **direct object**, but an **indirect object** is optional.

E. **Complement:**
A word or group of words that <u>provide additional information</u> about the **subject** or the **direct object**; it completes the **predicate**.
Subject complements appear after a **linking verb** and give more information about the **subject**.

CHAPTER 3. Phrases, Clauses, and Sentences **33**

Object complements appear after a *direct object* and give more information about the *direct object*. *Complements* are usually *nouns* or *adjectives*, but they can be or contain other types of words.

Now, returning to our original topic, the following are the <u>five</u> *basic sentence patterns* in English.

The following diagram presents *pattern 1*.

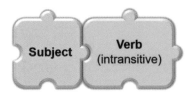

In sentences like this, the *subject* <u>performs a simple act</u> that does <u>not have a particular target</u> (i.e., an *object*). Correspondingly, the *verb* is *intransitive*—it does not require an *object*. *Intransitive verbs* that we can use in *pattern 1* sentences include **go**, **come**, **walk**, **talk**, **increase**, **rain**, and **sleep**. The following are examples of *pattern 1* sentences.

- **Henry swims well.**
- **She laughed loudly.**
- **We stayed at home all day.**
- **The medicine works.**

The following diagram presents *pattern 2*.

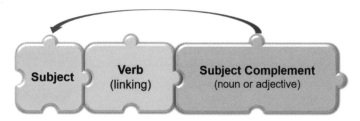

In sentences like this, the *subject* is not performing any act but is rather <u>being described</u> by the *subject complement*. Remember that the *subject complement* describes the *subject* and is usually either a *noun* or an *adjective*. The *verb* in use here is a *linking verb*; *linking verbs* include **be**, **remain**, **prove**, **feel**, **taste**, **fall**, and **make**. The following are examples of *pattern 2* sentences.

- **He seemed pleasant.**
- **The sea is very beautiful**
- **My brother was a teacher.**
- **You look tired.**

The following diagram presents *pattern 3*.

In sentences like this, the **subject** performs an action that has a particular target (i.e., an **object**). Correspondingly, the **verb** in use is *transitive*—it requires a **direct object**, at least. **Transitive verbs** used in *pattern 3* sentences include **write**, **borrow**, **bring**, **discuss**, **promise**, **offer**, and **have**. The following are examples of *pattern 3* sentences.

- **She eats cookies.**
- **We like our English teacher.**
- **He reads newspapers every day.**
- **Donovan brought his laptop today.**

The following diagram presents *pattern 4*.

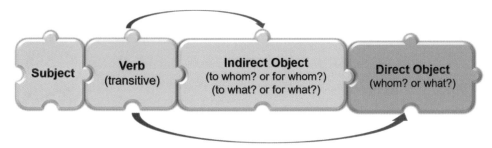

In sentences like this, the **subject** performs an action that has a particular target (i.e., a **direct object**) on another target (i.e., an **indirect object**). In other words, a specific person or thing (i.e., an **indirect object**) receives the action in this case. The following are examples of *pattern 4* sentences—try to spot the **direct objects** and the **indirect objects**. Note that the **indirect object** always appears before the **direct object**.

- **My mom baked me a birthday cake.**
- **The nurse gave the patient some medicine.**
- **My uncle bought me a bicycle.**
- **The students asked the teacher some questions.**

The following diagram presents *pattern 5*.

In sentences like this, the **subject** <u>performs an action</u> on the **direct object**, which is, in turn, <u>described</u> by the **object complement**. Recall that the **object complement** describes the **direct object** and is usually either a **noun** or an **adjective**. The following are examples of **pattern 5** sentences. Notice how some **object complements** contain other types of words like **verbs** and **prepositions**.

- **I think Tina is a great musician.**

- **Sam called her sister a genius.**

- **My son makes me laugh every day.**

- **The government advised people to stay at home.**

Books are the quietest and most constant of friends;
they are the most accessible and wisest of counselors,
and the most patient of teachers.

- Charles William Eliot (1834-1926) -

CHAPTER 04

Types of Verbs

verb: a word or group of words used to describe an action, experience, or state

4.1 The Crux of English

Do you know how many words the <u>shortest sentences</u> in English are made of? <u>Just one</u>. Such sentences are formed using just a single *verb*. For example, "**Run**" or "**Read.**" These are *imperative* sentences used only to give quick orders. What's interesting here is that of the nine *parts of speech*, <u>only</u> *verbs* can do this. In other words, the <u>only</u> *part of speech* that can <u>stand alone as a full sentence</u> is the *verb*.

In contrast, none of the other *parts of speech* can comprise independent sentences. In some cases, however, one-word *parts of speech* can be used to answer questions or react to events. For instance, "**Me!**" (a *pronoun*) might be the answer to the question, "**Who wants a chocolate bar?**" And "**Beautiful!**" (an *adjective*) might be a reaction to magnificent scenery or artwork. However, unlike our one-*verb* sentences, saying any of these out of nowhere (i.e., out of context) could render them meaningless. This is why the only *part of speech* that can stand alone as a sentence is the *verb*.

On that basis, the *verb* is the most crucial *part of speech* in any English sentence. A sentence can be devoid of other *parts of speech*, but it <u>must contain at least one *verb*</u>. Correspondingly, the most critical mistakes and the most dramatic differences in meaning often involve *verbs*. Accordingly, we're going to start our journey through the different *parts of speech* by looking at *verbs*.

4.2 What are Verbs?

So, what are *verbs*? A *verb* is a word that describes an <u>action</u> or <u>state</u> of a *noun* (usually the *subject*). And, as mentioned in *Section 3.4.3*, there are a number of different types of *verbs*. First, we can divide them into *action verbs* (which describe <u>actions</u>) and *linking verbs* (which describe <u>states of being</u>). Then, we can further split *action verbs* into *transitive verbs* (which require an *object*) and *intransitive verbs* (which do not require an *object*).

All of these explanations are good, but they sound too technical. They don't really tell us why or where we use *verbs*. Well, perhaps it's impossible to explain *verbs* in a single statement, but I think the following sentence does a pretty good job.

✓ **_Verbs_ reveal the narrator's intentions.**

The **_verb_** being used in the sentence allows us to immediately understand <u>the purpose of the sentence</u>. The **_verb_** type can tell us if the sentence describes an action or a state of being. And, as you'll soon see, the **_tense_** being used can tell us whether the sentence is discussing the **_past_**, the **_present_**, or the **_future_**. **_Verbs_** tell us a lot about the sentences in which they appear, and you'll gradually understand why this is so as we continue our English grammar journey.

4.3 Types of Verbs

4.3.1 Four Major Verb Types

English grammar can be quite subjective at times, especially in terms of categorizing words. If you search "**English verbs**" online, you'll find that different online grammar resources sort **_verbs_** differently—some say there are two types, others say three types, and so on. Such seeming discrepancies arise because different people prefer different levels of sophistication. None of these websites are wrong—people just want different levels of specificity.

In this book, I distinguish **_verbs_** into the following <u>four categories</u>.

Types of Verbs	What They Do	Examples
Action Verbs	Describe actions	read, smile, run
Linking Verbs	Describe states	appear, seem, look
Auxiliary Verbs	Help other verbs express deeper meaning	have, has, do, be
Modal Verbs	Modify other verbs' meanings	may, must, should

4.3.2 Main Verbs vs. Auxiliary Verbs

Before we discuss each type in detail, we must first consider **_main verbs_** and **_auxiliary verbs_**. Every sentence in English has a **_main verb_**. The **_main verb_** is <u>the most important **_verb_** in the sentence</u>, the one that shows the <u>action</u> or <u>state of being</u> of the **_subject_**. Most of the time, each sentence has precisely <u>one</u> **_main verb_**, but some complex sentences may have more.

In addition to **_main verbs_**, you have **_auxiliary verbs_**. As shown in the table above, **_auxiliary verbs_** <u>help</u> **_main verbs_** express <u>more complex meanings</u>. In a sentence, they often appear <u>directly before</u> the **_main verb_**. One more thing—**_modal verbs_** are actually a subcategory of **_auxiliary verbs_**. But, since **_modal verbs_** are special, I've placed them in a separate category.

Now let's consider some example sentences. When a sentence has exactly <u>one</u> **_verb_**, that **_verb_** is always the **_main verb_** of the sentence.

1. I <u>eat</u> lunch at 1 o'clock.

In #1 above, the **_verb_** "eat" is the **_main verb_**, and no **_auxiliary verbs_** are present in the sentence.

But, a lot of sentences in English have more than one **_verb_**, and many include multiple **_verbs_** in a row (i.e., **_verb phrases_**). In such a case, only one **_verb_** is the **_main verb_** and the other **_verbs_** are **_auxiliary verbs_**. Consider the following sentence.

2.   I am driving to work.

#2 uses two *verbs* in a row: "am" and "driving." Which one do you think is the *main verb*? The *main verb* in #2 is "driving." The *verb* "driving" states the action that "I," the *subject*, is performing. Then what type of verb is "am"? That's right, the *verb* "am" is used as an *auxiliary verb* in #2.

Finally, let's bring in the four types of *verbs* that I presented in the table above. Among these, *action verbs* and *linking verbs* can only be used as *main verbs*. Now, that does not mean that *auxiliary verbs* can never be used as *main verbs*. Some *auxiliary verbs* can act as the *main verb* of a sentence. However, when used as a *main verb*, the *verb* may have different meanings than when used as an *auxiliary verb*. In the next section I explain this further. One more thing—remember that *modal verbs* are actually a subset of *auxiliary verbs*.

4.3.3 Double Agents

As I hinted above, the four categories are not mutually exclusive. In other words, depending on how it's being used, a single *verb* can belong to multiple categories. Many English *verbs* have two (or more) meanings; though, of course, a *verb* cannot be two types or hold two meanings simultaneously in the same sentence.

This is also why you can never designate a *verb* as a certain type until after reading the entire sentence. The *verb* type is determined by what the sentence is saying. Therefore, you must reach to the end of it before you understand what kind of *verb* is in use. Keep this in mind as you go through each type. I'll show you some examples of these special *verbs* as we move along.

4.4   Action Verbs

4.4.1 Describe Actions

Action verbs describe actions. Wow, you'd have never guessed, right? These *verbs* tell us what the *subject* in the sentence is doing. As we covered earlier, the *subject* is the person or thing that performs the act or is described in the sentence. When the *verb* in the sentence indicates an action, we call that *verb* an "*action verb*." Consider the *verbs* in the following sentences.

1.   I painted the car.

2.   She is reading a newspaper.

3.   The bus arrived.

4.   She smiled.

Each underlined *verb* describes an action, something that the *subject* of the sentence is doing. Hence, they are all categorized as *action verbs*.

4.4.2 Transitive and Intransitive Verbs

Action verbs can be further divided into two additional types—*transitive verbs* and *intransitive verbs*. *Transitive verbs* act on something; they require an *object*. On the other hand, *intransitive verbs* do not act on anything; they do not require an *object*. The table below summarizes these two types. Pay attention to the *objects* as you go through the example sentences.

	Require *objects** (i.e., a person or thing on which the subject acts on)
Transitive Verbs	The teacher **addressed** *her student's question.* David **gave** *a laptop* to his sister as her birthday gift. Michael **borrowed** *the textbook* from the library. ** Objects Italicized*
	Do not require an *object*
Intransitive Verbs	Aiden **voted** yesterday for the first time in his life. Everybody **laughed** at his joke. Oil prices are rapidly **increasing** these days.

Remember our four sentences in *Section 4.4.1*? Well, #1, **I painted the car,** and #2, **She is reading a newspaper,** contain *transitive verbs*. In #1, the *subject*, "**I,**" is performing the action, "**painting,**" on the *object*, "**the car.**" Similarly, in #2, the *subject*, "**she,**" is performing the action, "**reading,**" on the *object*, "**a newspaper.**" In both cases, the *object* is a *direct object* that the respective *subjects* act upon. Neither sentence contains an *indirect object*; but, as we talked about before, when there is an *indirect object*, it appears <u>before</u> the *direct object* (see *Section 3.4.3*).

Now the other sentences: #3, **The bus arrived,** and #4, **She smiled,** contain *intransitive verbs*. In #3, the action, "**arrived,**" does not act on any particular *object*. The bus could have arrived at the station, but the station is not an *object*; the bus is not doing something to the station. Again, in #4, the action, "**smiling,**" does not act on an *object*. You may smile at someone, but that doesn't make that someone the *object* in the sentence.

4.5 Linking Verbs

Linking verbs describe <u>states of being</u>. Correspondingly, they're sometimes also called "***state verbs.***" They are used to <u>describe</u> the *subject* or <u>give more information</u> about the *subject*. The proper grammatical definition of the role of the *linking verb* is: "to link the *subject* to a *complement*." Recall that a *subject complement* is a word or group of words that provide additional information about the *subject* (see *Section 3.4.3*). Consider the following sentences.

1. **Harry <u>looks</u> just like his father.**

2. **This <u>seems</u> like a lovely house.**

3. **This pie <u>smells</u> delicious.**

All the underlined *verbs* describe a *subject*; they do not represent any form of action. In #1, the *verb* "looks" describes the *subject* "Harry" as bearing a resemblance to his father. That is, the *verb* "looks" links the *subject*, "Harry," to the *subject complement*, "his father." Similarly, the *verbs* in #2 and #3 link the *subjects* to the *subject complements* in order to give further information about such *subjects*.

Based on their meanings, *linking verbs* can be further distinguished into several categories.

of the senses	feel, hear, see, smell, taste …
of liking and disliking	like, love, hate, fear, detest, want, wish …
of mental states	agree, believe, forget, know, remember, suppose, think …
of permanent states	belong, contain, owe, own, possess …

Before we move on, let's talk briefly about the *verbs* "**see**" and "**hear**." These two *linking verbs* are interesting because for each one, at least one corresponding *action verb* exists. First of all, the *verb* "**see**" corresponds to the *verbs* "**look (at)**" and "**watch**."

✓ **See = *linking verb***

"**See**" refers to our natural ability to perceive the things around us. "**Seeing**" does not have a target; it's not planned. "**Seeing**" happens because our eyes are open, not necessarily because we want to observe something in particular.

I **see** many things in this room.
Can you **see** that sign on the street corner?
I **see** a man walking down the street.
I suddenly **saw** a bird fly in front of me.

✓ **Look (at) = action verb**

"**Look (at)**" refers to the conscious activity of observing something. When you "**look (at)**" something, there is always a specific target. The act of "**looking (at)**" something usually only lasts for a short period of time.

I'**m looking at** the clock. I want to know the time.
Look! It's snowing!
Look at the map to find out where we are.
Look at me when I'm talking to you.

✓ **Watch = action verb**

"**Watch**" has a similar meaning as "**look (at)**." However, "**watching**" usually suggests an action that lasts for a longer time (compared to "**looking (at)**").

We are **watching** the children play.
Are you **watching** the baseball game tonight?
They **watched** the FIFA World Cup on TV.
I do not have time to **watch** TV right now.

Next, "**hear**" corresponds to the *verb* "**listen (to).**"

✓ **Hear = linking verb**

"**Hear**" refers to our natural ability to detect sound using our ears. "**Hearing**" does not have a target; it's not planned. "**Hearing**" happens because you have ears, not necessarily because you want to listen to something in particular.

I'm in my apartment. I'm trying to study.
I **hear** music from the apartment next door. The music is loud.
I can't **hear** you. Could you speak louder please?
Did you **hear** the thunder last night?
I **heard** a strange noise outside.
I can't **hear** anything because of the loud music.

✓ **Listen (to) = action verb**

"**Listen (to)**" refers to the activity of consciously detecting and following a sound. "**Listening (to)**" something always involves a specific target.

I'm in my apartment. I'm studying. I have a tape recorder. I'**m listening to** music. I like to **listen to** music when I study.
My mother likes to **listen to** the radio.
The doctor is **listening to** Tom's heartbeat.
You should always **listen to** your mother's advice.

Action Verbs & Linking Verbs Exercises 01

✓ **Identify each of the underlined verbs as either an action verb or a linking verb.**

1) One day, I <u>want</u> to be famous.
2) We <u>play</u> soccer after school.
3) I <u>like</u> your new blouse, Katie.
4) Liam <u>goes</u> home at 4:30 pm.
5) Fay <u>cooks</u> wonderful meals.
6) Rob <u>takes</u> the bus to work.
7) This cheese <u>tastes</u> a bit strange.
8) The sommelier <u>tastes</u> the newly arrived wine.

Action Verbs & Linking Verbs Exercises 02

✓ **Identify each of the underlined verbs as transitive or intransitive.**

1) She <u>was crying</u> all day long.
2) We <u>showed</u> her the photo album.
3) The doctor <u>advised</u> me to exercise regularly.
4) It was <u>raining</u> at that time.
5) She <u>laughed</u> at the joke.
6) She <u>gave</u> a cookie to the child.
7) They <u>slept</u> in the street.
8) I <u>ate</u> the cherries.
9) My father <u>doesn't drink</u> coffee.

4.6.1 A Helping Hand (A Helping Verb)

"**Auxiliary**" is a rather big word, but its meaning is actually quite simple. "**Auxiliary**" is an *adjective* that holds a similar meaning to words like "**extra**," "**supplementary**," and "**additional**." *Auxiliary verbs* are basically "*extra verbs.*" *Auxiliary verbs* help the *main verb* express a deeper meaning. They usually appear before the *main verb* in a sentence.

Here is a list of common *auxiliary verbs*.

- **be, can, could, dare, do, have, may, might, must, need, ought, shall, should, will, would**

The following sentences each contain one *auxiliary verb*, which is underlined.

1. **Linda <u>has</u> *bought* a new shirt.**

2. **Cyan <u>is</u> *solving* the problems on his exam.**

Notice that they appear <u>directly before</u> the respective *main verbs*, "**bought**" and "**solving.**"

4.6.2 Where We Use Auxiliary Verbs

There are two main uses of *auxiliary verbs*: *modality* and *tense*. When we use *auxiliary verbs* for *modality*, that is, to <u>modify the meaning</u> of the *main verb*, we call them *modal verbs*. I'll handle *modal verbs* at length in *Section 4.7*.

We also use *auxiliary verbs* for *tense*. That is, we use *auxiliary verbs* to provide a <u>sense of time</u>, a sense of <u>when the action is happening</u>. Correspondingly, when we use *auxiliary verbs* for *tenses*, the *main verb* is often an *action verb* (though this is not always true). To modify the *tense* of the *main verb*, we use the *auxiliary verbs* "**be**," "**have**," and "**do**."

When we use these *auxiliary verbs* to modify *tenses*, they <u>don't hold any particular meaning of their own</u>. There are a number of set rules that tell us where to place *auxiliary verbs* and/or to modify the *main verbs* to form the desired *tense*. I'll tell you about these rules in the following chapters when we look at *tenses* in detail. Right now, I'll focus only on the types of *auxiliary verbs* that we use to form *tenses*. As noted above, we use <u>three</u> different *auxiliary verbs* to form *tenses*: "**be**," "**have**," and "**do**."

- <u>Be (is, am, are, was, were)</u>:
  We use "**be**" in sentences that involve a *continuous tense*.

  A. **He <u>is</u> *reading* a book. (Present continuous)**

  B. **He <u>was</u> *reading* a book. (Past continuous)**

- <u>Have (have, has, had)</u>:
  We use "**have**" in sentences that involve a *perfect tense*.

  A. **She <u>has</u> *left*. (Present perfect)**

    B. She <u>had</u> *purchased* a fancy dress. *(Past perfect)*

- **<u>Do (do, does, did)</u>:**
  We use "**do**" to form the <u>negative</u> in sentences that don't already include an ***auxiliary verb***.

    A. He <u>does not</u> *eat* sandwiches. *(Present simple negative)*

    B. My mom <u>didn't</u> *wait* for me. *(Past simple negative)*

We'll look into ***tenses*** in great detail in the upcoming sections, so I'll omit further explanation here.

4.6.3 The Negative Form

Unlike ***action verbs*** and ***linking verbs***, which <u>do not have negative forms</u>, ***auxiliary verbs*** <u>have negative forms</u>. In fact, we use negative ***auxiliary verbs*** to discuss the negatives of ***action verbs*** and ***linking verbs***. To form the <u>negative</u> of an ***auxiliary verb***, we place the word "**not**" <u>directly after</u> the ***auxiliary verb*** and <u>before</u> the ***main verb***.

Consider the following sentences.

1. **Maya <u>did not</u> *pass* her exam.**

2. **Gary <u>has not</u> *gotten* his tetanus shot yet.**

Pay attention to the position of "**not**" in these sentences (i.e., after the ***auxiliary verb***, before the ***main verb***). We'll talk a lot more about negatives when we look at ***tenses***, so I'll spare you further explanation here.

<u>Auxiliary Verbs Exercises</u>

   ✓ **In each sentence, circle the helping verb and underline the main verb.**

1) I am reading about the Junior Olympics
2) She was racing in a wheelchair race.
3) Sarah had joined the Wheelchair Athlete Club.
4) The racers were using special racing wheelchairs.
5) They are training several times a week.
6) They have lifted weights too.
7) Sarah has raced for several years.
8) She will race many more times.
9) She is practicing for next year's Olympics.

4.7 | Modal Verbs

4.7.1 Modify the Main Verb's Meaning

Now, on to the final type: *modal verbs*. As I mentioned, *modal verbs* are a subsection of *auxiliary verbs*; they are used to <u>modify the meaning</u> of the *main verb*. The following is a list of common *modal verbs* in English. They are also called the *principal modal verbs*.

- **can, could, may, might, must, shall, will, have to, would**

These *principal modal verbs* have various functions. The following tables summarizes the uses of *principal modal verbs*.

➢ *May and Might*

may		● permission (formal)
	e.g.	**May** I come in? **May** I ask you some questions about your experience? Students **may** not leave the class once their exams are complete.
		● possibility, probability
	e.g.	She **may** not arrive on time due to traffic. Dr. Kim **may** be your teacher next year. I'm worried that it **may** start raining soon.
might		● polite permission
	e.g.	**Might** I be excused from the table? **Might** I suggest an idea? **Might** I ask you a few questions?
		● suggestion
	e.g.	It's very flavorful overall, though you **might** add a bit more salt. You **might** try restarting your device; that could fix the problem. You **might** ask your brother to repay his loan the next time you run into him.
		● possibility, probability
	e.g.	Matilda **might** show up to the concert tonight. I **might** take a holiday to Australia next year. It looks nice, but it **might** be very expensive.

> *Can and Could*

can		● ability (= be able to)
		I **can** speak three languages. She **can** swim faster than anyone I know. I don't think my younger sister **can** read this book
		● permission (informal)
		Can I use your phone, please? **Can** I go to the bathroom, Mr. Brown? You **can't** have any dessert until you've finished your dinner.
		● possibility **and probability**
		Excessive smoking **can** cause lung cancer. It **can't** be Joe. He is in Sydney You **can** get help on your papers from your older brother
		● request and offer
		Can I do anything to help get dinner ready? **Can** I help you find what you need? **Can** I give you a ride home?
could		● ability in the past
		When I was younger, I **could** run fast. Last night, I **could** not keep my eyes open. He **couldn't** read until he was nearly 10 years old.
		● polite permission
		Could I borrow your car next week? Mom, **could** I sleepover at my friend's house tomorrow? I was wondering if I **could** take a short break from work.
		● request and offer
		Could you say it again more slowly? **Could** you please be quiet? **Could** we help you find what you need?
		● suggestion
		We **could** go to the movies after work on Friday. You **could** see if your boss would give you a raise. I know it must be difficult to convince your parents, but you **could** try.
		● possibility and probability
		I think it **could** rain tomorrow! Answer the phone! It **could** be your boss calling. Be careful, you **could** injure someone with that knife!

➢ *Will and Would*

will	● future tense
	e.g. Tomorrow I **will** be in New York. You **will** receive an e-mail from your teacher. He **will** be a scientist.
	● ability and willingness
	e.g. You wash the dishes; **I'll** take out the trash. This washing machine **won't** turn on. **Won't** the cat come out of her hiding place?
	● requests and offers
	e.g. **Will** you give me a chance? **Will** you walk the dog, David? **Will** you have a cup of tea, Henry?
would	● polite requests
	e.g. **Would** you make dinner? **Would** you let me know when I can expect your reply? **Would** you please take off your hat?
	● expressing desires
	e.g. I **would like to** go to the movies later. I **would like to** buy a new computer. Where **would** you **like to** go for your summer vacation?
	● habitual behavior in the past
	e.g. My dad **would** often go fishing. I **would** sit on the beach for hours. She **would** bring delicious snacks to the class.

➢ *Must*

must (= have to)	● strong obligation/necessity
	e.g. You **must** stop when the traffic lights turn red. All passengers **must** wear seat belts. You **must** not be late for your appointment.
	● logical deductions/certainty
	e.g. She **must** be very tired. She's been working all day long. He lied to the police. He **must** be the criminal. I **must** have left my keys on my desk at work.
must not	● prohibition
	e.g. You **must not** smoke in this restaurant. You **must not** tell anyone about what we saw. Cars **must not** be parked in front of the entrance.

➢ *Shall and Should*

shall* *used in many of the same ways as "will"*	• future tense	
	e.g.	I **shall** call when I arrive at the airport. We **shall** be staying at a guest house. We **shall not** be in attendance during this class.
	• offer, suggestion, and advice	
	e.g.	**Shall** I call a cab? **Shall** we walk along the lake?" **Shall** we stay or go out?
	➢ Note that "shall" is not often used in modern English, especially American English. In American English "shall" is mainly used in formal and/or legal documents.	
should	• 50 % obligation (polite obligations) (= ought to)	
	e.g.	I think she **should** take a rest. Guests **should** check out by 11 AM on the morning of their final reservation date. You **shouldn't** talk on your phone loudly when you're on the bus.
	• advice, suggestion	
	e.g.	You **shouldn't** eat so much fast food—it's not good for your health. You **shouldn't** smoke. It is unhealthy. You **should** visit your dentist at least twice a year.
	• logical deductions	
	e.g.	He **should** be exhausted. He's been working all day. I studied all day yesterday. I **should** be ready for the test. All you had was a glass of milk this morning. You **should** be hungry.

4.7.2 Modal Verbs for Ability

Now, let's briefly cover each use. To discuss abilities (of the *subject*), we often use the *modal verb* "can." Consider the following sentence.

1. I can *drive* a bus.

This sentence describes your ability to drive a bus. So, how is this sentence different if we don't include the *modal verb*?

2. I *drive* a bus.

When you remove the *modal verb* "can," the sentence suggests that you are a bus driver. #1 tells us only that you are qualified to drive a bus, but this doesn't necessarily mean that driving busses is your job. In contrast, #2 does suggest that driving a bus is your job. Can you see how important the *modal verb* is in this case?

4.7.3 Modal Verbs for Permissions, Requests, and Offers

Next, to ask for <u>permission</u> and make <u>requests</u> and <u>offers</u>, we use "**can**," "**may**," and "**could.**" These are mostly interchangeable, but the meaning of your sentence may vary slightly depending on which one you use. To ask for <u>permission</u>, we mostly use "**may**" or "**can**."

1. **You <u>may</u> *leave* now.**

"**May**" is more proper and formal than "**can**."

For <u>requests</u>, we mostly use "**can**" or "**could**."

2. **<u>Could</u> you *give* me a ride home?**

Like "**may**," "**could**" is more proper and formal than "**can**."

For <u>offers</u>, we mostly only use "**may**" or "**can**."

3. **<u>Can</u> I *loan* you my bike so you're not late to class?**

4. **<u>May</u> I *help* you?**

Note that while "**<u>May</u>** I *help* **you?**" is grammatically sound, it is not as natural as "**<u>Can</u>** I *help* **you?**" Using "**may**" in this case can be considered unnecessarily formal.

4.7.4 Modal Verbs for Suggestions and Advice

Next, to offer <u>suggestions</u> or <u>advice</u>, we use "**should**" and "**could**." However, just like the cases described above, the meaning of your statement changes depending on which *modal verb* you use. You can use "**should**" to strongly <u>advise</u> another person, i.e., when you really want that person to do what you recommend. In contrast, you can use "**could**" when <u>suggesting an option</u>. Since you're only presenting an option for the other person's consideration, you're not too concerned about the option being rejected. Consider the following examples.

1. **You <u>should</u> *go* to the doctor. You have been unwell for the past week.**

2. **You <u>could</u> *go* to the doctor if your symptoms get worse.**

When you say #1, you're seriously worried about the person, and you want them to pay a visit to the doctor. However, when you say #2, you're probably unsure or confused (about what the symptoms mean) and are suggesting an appointment with a doctor as an open option if things get worse.

4.7.5 Modal Verbs for Obligations

Now, on to <u>obligations</u>. Your obligations are your <u>responsibilities</u>, things that you have to do. To handle sentences with <u>obligations</u>, we mostly use two *modal verbs*: "**must**" and "**have to**." A quick note on "**have to**": in English, some *verbs* consist of <u>more than one word</u>. We call these "*phrasal verbs*," and they're usually made up of a *verb* followed by either a *preposition* or an *adverb*. I'll spare you further explanation of *phrasal verbs* because they are very common and you're probably already familiar with many of them.

Consider the following sentence.

1. **You <u>must not</u> *be* late for work.**

Speaking of <u>negatives</u>, we don't use "**have to**" for <u>negative obligations</u> (i.e., things that you <u>cannot</u> do). If we use "**have to**" in #1, it becomes the following.

2. **You <u>have to not</u> *be* late for work.**

This sentence is too wordy and difficult to say. That's why we rarely use such statements.

One more thing—you can use "**don't have to**" to talk about things that you <u>don't need to do</u> (i.e., things that you are <u>not responsible for</u>). Be careful, as this is <u>clearly different</u> from talking about negative obligations.

3. **Mark <u>doesn't have to</u> *drink* milk.**

Sentence #3 means that Mark gets the appropriate nutrients from other food sources so that he doesn't need milk in his diet. Note that this is very different to the following.

4. **Mark <u>must not</u> *drink* milk.**

Sentence #4 implies that Mark is probably lactose intolerant, and therefore should not consume milk. It's not that milk is unnecessary for Mark but rather that milk is actually harmful to him.

4.7.6 Modal Verbs for Logical Deductions

Finally, we arrive at <u>logical deductions</u>. Perhaps this one is a bit difficult to figure out based on its name alone. <u>Logical deductions</u> refer to your <u>suspicions</u> and <u>expectations</u> based on logic. In other words, instead of mere hopes, <u>logical deductions</u> are predictions based on information you already have. A bunch of different *modal verbs* are used for this purpose, including "**can**," "**could**," "**might**," "**must**," and "**may**."

1. **It <u>can't</u> *be* Jane because she's away right now.**

Before you speak this sentence, you probably saw someone who totally resembles Jane. However, you know that Jane is not in town right now. Now you're confused because even though Jane is away, you've just seen somebody that looks exactly like her.

2. **Tom <u>must</u> *have finished* school by now.**

You look at the time, and it's already pretty deep into the day. Hence, you suspect that Tom, who goes to school, must have completed the day's classes by that time.

As a side-point, note that #2 contains <u>two</u> *auxiliary verbs* that appear back-to-back: "**must**" and "**have**." As we just talked about, "**must**" is being used as a *modal verb* to signal a <u>logical deduction</u>, while "**have**" is being used as an *auxiliary verb* to form the correct *tense*. Again, we have plenty of chapters left to talk about *tenses*, so I'll skip further explanations here.

<u>Modal Verbs Exercises</u>

   ✓   **Pick the most appropriate modal verb out of the three options for each sentence.**

1) You (*must / should / shouldn't*) be 18 before you can drive in Spain.
2) You (*don't have to / mustn't / shouldn't*) go to bed so late. It's not good for you.
3) You (*don't have to / mustn't / shouldn't*) wear a school uniform in most Spanish state schools.
4) You (*must / mustn't / needn't*) come. I can do it without you.
5) (*Should / Could / Must*) you help me open this can, please?
6) I (*could / would / should*) like to have a better house.
7) We (*may / can / would*) go to Portugal this November.
8) He was afraid he (*mustn't / shouldn't / wouldn't*) arrive on time.

4.8 Double Agents Examples

I told you a while ago in this chapter that some *verbs* fit multiple categories. And some *verbs* possess distinctive meanings that allow them to be used as <u>more than one type</u> of *verb*. (Like *verbs*, many English words have <u>multiple meanings</u>.) Let's consider some examples.

A prime example of such a "double agent" is the *verb* "**look**." Mainly, the *verb* "**look**" can be used as follows: 1) to say that someone is <u>observing something with their eyes</u> or 2) to say that <u>something resembles something else</u> in physical appearances. Consider the following sentences.

1. He <u>looked</u> up at the sky.

2. He <u>looks</u> like his father.

In #1, the *subject* "he" is <u>using his eyes to look up</u> at the sky. Hence, in this sentence, the *verb* "**look**" is an *action verb*. On the other hand, in #2, the *subject* "**he**" <u>shares his father's looks</u> (i.e., appearance); he's not observing his father. Accordingly, in #2, "**look**" is a *linking verb*.

Here's another example: the *verb* "**be**" is very commonly used in English. However, ironically, the meaning of "**be**" is rather difficult to explain. Simply put, the *verb* "**be**" <u>equates</u> whatever appears before it with whatever appears after it; it's basically an equal sign ("**=**"). However, as you'll soon see, the *verb* is also frequently employed as an *auxiliary verb* to signal various *tenses*.

3. She <u>is</u> a professor.

4. She <u>is</u> *driving* to work.

In #3, the *verb*, "**is**" (a form of "**be**") is being used as a *linking verb* to indicate the <u>state of being</u> of the *subject* "**she**"; it tells us that the *subject* "**she**" is <u>equal</u> to the *subject complement* "**a professor.**" In contrast, in #4, the *verb* "**is**" is being used as an *auxiliary verb* to form the *present continuous tense* of the *main verb* "**drive**." Used as an *auxiliary verb*, "**is**" <u>holds no particular meaning</u>.

As you have seen, some *verbs* can act as <u>more than one type</u> depending on the usage. Remember that you can only figure out what type of *verb* you are dealing with after you've <u>read the sentence from beginning to end</u>.

CHAPTER 05

Tenses

forms of a verb that show actions or states in the past, the present, or in the future

5.1   All about Time

When we talk about any action, what do you think is the most important information we must provide? It's the time frame. When is the action happening? Is it happening right now? Did it happen in the past? Or has it not yet happened? Is it something that takes time to complete, or does it occur instantly? And, by any chance, is the action linked to another action in a different time? These types of questions must be answered clearly whenever we speak or write about any action.

In English, we answer questions like these by using *tenses*. *Tenses* are all about time! In English grammar, there is a set of rules we use to give *verbs* their *tenses*, that is, to give those *verbs* the exact sense of time we want them to express. As I hinted in the previous chapter, we do two things to form *tenses*: modify the *main verb* and/or add *auxiliary verbs*. But, before we learn about how to express *tenses*, we must investigate which *tenses* exist in English.

5.2   The Twelve Tenses

There are twelve *tenses* in English. Each *tense* is formed by the combination of one precise time point (*past*, *present*, or *future*) with one additional idea about the event (is the event instant? Is it continuous? Is it related to another event?). The following diagram shows how the twelve *tenses* in English are formed.

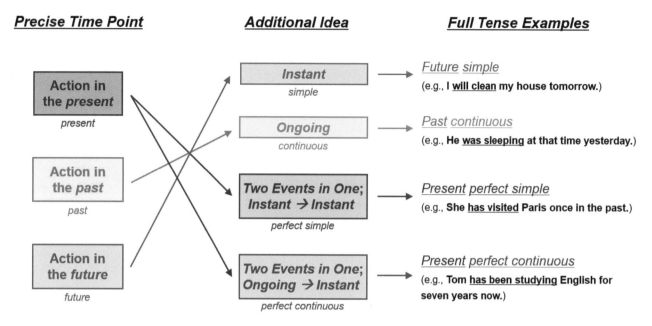

Precise Time Point | **Additional Idea** | **Full Tense Examples**

Action in the *present* (present)
Action in the *past* (past)
Action in the *future* (future)

Instant (simple)
Ongoing (continuous)
Two Events in One; Instant → Instant (perfect simple)
Two Events in One; Ongoing → Instant (perfect continuous)

Future simple
(e.g., I <u>will clean</u> my house tomorrow.)

Past continuous
(e.g., He <u>was sleeping</u> at that time yesterday.)

Present perfect simple
(e.g., She <u>has visited</u> Paris once in the past.)

Present perfect continuous
(e.g., Tom <u>has been studying</u> English for seven years now.)

In the table below, each of the twelve *tenses* is expressed as a <u>combination of a precise time point and an additional information</u>, following from my explanation above. The time points make up the columns, while the additional ideas make up the rows. While you may not learn the precise meaning of each *tense* from the table, I'd like you to use it to get an initial idea of where the twelve *tenses* come from.

The 12 Tenses	Past	Present	Future
Simple	I did my homework.	I do my homework.	I will do my homework.
Continuous	I was doing my homework.	I am doing my homework.	I will be doing my homework.
Perfect Simple	I had done my homework.	I have done my homework.	I will have done my homework.
Perfect Continuous	I had been doing my homework.	I have been doing my homework.	I will have been doing my homework.

Let's quickly compare each of the twelve sample sentences in the table. All twelve use the *main verb* "do." Notice how, among the *past*, *present*, and *future* sentences, either <u>the *main verb* changes</u> or *auxiliary verbs* <u>are added</u>. Sometimes, the *main verb* stays in its base form "**do**," e.g., in the *present simple tense*. However, it also changes its form sometimes, e.g., in the *past simple tense*, where it becomes "**did**." In addition, we sometimes have to add *auxiliary verbs*, e.g., in the *present continuous tense*, where we add the *auxiliary verb* "**is**." The point is, to form different *tenses*, we can do <u>two things</u>: 1) <u>modify</u> the *main verb* and/or 2) <u>add</u> *auxiliary verbs*.

The following diagram describes the time frames that the twelve *tenses* respectively refer to.

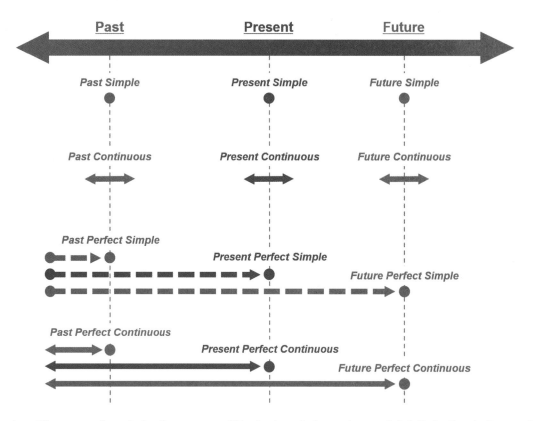

Even if you're still very confused, don't worry—we'll look at each *tense* in great detail starting in the next chapter.

5.3 The Additional Ideas

5.3.1 What are They?

I will omit explaining for the precise time points (i.e., the *past*, *present*, and *future*), as they should be pretty intuitable based on their names alone. However, the additional ideas about time—the *simple*, the *continuous*, the *perfect simple*, and the *perfect continuous tenses*—may not be so straightforward. Hence, I'll now explain what each one means.

5.3.2 The "Simple" Tenses

First, *simple* here refers to an event that happens relatively <u>instantly</u>. The following are three sentences, each in the *simple tense*.

1. *Present simple*: I <u>eat</u> cereal for breakfast every day.

2. *Past simple*: I <u>ate</u> breakfast at 8:00 AM yesterday.

3. *Future simple*: I <u>will eat</u> breakfast at 10:00 AM tomorrow.

It's true that "**eating**" is an activity that takes time; you can't just erase the food in front of you in an instant. However, you can still use the *verb* in a *simple tense*. When you use "**eat**" (in the *simple tense*), you are referring more to the <u>idea</u> of eating than the process. For example, in #1, you're not eating the cereal right now; instead, you're talking about the idea of having cereal for breakfast every day. Similarly, in #2, you're saying that an event—you having breakfast—happened at 8:00 AM yesterday. It's not important whether you were actively eating at exactly 8:00 AM yesterday. The same applies to #3: you're talking about your *future* plan rather than what your precise state will be at 10:00 AM tomorrow.

5.3.3 The "Continuous" Tenses

Next, *continuous* refers to events that <u>take some time</u> to happen, events that <u>occur over a certain duration</u>. However, the important thing to remember is that when we use the *continuous tenses*, we're not discussing the <u>entire duration</u> of an event. Instead, we're referring to a particular <u>point in time while the event is still happening</u>. Each of the following three sentences are in the *continuous tense*.

1. *Present continuous*: I <u>am cooking</u> dinner right now.

2. *Past continuous*: I <u>was cooking</u> dinner at 5:00 PM yesterday.

3. *Future continuous*: I <u>will be cooking</u> dinner at 4:00 PM tomorrow.

In contrast to the *simple tenses*, the *continuous tenses* actually tell us that <u>the action is in progress right now</u>. For example, in #1, you are cooking dinner right now. In #2, you were in the process of cooking dinner at exactly 5:00 PM yesterday, and in #3, you expect to be in the process of cooking at 4:00 PM tomorrow. What's important is that the event needs to <u>still be in progress</u>. Whenever you use the *continuous tense*, the action must have <u>already started</u> and must <u>not yet be over</u>.

5.3.4 The "Perfect Simple" Tenses

The *perfect tenses* may be a little more confusing than the two *tenses* above. Indeed, it's a lot more difficult to define the *prefect tenses* with a single sentence because, in fact, each of the *perfect tenses* has a different use/function. Essentially, the *perfect tense* is used to talk about <u>two related actions or ideas</u> in the same sentence. What's important is that the two actions and ideas take place <u>at different times</u>; they cannot be happening simultaneously.

The *perfect simple tenses* handle two related actions that both occur more or less <u>instantly</u>. In other words, they are conceptually very similar to the *simple tenses*, except you now have <u>two events</u> instead of one. The *perfect simple tenses*, therefore, also focus more on the <u>idea</u> of the activity, rather than the activity itself.

1. *Present perfect simple*: I <u>have been</u> to Paris before.

2. *Past perfect simple*: I <u>had been</u> to Paris before I went to Rome.

3. *Future perfect simple*: I <u>will have been</u> to Paris by next month.

The three *perfect simple tenses* are each quite different in nature, so I'll explain them one by one. First, the *present perfect simple* talks about an event in the recent *past* that is related to another in the *present*. It has various uses, but it's often associated with someone's *past* experience. In #1, you're stating that you've already visited Paris once. However, we have no idea of exactly when you visited Paris; we just know that you have already been there. When you use the *perfect tense*, you don't have to provide the exact time an event happened. Also, in #1, the second event in the *present* is not told. When you use the *perfect tense*, you can skip the second related event if it is obvious. In #1, the second idea in the *present* is that you have had the experience of visiting Paris. However, when you want to express a related idea that is not so obvious, you need to clearly write it out. Take the following sentence as an example.

4. *Present perfect simple*: I <u>have been</u> to Paris before, so I know the streets well.

Here, the second idea is clearly stated: you "**know the streets well.**" Notice how this part of the sentence is in the *present simple tense* as well. This *tense* shows that this second idea is in the *present*, as I've stated before.

Next, the *past perfect simple* talks about an event in the far *past* that is related to another in the nearer *past*. It's used to describe the order in which the events occurred in the *past*. In #2, you're stating that your visit to Paris happened before your visit to Rome. Note that both of these events are in the *past*—one is just further in the *past* than the other. When you use the *past perfect simple*, you almost always explicitly write out both events/ideas.

Finally, the *future perfect simple tense* talks about an event in the *past*, *present*, or *future* that is related to another event that is certainly in the *future*. What's important to remember is that the first event must occur before the second event that is definitely in the *future*. This *tense* is most often used to give an account about a *future* event that should be finished by a certain point of time in the *future*. From #3, we can realize that you've not yet been to Paris but that you will have visited the city by next month, because you already have a trip planned. You're safely projecting that the trip will have occurred by the next month.

5.3.5 The "Perfect Continuous" Tenses

Finally, the *perfect continuous tenses* are similar to the *perfect simple tenses*, except that the <u>preceding event occurs over time</u>. However, the <u>event that follows it is still instant</u>.

1. *Present perfect continuous*: I <u>have been studying</u> English for five years.

2. *Past perfect continuous*: I <u>had been studying</u> English for five years before I moved London.

3. *Future perfect continuous*: I <u>will have been studying</u> English for five years next month.

The *present perfect continuous* is used to talk about the duration of an event that started in the *past* and lasted until the *present*. Sentence #1 states that you started studying English five years ago. The duration of your English studies is measured from whenever you started up to right now. Just like before, you can add a particular idea to this, as in the following example.

4. *Present perfect continuous*: I <u>have been studying</u> English for five years, so I am not afraid to communicate with native English speakers.

Notice that the second idea is in the *present* and is instant.

The *past perfect continuous* is used to talk about the duration of an event that started in the *past* and also ended in the *past*. Sentence #2 states that you studied English for five years, leading up to the moment you moved to London. In other words, you had five years of English experience before moving. The duration of your English studies is measured from whenever you started to the day you moved to London. However, you might still be studying English—just because a sentence uses the *past perfect continuous tense*, doesn't mean that the activity is necessarily over now.

The *future perfect continuous* is used to measure the duration of an event up to a certain point in the *future*. Sentence #3 states that when the next month rolls around, five years will have passed since you started studying English. In other words, right now, you've been studying English for four years and eleven months. The duration of your English studies is measured from whenever you started up to that set point in the *future*. We use the *future perfect continuous* when we're close to hitting a nice whole number for the duration of a particular activity. "**Five years**" is more convenient and easier to understand than "**four years and eleven months.**"

5.4 This is Only the Start!

You think you know everything about **tenses** now? Well, perhaps you have a good idea about where each **tense** is used, that is, in which situations you will use each **tense**. However, you still have no idea how to change the **main verbs** or how to add **auxiliary verbs** in appropriate spots. We'll handle grammatical aspects such as these in the next few chapters—that is, we'll look at spelling rules, additional words, etc. Furthermore, in the above sections, I've only noted the main use for each of the twelve **tenses**. However, each **tense** actually has lots of different uses and purposes. In the following chapters, I'll talk all about these too. We'll start easy with the **present tenses** and then move along to the more complicated ones. So be ready for them.

Reading furnishes the mind only with materials of knowledge;
it is thinking that makes what we read ours.

- John Locke (1632-1704) -

The Present Tenses

the forms of a verb that show what is true, what exists, or what is happening now

6.1 A Present from the Present

6.2 The Present Simple

6.3 The Present Simple Negative

6.4 Present Simple Questions

6.5 Negatives and Questions

6.6 The Present Continuous

6.1 A Present from the Present

We often care so much about the *past* or the *future* that we end up neglecting the *present*. But, in reality, the *present* is where we should really focus our attention! We should always be thankful for everything the *present* offers us—for all the presents that the *present* gives us. (The "*present*" must be named so for some reason!) To help us celebrate the *present*, in this chapter, we're going to talk about the *present tenses* of English.

As we talked about in the previous chapter, the *present tenses* are all about the "now"; the time we're living in at this very moment. However, that doesn't mean that the *present tenses* only talk about events that are happening right now. In fact, compared to either the *past* or the *future tenses*, the *present tenses* have the largest variety of uses. The *present tenses* can describe not only events that are occurring right now but also events that happen on the regular (like habits), solid facts, and even your *past* experiences.

There are a total of four *present tenses*: the *present simple*, the *present continuous*, the *present perfect simple*, and the *present perfect continuous*. However, right now, I can only cover two of them—the *present simple* and the *present continuous*. This is because the *present perfect tenses* use *past tense verbs*. Hence, you need to learn the *past tenses* before you can form the *present perfect tenses*. Now, how ironic is that?

6.2 The Present Simple

6.2.1 Introduction

Out of all twelve *tenses*, the *present simple* is without doubt the easiest *tense* to form. You don't have to add any *auxiliary verbs* and you barely have to alter the *main verb* from its base form. Nevertheless, there is a very important rule in forming the *present simple tense*—the *verb* changes its form depending on the *subject* of the sentence.

6.2.2 The Seven Subject Pronouns of English

Before we can discuss this important rule, we must cover the seven *subject pronouns* in English. We will discuss these in more detail in *Chapter 12*. I'll keep it simple here.

By definition, **pronouns** are words that replace **nouns** such as the **subject** or the **object** in a sentence. We call the **noun** being replaced (by the **pronoun**) the "**target noun**" (see *Chapter 12*). Any **subject** in an English sentence can be represented by one of the following <u>seven</u> **subject pronouns**.

- **I, you, we, they, he, she, it**

The most important thing about **pronouns** is how we distinguish them. There are <u>six</u> categories that we use to sort the **subject pronouns**. Just like the twelve **tenses**, these **pronoun** categories are created based on a <u>combination of two criteria</u>.

1) <u>Whether the **target noun** is *singular* or *plural*</u> = whether the *subject pronoun* is *<u>singular</u>* or *<u>plural</u>*
   The first criterion focuses on <u>how many people</u> are in the **subject** of the sentence.

   A. **Subject** is a <u>single person/object</u> → use **<u>*singular*</u> subject pronoun**

   B. **Subject** contains <u>multiple people/objects</u> → use **<u>*plural*</u> subject pronoun**

2) <u>The relationship between the **target noun** and the narrator</u> = whether the *subject pronoun* is *<u>1st</u>* *<u>person</u>*, *<u>2nd person</u>*, or *<u>3rd person</u>*
   The second criterion focuses on <u>how the **subject** is related to the narrator</u>.

   A. If **subject** = <u>narrator</u> → use **1st *person* subject pronoun**

   B. If **subject** = <u>direct audience</u> → use **2nd *person* subject pronoun**

   C. If **subject** = <u>neither the narrator nor the direct audience</u> → use **3rd *person* subject pronoun**

Based on these criteria, the six categories are formed in the following ways.

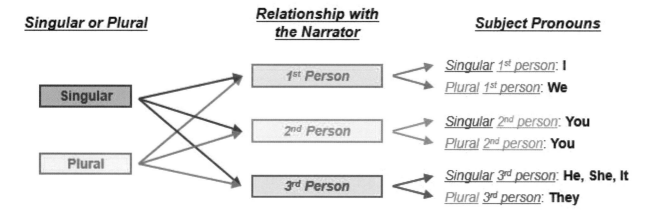

In the following table, I've arranged the seven **subject pronouns** into the six categories.

Subject Pronouns	1st Person	2nd Person	3rd Person
Singular	I	You	He, She, It
Plural	We	You	They

In the next table, below, I explicitly state the type of **subject** each **subject pronoun** stands for.

Perspective	Pronoun	What It Stands for
1st Person Singular	I	Yourself (the narrator).
1st Person Plural	We	A group of people including yourself (the narrator).
2nd Person Singular	You	The direct audience of your sentence.
2nd Person Plural	You	The group comprising the direct audience of your sentence.
3rd Person Singular	He	A male that is neither you nor the direct audience of your sentence.
	She	A female that is neither you nor the direct audience of your sentence.
	It	A thing that is neither you nor the direct audience of your sentence.
3rd Person Plural	They	A group of people that neither includes you nor the audience of your sentence.

6.2.3 How to Form the Present Simple

Now that we've covered the **subject pronouns**, it's time to look at how to form the **present simple tense**. When we speak in the **present simple tense**, we change the form of the **verb** to agree with the **subject**. A **verb** in the **present simple tense** can take one of two forms: 1) the base form (i.e., the dictionary form), or 2) the "base + -s" form. The following are the rules for when to use which; remember that it all depends on the **subject** in use.

1. <u>When to use the base form</u>:

   - For **1st person singular**, **1st person plural**, **2nd person singular**, **2nd person plural**, and **3rd person plural subjects**.

   A. I <u>exercise</u> every morning.

   B. You always <u>shop</u> in that market.

   C. We often <u>watch</u> movies in this theater.

   D. They <u>eat</u> lunch at noon.

2. <u>When to use the base + -s form:</u>

- For **3rd person singular subjects** <u>only</u>.

    A. He <u>enjoys</u> riding his bike.

    B. She <u>drives</u> to work.

    C. It always <u>rains</u> here in July.

Note that the rule applies to both the **subject pronouns** and the **nouns** that can be replaced by the **subject pronouns**. To give you an example, both "**he**" and "**Mr. Johnson**" are **3rd person singular subjects**.

6.2.4 Spelling Rules for the Present Simple

There are some spelling rules for how to change **verbs** in the **present simple tense** so that they agree with **3rd person singular subjects**. I describe them in the table below.

Verb Characteristics	Spelling Rule	Examples	
Verbs that end with -ch, -ss, -sh, -x, or -o	**Add -es**	watch → watches	miss → misses
		finish → finishes	mix → mixes
Verbs that end with a consonant + -y	**Remove -y and add -ies**	study → studies	reply → replies
		try → tries	cry → cries
Verbs that end with a vowel + -y	**Add -s**	buy → buys	enjoy → enjoys
		pay → pays	play → plays
Irregular verbs	**No unifying rule**	have → has	do → does
For all other verbs	**Add -s**	run → runs	wait → waits

Consider the following sentences. Pay attention to the type of **subject** being used in each sentence and how the spelling of the **verb** correspondingly changes to agree with that **subject**.

    1. Go

        A. I <u>go</u> to school on foot.

        B. She <u>goes</u> to school by bus, because she lives far away.

    2. Study

        A. They <u>study</u> chemistry.

        B. He <u>studies</u> physics.

3. *Pay*

    A. You never <u>pay</u> for the meals.

    B. Ben <u>pays</u> for everything with his credit card.

4. *Wait*

    A. I always <u>wait</u> for hours when I visit the dentist's office.

    B. The cat patiently <u>waits</u> for its owner to return home.

6.2.5 The "Be" Verbs

As such, ***present simple tense verbs*** take one of two forms, <u>except the **verb** "be."</u> The **verb** "be" takes one of <u>three</u> different forms when used in the ***present simple tense***.

What then is "**be**"? The **verb** "**be**" is one of the most commonly used **verbs** in English. It is mostly used as an **auxiliary verb** to form complex **tenses**, as you'll see later. However, it can also be used as a **main verb**. When used as a **main verb**, it acts like an equal sign ("**=**"); it equates the **subject** and the **subject complement**. "**Be**" is the most fundamental **linking verb**.

As I said, there are <u>three</u> different forms of "**be**" in the ***present simple tense***. The three forms of "**be**" are: "**am**," "**is**," and "**are**." Just like all the other ***present simple tense verbs***, which of the three forms you choose depends entirely on the **subject** in use. The table below matches the different **subjects** with the correct form of "**be**."

Subject	"be"	Rest of the sentence
I	am	
You / We / They	are	happy.
He / She / It	is	

Also, "**be**" is the only ***present simple tense verb*** that you can <u>contract</u> (i.e., <u>shorten</u>). This is because "**be**" holds a very simple meaning and the context is usually clear enough. The following examples show how we contract "**be**" in the ***present simple tense***.

I am → I'm	You are → You're	We are → We're
They are → they're	He is → He's	She is → She's
It is → it's	*(For more **contractions**, see Chapter 23)*	

6.2.6 Where to Use the Present Simple

Now that you've learned how to form the ***present simple tense verbs***, the next step is to learn <u>where to use them</u>. What's interesting about the ***present simple*** is that, despite its simple form, its <u>uses are not so intuitive</u>. Believe it or not, we rarely use the ***present simple*** to talk about what's happening right now. As I mentioned in *Chapter 5*, we need to use the ***continuous tense*** to talk about something in progress; the ***simple tense*** handles instant events and ideas only. Take the following sentence, for example.

- **I eat breakfast.**

Would you ever say this while you're actually having breakfast? No. That would be like you're narrating your own life, which is weird. The point is: you rarely use the *present simple* to actually talk about the *present*.

Rather, the major uses of the *present simple tense* are as follows.

1. <u>**To make simple statements of fact.**</u>

2. <u>**To discuss events that happen repeatedly.**</u>

3. <u>**To refer to things that are always true.**</u>

4. <u>**To discuss the future.**</u>

Let's look deeper into each use. First, the *present simple tense* is used to make <u>simple statements of fact</u>. Consider the following sentence.

1. **The sun <u>rises</u> in the east.**

Here, the *verb* "rises" is in the *present simple tense*. We know that the sun always rises in the east; it's an unchanging fact. We use the *present simple* to state facts, things that are always true.

Next, the *present simple tense* is also used to discuss <u>events that happen repeatedly</u>. Consider the following sentence.

2. **I <u>eat</u> lunch at noon every day.**

Here, the *verb* "eat" is in the *present simple tense*. The sentence tells us that you have lunch at noon repeatedly, in fact, every day. We use the *present simple* to talk about events that are repeated, things that happen at set intervals. For this type of sentence, we usually add <u>time interval expressions</u>, such as "**every day**" in #2, to state <u>how often the event is repeated</u>.

The final major use of the *present simple tense* is to refer to <u>things that are always true</u>. Consider the following sentence.

3. **We <u>start</u> work at 9 AM.**

Here, the *verb* "start" is in the *present simple tense*. The sentence talks about something that is always true. However, it's different from #1 in that it's <u>not a generic fact</u>. In other words, the fact that's stated here is <u>only true for the *subject* of the sentence</u>. Not everybody in the world starts work at 9 AM; however, the *subject*, "**we**" in #3 definitely must start work at 9 AM.

An interesting thing about the *present simple* is that we can use it <u>to talk about the *future*</u>. Consider the following sentence.

4. **She <u>starts</u> her new job tomorrow.**

Clearly, the event "**starting her new job**" is in the *future*—the sentence says that she'll start her new job "**tomorrow**." Nevertheless, the *main verb* "**start**" is in the *present simple tense*. As you can see, we can use the *present simple tense* to discuss the *future*. However, we can only handle a specific type of *future* events using the *present simple tense*: <u>*future* events that are fixed</u>. In other words, we can only use the *present simple tense* to speak of <u>*future* events that are already planned and that will likely happen</u>. Correspondingly, this usage is limited to things like public transportation timetables and scheduled events like concerts and ceremonies. I'll talk more about this in *Chapter 8*, when I discuss the *future tenses*.

The Present Simple Exercises

✓ **Fill in the gaps by putting the verbs in the present simple.**

1) I _____ (work) at a bank.
2) She _____ (live) with her parents.
3) Cows _____ (feed) on grass.
4) He _____ (earn) a handsome salary.
5) Janet _____ (want) to be a singer.
6) Emily _____ (be) a great cook.
7) Arti and her husband _____ (be) both Singaporeans.
8) I _____ (be) addicted to card games.
9) You _____ (be) a great writer.

6.3 The Present Simple Negative

6.3.1 How to Form the Present Simple Negative

Moving on to the *present simple negative*. The "*negative*" of any *tense* refers to the use of the word "**not**" with the corresponding *tense*. The *negative tense* is used to talk about something that's <u>not true</u> or <u>not correct</u>.

Again, to form the *present simple negative*, we need to add "**not**" somewhere in the sentence. What's important is to know where to add that "**not**." <u>The right location for "**not**" depends on the type of *verb* you're using</u>. Largely, there are <u>two</u> situations: 1) when we use "**be**" and 2) when we use any other *verb*.

1) <u>When we use "be":</u>

• We place "**not**" <u>after</u> "**be**."

    A. I *am* <u>not</u> a doctor.

    B. She *is* <u>not</u> happy.

    C. They *are* <u>not</u> invited.

2) <u>When we use any other *verb*:</u>

• We place the *auxiliary verb* "**do/does not**" <u>before</u> the *main verb*. We use "**does not**" for *3rd person singular subjects*; we use "**do not**" for all other *subjects*. The *main verb* <u>must always</u> be in its <u>base form</u>.

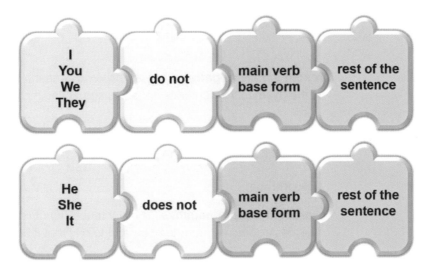

A. I <u>do not</u> *work* outside.

B. He <u>does not</u> *have* a car.

C. We <u>do not</u> *live* here.

Note that you no longer need to change the form of the **main verb** when you use the **present simple negative**. This is because you're using the **auxiliary verb** "**do**" here. The **subject** must agree with "**do**," which you change to "**does**" whenever you use a *3rd person singular subject*. Therefore, you don't have to change the **main verb** in such a case. Here's an important rule of thumb: <u>you only need the **subject** to agree with one **verb**</u>, the **verb** (be it **auxiliary** or **main**) that is <u>closest to it</u>.

6.3.2 Where to Use the Present Simple Negative

In terms of its uses, you'd obviously use the **present simple negative** in <u>situations that are the exact opposite</u> of those where you'd use the **present simple**. In other words, you'd use the **present simple negative** in the following situations.

1. <u>To state an incorrect fact (to point out error).</u>

2. <u>To discuss events that do not happen repeatedly.</u>

3. <u>To refer to things that do not occur.</u>

4. <u>To discuss what will not occur in the future.</u>

To make it easier, I'm going to bring back the example sentences from *Section 6.3.1*. With regards to case #1, consider the following sentence.

1. **The sun <u>does not rise</u> in the west.**

In this sentence, the **verb** "**rise**" is in the **present simple negative**. The sentence states an <u>incorrect fact</u>; the "**not**" points out that the statement is wrong.

For case #2, consider the following sentence.

2. **I <u>do not eat</u> lunch at noon every day.**

In this sentence, the **verb** "**eat**" is in the **present simple negative**. Notice that the sentence means that you <u>don't always</u> eat lunch at noon but that you <u>sometimes do</u>. When you <u>use a specific time expression</u> in this way, you're stating that an <u>event happens occasionally but not consistently</u>.

Case #3 presents a direct contrast to case #2. Consider the following sentence.

   3.   We <u>do not start</u> work at 9 AM.

In this sentence, the **verb** "**start**" is in the **present simple negative**. This sentence now means that you <u>never</u> start work at 9 AM. <u>Without a time expression</u>, the event in the sentence becomes <u>something that never occurs</u>. Be mindful of this distinction.

Finally, as the **present simple tense** can be used to discuss the **future**, the **present simple negative** can be used to discuss an <u>untrue</u> **future**. Consider the following sentence.

   4.   My semester <u>does not begin</u> until September.

In this sentence, the **verb** "**begin**" is in the **present simple negative**. The sentence denotes that <u>a certain statement about the **future** is incorrect</u>; your semester begins in September, and to say that it begins any time sooner would be wrong. Again, see *Chapter 8*.

6.3.3 We Don't Actually Use Negatives Often

Regarding **negatives**, I'd like you to keep one thing in mind. We generally use **negatives** <u>only for emphasis</u>. You might think that we simply use **negatives** in situations opposite to those in which we use the positive **tense**, but that's not true. In English many words have <u>corresponding words with exact opposite meanings</u>, i.e., "**antonyms**" In most situations, you use the opposite word instead of using the **negative** form. This way, you use <u>less words</u>—<u>the fewer words you use, the more effective your speech will be</u>. Consider the following case.

   1.   I <u>do not run</u> in the park.

   2.   I <u>walk</u> in the park.

Using the "**run**" in the **negative** costs you <u>three words</u> ("**do not run**"), but using the opposite word "**walk**" costs you only <u>a single word</u>. Correspondingly, #2 sounds a lot more natural and straightforward.

However, you might have seen a sign stating the following at, for example, a museum.

   3.   <u>Do not run.</u>

In such a case, the museum wants to <u>emphasize</u> that they're prohibiting the action of running. Therefore, they <u>deliberately</u> use the **negative** form. I'll talk more about **negatives** at the end of **tenses**, in *Chapter 9*.

<u>The Present Simple Negative Exercises</u>

    ✓   **Fill in the gaps by using the present simple negative forms of the verbs.**

1) He _____ (work, not) at a bank.
2) I _____ (live, not) with my parents.
3) Birds _____ (feed, not) on grass.
4) Tay _____ (earn, not) a handsome salary.
5) They _____ (want, not) to be singers.
6) Christian _____ (be, not) a great cook.
7) Kate and her husband _____ (be, not) both British; only Kate is.
8) Sam _____ (be, not) addicted to card games.
9) You _____ (be, not) someone to be ignored with.

6.4 Present Simple Questions

6.4.1 How to Form Present Simple Questions

You can also ask *questions* in the *present simple tense*. Again, in this case, the situation with "**be**" is different than with all the other *verbs*.

1) <u>When we use "be" to form a question:</u>

   A. The *subject* and "**be**" <u>swap places</u>; we <u>pull out</u> "**be**" and <u>bring it to the front of the sentence.</u>

   A. <u>Are</u> you Canadian?

   B. <u>Is</u> he your brother?

   C. <u>Am</u> I on the list?

2) <u>When we use any other *verb* to form a question:</u>

   A. We place the *auxiliary verb* "**do**" or "**does**" at <u>the start of the sentence</u>. Then, we add the *subject* and the *main verb* in its <u>base form</u>. We use "**does**" for *3rd person singular subjects*; we use "**do**" for all other *subjects*.

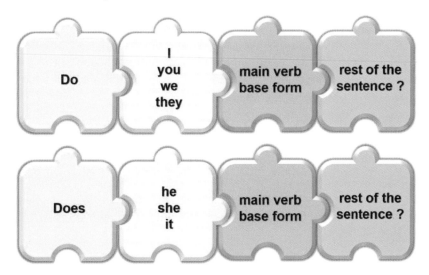

   A. <u>Do</u> you *know* where we are?

   B. <u>Does</u> she *work* in a school?

   C. <u>Does</u> Tom usually *finish* his work on time?

6.4.2 Where to Use Present Simple Questions

Questions are used to <u>ask</u> someone something, to <u>demand that someone provide an answer</u>. Hence, we use **present simple questions** to <u>ask about things (that we would state) in the</u> ***present simple tense***.

1. **<u>To ask about a fact.</u>**

2. **<u>To ask if an event happens repeatedly.</u>**

3. **<u>To ask if something is always true.</u>**

4. **<u>To ask about the future.</u>**

Again, we're going to reuse previous sample sentences.

1. **<u>Does the sun rise</u> in the east?**

In #1, we're asking <u>if certain information is correct</u>. In other words, you're asking someone to <u>confirm a fact</u>.

2. **<u>Do you eat</u> lunch at noon every day?**

In #2, we're asking <u>if an event happens repeatedly</u>.

3. **<u>Do we start</u> work at 9 AM?**

In #3, we're asking <u>if a rule is true</u>. In other words, we're asking <u>whether something is always true</u>.

4. **<u>Does the train arrive</u> at 9 PM?**

In #4, we're asking <u>if a scheduled event in the</u> ***future*** <u>is true</u>. In other words, we're asking <u>if something is supposed to happen in the</u> ***future***. Again, see *Chapter 8*.

6.4.3 How to Answer Present Simple Questions & How to Use Question Words/Phrases

For simple **present simple questions** like those shown above, the answer is always either "**yes**" or "**no.**" When you answer such questions, you can choose to repeat information from the question, for example, "**Yes, the sun rises in the east.**" But, in spoken conversations, you can usually omit that and just answer "**Yes.**" Note that <u>basic **present simple questions** are always yes/no questions</u>.

What if you want a more <u>specific answer</u>? Then you use **question words** and **phrases**. The following is the list of common **question words** and **phrases** used in English.

- **Who, where, when, why, what, what time, how, how often, how old, which, whose**

You can use these words/phrases at the <u>very start of your question</u> to ask for specific answers like the name of a person, someone's work methods, reasons that events occur, and times that events are scheduled to occur. Here are some examples.

1. **<u>Who</u> is that person?**

2. **<u>How much</u> does this cost?**

3. **<u>What time</u> does the movie start?**

4. **<u>Where</u> do you go to school?**

5. **<u>Why</u> does she talk so fast?**

6. **<u>When</u> do the farmers plant wheat?**

When someone asks you questions like these, <u>to answer "**yes**" or "**no**" would be insufficient</u>. You're being asked to provide more specific answers. For example, in #1, you're asked to provide the exact name of a person, and in #2, you're asked to provide the precise price of the object.

Present Simple Questions Exercises

✓ **Turn the following sentences into present simple questions.**

1) Mark is Korean.
2) Thomas is Ralph's brother.
3) You are a great singer.
4) She knows Tom Hanks.
5) You go to the gym every day.
6) They visit their grandparents every week.
7) Dolphins have high intelligence.
8) Harry wants to have Chinese food tonight.

6.5   Negatives and Questions

Technically, everything we've looked at so far belongs to just a single *tense*, the ***present simple***. The ***negatives*** and the ***questions*** are a given for each *tense*; you can form ***negatives*** and ***questions*** using any of the twelve *tenses*. We looked at ***negatives*** and ***questions*** in the ***present simple tense*** in such detail because it's the very first *tense* that we've handled. From now on, the ***negatives*** and ***questions*** for any *tense* will be taken for granted; I won't explain in detail when to use them or how to form them. Instead, I will simply provide a diagram that shows how to form them.

6.6   The Present Continuous

6.6.1 How to Form the Present Continuous

The ***present continuous tense*** is the second *tense* that we'll look at. You use the ***present continuous tense*** to talk about what's happening right now; it is used to describe continued actions that are happening presently. To form the ***present continuous tense***, you need to modify the ***main verb***. Fundamentally, you simply add "-ing" to the end of the ***main verb***. Here are the detailed spelling rules.

Verb Characteristics	Spelling Rule	Examples	
Verbs that end with -e	**Remove -e and add -*ing*** **if it ends with two e's, do not drop the e's; just add -ing*	drive → driving	take → taking
		make → making	write → writing
		smile → smiling	choose → choosing
		see → seeing	agree → agreeing
Verbs that end with -*ie*	**Replace -*ie* with -*y*, then add -*ing***	tie → tying	die → dying
Verbs that end with a vowel + a consonant	**Double the last consonant, then add -*ing***	get → getting	stop → stopping
		put → putting	swim → swimming
		run → running	shop → shopping
		sit → sitting	drop → dropping

For all other verbs	Add "-ing"	cook – cooking	speak – speaking
		eat – eating	start – starting
		fix – fixing	stay – staying

When we want to write a sentence in the *present continuous*, not only must we modify the *main verb* but we also must place the *auxiliary verb* "**be**" in front of it. Remember that the form of "**be**" to be used depends on the *subject* of the sentence. Also note that the form of the *main verb* remains the same regardless of which *subject* you use.

A. My sister is listening to music.

B. They are bringing a television set into the classroom.

C. I'm playing chess with my friend.

6.6.2 How to Form Present Continuous Negatives & Questions

Here are the ways you form *negatives* and *questions* using the *present continuous tense*. As I said, only brief explanations will be provided in the rest of the chapter (as well as in the rest of the book).

A. The students aren't watching TV.

B. I'm not sleeping.

C. They are not leaving now.

A. Is she studying in the library now?

B. Are you feeling sleepy?

C. Is he leaving his office now?

6.6.3 When to Use the Present Continuous

In whole, there are three uses of the *present continuous tense*.

1. **To talk about something that is happening right now.**

2. **To discuss the future.**

3. **To mention a repeated activity that annoys you or is unfavorable (+ "always")**

First, as I mentioned, the main purpose of the *present continuous tense* is to talk about actions that are in progress right now. Consider the following sentence.

1. **He is playing tennis.**

Here, you're saying that he's playing tennis right now; he's currently in the process of playing tennis. Correspondingly, you can use the *present continuous negative* to say that an action is not happening right now and the *present continuous question* to ask whether an action is happening right now.

1. **He is not playing tennis.**

1. **Is he playing tennis?**

Next, you can use the *present continuous tense* to talk about the *future*. Consider the following sentence.

2. **We are leaving Korea next week.**

Here, you're saying that you're planned to leave Korea in the *future* ("**next week**," to be exact). Just like with the *present simple tense*, we only talk about positive *future* plans using the *present continuous tense*. See *Chapter 8* for more. You can use the *present continuous negative* to say what will not occur in the *future*, and the *present continuous question* to ask about the *future*.

2. **We are not leaving Korea next week.**

2. **Are we leaving Korea next week?**

Finally, you can use the *present continuous tense* with the word "**always**" to talk about a repeated activity that annoys you. Consider the following sentence.

3. **My mom is always forgetting her keys.**

Here, you're saying that your mom forgets her keys time and time again and suggesting that it annoys you. Generally, we don't apply this use of the *present continuous tense* to *negatives* or *questions*.

 Linking (state) verbs are not used in the present continuous tense. Incorrect forms are highlighted with a strikethrough in the following table.

Correct sentence	Incorrect sentence
I hear a siren. Do you hear it too?	I'm ~~hearing~~ a siren. Are you ~~hearing~~ it too?
I'm hungry right now. I want some food.	I am ~~wanting~~ some food.
Jenny hates dogs.	Jenny is ~~hating~~ dogs.
I love chocolate.	I am ~~loving~~ chocolate.
I don't believe the news.	I am not ~~believing~~ the news.
This box contains a cake.	This box is ~~containing~~ a cake.

The Present Continuous Exercises

✓ **Complete the sentences using the present continuous forms of the provided verbs.**

1) He _____ (paint) the house.
2) She _____ (run) to her work.
3) I _____ (eat) breakfast.
4) They _____ (race) their toy cars.
5) Who _____ (chat, she) to now?
6) What _____ (do, you) at the moment?
7) I _____ (cook, not) right now.
8) Helen _____ (wear, not) her wedding ring today.

● **Present simple and Present Continuous Summary**

	Present simple	Present continuous
verb form	infinitive (=base form) he/she/it + '-s'	be(am/are/is) + infinitive + '-ing'
Positive	I work. You work. She works	I am working You are working. She is working.
Negative	I don't work. You don't work. She doesn't work.	I'm not working You aren't working. She's not working.
Question*	Do you work? Does she work?	Are you working? Is she working?
Negative question*	Don't you work? Does she not work? (Doesn't she work?)	Are you not working? Is she not working? (Isn't she working?)

* Generally speaking, it is uncommon to use a first-person subject in an interrogative sentence in the present simple.

✓ **Present simple signal words**

When the present simple tense is used to talk about events that happen repeatedly, we often use words like *always, regularly, every day, daily, normally, generally, usually, occasionally, sometimes, often, rarely, frequently, nowadays, naturally, seldom, constantly, never, every week, every year, once a year, once a week, at times, at present, every now and then, all the time, etc.*

✓ **Present continuous signal words**

When the present simple continuous is used to talk about events that are happening right now, we use words like *now, continually, perpetually, at this moment, at the moment, right now, this season, this year, forever, etc.*

CHAPTER 07

The Past Tenses

the forms of a verb that describes actions, events, or states from the past

7.1 Memory & The Past

The Giver by Lois Lowry is one of the most sophisticated books that I handle in my book club. The dystopian novel presents a seemingly attractive *future* society where there is no pain, fear, war, and hatred. However, to achieve such a state, the people had to surrender color, music, emotion, choice, and, most importantly, memory. To be more precise, the members of this community are blind to any history. Interestingly, memory hasn't been completely eliminated—there is exactly one person who looks after all the memories; that person is called the "receiver of memory."

Why do you suppose that memory hasn't been totally deleted? The book explains that one of the major tasks of the receiver of memory is to advise the community controllers in case of trouble. Whenever a problem occurs in the society, the controllers, having surrendered their memories as well, consult with the receiver of memory on how a similar problem was solved before. Even the all-powerful controllers are unable to solve certain issues without memory.

Furthermore, the elders in this book are treated with no respect; they are considered too inept to provide anything for society and no longer fit for labor. Hence, they are put in retirement homes and treated like children until they are killed off. However, in real life, we learn to always respect our elders. Why do you think there is this discrepancy between the world of the book and real life? It's because the most powerful gift the elders offer is their knowledge that stems from their memories. Elders gain respectability through their wisdom, built up by their years of experience. Elders need memory, in order to pass on their wisdom to the younger generations.

As such, *The Giver* highlights that our memories can give us wisdom to solve *future* problems. Similarly, our memory also allows us to avoid making the same mistakes over and over. We can see that Germany takes this lesson to heart as they educate their students about the Holocaust meticulously and exhaustively. The Holocaust occupies a big portion of history in German high schools, and it's mandatory for most students to visit concentration camps and/or synagogues throughout their education. The wrongness of racial hate is hammered deeply in their thoughts in order to avoid a similar event recurring.

To conclude, your memory serves a very important function in your life. *Past* experiences are some of the most common things we discuss when we talk to people in real life. This is why the *past tenses* are the most commonly used *tenses* in English. Now, we shall start our journey through the *past tenses*.

7.2.1 How to Form the Past Simple

In order to form the **past simple**, we need to modify the **main verb**, just as we do for the **present continuous**. Essentially, to form the **past simple tense**, we need to add "**-ed**" to the end of the **verb**. Just like with the **present continuous**, there are several spelling rules associated with how you turn **verbs** into the **past simple**, but we'll cover those a little later.

We saw that in the **present simple**, the **verb** form changes depending on the **subject**. Is there anything like that here? Yes, but only for "**be**." "**Be**" is the only **verb** in English that has two **past tense** forms: "**was**" and "**were**." We use "**was**" for "**I / he / she / it**," while we use "**were**" for "**you / we / they**." On the other hand, all other **verbs** have exactly one **past tense** form each. In other words, the **verb** takes the same form in the **past simple tense** with all seven types of **subjects**.

Here's how you'd write a sentence in the **past simple**.

1) **When we use a form of "be":**

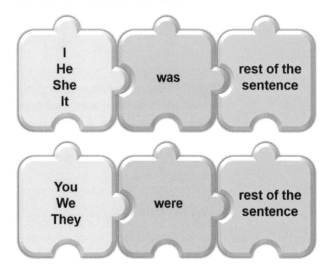

    A. I <u>was</u> exhausted.

    B. You <u>were</u> happy.

    C. He <u>was</u> in the garden.

    D. They <u>were</u> on the same school team.

2) **When we use any other _verb_:**

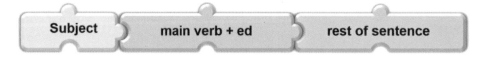

    A. Peter <u>washed</u> his car yesterday.

    B. Thomas Edison <u>invented</u> the light bulb in 1879.

    C. They <u>walked</u> to school together yesterday.

    D. We <u>visited</u> our uncle last week.

As I said, there are several spelling rules related to how you transform *verbs* into the *past simple*. In the table below, I show you those spelling rules. Note that <u>there are lots of *irregular verbs* in the *past simple*</u>. *Irregular verbs* are *verbs* that do not follow the regular rules. The *past simple* forms of these *verbs* often look very different than their respective base forms.

Verb Characteristics	Spelling Rule	Examples	
Verbs that end with *-e*	Just add *-d*	arrive → arrived	smile → smiled
		close → closed	like → liked
Verbs that end with a consonant + *-y*	Remove *-y* and add *-ied*	try → tried	hurry → hurried
		study → studied	cry → cried
Verbs that end with a vowel + *-y*	Add *-ed*	play → played	stay → stayed
		enjoy → enjoyed	
Verbs that end with a vowel + a consonant	Double the last consonant and add *-ed*	stop → stopped	pat → patted
		drop → dropped	grab → grabbed
Irregular verbs	No unifying rule	buy → bought	drive → drove
		see → saw	eat → ate
For all other verbs	Add *-ed*	ask → asked	push → pushed
		listen → listened	need → needed

The Past Simple Exercises

   ✓   **Complete the following sentences using the past simple forms of the verbs given in brackets.**

1) I accidently _____ (arrive) at school late yesterday.
2) The play tonight _____ (be) excellent.
3) The last time Taylor and I _____ (play) with each other _____ (be) already a week ago.
4) After he _____ (get) his test results, Doug _____ (become) very pleased.
5) You _____ (be) at home when I _____ (call) you yesterday so you can't be the criminal.
6) As it turns out, the dinner Gary _____ (buy) us yesterday _____ (cost) him over $300!
7) We _____ (be) in such a hurry that we almost _____ (forget) to bring our child!

Like in *Chapter 6*, I'll handle the *negatives* and *questions* for the *past simple tense* only briefly. First, the *past simple negative*. Similar to the *past simple*, we must handle "**be**" differently than we handle all other *verbs*. When we use a form of "**be**," we simply place "**not**" <u>after</u> it. However, when we use any other *verb*, we need to place the *auxiliary verb* "**did not**" <u>before</u> the *main verb*. We use "**did not**" for all seven types of *subjects*. Meanwhile, the *main verb* is used in its <u>base form</u>.

1) <u>When we use a form of "be":</u>

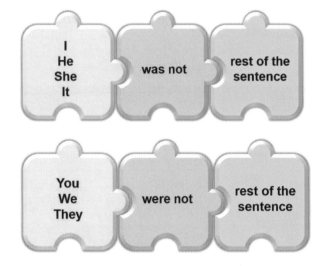

    A. They <u>were not</u> impressed.

    B. We <u>were not</u> tired.

    C. It <u>was not</u> cold.

    D. He <u>was not</u> pleased.

2) <u>When we use any other *verb*:</u>

    A. Nadia <u>did not go</u> outside today.

    B. Ben <u>did not eat</u> anything yesterday.

    C. I <u>didn't remember</u> to buy milk.

<u>The Past Simple Negative Exercises</u>
  ✓ **Complete the following sentences using the past simple negative forms of the verbs given in brackets.**

1) I _____ (go, not) out last night because I felt sick.
2) You _____ (come, not) to the party last week. Where were you?
3) He _____ (feel, not) well after watching the slasher movie.
4) David and I _____ (do, not) a good job in our presentations yesterday.
5) The book _____ (be, not) very fun; I _____ (enjoy, not) it much.
6) The comedians on stage last night _____ (be, not) entertaining at all.
7) I _____ (buy, not) chocolates today because you need to start staying away from them.

Next, the *past simple questions*. Again, we handle "**be**" differently than all other *verbs*. When we use "**be**," the *subject* and "**be**" <u>swap the places</u>; in other words, we <u>pull out "**be**" and move it to the front</u>. However, when we use any other *verb*, we need to <u>place the *auxiliary verb* "**did**" at the front of the sentence</u>. Then we write the *subject* and then the *main verb* in its <u>base form</u>.

1) <u>When we use a form of "be":</u>

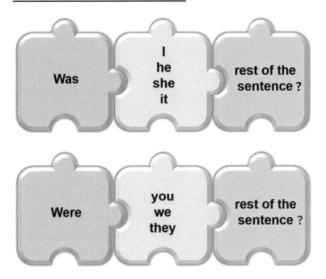

    A. <u>Were</u> you disappointed?

    B. <u>Was</u> she a good student?

    C. <u>Were</u> they in the class last week?

    D. <u>Was</u> I excited?

2) <u>When we use any other *verb*:</u>

    A. <u>Did you go</u> to the movies last week?

    B. <u>Did he get</u> into a car accident?

    C. <u>Did you have</u> fun at the party?

    D. <u>Did it snow</u> last winter?

Just as for the *present simple questions*, <u>these questions require yes/no answers</u>. <u>To require more specific answers, you need to use the *question words*</u>.

    A. <u>Where</u> did she meet that person?

    B. <u>When</u> did you go to the gym?

    C. <u>Why</u> did you come here?

    D. <u>Who </u>did you meet at the party?

Past Simple Questions Exercises

✓ **Complete the following questions using the correct past forms of the verbs and the subjects given in brackets.**

1) (buy, you) _____ a new dress?
2) (come, not, you) Why _____ to the party last week?
3) (leave, he) When _____ work yesterday?
4) (be, he) _____ always this tall?
5) (be, you) _____ in the gym anytime during the last week?
6) (eat, you) _____ the cookies that were left here?
7) (be, not, they) _____ over 40 years-old already?

7.2.2 Where to Use the Past Simple

As I said before, the **past simple** is one of the most used **tenses** in English. Just think about your daily conversations—you frequently talk about what you did in the **past**: what you ate yesterday, where you visited last week, and where you lived a few years ago. To discuss such simple events from the **past**, we must use the **past simple tense**. Hence, the **past simple** is definitely one of the most important **tenses** in English.

The major function of the **past simple tense** is to talk about an event from a fixed time in the **past**. Note that we must provide a specific time of occurrence, as we use a different **tense** to talk about an event for which the time in the **past** is unknown or unspecified. Another important aspect of **past simple** events is that they are usually already completed. In other words, such an event is either no longer happening or is no longer the case.

Specifically, we can spotlight three common uses of the **past simple**.

1. **To talk about actions completed in the past.**

2. **To talk about past habits.**

3. **To discuss durations of past events.**

The most frequent use of the **past simple** is to talk about actions completed in the **past**. Consider the following sentences.

1. **To talk about actions completed in the past.**

   A. **I bought a new laptop yesterday.**

   B. **The grizzly bear gave birth to a cub last week.**

> ✓ **Time words for talking about the past**
> **yesterday:** yesterday, yesterday morning, yesterday evening…
> **last:** last night, last week, last year, last summer, last Sunday…
> **ago:** ten minutes ago, two days ago, three weeks ago, two years ago…

Can you tell that the events in the **past** in both sentences are already over? In #1A, you're not purchasing the laptop right now—you already own the laptop; the buying process is over. Similarly, in #1B, the grizzly is not giving birth right now—the cub is already born; the delivery is over. Furthermore, notice how each sentence includes an expression of a definite time in the **past**. As was mentioned, whenever we talk in the **past simple**, we must provide a specific time of occurrence.

The other two uses don't involve events; rather, they mostly refer to states or facts from the **past**. First, we use the **past simple** to talk about **past** habits. Consider the following sentences.

2. <u>**To talk about past habits.**</u>

   A. I *always* <u>arrived</u> at school on time *when I was a student*.

   B. I *rarely* <u>had</u> cereal for breakfast *when I was young*.

Both #2A and #2B talk about <u>repeated events from the **past**</u> (i.e., ***past*** habits). This understanding is based on two parts that both sentences contain: 1) an ***adverb of frequency*** (see *Chapter 15*) and 2) a range of time expression. When you're handling habits, you need to let the listener know: 1) how often you practiced the habit (with an ***adverb of frequency***) and 2) the time period during which you practiced the habit (with a range of time expression). Another important thing to note: <u>the ***past*** habit must not still be a ***present*** habit</u>. As I mentioned, the ***past simple*** generally talks about <u>completed ***past*** events</u>. Hence, when you use the ***past simple*** to discuss a ***past*** habit, you must have <u>stopped the habit in the past</u>.

In #2A, 1) the ***adverb of frequency*** "always" tells us that you practiced the habit all the time, and 2) the range of time expression "**when I was a student**" tells us that this habit persisted only during your school years. This means that #2A indirectly suggests that you're no longer a student. Similarly, in #2B, 1) the ***adverb of frequency*** = "**rarely**" and 2) the range of time expression = "**when I was young.**" Again, #2B suggests that you're no longer young.

Finally, another common use of the ***past simple*** is to discuss <u>durations of ***past*** events</u>. Consider the following sentences.

3. <u>**To discuss durations of past events.**</u>

   A. I <u>lived</u> in Paris *for two years*.

   B. We <u>talked</u> on the phone *for an entire hour*.

Despite #3A and #3B both using the ***past simple tense***, they both discuss ***past*** events that <u>occurred over certain durations</u> (i.e., <u>not instantly</u>). However, the ***past simple tense*** does not place the audience in the middle of these events—as you'll see later, that's the job of the ***past continuous tense***. Rather, here, the events are <u>treated as facts</u>, as if they're instantaneous events. For this usage, we must include a duration of time expression to denote how long the event persisted. Again, since we're using the ***past simple tense***, <u>the events must not still be going on</u>; they must be <u>already completed</u> or <u>no longer the case</u>.

Sentence #3A states that you once lived in Paris for two years, but it's not referring to any event that happened during those two years in Paris; it treats your residency in Paris as a fact. Notice the duration of time expression "**for two years**" in #3A. Finally, if you are stating sentence #3A, then you must not still be living in Paris. Similarly, #3B treats the phone call as a fact, something that occurred, rather than focusing on the actual process of talking on the phone. It contains the duration of time expression "**for an entire hour**." If you say this, the phone call must now be over.

Following from above, we use the ***past simple negative*** in the following situations.

1. <u>**To talk about actions that didn't happen in the past.**</u>

   A. I <u>did not buy</u> a new laptop yesterday.

   B. The grizzly bear <u>did not give</u> birth last week.

2. <u>**To talk about past habits that you did not have.**</u>

   A. I <u>did not *always* arrive</u> at school on time *when I was a student*.

   B. I <u>did not *always* have</u> cereal for breakfast *when I was young*.

3. <u>**To clarify incorrect statements or assumptions about the durations of past events.**</u>

   A. I <u>did not live</u> in Paris *for two years*.

B. We <u>did not talk</u> over the phone *for an entire hour*.

Finally, we use ***past simple questions*** in the following situations.

1. <u>To ask about actions that may have been completed in the past.</u>

    A. <u>Did you buy</u> a new laptop yesterday?

    B. <u>Did the grizzly bear give</u> birth last week?

2. <u>To ask about past habits.</u>

    A. <u>Did you *always* arrive</u> at school on time *when you were a student*?

    B. <u>Did you *rarely* have</u> cereal for breakfast *when you were young*?

3. <u>To ask about the durations of past events.</u>

    A. <u>Did you live</u> in Paris *for two years*?

    B. <u>Did we talk</u> over the phone *for an entire hour*?

7.3   The Past Continuous

7.3.1 How to Form the Past Continuous

We use the ***past continuous*** to talk about <u>events that were in progress at some time in the *past*</u>. Forming sentences in the ***past continuous*** is very similar to forming sentences in the ***present continuous***—we <u>add the *auxiliary verb* "be"</u> to the front of a ***main verb*** that's in the ***continuous*** form (i.e., "**main verb + -ing**"). But, since we're now talking in the ***past tense***, we need to use one of the two ***past tense*** forms of "**be**" as the ***auxiliary verb***. In other words, <u>we use "**was**" and "**were**" as *auxiliary verbs*</u> when we speak in the ***past continuous***.

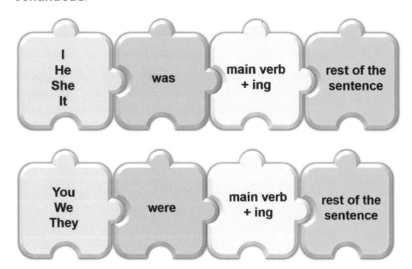

A. She <u>was packing</u> her books into her schoolbag.

B. They <u>were washing</u> the paint brushes.

C. I <u>was listening</u> to music last night.

D. He <u>was playing</u> tennis at three o'clock yesterday.

To form the *past continuous negative*, we <u>add "**not**" after "**was/were.**"</u>

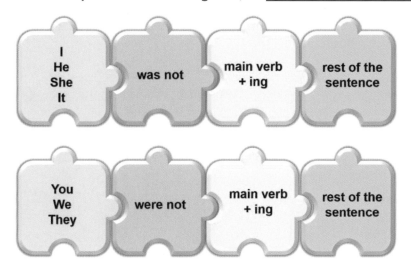

- A. I <u>was not sleeping</u> when you got home late last night.
- B. She <u>was not cooking</u> when I telephoned her.
- C. He <u>wasn't drinking</u> coffee in the library.
- D. They <u>weren't playing</u> tennis at three o'clock yesterday.

To form a *past continuous question*, <u>the positions of the *subject* and "**was/were**" are swapped</u>.

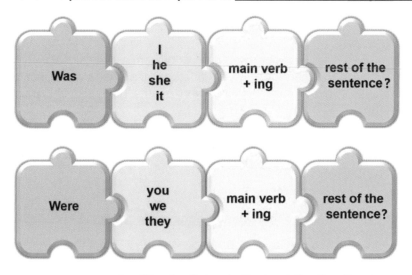

- A. <u>Was</u> he living in Paris at the time?
- B. <u>Was</u> it snowing when you arrived?
- C. <u>Were</u> they studying then?
- D. <u>Were</u> you working at 8 PM yesterday?

7.3.2 When to Use the Past Continuous

As I said, we use the **past continuous** to talk about an <u>action that was occurring at some time in the past</u>. Consider the following sentence.

1. I <u>was having</u> lunch at noon.

In #1, you're saying that at 12 o'clock today, you were <u>in the middle</u> of your lunch; you were <u>in the process</u> of having lunch at that time.

Following this, the **past continuous negative** (see #2 below) is used to say that <u>something was not in process at a certain time in the *past*</u>, while the **past continuous question** (see #3 below) <u>asks if something was in progress at a certain time in the *past*</u>.

2. He <u>was not watching</u> TV at that time.

3. <u>Were you sleeping</u> at 8 o'clock yesterday?

7.3.3 The Past Simple + the Past Continuous

An interesting way to use the **past continuous** is to <u>include it along with the **past simple** in the same sentence</u>. Consider the following.

1. I <u>was taking</u> a photo when a monkey <u>grabbed</u> my camera.

Here, the **verb** "take" is in the **past continuous** form, while the **verb** "grab" is in the **past simple** form. In sentences like this, the **past continuous** <u>describes an ongoing background event</u>, while the **past simple** <u>describes an interrupting event</u>. In the sentence above, you were already trying to take a photo of the monkey; you were obviously taking your time to line up the shot. Then, suddenly, the monkey grabbed your camera, interrupting the process. Using the **past continuous** and the **past simple** like this in the same sentence can lead to an interesting expression of a situation.

A tip to using this mode of expression effectively involves incorporating <u>time signal words</u>. Time signal words are words like "**suddenly**," "**before**," "**while**," and "**until**." Interrupting events (stated in the **past simple**) would come after words like "**suddenly**," "**before**," and "**until**," while ongoing **past** events (stated in the **past continuous**) would come after words like "**while**," and "**during**."

2. We <u>witnessed</u> a robbery *while* we <u>were walking</u> our dogs yesterday.

3. She <u>was screaming</u> her lungs out *before* you <u>showed</u> up.

4. They <u>were fighting</u> *until* their teacher <u>entered</u> the room.

5. I <u>was relaxing</u> in bed, *and then* I *suddenly* <u>realized</u> that I hadn't done my laundry.

The Past Continuous Exercises

✓ **Complete each of the following sentences using the past continuous form of one verb and the past simple form of the other verb given in brackets.**

1) I _____ (walk) to the bus stop when it suddenly _____ (start) to rain.
2) She _____ (try) really hard already to fix it before you _____ (arrive).
3) I _____ (hear) the postman knocking on the front door while I _____ (talk) on the phone yesterday.
4) They _____ (stop) by the grocery store while they _____ (drive) home yesterday to buy some onions.
5) Students _____ (whisper) to each other until the principal _____ (tell) them to be quiet.

- **Past simple and Past continuous**

	Past simple	Past continuous
verb form	infinitive + "ed"	was/were + present participle
Positive	I worked. You worked. She worked.	I was working You were working. She was working.
Negative	I did not work. You didn't work. She did not work.	I was not working You weren't working. She wasn't working.
Question	Did you work? Did she work?	Were you working? Was she working?
Negative question	Didn't you work? Did she not work? (Didn't she work?)	Were you not working? Was she not working? (Wasn't she working?)

7.4 Participles

7.4.1 Verb-Based Adjectives

Now, we arrive at the first "difficult" topic in this book. Hopefully, everything we've looked at so far has been somewhat familiar to you. But this might be something you've never considered before. Don't worry though. I will walk you through it. To start, let's define *participles.* First, a *participle* is a word derived from a *verb* and which we use as an *adjective*. In other words, each *participle* is an adjective that carries a message related to a certain action. You'll see later that *adjectives* are words that describe *nouns* (see *Chapter 14*).

7.4.2 The Present Participle

There are two types of *participles* in English: the *present participle* and the *past participle*. Let's start by looking at the *present participles. Present participles* take the *present continuous* forms of the respective *verbs* (i.e., "*verb* + -ing"). Here are some examples of how we'd use *present participles* as *adjectives*.

1. the <u>laughing</u> *face*

2. the <u>crying</u> *girl*

Here, "**laughing**" and "**crying**" are *present participles*. While they may take the respective *present continuous* forms of the *verbs* "**laugh**" and "**cry**," they are not used as *verbs* in these phrases. Instead, they are used as *adjectives* that describe the "**face**" and the "**girl**," respectively.

What then do *present participles* mean? Whenever a *noun* is described by a *present participle*, it means that the *noun* is currently performing the action represented by the root verb of the *present participle*. In #1 above, we mean that the "**face**" (*noun*) is currently performing the action "**(to) laugh**" (root verb). The same goes for #2: the "**girl**" (*noun*) is currently performing the action "**(to) cry**" (root verb).

7.4.3 The Past Participle

Now, let's look at *past participles*. Fundamentally, the *past participle* form of a *verb* matches its *past simple* form (i.e., "**verb + -ed**"). However, there are <u>more *irregular verbs* than *regular verbs*</u>. In other words, there are lots of *verbs* whose *past participles* take <u>completely different forms</u> than their respective *past simple* forms. The following tables list the *past simple* forms and the *past participles* of some common *verbs*. Separate tables are provided for *regular verbs* and *irregular verbs*.

- **Common regular Verbs**

Infinitive	Past Simple	Past Participle	Infinitive	Past Simple	Past Participle
accept	accepted	accepted	identify	identified	identified
act	acted	acted	invite	invited	invited
bake	baked	baked	join	joined	joined
behave	behaved	behaved	love	loved	loved
close	closed	closed	manage	managed	managed
compare	compared	compared	need	needed	needed
compete	competed	competed	open	opened	opened
disagree	disagreed	disagreed	organize	organized	organized
dry	dried	dried	pass	passed	passed
end	ended	ended	protect	protected	protected
enjoy	enjoyed	enjoyed	shop	shopped	shopped
fix	fixed	fixed	slow	slowed	slowed
follow	followed	followed	turn	turned	turned
guess	guessed	guessed	underline	underlined	underlined
hunt	hunted	hunted	want	wanted	wanted

- **Common Irregular Verbs**

Infinitive	Past Simple	Past Participle	Infinitive	Past Simple	Past Participle
be	was/were	been	lend	lent	lent
become	became	become	let	let	let
bend	bent	bent	lose	lost	lost
bite	bit	bitten	make	made	made
blow	blew	blown	meet	met	met
break	broke	broken	pay	paid	paid
begin	began	begun	put	put	put
bring	brought	brought	read	read	read

buy	bought	bought	ride	rode	ridden
catch	caught	caught	ring	rang	rung
choose	chose	chosen	run	ran	run
come	came	come	say	said	said
draw	drew	drawn	see	saw	seen
do	did	done	sell	sold	sold
drink	drank	drunk	send	sent	sent
drive	drove	driven	shake	shook	shaken
eat	ate	eaten	shoot	shot	shot
fall	fell	fallen	sing	sang	sung
feed	fed	fed	sit	sat	sat
fell	felt	felt	sleep	slept	slept
fight	fought	fought	speak	spoke	spoken
find	found	found	spend	spent	spent
fly	flew	flown	stand	stood	stood
forget	forgot	forgotten	steal	stole	stolen
get	got	gotten	swim	swam	swum
give	gave	given	take	took	taken
go	went	gone	teach	taught	taught
grow	grew	grown	tear	tore	torn
hang	hung	hung	tell	told	told
have	had	had	think	thought	thought
hear	heard	heard	throw	threw	thrown
hide	hid	hidden	understand	understood	understood
hold	held	held	wake	woke/waked	woken/waked
keep	kept	kept	win	won	won
know	knew	known	wear	wore	worn
leave	left	left	write	wrote	written

Here's one thing about the spelling of **past participles**: there seems to be another <u>minor pattern</u> where some **verbs** receive an "**-en**" at the end to transform into their respective **past participle** forms (e.g., be → been, eat → eaten, beat → beaten, and bit → bitten). However, <u>this is not a proper rule</u>, simply a pattern we can keep in mind.

Here are some examples of how we'd use *past participles* as *adjectives*.

1. the <u>abandoned</u> house

2. the <u>forgotten</u> time

Again, the words here, "**abandoned**" and "**forgotten**," are <u>not actually *verbs*; in these phrases, they are</u> <u>*adjectives*</u>.

In terms of their meanings, *past participles* indicate a stance similar to that of the *passive voice* (see *Chapter 20*). In other words, a *past participle* describes an <u>action done by someone else on the *target noun*</u>. In #1, the *target noun* is the "**house**"; the *past participle* "**abandoned**" is describing the "**house.**" Here, the *past participle* "**abandoned**" signifies that the "**house**" <u>has been vacated by its previous owners and is no longer cared for by anyone</u>. Obviously, a "**house**" cannot abandon itself. Similarly, in #2, the *target noun* "**time**" (referring to a certain time in the *past*) has been erased and so <u>is no longer remembered by a person, a group of people, or by people in general</u>; "**time**" cannot forget itself. As such, *past participles* are *adjectives* that describe actions being performed by others on the respective *target nouns*.

7.4.4 Present Participles and Past Participles Used in Verb Tenses

So, you might be wondering why we suddenly diverted to *participles* when we were looking at *tenses*. After all, *tenses* are all about *verbs*, and *participles* are not even *verbs*—they're *adjectives*! Here's a hint: where did we see *present participles* before? *Continuous tenses*. That's right—*participles* <u>are used in *tenses*</u>.

1. *Present participles* are used in *continuous tenses*.

2. *Past participles* are used in *perfect tenses*.

We've already looked at a couple of *continuous tenses*—the *present continuous* and the *past continuous*. Recall how both of these *continuous tenses* require use of the *present participle* forms of the *main verb*.

However, we haven't looked at the *perfect tenses* yet. This is exactly why we just covered the *participles*—I needed to introduce you to the *past participles* in order to move on to the *perfect tenses*. We'll start looking at the *perfect tenses* in the next section.

Before moving on, here's a table that shows where *present* and *past participles* are used for each of the twelve *tenses* in English. As you'll see, *present* and *past participles* appear in many different *tenses*.

- **present participle / past participles**

Past Tenses	Example
Past simple	I **did** my homework.
Past continuous	I **was doing** my homework
Past perfect simple	I **had done** my homework.
Past perfect continuous	I **had been doing** my homework.

Present Tenses	Example
Present simple	I **do** my homework.
Present continuous	I **am doing** my homework.
Present perfect simple	I **have done** my homework.
Present perfect continuous	I **have been doing** my homework.

Future Tenses	Example
Future simple	I **will do** my homework
Future continuous	I **will be doing** my homework.
Future perfect simple	I **will have done** my homework.
Future perfect continuous	I **will have been doing** my homework.

7.5 The Present Perfect Simple

7.5.1 Perfection

The main reason we've handled *participles* is so we can progress to the *perfect tenses*. The term "*perfect*" in *perfect tenses* is pretty confusing, isn't it? What's so "*perfect*" about them? Well, to truly understand the name, we must go back to the origin of the word "*perfect*," that is, the Latin word "*perfectum*." "*Perfectum*" means "complete." In fact, "complete" is one of the dictionary definitions of the English word "*perfect*." Now that I've mentioned it, doesn't the word, "*perfect*" make you feel a certain sense of completion? When you say that something is "*perfect*," it feels like there's nothing more you can do to it to make it better; everything has already been done. Let's extend this line of thought.

Perfect tenses mainly discuss events that are already completed. But wait, there's more. *Perfect tenses* also handle the relationship between a completed event and a *future* event. Any sentence that's in a *perfect tense* is handling two events at the same time: 1) a main, completed event and 2) an event that occurred later, which is influenced by the main event.

7.5.2 Introduction to the Present Perfect Simple

The first case of the *perfect tense* that we're going to cover is the *present perfect simple*. The *present perfect simple* is used to talk about: 1) an event from the recent *past* that affects 2) the *present* moment; that is, 1) the main event is from the near *past*, while 2) the related event unfolds in the *present*. To make things simpler, I'll now refer to the two parts as 1) the *main past* and 2) the *related present*, respectively.

The Present Perfect Simple

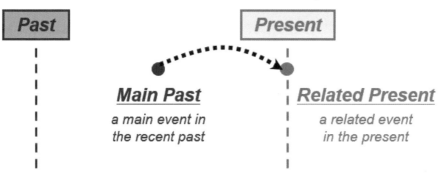

Note carefully that although the name "*present perfect simple*" includes "*present*," the <u>main event is from the</u> <u>*past*</u>.

7.5.3 How to Form the Present Perfect Simple

In order to speak in the *present perfect simple*, <u>we use *auxiliary verbs* "**has**" and "**have.**"</u> We use "**has**" for the *subjects* "**he**," "**she**," and "**it**," while we use "**have**" for all other *subjects*. <u>We place the *auxiliary verb*</u> "**has/have**" before the *past participle* form of the *main verb*. (Now do you see why we covered *participles*?)

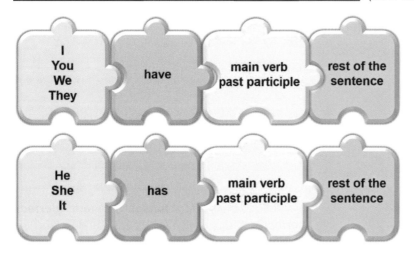

A. He <u>has scored</u> two goals.

B. I<u>'ve</u> just <u>finished</u> my homework.

C. They <u>have moved</u> to Sydney.

D. She <u>has</u> already <u>reached</u> there.

To form the *present perfect simple negative*, we add "**not**" after "**has/have**."

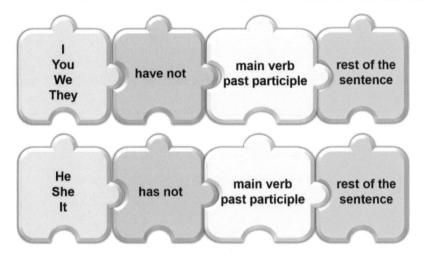

A. It <u>has not rained</u> for months.

B. I <u>have not finished</u> my homework yet.

C. They <u>have</u> still <u>not arrived.</u>

D. She <u>hasn't mastered</u> English yet, but she can communicate.

 tip   We use the following words frequently with the present perfect simple tense: *just, already, yet, just now, ever, lately, and recently. Already* comes between have/has and the main verb past participle; *yet* only appears at the end of negative sentences.

To form the *present perfect simple question*, <u>the positions of the **subject** and "**has/have**" are swapped.</u>

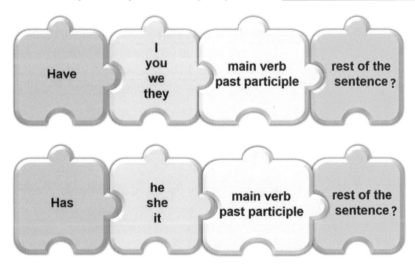

A. <u>Have</u> you <u>read</u> the book yet?

B. <u>Have</u> I <u>met</u> you before?

C. <u>Has</u> he <u>heard</u> any news?

D. How much coffee <u>have</u> you <u>drunk</u> today?

7.5.4 Where to Use the Present Perfect Simple

Remember when I said the *past simple* is one of the most frequently used *tenses* in English? Well, the *present perfect simple* is the other one. In other words, the *past simple* and the *present perfect simple* are the two most commonly used *tenses* in English.

The *present perfect simple*, however, offers even more uses than the *past simple*. Here are the different situations where we use the *present perfect simple tense*.

1. **For events from the recent past that affect the present**

2. **For events from the recent past that are still happening**

3. **For past experience where the time does not matter (or is unclear)**

4. **Repeated action from an unspecified period in the past**

5. **For just completed events (+ "just")**

Before we look at each one, let me remind you that the *present perfect simple* describes two events at once: the 1) *main past* and the 2) *related present*. Keep this in mind as you go through the following sections.

First, the most fundamental use of the *present perfect simple* is to discuss a main event from the recent *past* that affects the *present*. Consider the following sentences.

1. **For events from the recent past that affect the present**

    A. I have cooked dinner for us.

    B. I have arrived in America.

Sentences #1A and #1B both describe events from the recent *past*. You cooking dinner and you arriving in America are both finished events. What's peculiar in both #1A and #1B is that the respective *related presents* are missing. I told you that every sentence in the *present perfect simple* handles two events at once: 1) the *main past* and 2) the *related present*. But, neither of these sentences mention anything about 2) the *related present*. Why not? Is it okay to do this? Well, yes, it sure is.

As a matter of fact, most sentences in the *present perfect simple* omit the *related present*. This is because the *related present* is often so obvious that it does not need to be stated. What do you think the *related present* in #1A is? That's right, it's that dinner is ready to be served to "**us**." What about #1B; what's the *related present* there? It's that you're now in America; your current location is America. As such, the *related present* is often omitted because it's so obvious that it can "go without saying."

As a side point, notice that in both sentences the omitted *related present* is more of an idea than an event. In this way, the *related present* part of the *present perfect simple* can stand for an idea as well as an event. However, the *main past* part must be an event/action.

You only explicitly state the *related present* when it is specific and/or less apparent. Consider the following sentence.

    C. I have arrived in America, and I am exhausted.

You being exhausted from the trip is not a *related present* that your audience can take for granted from the first part of that sentence alone. Therefore, you need to clearly state the *related present* here. Also, notice that the *related present* part of the sentence is expressed in the *present simple tense*.

Next, we also use the *present perfect simple* for events in the recent *past* that are ongoing in the *present*. Consider the following sentences.

2. **For events from the recent past that are still happening**

A. Olivia <u>has gone</u> on a trip to Egypt.

B. She <u>has been</u> to the cinema twice *this week*.

Notice again how the ***related presents*** are not explicitly stated in either of these sentences. Here, <u>the idea that these events are still occurring can be considered the **related present** part</u>. In #2A, the ***related present*** is that Olivia left for Egypt sometime in the ***past***, and she is still on her trip. At the same time, a secondary ***related present*** is that, since her trip is still happening, Olivia is not in her office, home, or wherever she usually is at a given time. Next, #2B, which is quite a peculiar one. The important aspect of this sentence is that "**this week**" must not yet be over. You'd most likely say this later in the week, maybe on Saturday or Sunday, to indicate that "**she**" had paid two visits to the cinema earlier this week. If she paid two visits to the cinema last week (i.e., the week that's over), we'd say the following instead.

C. She <u>visited</u> the cinema twice *last week*.

Notice how that sentence is in the ***past simple tense***. <u>We use the ***past simple*** when an event is simply completed</u>; <u>we use the ***present perfect simple*** when an event is still going on</u>. I'll talk more about the differences between these two later.

The next example represents what is probably the most common use of the ***present perfect simple tense***—that is, <u>to talk about ***past*** experiences</u>. Consider the following sentences.

3. <u>**For past experience where the time does not matter (or is unclear)**</u>

A. She <u>has seen</u> the movie already.

B. I <u>have been</u> to the police station once.

In #3A, we learn about someone's experience with the movie—"**she**" has already experienced the movie in the ***past***. However, note that no further information about exactly when the event happened is provided here. We know that she's definitely seen the movie before, but we don't know how long ago. Similarly, in #3B, we understand that you've been to the police station once in the ***past***, but we have no idea when. Again, we <u>do not provide specific time details</u> when we talk about our ***past*** experiences in the ***present perfect simple tense***. Keep this in mind.

Another way of using the ***present perfect simple*** to discuss your ***past*** experiences is to talk about <u>repeated events from the ***past***</u>.

4. <u>**Repeated action from an unspecified period in the past**</u>

A. We <u>have visited</u> Korea several times.

B. I <u>have visited</u> California every summer since I was 18.

Again, similar to the case above in #3, <u>the specific timeframe is not provided here</u>. In fact, #4A provides absolutely no information about when your visits to Korea happened. In #4B, however, a starting point is provided—you started those visits to California after you turned 18. Still, we don't know the exact dates of all of those visits to California for all those years. Also, the word "**since**" in #4B implies that you have not stopped visiting California; you must still be visiting California every summer.

Here's an interesting way of using the ***present perfect simple***—add the ***adverb*** "just." When you use the ***tense*** with "**just**," you can signify that <u>the ***past*** event was completed moments ago</u>.

5. <u>**For just completed events (+ "just")**</u>

A. I <u>have just finished</u> my homework.

     B. **I <u>have just finished</u> doing the dishes.**

Sentence #5A indicates that you finished doing your homework just moments ago. Compare #5A with the following sentence.

     C. **I <u>have finished</u> my homework**

In #5C, we don't know exactly how long it's been since you finished your homework. From such a sparse statement, we may be able to guess that you finished it in recent times, but we don't know if that was a day ago or just half an hour ago. When we add the word "**just**," as in #5A, it signals that the homework was completed only moments ago. Although the exact time sense would still depend on the context, a sentence like #5A would generally imply that you finished your homework within the past five minutes or so. The same goes for #5B; you probably completed the action of washing the dishes within the past five minutes or so.

7.5.5 Gone vs. Been

An interesting topic related to the *present perfect simple* is the difference between "**gone**" and "**been**." "**Gone**" is the *past participle* of "**go**" and "**been**" is the *past participle* of "**be**." Both are often associated with the *present perfect simple*. "**Gone**" and "**been**" may sound like similar things, but their meanings are clearly different. The contrast between the two can be explained as follows.

    1. <u>"Gone" = the event is still happening.</u>

    2. <u>"Been" = the event is no longer happening.</u>

Consider the following sentences.

    1. **Jack has <u>gone</u> to the mall**

    2. **Jack has <u>been</u> to the mall.**

#1 indicates that Jack left for the mall a few moments ago, and he's no longer here. It also implies that Jack is most likely at the mall right now, or will be soon. In contrast, #2 states that Jack has recently visited the mall, but he's no longer at the mall.

The following conversations should give you more clues about how "**gone**" and "**been**" differ.

    3. **Where's Ben? / He's <u>gone</u> to the mall.**

    4. **I've never seen you wear that jacket. / Yeah, I've <u>been</u> to the mall recently.**

7.5.6 The Present Perfect Simple vs. the Past Simple

As mentioned, the *present perfect simple* and the *past simple* are the <u>two most-used *tenses*</u> in English. Plus, as you now know, they are used in quite similar ways—fundamentally, they both discuss <u>events from the *past*</u>. Therefore, it's easy to confuse them. However, as they are clearly grammatically different, they can never be used interchangeably. So, what's the difference between these two *tenses*? And how do we decide which one to use where?

We use the *past simple* to talk about <u>something that happened at a definite time in the *past*</u>. On the other hand, we use the *present perfect simple* to talk about <u>something that happened at an unspecified time</u> or an <u>unknown time in the *past*</u>. Let's have a look at the following two conversations.

    1. **Have you ever been to France? / Yes, I <u>visited</u> Paris in 2010.**

    2. **Have you ever been to France? / Yes, I <u>have visited</u> Paris several times.**

In #1, a definite time for your visit to Paris is provided: the year 2010. Therefore, it is correct to use the *past simple*. However, in #2, a definite time for your Paris visit is not provided. Therefore, it is correct to use the *present perfect simple*.

As such, the choice between the *past simple* and the *present perfect simple* depends on whether you provide a definite time for an event. If you do, you use the *past simple*, and if you do not, you use the *present perfect simple*.

By the way, the reason for not providing the definite time doesn't have to be because you don't remember. Sometimes, the time is irrelevant. Consider the following sentences.

3. **John <u>fixed</u> the car a few hours ago.**

4. **John <u>has fixed</u> the car.**

If you simply want to emphasize the fact that the car is now fixed, then you'd say #4. The time sense is irrelevant here because the only thing that's important is that the car works again. On the other hand, #3 highlights that John is the person who fixed the car, and that the repair process was finished a few hours before.

The Present Perfect Simple Exercises 01

✓   **Complete the following sentences using the present perfect simple tense of the verbs given in brackets.**

1) Today's the due day and he still _____ (do, not) his homework.
2) I _____ (visit) the nurse's office several times during last week because of the flu.
3) My parents _____ (be, not) on a plane before so they're feeling quite anxious now.
4) She _____ (receive) an eviction notice from her landlord recently; that's why she's so stressed out.
5) He _____ (know) David for years; they're very close friends.
6) We _____ (be) here for two weeks already!
7) Ray _____ (meet, not) my new sister yet.

The Present Perfect Simple Exercises 02

✓   **Complete the following questions in the present perfect simple tense.**

1) (clean) _____ your room yet?
2) (see, not) _____ the notice yet? They're renovating the gym!
3) (be) _____ sick lately? I haven't seen you in class recently.
4) (receive) _____ any news from David recently? I haven't heard him in ages.

✓   **Choose the correct word for each sentence.**

1) I've (gone/been) to New York only once in my life.
2) She's (gone/been) to the hospital because she hurt herself badly while cooking.
3) They've (gone/been) to Paris to meet their business partners.
4) I've (gone/been) to the principal's office twice this week because I got into a fight with my classmate.

✓ **Use either the past simple tense or the present perfect simple tense to complete the sentences.**

1) He _____ (visit) the principal's office five times already this week. He _____ (go) there yesterday too! I swear he's such a troublemaker!
2) I _____ (be) to China many times. In fact, I _____ (be) in China this very moment last week!
3) Jack _____ (get) out of the hospital two days ago. He _____ (be) in there over the last two weeks.
4) Michael _____ (be) to prison a couple of times in the past, but he _____ (be, not) in prison in March 2021.

7.6 The Present Perfect Continuous

7.6.1 Introduction to the Present Perfect Continuous

There's really only <u>one</u> purpose for the ***present perfect continuous***. By definition, we use this ***tense*** to talk about an <u>event with a certain duration that started in the recent ***past*** and affects the ***present*** moment</u>. The event in focus <u>may be either finished or still in progress</u>. Consider the following diagram.

The Present Perfect Continuous

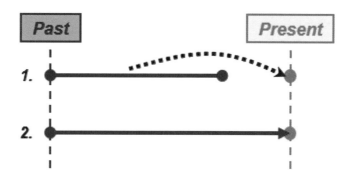

7.6.2 How to Form the Present Perfect Continuous

To speak in the *present perfect continuous*, we need to <u>use two *auxiliary verbs*</u>: "**has/have**" and "**been.**" They occur in this exact order in a sentence: "**has/have been**". The *main verb* in its *present participle* form (i.e., "**main verb + -ing**") is placed after "**has/have been.**"

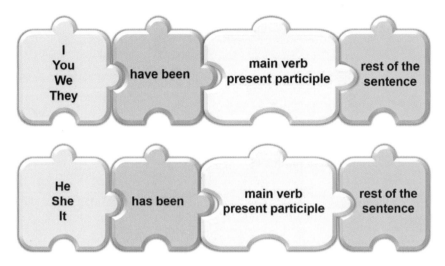

A.   He <u>has been playing</u> computer games for three hours.

B.   We <u>have been living</u> together for three years.

C.   I <u>have been waiting</u> for you since 3 o'clock.

D.   She <u>has been working</u> here for 15 years.

In the *negative*, <u>the first *auxiliary verb*</u> "**has/have**" receives the "**not**"; on the other hand, "**been**" is left as is.

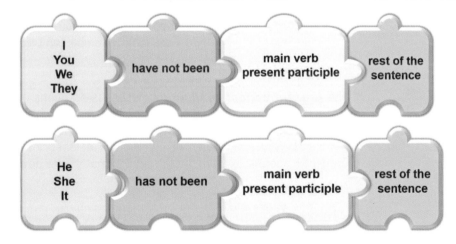

A.   He <u>has not been practicing</u> his English.

B.   She <u>has not been watching</u> TV much recently.

C.   They <u>haven't been living</u> here for very long.

D.   It <u>hasn't been snowing</u> this winter.

For *questions*, the positions of the *subject* and "has/have" are swapped. Note that the position of "**been**" does not change. However, given the above swap, "**been**" now appears directly after the *subject*.

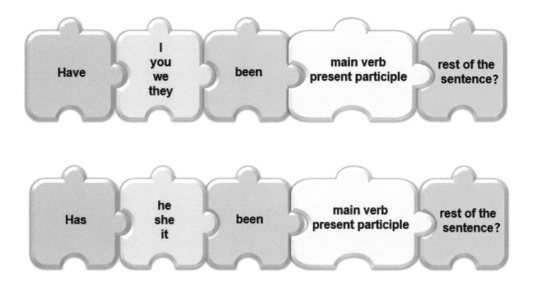

    A.   <u>Has it been raining</u>?

    B.   <u>Has he been working</u> in this company for more than two years?

    C.   <u>Have you been studying</u> English for a long time?

    D.   How long <u>have you been living</u> here?

7.6.3 Where to Use the Present Perfect Continuous

As I said above, the *present perfect continuous* only has a <u>single use</u>: to talk about an <u>event of a certain duration that started in the *past* and affects the *present*</u>. In more practical terms, we use the *present perfect continuous* to <u>discuss the duration of a *past* event</u>; how long something's been happening. Again, the event must have <u>started in the *past*</u>, but it <u>either has finished recently or is still happening</u>. Let's look at some examples.

    1.   **I have been painting the house all day. I'm exhausted.**

First, notice the time expression in #1: "**all day**." As the *present perfect continuous* discusses durations of events, we must include a time expression in this type of sentence. In #1, a time expression that directly states the duration has been used. Moving along, the way #1 is written suggests that the activity is now over; the house is now completely painted. However, if you're saying this, it is likely already pretty late into the day, at least close to sunset. Finally, in #1, the effect on your *present* moment is clearly explained: the result is that you're now exhausted.

    2.   **She has been studying English since she was five years-old.**

Can you spot the time expression in #2? It's "**since she was five years-old**." Here, the important word is "**since**"; that word marks the starting point of an event. Next, #2 implies that the activity is not yet over; she's still studying English in the *present*. Finally, #2 does not explain the effect on the *present*. Hence, the only "effect" we can extract from #2 is a rough estimate of her current level of English—the level would be similar to most people her age who've been studying English since they were five.

    3.   **I haven't been paying attention to this class.**

Sentence #3 has no time expression. This is because the time sense is obvious enough. When you say #3, the duration of you not been paying attention is equal to the duration of "**this class**" at the moment you spoke. Even if your distraction did not span the entire class period, we know that it occurred within the duration of the class.

As such, <u>in situations where the duration is obvious enough, we don't have to explicitly provide it</u>. Note also that the effect on the **present** is not explained either. Nevertheless, we can deduce the result: "I've learned nothing from the class."

> **4. Have you been working out? You look good!**

Sentence #4 also has no time expression. On top of that, there are no clues like in #3. However, an important thing about **present perfect continuous questions** is that <u>they always ask about the recent **past**</u>. Since #4 is in the **present perfect continuous tense**, we can figure out that the speaker is asking if you've been going to the gym <u>in recent times</u>.

7.6.4 The Present Perfect Continuous vs. the Present Perfect Simple

Another important difference we must investigate is the difference between the **present perfect continuous** and the **present perfect simple**. Both tenses talk about events that began in the **past**. The contrast is in <u>whether the event is finished or is still in progress</u>.

When we use the **present perfect continuous**, the event that started in the **past** can <u>be either finished or still in progress</u>. However, when we use the **present perfect simple**, the event that started in the **past** is <u>always completed</u>. Let's have a look at three cases.

> **1. I've been fixing my car for the last two hours. It's working now.**
>
> **2. I've been fixing my car for the last two hours. I'm covered in oil.**
>
> **3. I've fixed my car. Now I can drive again.**

In #1 and #2 the **present perfect continuous tense** is used; in #3, the **present perfect simple tense** is used. In #1, the second sentence lets us know that the event of fixing the car is now over, as the car is working again. However, in #2, we don't know if the fixing of the car is completed or not. We just know that you've had such an intense battle with your car during the last two hours that it looks like you've been completely dipped in oil. As such, the **present perfect continuous** can be used <u>both for completed events and for events still in progress</u>.

In contrast, in #3, the event is most definitely finished. Relatedly, it'd be wrong to say the following.

> **4. I've fixed my car. It's still not working.**

Together, the sentences in #4 do not make sense. When you've fixed your car, then the fixing process is surely over, and you must be able to drive the car again. As such, you should only use the **present perfect simple tense** <u>when the event from the recent **past** is finished</u>.

The Present Perfect Continuous Exercises

> ✓ **Use either the present perfect simple or the present perfect continuous to complete the following paragraph.**

Hello, my name is Sam. I _____ (play) for Leeds United for three years now. I _____ (dream) of becoming a professional football player ever since I was a kid. To achieve that goal, I started training as early as when I was nine years-old. When I turned 15, I was accepted into the Leeds United academy. Ever since then, I _____ (train) for over six hours every day, even after being accepted into the professional team. All the training definitely _____ (pay off), as I _____ (score) 26 goals for my team already in my 34 appearances. Especially, in the recent matches, I _____ (score) almost every match! But, as you'd agree, I _____ (work) hard to achieve this form. And I will continue to work hard to keep my performance up.

- **Present Perfect Simple and Present Perfect Continuous**

	Present Perfect Simple	Present Perfect Continuous
verb form	have/has + past participle	have/has + been + present participle
Positive	I have worked. You have worked. She has worked.	I have been working You have been working. She has been working.
Negative	I have not worked. You haven't worked. She hasn't worked.	I have not been working You haven't been working. She hasn't been working.
Question	Have you worked? Has she worked?	Have you been working? Has she been working?
Negative question	Haven't you worked? Has she not worked? (Hasn't she worked?)	Have you not been working? Has she not been working? (Hasn't she been working?)

7.7 The Past Perfect Simple

7.7.1 Introduction to the Past Perfect Simple

The ***past perfect simple*** handles <u>1) a main event that occurred in the ***far past*** that affected 2) the more ***recent past***</u>. I'll now refer to the two as 1) the ***main far past*** and 2) the ***related recent past***, respectively.

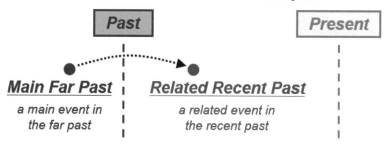

The Past Perfect Simple

Past | Present

Main Far Past | **Related Recent Past**
a main event in the far past | *a related event in the recent past*

Do you remember our talk about being able to omit the second part (i.e., the ***related recent past***) if it's obvious enough? Well, with regards to the ***past perfect simple tense***, the second part is usually not so obvious. Hence, <u>we often talk explicitly about both events</u> in the ***past perfect simple***; <u>the ***related recent past*** is rarely left out</u>.

7.7.2 How to Form the Past Perfect Simple

Principally, we form the *past perfect simple tense* by placing the *auxiliary verb* "had" in front of the *past participle* form of the *main verb*.

    A. The police <u>had known</u> about the incident for a while.

    B. I <u>had finished</u> my homework before.

Following this, we form the *past perfect simple negative* by adding "**not**" after "**had**."

    A. They <u>had not visited</u> New York City until then.

    B. She <u>had not had</u> time to explain herself yet.

Finally, we form *past perfect simple questions* by swapping the positions of the *subject* and "**had**."

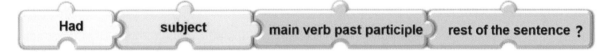

    A. <u>Had you cleaned</u> up your house by then?

    B. <u>Had he discussed</u> his salary with his boss before?

However, as I said above, we rarely omit the *related recent past* in the *past perfect simple tense*. Then, how do we provide the *related recent past* in a sentence? We do so by adding a clause in the *past simple tense*. Then, the *past perfect simple* describes the *main far past*, while the *past simple* describes the *related recent past*. In other words, most of the time, a sentence in the *past perfect simple* consists of two clauses: one in the *past perfect simple tense* and one in the *past simple tense*. The order of the clauses can be reversed.

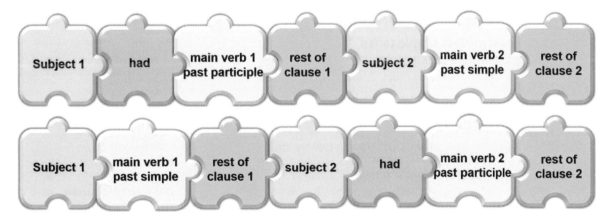

A. After Michael <u>had finished</u> his work, he <u>went</u> to see a movie.

B. I <u>cleaned</u> my house once the plumber <u>had gone</u> away.

C. It was only after she <u>had run</u> away that they <u>realized</u> she suffered from bullying at school.

D. By the time he <u>called</u> her, she <u>had left</u> work.

As you can see from the example sentences, we often use time signal words like "**before**," "**already**," and "**after**" in these types of sentences to clearly illustrate the time relationship between the two events. The time signal word is usually placed before either of the clauses.

Okay then, what's up with the sentences above that don't include the second part? Are they incomplete? No. We saw with the *present perfect simple tense* that <u>when the second part is obvious enough, we can omit it</u>. <u>The same applies here</u>—sometimes the *related recent past* is obvious enough. Let's look at one of our examples again.

1. The police <u>had known</u> about the incident for a while.

This sentence does not contain the extra clause in the *past simple tense*. What do you think the *related recent past* is here? If we were to write out a full version of this sentence, it could be as follows.

2. The police <u>had known</u> about the incident for a while *before the public <u>learned</u> about it as well*.

As you can see, the *related recent past* is somewhat obvious here. So, we can drop it. However, do remember that <u>it's always a good idea to explicitly state the *related recent past* whenever you're speaking in the *past perfect simple tense*</u>.

7.7.3 Where to Use the Past Perfect Simple

While the main use of the *past perfect simple* is to talk about <u>two related events from the *past*</u> there are a couple of other interesting ways to use the *tense*. Let's look more into where we can use the *past perfect simple*.

1. <u>For two related events from the past</u>

2. <u>To discuss an insight from the past</u>

3. <u>For the third conditional</u>

Again, the main use of the *past perfect simple* is to talk about <u>two related events from the *past*</u>. Consider the following example.

1. The train <u>had left</u> before we <u>arrived</u> at the station.

The first clause in the *past perfect simple tense*, "**the train had left**," describes the *main far past*, while the second clause in the *past simple tense*, "**we arrived at the station**," describes the *related recent past*. The time signal word "**before**" clearly tells you that the leaving of the train happened before you arriving at the station.

An interesting way of using the *past perfect simple* is to describe <u>an insight from the *past*</u>. Consider the following sentence.

2. <u>I'd never known</u> the importance of friends before one of my closest friends <u>left</u> me.

The first clause in the *past perfect simple tense*, "**I'd never known the importance of friends**," describes <u>something you realized after a certain *past* event</u>, while the second clause in the *past simple tense*, "**one of my closest friends left me**," pinpoints <u>the *past* event that made you have the realization</u>. Again, this sentence contains a time signal word, "**before**," to make this clarification.

As such, in this kind of sentence, you'd use expressions like "**I had never known**," or "**I had never realized**." Then, using the **past simple tense**, you present the life-changing event that led to your epiphany.

Finally, we use the **past perfect simple** for **_third conditional_** sentences. We discuss **conditionals** near the end of the book—see _Chapter 21_. I'll only provide an example here.

   3.   **If you <u>had attended</u> your classes properly, your grades would have been better.**

As you can see, this type of sentence provides an <u>alternative outcome for a **past**</u> event. Again, we'll talk more about **conditionals** in _Chapter 21_.

7.7.4 The Past Perfect Simple vs. the Present Perfect Simple

To compare the **past perfect simple** and the **present perfect simple**, we need to focus on <u>when a given event happens</u>. When we use the **past perfect simple tense**, <u>the main event happens in the **far past**, and it affects the **recent past**</u>. However, when we use the **present perfect simple**, <u>the main event happens in the **recent past**, and it affects the **present**</u>.

Consider the following examples.

Present Perfect Simple	Past Perfect Simple
I **am** so relieved. I **have** just **passed** my test.	I **was** so relieved. I **had** just **passed** my test.
We**'ve finished** the match, and now it**'s** time for a feast.	We**'d finished** the game when our coach **called** us for dinner.
His team **has won**, and he**'s** ecstatic.	His team **had won**, so they **went** to the restaurant to celebrate.

The Past Perfect Simple Exercises 01

   ✓   **Complete the following sentences using the past perfect simple or the past simple.**

   1)   Before I _____ (come) here, I _____ (speak) to Jack. I can confirm that he is not responsible for this case.
   2)   I _____ (watch) the movie three times already by the time Jenny _____ (see) it for the first time. In fact, I'm the one who recommended her to watch it in the first place.
   3)   I _____ (go over) the topic five times yesterday, so I _____ (do, not) find the test difficult at all, unlike some others.
   4)   If I _____ (read) the book earlier, I would have been able to have a deeper conversation about it with you. It's a shame I haven't.

The Past Perfect Simple Exercises 02

✓ **Complete the following sentences using either the past perfect simple or the present perfect simple.**

1) You _____ (change) your style recently. Did something happen to you?
2) I _____ (notice) that my car was struggling by then, but it was too late to turn around.
3) There _____ (be) a change to the company policies. You should read up on them as soon as possible.
4) _____ (see, you) my car keys? I swear I left them on the dinner table yesterday.
5) Emily _____ (stay) in her house for a whole week already when her friend Jane realized that she's under quarantine.

7.8 The Past Perfect Continuous

7.8.1 Introduction to the Past Perfect Continuous

We use the *past perfect continuous* to describe a situation where 1) an event with a certain duration in the *far past* influences 2) a moment in the *recent past*. In other words, the main event from the *past* continues up to another point in the *past*. Events described in the *past perfect continuous* never reach the *present*.

The Past Perfect Continuous

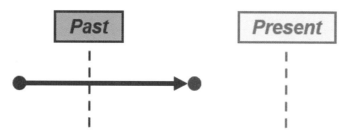

7.8.2 How to Form the Past Perfect Continuous

To form the *past perfect continuous*, we use the following two *auxiliary verbs*: "had" and "been." The two *auxiliary verbs* are placed before the *main verb* in its *present participle* form.

A. He <u>had been working</u> for five hours by then.

B. I <u>had been studying</u> English for six years before that happened.

To form the *past perfect continuous negative*, we add "**not**" after "**had**." The second *auxiliary verb* "**been**" and the *main verb* are untouched.

A. We <u>had not been waiting</u> for too long for the taxi.

B. She <u>had not been crying</u> for long.

Finally, to form *past perfect continuous questions*, the *subject* and "**had**" swap places. Note that the position of "**been**" does not change.

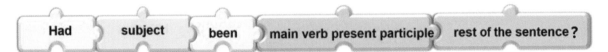

A. <u>Had he been studying</u> French for a long time before moving?

B. <u>Had his boss been complaining</u> about Jerry before Jerry did that?

However, just like with the *past perfect simple tense*, we regularly provide the *related recent past* when we use the *past perfect continuous tense*. Again, we use the *past simple tense* to do so here as well.

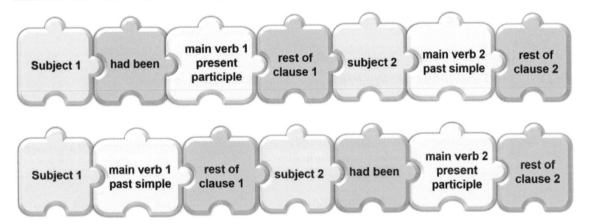

A. Simon <u>had been studying</u> English for five years before he <u>moved</u> to England.

B. My teacher <u>ended</u> the class early because she <u>hadn't been feeling</u> well.

C. By the time the shop owner <u>returned</u>, we <u>had been waiting</u> for twenty minutes.

D. Paul <u>had been cleaning</u> the house for two hours when Samantha <u>came</u> home.

7.8.3 Where to Use the Past Perfect Continuous

There are two main situations where you'd use the *past perfect continuous*. Fundamentally, as I said above, you'd use this tense to talk about a continuing event from the *far past* which ended up influencing a more *recent past* occurrence. Perhaps a less intuitive use of the *tense* is to handle a repeated event from the *far past*.

1. **To discuss the effect of a continuing activity from the far past**

2. **To discuss the effect of a repeated action from the far past**

Again, the main use of the *past perfect continuous* is to discuss a continuing event from the *far past* that affected an occurrence in the more *recent past*. Consider the following sentence.

1. **I went to see the doctor after I had been feeling unwell for a few days.**

In #1, the second clause that uses the *past perfect continuous tense*, "**I had been feeling unwell for a few days**," describes a certain continuing occurrence from the *past*: that you had already been ill for a few days. On the other hand, the first clause that uses the *past simple tense*, "**I went to see the doctor**" explains the result, which is that you ended up visiting the doctor. As such, we can discuss the influence that a certain continuing occurrence from the *far past* has had on the more *recent past*.

Next, the *past perfect continuous* can be used to discuss a repeated event from the *far past* that affected a more *recent past* occurrence. Consider the following sentence.

2. **The band had been rehearsing every day, so they won the competition.**

In the sentence above, the first clause, "**the band had been rehearsing every day**," which contains the *past perfect continuous tense*, describes a certain repeated action from the *past*: the band rehearsed every day. The second clause, "**so they won the competition**," which is in the *past simple tense*, explains the result of this repeated event: the band ended up winning the competition. As such, we can describe the influence of a certain repeated event from the *far past* on the more *recent past*.

7.8.4 The Past Perfect Continuous vs. the Present Perfect Continuous

The distinction between the *past perfect continuous* and the *present perfect continuous* is very similar to the distinction between the respective *perfect simple tenses*—the key is timing, which involves when two events occur. The *past perfect continuous* handles main events that occurred in the *far past* and influenced the more *recent past*, while the *present perfect continuous* handles main events that occurred in the *recent past* that influence the *present*.

To say this in another way, the *present perfect continuous* talks about events that started in the *past* and continue up to the *present*. The activity may or may not be finished, but it has to continue up to the *present*. On the other hand, the *past perfect continuous* is used to describe events that started in the *past* and ended in the *past*. The activity never reaches the *present* in such cases.

Consider the following examples.

Present Perfect Continuous	Past Perfect Continuous
I**'m** really thirsty. I **have been exercising** for three hours.	I **was** really thirsty. I **had been exercising** for three hours.
They **have been playing** tennis all day long, and now they **are** exhausted.	They **had been playing** tennis all day long before they **got** exhausted and **went** home.
Ann **hasn't been doing** well at school recently, and her test results **are** poor.	Ann **hadn't been doing** well at school recently, and she **failed** her final tests.

The Past Perfect Continuous Exercises

✓ **Complete the following sentences using either the past perfect continuous or the present perfect continuous.**

1) Ryan _____ (study) about space ever since he was a kid. That's why he took the astrophysics major.
2) They _____ (construct) new buildings left and right around here recently. I bet this town is destined for a redevelopment.
3) Since 1929, America's economy _____ (fall) continuously until the recession in 1937, which is when Roosevelt's New Deal Policies started to show positive results.
4) By the time Ray finally answered the phone, his parents _____ (try) to reach him for hours already.

● **Past Perfect Simple and Past Perfect Continuous**

	Past Perfect Simple	Past Perfect Continuous
verb form	had + past participle	had + been + present participle
Positive	I had worked. You had worked. She had worked.	I had been working You had been working. She had been working.
Negative	I had not worked. You hadn't worked She hadn't worked.	I had not been working You hadn't been working. She hadn't been working.
Question	Had you worked? Had she worked?	Had you been working? Had she been working?
Negative question	Hadn't you worked? Had she not worked? (Hadn't she worked?)	Hadn't you been working? Had she not been working? (Hadn't she been working?)

Hey, we've finally arrived at the last section of the chapter on *past tenses*! This chapter had a pretty heavy load, for sure. But that's because it covers the two most important *tenses* in English: the *past simple* and the *present perfect simple*. It is essential that you understand exactly where you use these two *tenses*. The other *tenses*, though used less frequently, are still important, so don't overlook them.

This final part is quite easy. We've established that we use the *past tenses*, especially the "duo," to describe *past* habits or conditions. Another common way to describe the *past* is to use "**used to**" or "**would**." The main between them is that while we can use "**used to**" for both *past* habits and for states, we can only use "**would**" for *past* habits; it's impossible to use "**would**" for *past* states. Also, one more important thing that applies to both "**used to**" and "**would**" is that the *past* habits or the *past* states being mentioned must no longer be occurring or the case. You can only use the two expressions to talk about your *past* when it is different than your *present*.

A. We <u>used to</u> live in Australia (but now we live in Korea).

B. He <u>used to</u> smoke (but now he doesn't).

C. She <u>used to</u> long hair (but now she has short hair).

D. I <u>would</u> always lose when I played chess with my brother.

E. My mom <u>would</u> drink a cup of coffee after dinner every night.

F. When I lived in Australia, we <u>would</u> go to a little cafe near our house.

"Used to" is in the past tense. With negatives and questions, we use the auxiliary verbs "did" or "did not," which are both already in the past tense. Therefore, with negatives and questions, we use "use to" not "used to."

He didn't <u>use to</u> like candy, but he does now.
Did she <u>use to</u> study English?
Did they <u>use to</u> go to the beach every summer?

Consider the following two sentences.

1. I <u>used to</u> play tennis, but now I prefer golf.

2. I <u>would</u> play tennis, but now I prefer golf.

Both sentences are describing your *past* habit of playing tennis. Both sentences make sense, but #2 is a little awkward, as you probably noticed. That's because "**would**" is rarely used without a reference to a certain time or a time range. So, to make #2 more natural, you can say the following.

3. *Up until I was 24 years-old*, I <u>would</u> play tennis, but now I prefer golf."

Now, consider the following two sentences.

4. We <u>used to</u> live in London before we moved to Sydney.

5. ~~We would live in London before we moved to Sydney.~~

Here, only #4 is correct; #5 is incorrect. You cannot use "**would**" with *past* states. This is because "**would**" has another, more common use as a *conditional* (see *Chapter 21*). Consider the following sentence.

6. We <u>would</u> live in London if the prices of everything weren't so high!

Since it is very easy to confuse these two senses of "**would**," we do not use "**would**" to talk about *past* states.

Used to vs. Would Exercises 01

✓ **If it's possible, make a sentence with 'would'. If it's not possible, use 'used to'.**

1) She _____ love playing tennis before she hurt her wrist.
2) He _____ walk along the beach every morning before breakfast.
3) We _____ live in Sydney.
4) My family _____ often go to the zoo for the weekend when I was young.
5) She _____ have long hair when she was a teenager.
6) We _____ go to the same cafeteria for lunch every day when I was a student.

Used to vs. Would Exercises 02

✓ **Find sentences with mistakes and fix them (some sentences may not have any mistakes).**

1) Yes, I remember the time when we would play in the woods every day.
2) We used to live in LA before moving to New York City. That's why we're so unaccustomed to the coldness around here during winter.
3) Based on my looks now, maybe you'd be surprise to hear that I would be extremely overweight up until just a few months ago.
4) I would visit my uncle almost every month when I was young. Unfortunately, now, we're not that close anymore.
5) I would love watching reality TV shows when I was a kid, but, these days, none of the shows are funny to me anymore.

'Classic' – a book which people praise and don't read.

- Mark Twain (1835-1910) -

CHAPTER 08

The Future Tenses

the forms of a verb that describe actions, events, or states that may occur or may become the reality in the future

8.1   J or P?

Any of you guys interested in the Myers-Briggs Type Indicator, a.k.a. the MBTI? It's a system that expresses one's personality in four-letter codes. Each letter corresponds to a certain element of the human personality. There are two sides/options available for each component: 1) **E**xtraversion vs. **I**ntroversion; 2) **S**ensing vs. i**N**tuition; 3) **T**hinking vs. **F**eeling; 4) **J**udging vs. **P**erceiving. Through your answers to a set of introspective questions, your complete personality is determined and expressed via that four-letter code, with one letter designated from each category.

Too Gen Z for you? Hold on, there's a point to all this. Let's look more into the final category: **J**udging vs. **P**erceiving. This class of personality indicator inquires one's tendency to prepare for the *future*. The "Judging" type prefers clear, detailed plans, considers deadlines absolute, and attempts to thoroughly study the ins-and-outs of any *future* possibility. On the other hand, the "Perceiving" type prefers to leave all options open, understands deadlines as flexible, and appreciates spontaneity.

The way English handles the *future* is similar to this **J**udging vs. **P**erceiving distinction. In short, there are two expressions that English utilizes to describe the *future*. One of them suggests spontaneous decisions or uncertain plans (i.e., the "**P**erceiving" type), while the other suggests solid plans that we reasonably expect to occur (i.e., the "**J**udging" type). Isn't it interesting that there are two ways to discuss the *future*, when there's only one way to discuss the *present* and only one way to discuss the *past*? Isn't it also interesting that the two ways to discuss the *future* are distinguished by the level of uncertainty or spontaneity in a given sentence?

8.2   The Future is Special (... Grammatically)!

Recall the previous chapters wherein we looked at the ***present simple*** and the ***past simple***. For both ***simple tenses***, we had to modify the ***main verb*** to indicate the ***tense***. In the ***present simple tense***, we either kept the ***main verb*** in its dictionary form, or added an "**-s**" at the end. And in the ***past simple tense***, we added "**-ed**" at the end of the ***main verb***. However, for the ***future simple,*** we do not do these things.

In English, we use <u>auxiliary verbs</u> to talk about the **future**. We've already seen several occasions for the use of **auxiliary verbs** to form **tenses**. Specifically, we had to use the **auxiliary verb** "**be**" for **continuous tenses**, "**have**" for **perfect simple tenses**, and "**have been**" for **perfect continuous tenses**. As such, I hope you're now comfortable using **auxiliary verbs** to form **tenses**.

As I mentioned, <u>we use two major **auxiliary verbs**</u> to explain the **future**: "**will**" and "**be + going to.**" In a sentence, we can <u>place either one of these before the **main verb**</u>, which is kept in its base form (i.e., <u>dictionary form</u>).

8.3 "Will"

8.3.1 How to Use "Will"

"**Will**" is one of the most common words used in English when expressing the **future**. Unlike some of the **auxiliary verbs** we've looked at so far, "**will**" does not change according to the **subject** of the sentence. To speak or write in the **future simple** with "**will**," <u>we place "**will**" before the base form of the **main verb**</u>.

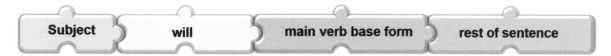

D. I <u>will make</u> lots of friends in my new class.

E. They <u>will enjoy</u> visiting Canada.

F. He <u>will finish</u> the job next week.

To form the **future simple negative** using "**will,**" <u>we add "**not**" after "**will.**"</u>

A. Julia is ill. She <u>will not be</u> at the party.

B. They <u>won't change</u> the telephone number.

C. He <u>will not tell</u> his sister about the surprise party.

To form **future simple questions** using "**will,**" <u>the positions of "**will**" and the **subject** are swapped</u>. The **main verb**, in its base form, appears after the **subject**.

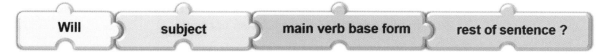

A. <u>Will</u> they <u>come</u> early?

B. <u>Will</u> you <u>give</u> me a hand?

C. <u>Will</u> she <u>arrive</u> soon?

8.3.2 Where to Use "Will"

So, which one is "will"—the Judging type or the Perceiving type? It's the Perceiving type. In other words, you use "will" in situations where a degree of uncertainty exists or where a *future* decision or plan has just been made spontaneously.

Now let's examine uses of "will" in more detail. We use "will" in the following situations.

1. **To make a prediction.**

2. **To offer someone something.**

3. **To describe spontaneous decisions.**

4. **To make promises.**

5. **For decisions that you're particularly unsure about (+ "think").**

First, we use "will" to make predictions about the *future*. Consider the following sentence.

1. **I'm sure Tommy will love the movie.**

In #1, you're speculating that Tommy will enjoy the movie.

Next, we use "will" to make someone an offer. Consider the following sentence.

2. **You seem busy. I will do the dishes tonight.**

In #2, you're offering to do the dishes so your friend (i.e., the *subject*, "you") doesn't have to. Usually, such offers stem from logical deductions based on *present* observations. In #2, you see that your friend is busy right now, so you offer to help them; you say that you'll do the dishes instead of them. How nice of you!

Next, we use "will" to discuss spontaneous decisions. Consider the following sentence.

3. **Oh, it's raining! I will take my umbrella.**

In #3, you've just made the spontaneous decision to take your umbrella. Again, such decisions are often based on *present* observations. In #3, you probably just opened the front door and realized for the first time that it's raining. Hence, you've come to the quick conclusion that you should take your umbrella.

Next, we use "will" to make promises. Consider the following sentence.

4. **I will pick Michael up from school at 4 o'clock.**

In #4, you're making a promise that you'll arrive at the school by 4 o'clock to pick up Michael.

Finally, we use "will" with the word "think" to talk about plans or decisions that you are particularly unsure about.

5. **I'm tired. I think I will go to bed.**

No, you're not. The fact that you've used "think" and "will" together in #5 tells us that you most likely do not plan on going straight to sleep. Instead, maybe you'll stay up a bit more, despite already being tired. When you use "think" with "will" in this way, you're indicating that your plan is very uncertain.

8.3.3 "Will" and Questions

Here's something fun about "**will**": <u>we rarely use "**will**" in **questions**</u>. The reason for that is because **questions** <u>always demand clear answers</u>; the receiver of the question is expected to answer either "**yes**" or "**no**." However, as I've mentioned several times, <u>the word "**will**" includes an inherent uncertainty</u>. Therefore, we don't use "**will**" much for **questions** about the **future**.

In fact, **questions** starting with "**will**" <u>hold a forceful tone</u>; <u>they are not neutral questions</u>. Take the following as an example.

1. **Will you come to the party tomorrow?**

While it may be not too obvious, #1 has a hint of assertiveness. In other words, #1 is not understood as the following.

2. **Will I be able to find you at the party tomorrow?**

But rather, it's understood as the following.

3. **Can you please come to the party tomorrow?**

Using "**will**" this way applies a demanding or begging tone to your question. Be careful of using "**will**" in questions.

<u>**The "Will" Exercises**</u>

✓ **Use "will" to complete the following sentences in the future tense.**

1) I'm feeling too tired right now. Maybe I _____ (exercise) later.
2) I get a feeling that it _____ (rain) tomorrow.
3) We bought a lot of stuff today. Maybe I _____ (carry) the bags.
4) I'm excited to meet you tomorrow. You _____ (be) surprised at how much I've changed.
5) Something just came up. I _____ (look) at that later.
6) If we keep going this slow, we _____ (make it, not) to the party in time.
7) There seems to be another thunderstorm on the way. We _____ (leave, not) the house tonight.
8) _____ (go, you) to the party tonight?

8.4.1 How to Use "Be Going to"

At the opposite end of the spectrum from "**will**" we have "**be going to**." "**Be going to**" is the Judging type, in terms of handling the *future*. To speak in the *future simple* with "**be going to**," we place "**be going to**" before the base form of the *main verb*. Note that "**be**" must be adjusted to account for the *subject* here, just like with the *present simple tense*.

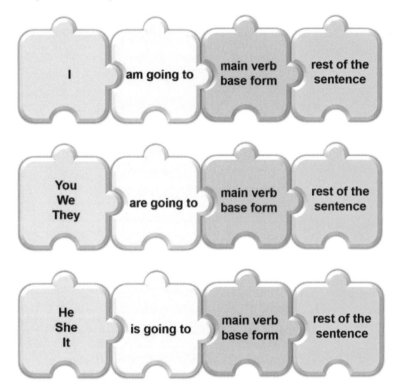

    A. We <u>are going to bake</u> a cake this afternoon.

    B. I'm sure my parents <u>are going to be</u> proud of me.

    C. She<u>'s going to go</u> on a holiday next week.

To form the *future simple negative* with "**be going to**," <u>we add "**not**" after "**be**.</u>" All the other parts remain the same.

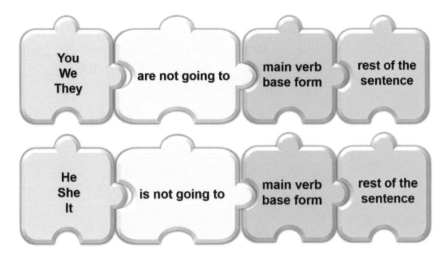

A. I'm not going to get up early.

B. They aren't going to visit Grandma.

C. She is not going to work on Sunday.

To form *future simple questions* with "**be going to**," the positions of "**be**" and the *subject* are swapped. Again, all the other parts remain the same.

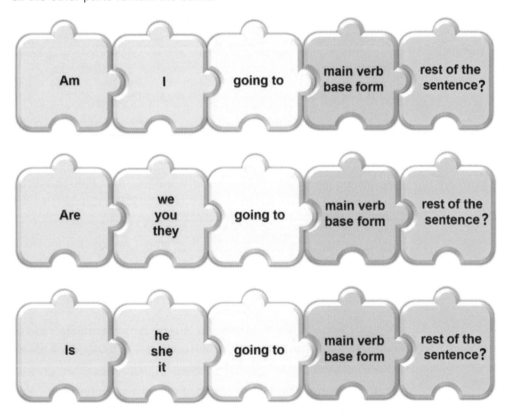

A. Are you going to go to the library?

B. Is she going to make Matilda's birthday cake?

C. Are they going to drive all the way to Alaska?

8.4.2 Where to Use "Be Going to"

As mentioned above, "**be going to**" is the Judging way of talking about the *future*. In other words, "be going to" is used for definite *future* plans. Now let's look at some specific situations for using "**be going to**."

1. **Guesses that you're certain about.**

2. **Scheduled public events.**

3. **Discussing the opinions of experts.**

4. **Events that have been planned for a long time.**

5. **Questions about the future.**

First, we use "**be going to**" to make guesses that we're certain about. Consider the following sentence.

1. **I bet Miranda is going to get a perfect score on this test.**

In #1, you're making a confident guess that Miranda will do very well on the test. Usually, you'd only be this certain if you had some evidence. In the case of #1, perhaps you've seen Miranda studying hard for the test lately; that's why you're so sure that she's going to get a perfect score. Also, when you use "**be going to**" in this way, you often include guessing words that express certainty like "**bet**," "**know**," and "**be sure that**" in your sentence.

Next, we use "**be going to**" to talk about scheduled public events. Consider the following sentence.

2. **The train is going to arrive at 7:00 PM.**

#2 states a fact about a pre-scheduled public event. We use "**be going to**" for these events because they've been fixed by officials. Although there's always room for adjustments and delays, such public occasions deserve the certainty provided by "**be going to**." Similar situations include concerts, ceremonies, TV shows, etc.

Next, we use "**be going to**" to discuss the words of experts. Consider the following sentence.

3. **According to scientists, it is not going to be possible to develop a cure for the disease in the next few years.**

Words from experts like scientists are considered trustworthy. If they talk about the *future*, their ideas deserve to be discussed with the confidence provided by "**be going to**." In fact, experts themselves often prefer "**be going to**" over "**will**" to reinforce the reliability of their words. In addition to experts' predictions, you can use "**be going to**" to talk about *future* events mentioned in the news and weather forecasts.

Next, we use "**be going to**" to talk about events that have been planned for a long time. Consider the following sentence.

4. **I am going to visit my grandparents this weekend because this Saturday is my grandfather's birthday.**

You've probably known that this Saturday is your grandfather's birthday for a long time. Therefore, you've planned in advance to visit your grandparents this coming weekend to celebrate his birthday. As a direct contradiction to this, consider the following sentence.

*   **I just realized that I haven't visited my grandparents in a while. I guess I will visit them this weekend.**

Can you feel the spontaneity of the decision in this sentence? You've just realized that you haven't been to your grandparents' in a long time, and hence you've impulsively decided to pay them a visit this weekend. Therefore, it's more correct to use "**will**" in this sentence. Again, for long-planned events, you use "**be going to**," while for spontaneous decisions, you use "**will**."

Finally, we use "**be going to**" for *questions* about the *future*. Consider the following example.

5. <u>**Are you going to come** to the meeting tomorrow?</u>

As we looked at before, there are some problems involved in asking *questions* about the *future* with "**will**." First of all, "**will**" is inherently uncertain, and *questions* with "**will**" are not neutral. However, "**be going to**" doesn't involve any of these problems. First of all, <u>we use "**be going to**" for definite events and plans</u>. In addition, "**be going to**" allows for more neutral sounding *questions*. As you can see, #5 has barely any coercive or assertive undertones. As such, we often use "**be going to**" to ask *questions* about the *future*.

The "Going to" Exercises

✓ **Use "going to" to complete the following sentences in the future tense.**

1) I bet she _____ (get) a perfect score on this test.
2) The train _____ (arrive) at 7:00 PM. We should get going now to pick her up in time.
3) The weather forecast says it _____ (rain) tomorrow.
4) According to the scientists, it _____ (be, not) possible to develop a cure for this disease in the next few years.
5) Within the next decade, newspapers _____ (be, not) printed anymore.
6) _____ (come, you) to the meeting tomorrow?
7) _____ (tell, she) him about what happened to his car?
8) _____ (be, they) promoted today?

The "Will" vs. "Going to" Exercises

✓ **Use either "will" or "going to" to complete the following sentences in the future tense. Choose carefully.**

1) I just realized that I haven't visited my grandparents in a while. I guess I _____ (visit) them this weekend.
2) I _____ (visit) my grandparents this weekend because this Saturday's my grandfather's birthday.
3) _____ (you, attend) the meeting this weekend?
4) I baked these cookies. I'm sure you _____ (love) them!
5) You seem pretty occupied. I _____ (take out) the garbage.
6) I'm genuinely excited for this concert. My favorite singer _____ (be) on stage tonight.
7) Jack _____ (leave) school a little early today because he has a dentist's appointment in the afternoon.

8.5 Other Ways to Discuss the Future

As we have seen, we use *auxiliary verbs* to handle the *future* in English. The two we've looked at so far: "**will**" and "**be going to**" are the most frequently used ones. However, they're not the only *auxiliary verbs* used to talk about the *future*. In fact, you can use any *auxiliary verb* with a predictive or a prospective tone to discuss the *future*. For example, you can use words like "**might**," "**be planning to**," "**may**," "**shall**," and "**must**" to talk about the *future*. Below are some examples.

1. I <u>might</u> not be attending school tomorrow.

2. I <u>am planning to</u> leave town today.

3. I <u>may</u> not be able to accompany you to the party.

4. <u>Shall</u> I pick you up after school today?

5. It <u>must</u> rain soon; look at the sky.

8.6 The Present for Future Events

As you can probably tell by now, discussing the *future* in English has many degrees of freedom. Numerous different *auxiliary verbs* can be used to signal the *future*. Here's a bit of a ridiculous idea: <u>we can use the</u> <u>**present tenses**</u> <u>to talk about the</u> *future* <u>too</u>! Do you remember looking at this before?

We can use the *present simple* to discuss the *future*. Recall that we use the *present simple* to state facts and truths. Hence, <u>when we use the</u> *present simple* <u>to mention the</u> *future*, <u>the event must be a planned one</u>. In other words, <u>the</u> *present simple* <u>has a similar vibe to</u> "**be going to**"—but the *present simple* <u>is usually</u> <u>regarded as having an even stronger level of certainty</u>. Correspondingly, we often include a clear indicator of time in these sentences that tells us when the event is planned. Despite its strict certainty, the *present simple* is used quite often to talk about the *future*; practically, it can take the place of "**be going to**." Consider the following examples.

1. The train <u>arrives</u> at *10 PM tonight*.

2. Don't forget we <u>have</u> a meeting *early tomorrow morning*.

3. The concert <u>is</u> *next Wednesday*.

You can also use the *present continuous* to express the *future*. <u>Unlike its other usage, the</u> *tense* <u>here has</u> <u>nothing to do with whether the</u> *future* <u>event is expected to have a certain duration; you can use it for instant</u> *future* <u>events as well</u>. Just like the *present simple*, <u>the</u> *present continuous* <u>is also only used for relatively</u> <u>certain</u> *future* <u>events; it more or less replaces</u> "**be going to**." However, <u>the</u> *present continuous* <u>is used more</u> <u>commonly in spoken English, while the</u> *present simple* <u>is used more commonly in written English</u>. Consider the following examples.

1. Jack<u>'s playing</u> soccer tomorrow.

2. I<u>'m seeing</u> a movie later.

3. The train <u>is arriving</u>. Please stand back.

You have probably heard something like #3 announced at a train station. The announcer never says: "**the train will arrive soon**," or "**the train is going to arrive soon**." Instead, the *present continuous* is used, because it's simpler and shorter.

The Present for Future Events Exercises

✓ Rewrite each sentence using <u>both</u> the present simple and the present continuous to express the future

1) We are going to have a party tomorrow.
   → (present simple) / (present continuous)
2) A storm will come to Korea this week.
   → (present simple) / (present continuous)
3) The train will arrive soon.
   → (present simple) / (present continuous)
4) The movie is going to start now.
   → (present simple) / (present continuous)

8.7 The Future Continuous

8.7.1 How to Form the Future Continuous

Just like the *future simple*, <u>we can use either "**will**" or "**be going to**"</u> for the *future continuous*. Do you recall when we've looked at the other *continuous tenses*? We placed the *auxiliary verb* "**be**" in front of the *present participle* form of the *main verb*. The same idea holds here, but we have other *auxiliary verbs* to work with (i.e., "**will**" or "**be going to**"). Where do you think "**be**" fits into all of this?

To speak in the *future continuous*, <u>first, you start with "**will**" or "**be going to**,"</u> then, you add "**be**," and finally, <u>you add the *main verb* in its *present participle* form</u>. Note that <u>the extra *auxiliary verb* "**be**" (that appears after "**will**" or "**be going to**") remains in its base form.</u>

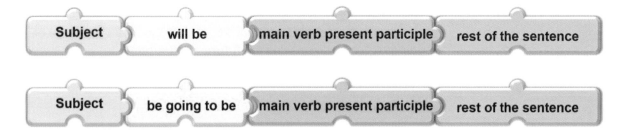

A. They<u>'ll be studying</u> in the library at 9 a.m. tomorrow.

B. Take your umbrella. It <u>will be raining</u> when you return.

C. Mark <u>is going to be waiting</u> for her when her plane arrives tonight.

To form the *future continuous negative*, you basically flip the meaning of "**will**" or "**be going to**." In other words, <u>you use either "**will not**" or "**be not going to**,"</u> followed by "**be**," and followed by the *main verb* in its *present participle form*.

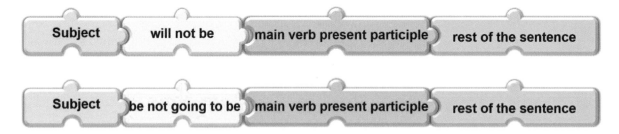

A. He <u>will not be sleeping</u> when you call him.

B. They <u>won't be watching</u> TV when she arrives.

C. She<u>'s not going to be staying</u> at a Hilton Hotel.

To form *future continuous questions*, you do something similar to what you've done for the *future simple tense* —you either <u>swap "**will**" and the *subject*</u> or <u>swap "**be**" from "**be going to**" and the *subject*</u>.

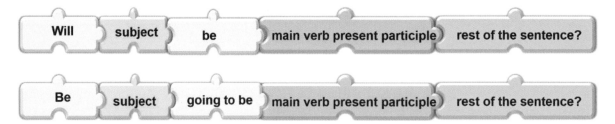

A. <u>Will</u> David and Aiden <u>be discussing</u> the new project?

B. <u>Will</u> you <u>be traveling</u> at this time on Sunday?

C. <u>Are</u> you <u>going to be helping</u> Julia tomorrow?

Before we move on, I must say that <u>we usually avoid using "**be going to**" for the *future continuous*</u>. This is because it requires <u>too many extra words</u>. To use "**be going to**" in the *future continuous*, you need four words: "**be going to be**" to express yourself. As I always say, the less words you use, the more effective your communication will be. Using so many additional words that hold no individual significance is considered bad technique. Therefore, we rarely use "**be going to**" when we're using the *future continuous*.

8.7.2 Where to Use the Future Continuous.

Like most *continuous tenses*, the *future continuous* has one major purpose: <u>to talk about *future* events that will be ongoing or in progress</u>. However, it has some other functions as well.

Largely, there are <u>three</u> common uses of the *future continuous*.

1. <u>To talk about future ongoing or in progress events.</u>

2. <u>To talk about events that are expected to happen as a matter of course (+ "anyway").</u>

3. <u>To ask neutral questions.</u>

Again, the major use of the *future continuous* is to talk about <u>events that will be in progress at a certain time in the *future*</u>. Consider the following example.

1. This time next week, I <u>will be travelling</u> through Italy.

One caution. When using the *future continuous* like this, you must be planning to have <u>already commenced</u> <u>the activity by the time that you've specified</u>. Applying this logic to #1, you must be planning to be in Italy in exactly a week's time or less. In other words, your trip must be planned to commence before a week from now has passed.

Next, we can also use the *future continuous* <u>with the word "**anyway**" to discuss an event that is expected to</u> <u>happen as a matter of course</u>. Consider the following example.

> 2. **You can send the parcel directly to my house; <u>I'll be working</u> at home today *anyway*.**

In #2, you're saying that your friend (i.e., the *subject*, "**you**") can send the package directly to your home, since you know you'll be at home all day; the delivery will likely occur during the natural course of your day. The second clause in #2 uses the *future continuous* to outline your prearranged *future*, while the first clause in #2 describes an event that can fit into that prearranged *future*.

Finally, you can use the *future continuous* to <u>ask the most neutral questions about the *future*</u>. Consider the following example.

> 3. <u>**Will you be coming**</u> **to work tomorrow?**

Of all the ways to ask someone about their *future* plans, this is the most polite. As mentioned, *questions* with "**will**" in the *future simple* often sounds quite forceful or demanding. And, although *questions* with "**be going to**" in the *future simple* are a bit better, they still might sound slightly assertive. However, questions like #3 generally puts the least amount of pressure on the receiver; in #3, the narrator is just genuinely curious if their coworker will be at work the next day. Compare #3 to the following two *questions*; see if you can notice the tone differences.

> 4. <u>**Will you come**</u> **to work tomorrow?**

> 5. <u>**Are you going to come**</u> **to work tomorrow?**

However, note that <u>this level of politeness is often unnecessary</u>. You'd only ask questions in the *future continuous* to people who you are still awkward to be with. In general, <u>the best way to ask questions about the</u> *future* is to use "**be going to**" in the *future simple tense*.

The Future Continuous Exercises

> ✓   **Complete the following sentences in the future continuous form.**

1) I _____ (will, start) a business in November.
2) This time tomorrow, she _____ (be going to, visit) her parents.
3) At three o'clock tomorrow, they _____ (be going to, evacuate) the building due to a pre-scheduled disinfection job.
4) I can finish the report by 11:00 PM, but I guess you _____ (will, sleep) by then.
5) Our guests _____ (be going to, arrive) at two o'clock tomorrow. Be ready to greet them politely.
6) I _____ (will, not, play) golf this afternoon. I just got an urgent business that I need to take care of.
7) They _____ (will, have) a good time in Spain by the end of this week

- **Summary of the Future Simple and Future Continuous**

	Future simple	Future Continuous
verb form	will + infinitive (=base form) am/are/is + going to + base form	will be + present participle am/are/is + going to be + present participle
Positive	I will work. You will work. She will work.	I will be working You will be working. She will be working.
Negative	I will not work. You won't work. She will not work.	I will not be working You won't be working. She will not be working.
Question	Will you work? Will she work?	Will you be working? Will she be working?
Negative question	Won't you work? Will she not work? (Won't she work?)	Will you not be working? Will she not be working? (Won't she be working?)

8.8 The Future Perfect Tenses

8.8.1 The Future Perfect Introduction

The *future perfect tenses* are not very frequently used in English. Hence, we'll handle the *future perfect simple* and the *future perfect continuous* collectively in this single section.

Before we move on, you can imagine that if we use "**be going to**" here, we'll run into the same problem we did with the *future continuous*. There would simply be too many *auxiliary verbs*—"be going to" is already three words, and as you know, we have to add even more words for the *perfect tenses*. As such, we do not use "**be going to**" for the *future perfect tenses*—it's practically forbidden—we only use "**will**."

8.8.2 How to Form the Future Perfect Tenses

The *future perfect simple* is formed by employing two *auxiliary verbs*: "**will**" to denote the *future* tone of the tense and "**have**" to denote the *perfect* tone of the *tense*. Then, the *main verb* is written in its *past participle* form.

To form the *future perfect simple negative*, we add "**not**" after "**will.**"

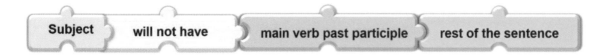

To form the *future perfect simple question*, the positions of "**will**" and the *subject* are swapped.

A. We <u>will have perfected</u> our English by the time we come back from the U.K.

B. We <u>will not have perfected</u> our English by the time we come back from the U.K.

C. <u>Will</u> we <u>have perfected</u> our English by the time we come back from the U.K.?

On the other hand, the *future perfect continuous* is formed by employing three *auxiliary verbs*: "**will**" for the *future* part and "**have been**" for the *perfect* part. Then, we use the *present participle* form of the *main verb* to denote the activity in focus.

To form the *future perfect continuous negative*, we add "**not**" after "**will**."

To form the *future perfect continuous question*, the positions of "**will**" and the *subject* are swapped.

A. He <u>will have been studying</u> English for two years when he takes the exam.

B. He <u>will not have been studying</u> English for two full years yet when he takes the exam.

C. <u>Will</u> he <u>have been studying</u> English for two years when he takes the exam?

8.8.3 Where to Use the Future Perfect Tenses

We can use the *future perfect simple* to describe planned deadlines for activities. A sentence in this **tense** marks a certain time in the **future** and describes an event that will finish by that time. What's interesting is that the beginning of the event can be in either the **past**, the **present**, or the **future**. Unless it is explicitly stated, we don't know when the event started; all we know is when it will finish.

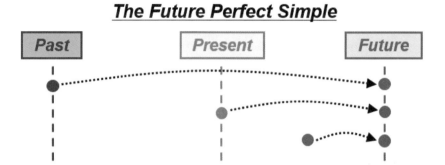

The Future Perfect Simple

Consider the following example.

1. Sam **will have finished** reading *Wonder* by next week.

In #1, we know that Sam is going to finish reading the book *Wonder* by next week. However, we have no idea when he started reading it. He might have already started reading the book (i.e., in the **past**), be just about to start reading the book (i.e., in the **present**), or hasn't even started reading it at all (i.e., in the **future**). All we know is that Sam is expected to finish the book next week.

If you want to state the precise starting point of the action, you must explain it in a separate sentence or at least in a separate clause. Consider the following example.

2. Sam **will have finished** reading *Wonder* by next week. He started reading yesterday. / Sam **will have finished** reading *Wonder*, which he started yesterday, by next week.

Now, consider the following example.

3. By next week, I **will have had** a haircut.

A haircut usually doesn't take as long as it takes to read a book. As such, we can safely assume that the haircut has not started yet. As in this example, sometimes we can guess the starting point even if it's not denoted clearly.

Next, we can use the *future perfect continuous* to describe the length of an activity from its start to a certain time in the *future*. Wait, what? Why would you set a certain time in the *future* as the marker instead of the *present*? Well, let's imagine that you've been working at a company since July of last year. It's currently June, so if someone asks you how long you've been working there, you'd have to answer "**11 months.**" However, "**11 months**" is a bit awkward; your audience will need to take some time to process how long that actually is. On the other hand, "**a year**" is direct and easy to understand. However, it'd be untrue to answer "**a year**" because you have not yet completed 12 months. You need to deliver the idea that: *when it becomes July, my experience working there will comprise a full year*. You can express such an idea by using the *future perfect continuous* *tense*. In other words, we use the *tense* in a situation where there's just a bit more time left until you get a nice whole duration.

Similar to the *future perfect simple*, the start of the event can be in either the *past*, the *present*, or the *future*. However, we most often use the *future perfect continuous* for events that started in the *past*.

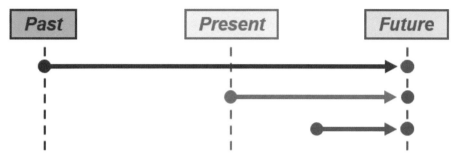

Consider the following example.

1.   By the time the dinner is served, Andy <u>will have been cooking</u> for hours!

In #1, we know that Andy will have been cooking for hours by dinnertime. But we don't exactly know when he started. He could have already started cooking (i.e., in the *past*), be just starting (i.e., in the *present*), or be starting later (i.e., in the *future*). Maybe Andy's the chef today, and he's cooking for you right now, or maybe he's the chef for this Sunday's party, and he hasn't even started yet.

Now, consider the following example.

2.   By this time next month, I <u>will have been studying</u> English already for six years!

In this case, we know definitely that you already commenced your English studies, because the time remaining, "**one month**," is a lot shorter than the full duration, "**six years**."

<u>**The Future Perfect Exercises**</u>

✓   **Complete the sentences using the future perfect simple tense.**

1)   Hopefully, by this time tomorrow, I _____ (complete) my homework.
2)   By next year, they _____ (redevelop) this town. Everything will be different.
3)   I _____ (lost) some weight by then, because I need to attend my sister's wedding.
4)   You _____ (receive) your test scores by this Sunday.

✓   **Complete the sentences using the future perfect continuous tense.**

1)   By next month, they _____ (work) on that skyscraper for already a year.
2)   In just a few weeks, this restaurant _____ (run) for 40 years.
3)   In three years, Lionel Messi _____ (play) professional soccer for 20 years.
4)   If it rains tomorrow as well, it _____ (rain) for a week straight

Isn't that an ironic title? Well, once I explain it, it'll become a lot clearer. By using the **past tense** of "be" in "**be going to**," we can talk about failed predictions and unfulfilled plans.

Consider the following example.

1. I <u>was going to start</u> a new book today, but I didn't have time.

You plan to start that new book today fell through due to your lack of free time. Notice that although we're using "**be going to**" in this sentence, we're actually talking about the **past**.

For the same purpose, we can also use "**would**" or the **past continuous** for this purpose. Consider the following examples.

2. I thought I <u>would</u> finish my homework today, but the load was heavier than what I expected.

3. Hugo went to bed early because he <u>was flying</u> early the following morning.

<u>Did you know that "**would**" is also the **past tense** of "will"</u>? We saw that "**will**" and "**be going to**" are both ways of discussing the **future**. If we can use the **past tense** of "**be going to**" for this purpose, then <u>we should be able to use the **past tense** of "will" as well</u>. We also saw that we can use the **present continuous** to talk about the **future** (see section 8.6). Similarly, <u>we can use the **past continuous** to talk about **past** predictions</u>.

Can you see the pattern now? <u>We can use the **past tense** of expressions used to discuss the **future** to handle **past** predictions and unfulfilled plans</u>.

The Future for Past Predictions Exercises

✓ **Use the future tense to complete the following past predictions.**

1) The ceremony _____ (take) place today, but it was delayed due to the rain.
2) Jake _____ (leave) for Paris yesterday, but he had some urgent business to take care of. He's leaving this afternoon.
3) I went home early yesterday because I _____ (clean) the house. But by the time I got home, I was too tired that I ended up not doing it.
4) They _____ (close) the school during the holidays, but they decided not to after realizing that many students were planning to stay on campus.

- **Summary of the Future Perfect Simple and Future Perfect Continuous**

	Future Perfect Simple	Future Perfect Continuous
verb form	will have + past participle	will have been + present participle
Positive	I will have worked. You will have worked. She will have worked.	I will have been working You will have been working. She will have been working.
Negative	I will not have worked. You won't have worked. She will not have worked.	I will not have been working You won't have been working. She will not have been working.
Question	Will you have worked? Will she have worked?	Will you have been working? Will she have been working?
Negative question	Won't you have worked? Will she not have worked? (Won't she have worked?)	Will you not have been working? Will she not have been working? (Won't she have been working?)

Live always in the best company when you read.

- Sydney Smith (1771-1845) -

Overview of Tenses

9.1 Master of Time

9.2 Negatives

9.1 Master of Time

Now that we've discussed all twelve *tenses* in detail, hopefully the following diagram will hit you differently now. You saw this before when we discussed each *tense* in detail. Does it make more sense to you now?

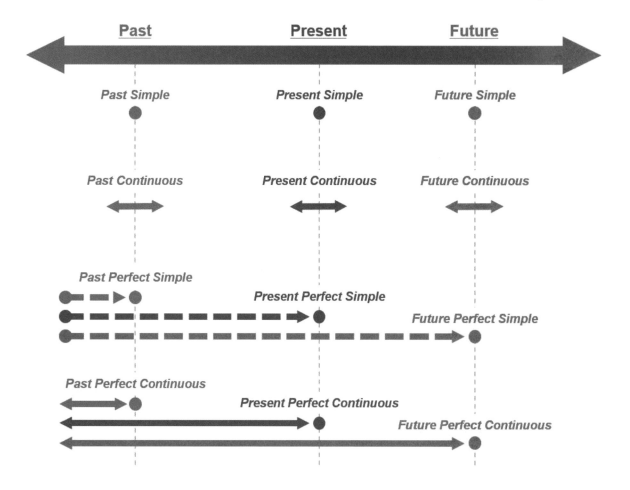

Also, here's a table that summarizes the main uses and the frequency of use for each *tense*.

Main	Specific Tense	Main Uses	Frequency
The Present	Simple	Facts, repeated acts	★★☆☆☆
	Continuous	Cont'd actions now	★★★☆☆
	Perfect Simple	Experiences, recent past	★★★★★
	Perfect Continuous	Cont'd actions in recent past	★★★★☆
The Past	Simple	Past events	★★★★★
	Continuous	Cont'd actions in past	★★★★☆
	Perfect Simple	Preceding events in far past	★★★☆☆
	Perfect Continuous	Cont'd actions in far past	★★☆☆☆
The Future	Simple	Predictions, plans, decisions	★★★☆☆
	Continuous	Cont'd actions in future	★★☆☆☆
	Perfect Simple	Planned deadlines	★★☆☆☆
	Perfect Continuous	Length of activities	★☆☆☆☆

Notice that the top two most frequently used *tenses* are the *present perfect simple* and the *past simple*. This is because in everyday life you often talk about events from the *past* and your *past* experiences. What do you say? Do you agree? Do you think you discuss your *past* events and *past* experiences a lot in real life?

That said, all the twelve *tenses* of English are important. And what's even more important than knowing how to form them is knowing where to use them. Anyone can easily look up how to form each *tense* online, but knowing where to use each one is what separates expert writers from novice writers. Keep striving to make yourself comfortable with the uses of all the *tenses*.

As we finish off *tenses*, I'd like to tell you one thing about *negatives*. The truth is: we don't use *negatives* to state the opposite in English. As many words as English has, there are multiple *synonyms* and *antonyms* for most words. A word's *synonyms* are other words that have a similar meaning while its *antonyms* are words that mean the opposite. In English, there are lots of *antonym* pairs—pairs of words that hold opposite meanings to one another. Consider the following examples. In each example, I present two ways of saying the same thing.

1. It's not going to be <u>possible</u> … / It's going to be <u>impossible</u> …

2. I may not be <u>present</u> … / I may be <u>absent</u> …

3. It's not <u>nice</u> to … / It's <u>mean</u> to …

In these sentences, the underlined words are *antonym* pairs (i.e., **possible** and **impossible**, **present** and **absent**, and **nice** and **mean**).

In English, concise writing is more effective than wordy writing. As you can see in #1-#3, using the *antonym* rather than the word "**not**" allows you to use one less word. Hence, whenever we're simply stating the opposite, use of the *antonym* is preferable.

On the other hand, we often use "**not**" to emphasize negativity. While using the *antonym* may allow us to state the opposite, it does not allow us to put weight on the negativity. If we wish to stress an implied contrast between positive behavior and negative behavior, "**not**" is clearly an excellent option. Consider the following case.

1. That's *not* polite! Don't do it.

2. That's <u>rude</u>! Don't do it.

Here, "*not* polite" has a slightly stronger tone than "**rude**"; #1 is stricter and more assertive than #2. To be clear, it helps to emphasize "*not*"—we do this by *italicizing* the font in written English, and by pronouncing the word loudly in spoken English.

Now, consider the following case.

3. That's <u>not</u> going to be <u>possible</u>.

4. That's going to be <u>impossible</u>.

Generally, #3 suggest an absolute 0% chance, while #4 suggests a less than 10% chance. In addition, if you use #3 or #4 to respond to someone's request, #3 means that you refuse to fulfill the request, while #4 means that the request is out of your hands. Can you tell the difference?

All in all, the main take here is that we do not use "**not**" for simple negatives in English. We use an *antonym* if at all possible in a case, and we use "**not**" to emphasize the negative.

The table below lists some common *antonym* pairs in English.

abundant ↔ scarce	follow ↔ lead	kind ↔ cruel
succeed ↔ fail	major ↔ minor	knowledge ↔ ignorance
admit ↔ deny	native ↔ foreign	lazy ↔ diligent
arrogant ↔ humble	foolish ↔ wise	loose ↔ tight
artificial ↔ natural	frank ↔ evasive	lower ↔ higher
attack ↔ defend	fresh ↔ stale	messy ↔ neat
attractive ↔ repulsive	frequent ↔ seldom	offer ↔ receive
blame ↔ absolve/forgive	gentle ↔ violent	order ↔ mess
blunt ↔ sharp	frank ↔ secretive	peace ↔ war
unlimited ↔ limited	fresh ↔ stale	permanent ↔ temporary
bravery ↔ cowardice	frequent ↔ seldom	permit ↔ forbid
build ↔ destroy	gentle ↔ rough	poverty ↔ wealth
capture, catch ↔ release	gloomy ↔ cheerful	powerful ↔ weak
cause ↔ effect	grow ↔ shrink	refuse ↔ agree, accept
clever ↔ stupid	guest ↔ host	rough ↔ smooth
combine ↔ separate	guilty ↔ innocent	same ↔ opposite, different
common ↔ rare	hasten ↔ dawdle	serious ↔ negligible, minor
complex ↔ simple	hero ↔ villain	sense ↔ nonsense
continue ↔ interrupt	honest ↔ dishonest	shallow ↔ deep
decrease ↔ increase	horizontal ↔ vertical	throw ↔ catch
definite ↔ indefinite	ignore ↔ notice	transparent ↔ opaque
demand ↔ supply	important ↔ trivial	true ↔ false
despair ↔ hope	inferior ↔ superior	unity ↔ division
diseased ↔ healthy	intelligent ↔ stupid	vanish ↔ appear
excited ↔ calm	intentional ↔ accidental	visible ↔ invisible
export ↔ import	justice ↔ injustice	voluntary ↔ compulsory
external ↔ internal	private ↔ public	win ↔ lose
float ↔ sink	junior ↔ senior	wisdom ↔ folly, stupidity

CHAPTER 10

Nouns

a word or group of words that represent a person, place, thing, quality, action, or idea.

10.1　What are Nouns?

What's your name? Who are you? What are you? What's in front of you right now? Where are you right now? What do you do for a living? To answer these questions, you need *nouns*. You need *nouns* to talk about yourself and the beings and <u>things</u> around you; *nouns* are <u>the words we use to identify a person, place, thing, or idea</u>.

- **Type of nouns**

Concrete Nouns	Things that we can experience with our five senses (i.e., taste, touch, sight, hearing, and smell).				
	apple	ball	bear	book	car
	coffee	doctor	finger	foot	child
Abstract Nouns	Abstract ideas or concepts that you cannot see, hear, touch, smell, or taste.				
	joy	anger	success	courage	happiness
	hate	fear	knowledge	freedom	love
Common Nouns	A general person, place, or thing.				
	mother	boy	jacket	television	dog
Proper Nouns	A specific person, place, or thing.				
	South Korea	Eiffel Tower		Joe Biden	Dr. Smith
Collective Nouns	A group of people, animals or a collection of things taken as a whole.				
	a **herd** of buffaloes		a **swarm** of insects		a **crew** of sailors
	staff (**group** of employees)		a **group** of engineers		a **class** of students

Compound Nouns	Nouns that are made with two or more words.				
	boyfriend	battleship	ladybug	goldfish	fingerprint
Countable Nouns	Objects, people, places, etc., that can be counted.				
	car	house	frog	chair	apple
Uncountable Nouns	Materials, concepts, information, etc. that cannot be counted.				
	water	information	music	coffee	knowledge

10.2 Common Nouns vs. Proper Nouns

Nouns can be divided into <u>two</u> principal categories—**common nouns** and **proper nouns**. <u>A **common noun** identifies any of a class of people, places, or things</u>, while <u>a **proper noun** names a particular one of these</u>. Since a **proper noun** refers to a specific entity, we must differentiate it from a **common noun** <u>by starting it with a capital letter</u>. In the following table, I give you some examples of **common** and **proper nouns**.

- **Common Nouns**

types of people	actor	artist	aunt	baby	baker
	boy	businessman	cook	dentist	doctor
	engineer	firefighter	giant	girl	lawyer
	judge	man	musician	nurse	painter
	police officer		soldier	student	teacher
types of animals	alligator	butterfly	cat	cow	crab
	dog	dolphin	eagle	fly	frog
	goat	goldfish	horse	lizard	mosquito
	mouse	octopus	owl	parrot	penguin
	pig	pigeon	rabbit	scorpion	shark
types of places	airport	bakery	bank	beach	cave
	church	farm	hill	hospital	hotel
	island	library	mall	market	mountain
	park	restaurant	school	stadium	temple
	theater	subway station		gas station	zoo
types of things	bag	basket	bed	blanket	bookcase
	box	bread	cake	can	candle
	egg	gate	ladder	lamp	mirror
	picture	pillow	scissors	soap	table
	toothbrush	towel	train	truck	window

- **Proper Nouns**

names of people	Harry Potter	Pinocchio	Robin Hood	Santa Claus
	Beethoven	Jack	Annie	Alice

names of cities, buildings and landmarks	Seoul	Bangkok	Sydney	Paris
	Eiffel Tower	Central Park	Grand Canyon	
	New York City	Leaning Tower of Pisa	Great Wall of China	
	Brooklyn Bridge	Empire State Building	Statue of Liberty	

days of the week and months of the year	Sunday	Monday	Tuesday	Wednesday
	August	September	November	December

names of mountains, seas, rivers and lakes	Lake Michigan	Lake Victoria	Great Salt Lake	
	Alps (the highest mountains)	Himalayas (more mountains)	Rocky Mountains	
	Pacific Ocean	Atlantic Ocean	Arctic Ocean	
	Dead Sea	Mediterranean Sea	Arabian Sea	
	Yellow River	Thames (another river)	Niagara Falls	
	Mount Everest (Mt. Everest)		Mount Fuji (Mt. Fuji)	

names of specific festivals, special events, and holidays	Christmas	Parents' Day	Memorial Day
	Easter	Thanksgiving Day	Halloween

- **The names of countries and their people are also proper nouns.**

Country	People	Country	People
South Korea	Korean	Argentina	Argentinean
England	English	Australia	Australian
Italy	Italian	Germany	German
Spain	Spanish	Canada	Canadian
China	Chinese	Egypt	Egyptian
France	French	Malaysia	Malaysian
Portugal	Portuguese	Japan	Japanese
United States of America	American	Thailand	Thai

10.3 Countable Nouns vs. Uncountable Nouns

10.3.1 The Definitions

A very important distinction that we make among **common nouns** is whether or not they're countable. In general, "people, places, and things" are countable most of the time; for example, there are always a certain number of cars, dogs, cups, plates, and houses. If you can express the exact amount of a thing using a number, then you are surely dealing with a **countable noun**. On the other hand, ideas and abstract concepts are generally difficult, if not impossible to count; for example, how much intelligence, happiness, anger, information, or sadness do you have? If you cannot answer with a number, then you are surely dealing with an **uncountable noun**. Of course, we can count how many ideas or concepts or rules exist, but an idea, concept, or theory, for the purpose of grammar, cannot be counted. In addition, things that you can count but are useless to count are often treated as **uncountable nouns** as well. For example, you can count individual grains of rice or sugar, but it's pointless to do so. Hence, we consider "rice" and "sugar" **uncountable nouns**. The same applies to "spaghetti," as there's no use counting individual noodles.

Fundamentally, we can define **countable** and **uncountable nouns** as follows.

1. _Countable Nouns_: **Things that you <u>can count</u>, most commonly solid objects,**
   e.g., sandwich, apple, banana, egg.

2. _Uncountable Nouns_: **Things that you <u>cannot</u> or you <u>do not count</u>, including non-solid objects, some types of ideas or thoughts, and high numbers of things that are usually bunched up together,**
   e.g., milk, water, spaghetti, sugar, rice, dust, information, intelligence.

Before I move on, I'd like to point out some **uncountable nouns** that you might find confusing to identify (as either countable or uncountable). The following **uncountable nouns** are commonly mistaken for **countable nouns**: "**data**," "**information**," "**equipment**," "**homework**," "**research**," "**evidence**," and "**music.**"

Countable and Uncountable Nouns Exercises

   ✓   **Write "C" in front of countable nouns and "UC" in front of uncountable nouns**

1) _____ Car	5) _____ Music	9) _____ Homework
2) _____ Oil	6) _____ Paper	10) _____ Equipment
3) _____ House	7) _____ Internet	11) _____ Information
4) _____ Time	8) _____ Year	12) _____ Hat

10.3.2 The Plural Form

For **countable nouns**, if we have more than one of a particular thing, we discuss it using its **plural** form. On the other hand, if we only have one, we discuss it using its **singular** form. The **singular** form of a **noun** is the base form (e.g., dog, cat, book). To form the **plural** of a **noun**, we usually add an "-s" to the end of the **singular noun** (e.g., dogs, cats, books). However, for many **nouns**, forming the **plural** is a bit more complicated. There is a set of spelling rules that will help you out in that department.

The following are the spelling rules for forming the **plurals** of **countable nouns**.

✓	**For regular nouns, add "-s" to the end.**		
e.g.	bird → birds	broom → brooms	camel → camels
	egg → eggs	flower → flowers	fork → forks
	house → houses	shirt → shirts	star → stars

✓	**For nouns ending in "-s," "-ss," "-sh," "-ch," "-x," or "-z," add "-es" to the end.**		
e.g.	beach → beaches	box → boxes	branch → branches
	brush → brushes	bus → buses	bush → bushes
	church → churches	class → classes	dish → dishes
	dress → dresses	lunch → lunches	blitz → blitzes
	fox → foxes	glass → glasses	match → matches
	sandwich → sandwiches	tax → taxes	witch → witches

✓	**For nouns ending with a vowel + "-s" or "-z," you need to add another "-s" or "-z," and then add "-es."**	
e.g.	fez → fezzes	gas → gasses

✓	**For nouns ending in "-f" or "-fe," remove the "-f" or "-fe," and add "-ves."**		
e.g.	calf → calves	elf → elves	half → halves
	knife → knives	leaf → leaves	life → lives
	loaf → loaves	self → selves	sheaf → sheaves
	thief → thieves	wife → wives	wolf → wolves

	✓ **Exceptions:** simply add "-s"		
e.g.	belief → beliefs	chef → chefs	chief → chiefs
	cliff → cliffs	handkerchief → handkerchiefs	roof → roofs

✓	**For nouns ending with a consonant + "-y," remove the "-y," and add "-ies."**		
e.g.	baby → babies	strawberry → strawberries	puppy → puppies
	story → stories	dictionary → dictionaries	city → cities

fairy → fairies	butterfly → butterflies	family → families
lady → ladies	lily → lilies	fly → flies
candy → candies	library → libraries	diary → diaries

✓ **For nouns ending with a vowel + "-y," simply add "-s" to the end.**

e.g.	boy → boys	chimney → chimneys	day → days
	key → keys	kidney → kidneys	jersey → jerseys
	toy → toys	tray → trays	monkey → monkeys

✓ **For nouns ending in "-o," add "-es" to the end.**

e.g.	hero → heroes	potato → potatoes	tomato → tomatoes
	echo → echoes	embargo → embargoes	veto → vetoes

✓ **Exceptions:** simply add "-s"

e.g.	photo → photos	hippo → hippos	kangaroo → kangaroos
	rhino → rhinos	video → videos	zoo → zoos
	piano → pianos	halo → halos	radio → radios

✓ **Exceptions:** we can form the plural by adding either "-s" or "-es"; both are accepted.

e.g.	mango → mangoes / mangos	zero → zeroes / zeros
	mosquito → mosquitoes / mosquitos	volcano → volcanoes / volcanos

✓ **For nouns ending in "-us," remove the "-us," and add "-i" to the end.**

e.g.	cactus → cacti	focus → foci	radius → radii

✓ **Exceptions:** there are <u>three</u> accepted forms of the plural of octopus—octopi (the oldest form), octopuses (perhaps the most commonly used), and octopodes (less common).

✓ **For nouns ending in "-is," remove the "-is," and add "-es" to the end.**

e.g.	analysis → analyses	ellipsis → ellipses	synopsis → synopses

✓ **For nouns ending in "-on," remove the "-on," and add "-a" to the end.**

e.g.	phenomenon → phenomena	criterion → criteria

✓ **For some nouns, the singular and the plural are exactly the same.**

e.g.	aircraft → aircraft	deer → deer	fish → fish
	sheep → sheep	series → series	species → species

✓ **Exception:** You can use fishes as the plural of fish when you are talking about different species of fish: e.g., the **fishes** of the Pacific Ocean

✓ **Some nouns are irregular and do not follow any of the above rules.**

e.g.	child → children	foot → feet	goose → geese
	man → men	ox → oxen	tooth → teeth
	woman → women	person → people	mouse → mice

✓ **Some nouns are generally considered plural.**

e.g.	binoculars	goggles		jeans	pajamas
	pants	stockings		sandals	scissors
	trousers	shorts		slippers	sneakers

e.g.	✓ **Exceptions:** You can make these plural nouns singular by attaching appropriate units to the front.		
	a pair of binoculars	a pair of goggles	a pair of scissors

Quite a lot of rules, right? As I said at the start of the book, English takes words from many different languages, and the root of a word usually determines how we pluralize it. For example, "**cactus**," "**focus**," and "**radius**" all come from Latin, and so you do the "**-i**" thing at the end to pluralize them. However, "**octopus**" comes from Greek, which is why many linguists argue that only the form with "**-es**" at the end is correct. As such, words from different root languages often have different pluralization rules from one another. And that's one reason there are so many exceptions to each case/rule.

The Plural Form Exercises

✓ **Write the plural forms of the given nouns.**

1) Cat
2) Desk
3) Trip
4) Lock
5) Thought
6) Try
7) Day
8) Fox
9) Wish

10) Stair
11) Dish
12) Stone
13) Store
14) Bay
15) Hoof
16) Domino
17) French fry
18) Ice cream

10.4 How to Use Nouns in Sentences

10.4.1 The Extra Words (the Determiners)

We don't usually use a *noun* or *noun phrase* by itself in a sentence; we are often required to place an extra word in front of it. As discussed in more detail later, we call these words *determiners*. The main purpose of a *determiner* is to provide information about the particular *noun* that follows it, but you also need *determiners* when you're speaking in general.

Under general situations (i.e., when you're not pointing to a particular *noun*), there are <u>three sets</u> of *determiners* that you can choose from. You decide which set you need based on the type of noun you're using. *Singular countable nouns*, *plural countable nouns*, and *uncountable nouns* each call for a different set. Here are the rules.

1. **For *singular countable nouns*, we use "a" or "an."**
   We use "a" for words that start with a consonant sound,
   e.g., a dog, a car.
   We use "an" for words that start with a vowel sound,
   e.g., an egg, an hour.

2. **For *plural countable nouns*, we use numeral or "some,"**
   e.g., four eggs, some brownies. (See the chart below for more.)

3. **For *uncountable nouns*, we use "some,"**
   e.g., some rice, some time. (See the chart below for more.)

I presume that most of these rules are pretty self-explanatory, but I'll cover the difference between "**a**" and "**an**" in a bit more detail. The important thing is that <u>we focus on the sound of the word, not the spelling</u>. A word can start with a consonant but be pronounced with a vowel sound. A great example of such a word is "**hour**." It starts with "**h**," a consonant, but it's pronounced "**our**" (i.e., the "**h**" is silent). Therefore, we use "**an**" with the *noun* "**hour**": "**an hour**." Conversely, a word may start with a vowel but be pronounced with a consonant sound— consider the word "**European**." Though it starts with an "**e**," which is a vowel, it's pronounced as "**yuro-pian**," i.e., it begins with a consonant sound. Therefore, we place an "**a**" in front of it: "**a European**." (*For more on this, see Section 13.2.2.*)

	Countable nouns	Uncountable Nouns
Definition	Can be counted	Cannot be (or are not) counted.
Subject-Verb Agreement	Can take singular or plural verbs.	Always take singular verbs.
General Determiners* *** Also, see Chapter 13 "Determiners"**	<u>**Singular nouns**</u> accept **a/an, the**.	<u>Cannot</u> accept **a/an**.
	<u>**Plural nouns**</u> accept *some, any, [number], many, few, a number of, several*.	Accept *some, any, much, little, a bit, a great deal of, a large quantity/amount of.*

10.4.2 Making Uncountable Nouns Countable

Here's an interesting thing about *uncountable nouns*. <u>We can make them countable by placing appropriate units in front of them</u>. Here are some examples.

1. Some sugar → <u>**One bag**</u> of sugar

2. Some coffee → <u>**Two cups**</u> of coffee

3. Some water → <u>**Three bottles**</u> of water

4. Some cereal → <u>**A bowl**</u> of cereal

For most *uncountable nouns*, which units to use should be quite intuitable. Nonetheless, here's a tip for you: when it's not so intuitable and you're unsure which unit to use, "**<u>a piece of</u>**" usually <u>fits</u>. For example, "**a piece of information**," or "**two pieces of equipment**."

- **Measurements with uncountable nouns**

Here are some common units of measure and some of the *uncountable nouns* they are used with. Note that these are not the only units you can use for each of the *uncountable nouns* listed.

a bag of flour/rice	**a bar of** soap
a bottle of beer/wine	**a bowl of** cereal/rice/soup
a box of candy/cereal	**a bunch of** bananas
a can of corn	**a carton of** ice cream/milk
a container of shampoo	**a cube of** ice
a cup of coffee/tea	**a dish of** spaghetti
a drop of rain	**a gallon of** juice
a glass of water	**a head of** lettuce
a jar of peanut butter/pickle	**a loaf of** bread
a pair of scissors	**a piece of** cake/pie/cheese/paper
a pound of meat	**a roll of** tape/toilet paper
a sheet of paper	**a tube of** toothpaste

Countable and Uncountable Nouns in Sentences Exercises 01

   ✓ **Fix the errors in the following sentences (some sentences may not have any errors).**

Answer
1) There are some egg in the fridge.
2) I'd like to order two cup of black coffees.
3) Here, have some rice.
4) This recipe calls for two cups of milk.
5) Can we place an order for two spaghettis?
6) There is a three sandwiches in my lunch bag.
7) I've had some thoughts about your suggestion.
8) Two different opinions were raised in today's meeting.

Countable and Uncountable Nouns in Sentences Exercises 02

   ✓ **Make the following uncountable nouns countable by using appropriate units.**

1) Rice
2) Water

3) Music
4) Time

10.4.3 Negatives

We form negatives differently for **singular countable nouns**, **plural countable nouns**, and **uncountable nouns**. Interestingly, for each such case, there are exactly two methods you can use to form negatives. For each type of **noun**, both methods are used with similar frequencies. Here are the rules.

1. **For _singular countable nouns:_**
   "There is not a/an" + *[singular countable noun].* OR
   "There is no" + *[singular countable noun].*

2. **For _plural countable nouns:_**
   "There are not any" + *[plural countable noun].* OR
   "There are no" + *[plural countable noun].*

3. **For _uncountable nouns:_**
   "There is not any" + *[uncountable noun].* OR
   "There is no" + *[uncountable noun].*

Consider the following examples.

1. There <u>isn't a</u> freezer in the kitchen. / There <u>is no</u> freezer in the kitchen.

2. There <u>aren't any</u> eggs in the fridge. / There <u>are no</u> eggs in the fridge.

3. There <u>isn't any</u> rice. / There <u>is no</u> rice.

<u>**Countable and Uncountable Nouns in Sentences Exercises 03**</u>

✓ **Turn the following sentences into negative forms.**

1) There is some cereal left in the cupboard.
2) There is water in the Sahara Desert.
3) There are some children playing in the playground.
4) There is a guest bed in my house.
5) There are some people in the cafeteria.
6) There is a smoking lounge in this hotel.
7) There is music playing in the café.
8) There are some pets in my house.
9) There is some news you need to hear.

10.4.4 Questions

We form questions differently for **singular countable nouns**, **plural countable nouns**, and **uncountable nouns**. Unlike with **negatives**, there's only one way to form questions for each case. Here are the rules.

1. **For _singular countable nouns:_** "Is there a/an" + *[singular countable noun]?*

2. **For _plural countable nouns:_** "Are there any" + *[plural countable noun]?*

3. **For _uncountable nouns:_** "Is there any" + *[uncountable noun]?*

Consider the following examples.

1. <u>Is there a</u> toilet on this train?

2. <u>Are there any</u> trains leaving for London today?

3. <u>Is there any</u> rice left in the bag?

Notice that <u>these questions all require a "**yes/no**" answer</u>. You're asking whether the **_noun_** in focus exists in a certain location. An answer of "**yes**" means that the thing exists, while an answer of "**no**" means that it does not.

How do we, then, <u>ask about a quantity of a particular thing</u>? For such purposes, <u>we use the **_question words_**</u> "**how much**" and "**how many**." We use "**how much**" for **_uncountable nouns_**, <u>while we use "**how many**" for **_countable nouns_**</u>. A very important aspect of asking questions about quantity is that <u>you always use a **_plural countable noun_**</u>. You cannot use a **_singular countable noun_** when asking for a quantity. Here are the rules.

1. For *countable nouns:*

   e.g.) **How many** *eggs* **are there** in the fridge?

   "**How many**" + *[plural countable noun]* + "**are there**"?

2. For *uncountable nouns:*

   e.g.) **How much** *time* **is there** before the show starts?

   "**How much**" + *[uncountable noun]* + "**is there**"?

Countable and Uncountable Nouns in Sentences Exercises 04

✓ **Turn the following sentences into simple questions (i.e., no quantities).**

1) There is some sugar left in the bag.
2) There is a plane leaving for New York today.
3) There are some fishes in this lake.
4) There is water on Mars.

Countable and Uncountable Nouns in Sentences Exercises 05

✓ **Turn the following sentences into questions asking for quantities.**

1) There are some oranges in the fridge.
2) There is some time before the ceremony.
3) There is some coffee left in the cup.
4) There are some guests in the house tonight.

10.4.5 Negatives & Questions—Singular vs. Plural

Now here's an interesting conundrum—what's the difference between using a **_singular noun_** and a **_plural noun_** for negatives and questions? The fundamental meaning is actually the same for both forms! Consider the following sentences.

1. **There aren't any eggs.**

2. **There's no egg.**

Both sentences are telling you that there is absolutely no egg available; zero eggs are available. So then, what's the difference between them? <u>The first version (i.e., the **_plural form_**) resulted from genuine curiosity</u> rather than absolute need, and it highlights that you were previously oblivious to the level of your egg supply. That is, you just checked the fridge and found out that, to your surprise, you'd run out of eggs. In shock, you say: "**There aren't any eggs!**" <u>The second version (i.e., the **_singular form_**) resulted from absolute need for eggs</u>, and <u>it</u>

emphasizes the *noun* in focus. In other words, the recipe that you're following right now calls for eggs, so you opened the fridge, but found not a single egg. In frustration, you yell: "**There's no egg!**" Another situation where you'd use this expression is shopping at the grocery store. You're appalled that the grocery store is missing, of all things, the eggs! This realization makes you shout: "**There's no egg in this store!**"

The situation is similar with questions. Consider the following examples.

1. **Are there toilets on this train?**

2. **Is there a toilet on this train?**

Both questions can simply be answered with a "**yes**" or a "**no**" that either confirms or denies the existence of toilets on the train. However, the first version (i.e., the *plural form*) stems from your curiosity. You're just curious whether the train is an advanced model with built-in toilets. On the other hand, the second version (i.e., the *singular form*) stems from your need. You need to use the toilet, so you're asking if there's one on the train. At the same time, you're desperately hoping that the answer is "**yes**."

10.5 Subject-Verb Agreement

This part handles a rule that's so obvious that we've already been using it in the previous parts. However, it should be clearly stated at least once, so here it is.

Subjects and *verbs* must agree in number. In other words, if a *subject* is *singular*, the *verb* must also be *singular*, and if a *subject* is *plural*, the *verb* must also be *plural*.

Recall several chapters back when we looked at the *present simple tense*. There, we said that when the *subject* of the sentence is "**I**," "**you**," "**we**," or "**they**," the base form of the *verb* is used, while when the *subject* is "**he**," "**she**," or "**it**," the base form with an "-s" added to the end is used. Back then, we focused on the *verb*, but now, our focus is on the *subject* (i.e., the *noun*). A *singular countable noun* can be replaced with "**he**," "**she**," or "**it**," while an *uncountable noun* can be replaced with "**it**." Therefore, when a *singular countable noun* or an *uncountable noun* is our *subject*, we must use the "-s" form (i.e., the *singular* form) of the *verb*. On the other hand, a *plural countable noun* can be replaced with "**we**," "**you**," or "**they**." Hence, we must use the base form (i.e., the *plural* form) of the *verb* in that case. Under normal situations, there's no *noun* that can replace "**I**." Here are the rules.

1. **For *singular countable nouns* & *uncountable nouns*: use the "-s" form,**
    e.g., is, was, has, does, runs, eats.

2. **For *plural countable nouns*: use the base form,**
    e.g., are, were, have, do, run, eat.

We call the *verbs* we use for **situation 1** *singular verbs*, while we call the ones we use for **situation 2** *plural verbs*. Conversely, we say that *singular countable nouns* & *uncountable nouns* are *singular* and that *plural countable nouns* are *plural*.

Here are some more specific rules for situations that may be confusing.

1. ***Proper nouns* can be *singular* or *plural*,**
   e.g., <u>Wonder</u> is …, <u>Jack</u> is …, <u>The University of Cambridge</u> is …, <u>Londoners</u> are...

2. ***Collective nouns* are almost always *singular*,**
   e.g., My <u>team</u> is …, My <u>class</u> is …

3. **Just because a noun ends with"-s" doesn't mean it's *plural*.**
   e.g., <u>Los Angeles</u> is … <u>Paris</u> is … <u>Physics</u> is …. <u>Mathematics</u> is ….

<u>Subject-Verb Agreement Exercises 01</u>

✓ **Choose the correct verb from the bracket for each sentence.**

1) Paris (is / are / was) often referred to as the "city of love".
2) This coffee (is / has / was) a very bitter flavor.
3) The United States (are / is / was) officially founded in 1776.
4) Jack and Emily (have / are / was) great friends for each other.
5) My team (has / is / have) reached the semi-finals in this tournament.
6) The workers' union (were / was / is) formed two years ago after the mistreatment of one of the workers by the company.
7) The Harvard University (is / has / was) currently one of the most respected universities in the world.

10.6 Abstract vs. Concrete Nouns

Another very common way of distinguishing ***nouns*** is by determining <u>whether they're</u> ***abstract*** or ***concrete***. ***Abstract nouns*** <u>represent ideas, concepts, feelings, and qualities and are often uncountable</u>. ***Concrete nouns*** <u>represent things that can be seen, touched, heard, or smelled and are often countable</u>. Here are some examples.

Abstract Nouns	Concrete Nouns
love, freedom, knowledge, health,	teacher, classroom, chair, paper, exam

● **Common Abstract Nouns**

ability	advantage	adventure	anger	beauty	belief
bravery	brilliance	calm	care	comfort	compassion
confidence	confusion	death	delay	dream	education
elegance	envy	evil	fascination	fear	friendship
growth	happiness	hate	hope	horror	hurt
idea	intelligence	joy	justice	kindness	life
loss	luck	luxury	movement	need	opinion
opportunity	pain	peace	pleasure	power	pride
right	shock	skill	strength	success	surprise
talent	trend	trust	victory	weakness	worry

Some *nouns* can be either *abstract* and *concrete* depending on the situation and the usage. The *abstract* version and the *concrete* version often have different meanings. Remember that only *concrete nouns* can ever be countable. Consider the following examples.

1. **These <u>waters</u> are dangerous.** → *bodies of water like oceans & seas (i.e., concrete).*
   Here's a cup of <u>water</u>. → *the liquid that you drink (i.e., abstract)*

2. **He has many good <u>qualities</u>.** → *characteristics of a person, like personality & skills (i.e., concrete)*
   This wine is of high <u>quality</u>. → *standard (i.e., abstract)*

3. **I've had some <u>thoughts</u> about it.** → *several specific & separate thoughts or ideas (i.e., concrete)*
   This task requires <u>thought</u>. → *the process of thinking; consideration (i.e., abstract)*

As you can see, *nouns* can have multiple meanings, both *abstract* and *concrete*. You should consider the circumstances and contexts carefully when evaluating whether a *noun* is *abstract* or *concrete*.

Here are some more examples of *nouns* that can be either *abstract* (**A**) or *concrete* (**C**).

memory	A	✓ the ability to remember I have a very good **memory** for people's names.
	C	✓ specific memories of past events He has lots of exciting **memories** about his grandmother.
glass	A	✓ material **Glass** bottles can be recycled.
	C	✓ container Please bring two wine **glasses** from the kitchen.
time	A	✓ length of an activity How much **time** did it take for you to prepare for this test?
	C	✓ number of instances I've already seen the movie many **times**.
chicken	A	✓ food We had **chicken** at the big family meeting.
	C	✓ kind of animal Our grandparents have three **chickens** that they are raising in their backyard.
room	A	✓ space Can you guys make some **room** for me?
	C	✓ place There are two meeting **rooms** on this floor that can hold up to 50 people each.
experience	A	✓ knowledge or skill Lack of **experience** affects even the greatest football players in big competitions.
	C	✓ an incident that affects you Hearing about his **experiences** during the war is interesting and horrifying at the same time.

Abstract and Concrete Nouns Exercises 01

✓ **Identify the nouns in bold as either abstract ("A") or concrete ("C").**

1) _____ You need high **intelligence** to tackle this problem.
2) _____ This **picture** is breathtakingly beautiful.
3) _____ I respect your high **confidence**.
4) _____ It took a while for me to earn the **trust** of this street cat.
5) _____ One of my front **teeth** fell out today.
6) _____ I am going to visit my grandparents this **summer**.
7) _____ I took a math **exam** today.
8) _____ I went outside to take in some fresh **air**.
9) _____ The **air** around the house felt different today.

10.7 Compound Nouns

Compound nouns are *nouns* formed by joining two (or more) words. Sometimes these mergers are expressed as single, complete words (e.g., **bedroom**, **toothbrush**), sometimes as two separate words with a space between them (e.g., **picture book**, **table tennis**), and sometimes as two separate words with a **hyphen ("-")** between the words (e.g., **six-pack**). Some *compound nouns* have very different meanings than their individual components, so watch out.

To form the *plural* of a *compound noun*, you make the final *noun plural*. For example, the *plural* of "**bus stop**" is "**bus stops,**" and that of "**bookcase**" is "**bookcases**".

Compound nouns needn't always be formed by joining exactly two words. However, when you have three or more *nouns* in a row, it may be difficult to read your sentence. Such expressions are usually limited to newspaper titles, where as much concision as possible is needed.

- **Ways to form compound nouns**

Noun + Noun	football, girlfriend, greenhouse, grandmother, homework
Noun + Verb	haircut, handmade, raindrop, heartbeat, sunrise
Adjective + Noun	full moon, blackboard, software, highway
Adverb + Noun	online, overdue, overdose, outside, outdoor
Verb + Noun	breakfast, washing machine, swimming pool
Adverb + Verb	output, intake
Verb + Adverb	takeover
Adverb + Noun	upstairs, downstairs
Verb + Preposition	check-out
Preposition + Noun	underworld

- **Common Compound Nouns**

airport	anymore	armchair	background
bookshelf	boyfriend	chopstick	classmate
dishwater	dry-cleaning	earthquake	evergreen
everything	eyeball	fire-fly	footprint
friendship	gentleman	goldfish	great-grandmother
hallway	headache	ladybug	leadership
moonlight	mother-in-law	newspaper	nobody
overboard	pancake	postman	railway
rainbow	raincoat	sandcastle	seafood
skateboard	snowboard	strawberry	sunlight
sunshine	teapot	thunderstorm	timetable
toolbox	website	weekend	yourself
mother-in-law	merry-go-round	commander-in-chief	

Compound Nouns Exercises 01

✓ **Form the plural forms of the following compound nouns.**

1) Bedroom
2) Motorcycle
3) Washing machine
4) Driver's license
5) Rainfall

6) Haircut
7) Policeman
8) Swimming pool
9) Greenhouse

10.8 Collective Nouns

As we saw briefly in *Section 10.1* above, ***collective noun*** refers to a ***noun*** used to describe a group of more than one person, animal or thing. While most ***collective nouns*** such as "**class**" and "**herd**" do not refer to specific quantities, some, such as "**pair**" and "**gallon**" provide exact quantities.

The most important thing about ***collective nouns*** is that they are almost always treated as ***singular***. Although each ***collective noun*** refers to a group consisting of more than one thing, the group in whole is usually the topic, rather than the individual entities that make up the group, and so is treated as ***singular***. For example, consider the following situation.

1. *My team* <u>have</u> placed third. → *Wrong!*

2. *My team* <u>has</u> placed third. → *Correct!*

The following table shows some common *collective nouns*. They are categorized by whether they represent groups of people, animals, things, or foods and drinks.

for people	a **band** of musicians		a **class** of students		a **crowd** of people
	a **team** of players		a **cast** of actors		a **gang** of thieves
for animals	an **army** of ants		a **flock** of birds		a **herd** of cows
	a **pack** of wolves		a **school** of fish		a **swarm** of bees
for things	a **bouquet** of flowers		a **forest** of trees		a **galaxy** of stars
	a **bunch** of keys		a **pack** of lies		a **drop** of rain
	a **ball** of wool			a **set** of tools	
	an **album** of photographs			a **tube** of toothpaste	
	a **collection** of books			a **gallon** of gasoline	
for food and drinks	a **bar** of chocolate		a **bottle** of milk		a **can** of soda
	a **jar** of honey			a **slice** of pizza	

10.9 Masculine and Feminine Nouns

Some *nouns* can be classified as either *masculine* or *feminine*. *Masculine nouns* represent males while *feminine nouns* represent females. *Masculine* and *feminine nouns* apply to both people and animals.

Masculine	Feminine	Masculine	Feminine	Masculine	Feminine
actor	actress	boy	girl	bridegroom	bride
brother	sister	father	mother	gentleman	lady
hero	heroine	host	hostess	king	queen
lion	lioness	man	woman	master	mistress
nephew	niece	prince	princess	son	daughter
rooster	hen	sir	madam	wizard	witch
uncle	aunt	waiter	waitress	husband	wife

- **Many nouns are used for both males and females**

accountants	artists	children	dancers	designers
doctors	engineers	lawyers	managers	parents
pupils	scientists	singers	students	teachers

Infinitives and Gerunds

infinitive: the basic form of a verb, e.g., "be," "make," and "go"... usually used with "to," e.g., "to be," "to make," "to go," etc. to denote an action or an experience itself

gerund: a noun in the form of a PRESENT PARTICIPLE that describes an action or experience, e.g., "shopping," "reading," etc.

11.1 Verb-Based Nouns

To discuss activities and actions, we generally use **verbs**. However, you sometimes encounter situations where you need **nouns** to talk about these concepts. A good example of such a situation is when you want to discuss the activity itself rather than the idea of performing it. For example, "**think**" is a **verb** that implies the act of using the brain to consider an idea. But what if you want to talk about the practice of the act? That's when you use **infinitives** and **gerunds**. They are ways to turn **verbs** into **nouns**.

   ✓   **An act during which you think = "to think" (*infinitive*) = "thinking" (*gerund*)**

11.2 How to Form Infinitives and Gerunds

The word "**infinitive**" actually refers to the base form of a **verb** (i.e., the form you use for the **present simple tense**). However, we often use "**infinitive**" to describe the above technique of turning **verbs** into **nouns**. In reality, the "full name" of this form/technique is "**'to'-infinitive.**" And that's a big hint about how to form it. As the alternative name suggests, you place "**to**" in front of the infinitive form of the **verb** when using this technique.

   ✓   run = a **verb** that identifies the activity.
        to run = a *noun* that denotes the practice of the activity.

Next, the **gerund** form of a **verb** is equal to its **present participle** form; in other words, it is the version ending with "**-ing**."

   ✓   talk = a **verb** that identifies the activity.
        talking = a *noun* that denotes the practice of activity.

Consider the following sentence examples.

1. He <u>runs</u>.
   He decided <u>to run</u> to work.
   He loves <u>running</u> on weekends.

2. She <u>talks</u>.
   She deserves <u>to talk</u> now.
   She enjoys <u>talking</u> with strangers.

11.3 Verb Patterns of Infinitives and Gerunds

11.3.1 Why Infinitives and Gerunds Are Stupid

As you can see in the examples above, we often place an *infinitive* or a *gerund* right after a *verb*. The thing is, <u>often, only one of the two is grammatically correct</u>; <u>which one to use depends on the *verb* that directly precedes it</u>. Personally, I consider *infinitives* and *gerunds* some of the trickiest grammar components. This is because **there is no rule to help us decide which one fits where**. If you really want to perfect your *infinitive* and *gerund* skills, the only way is to memorize all the *verbs* that can only be followed by *infinitives* and all the *verbs* that can only be followed by *gerunds*. That said, with extensive reading experience, you will eventually develop a "body memory" of which one fits where; it's similar to developing an instinct. All in all, here's a crucial piece of advice: **if you're unsure, look it up on the internet.**

Despite there being no rules for which one fits where, I will provide some examples of special *verbs* that can be followed by only one form (i.e., either an *infinitive* or a *gerund*). Perhaps you're already familiar with some of them.

11.3.2 Verbs that Can Only be Followed by Infinitives

Some people argue that *verbs* with <u>prospective tones</u> or *verbs* used to <u>discuss one's plans</u> can be followed by *infinitives* only. But, again, that's not an absolutely inclusive way of grouping these special *verbs*. Here is the list of *verbs* that can only be followed by *infinitives*.

advise	decide	intend	plan	teach
agree	deserve	invite	pretend	threaten
appear	expect	learn	prepare	tell
arrange	fail	manage	promise	wait
choose	happen	offer	refuse	want
claim	hope	order	seem	wish

Kate <u>learned</u> ***to speak*** Spanish very quickly.
They <u>decided</u> ***to visit*** England for their wedding anniversary this year.
Lucy <u>planned</u> ***to study*** French during the vacation.
My brother <u>hopes</u> ***to be*** a baker in the future.
She <u>promised</u> ***to take*** us with her next time.

11.3.3 Verbs that Can only be Followed by Gerunds

Again, some argue that **verbs** involving one's emotions, especially positive emotions can be followed by **gerunds** only, but this is not absolute either. Here's a list of **verbs** that can only be followed by **gerunds**.

admit	consider	enjoy	keep	recommend
allow	delay	finish	mind	risk
appreciate	deny	imagine	miss	stop
avoid	discuss	involve	practice	suggest
complete	dislike	justify	prevent	understand

He enjoys **playing** baseball.
My dad stopped **drinking** alcohol.
We finished **cleaning** our rooms.
The team practiced **kicking** the ball into the goal.
She considered **quitting** her school.

11.3.4 Verbs that Can Followed by Either with No Difference in Meaning

Some **verbs** can be followed by either form with no resulting difference in the meaning of your sentence. The following is a list of some such **verbs**.

begin	continue	like	neglect	propose
cease	hate	love	prefer	start

I like **to listen / listening** to classical music.
My family loves **to watch / watching** horror movies.
Sam hates **to take / taking** a shower in the morning.
The temperature will continue **to rise / rising** in the next few days.
He prefers **to eat / eating** dinner before 7 PM.

11.3.5 Verbs that Can Be Followed by Either... with Differing Meanings

Some **verbs** can be followed by either form, but the meaning changes depending on which one you use. The following is a list of some such **verbs**.

stop	forget	try	regret	remember

He stopped **to talk** to her in the office before lunch.
≠ He stopped **talking** to her in the office before lunch.

Let's look at the two sentences in more detail. To explain the first sentence further: "he" was passing by her office, probably on his way to lunch, but he decided to stop by and say hi to "her." On the other hand, in the second sentence, "he" and "she" were both in the office to start with, and were on speaking terms previously. But, something went wrong before lunch and "he" decided to no longer speak to "her" at all. Most likely, they'd just gotten into a fight. Can you spot the difference now?

Often, the *infinitive* is used to indicate the purpose of the action defined by the *main verb*, while the *gerund* is usually used to talk about an action that is happening in parallel with the *main verb's* action. Another distinction is that we often use the *infinitive* for *future* prospective situations, while we use the *gerund* for reflecting on the *past*. For example, "**remembering**" is often used for reminiscing about the *past*, while "**to remember**" is used to remind yourself about something that you have to do in the *future*.

Verb Patterns Exercises

✓ **Use either the infinitive or the gerund to complete the following sentences.**

1) I hope _____ (run) my own restaurant in the near future.
2) I enjoy _____ (ride) my bicycle to work.
3) She's kept quiet for long enough. She deserves a chance _____ (speak) now.
4) I love _____ (eat) sweets whenever I feel down.
5) This appears _____ (be) a serious problem.
6) I usually avoid _____ (go) to sleep too late, but sometimes, I can't help it.
7) I intend _____ (lose) at least 10 kilos before my brother's wedding arrives.
8) I prefer _____ (watch) movies at home rather than going to the theaters.

11.4 Verb Patterns with Objects

11.4.1 Verbs That Require an Object Before the Infinitive

We know that some *verbs* always need an *object*. Recall that we call these *transitive verbs*. The following list provides the *verbs* that require an *object* and that can only be followed by *infinitives*. Remember that the *object* always comes between the *verb* and the *infinitive*.

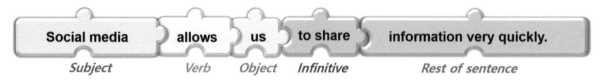

Social media	allows	us	to share	information very quickly.
Subject	*Verb*	*Object*	*Infinitive*	*Rest of sentence*

advise	buy	expect	remind	want
allow	cause	force	remind	will
ask	encourage	invite	tell	

I <u>want</u> the clerk *to find* the exact product for me.
The wind last night <u>caused</u> a lot of street signs *to fall*.
Social media <u>allows</u> us *to share* information very quickly.

11.4.2 Verbs That Require an Object Before the Gerund

Now, here's the list of ***transitive verbs*** that can only be followed by ***gerunds***. Again, remember that <u>the **object** always comes between the **verb** and the **gerund**</u>.

Subject   Verb   Object   Gerund   Rest of sentence

dislike	imagine	leave	mind	see
hear	keep	like	remember	spend

e.g.

My parents <u>dislike</u> me ***going*** to sleep late at night.
Our teacher <u>left</u> us ***studying*** by ourselves for hours.
Elizabeth <u>spends</u> every winter ***skiing*** in the Alps.

Verb Patterns with Objects Exercises

✓ **Complete each sentence using the given noun as the object and the given verb as either the to-infinite or the gerund form.**

1) My mother wants _____ (me, want) law but I really don't want to.
2) On my way home, I remembered _____ (my father, ask) me to buy some flowers. So, I stopped by at the florist store.
3) My friend always reminds _____ (me, clean) my bathroom. Without her, it'd normally be much dirtier than it is now.
4) While driving by the tennis court yesterday, I saw _____ (Tom, play) tennis with his girlfriend, Taylor.

11.5   Verb Patterns with Prepositions

11.5.1 Gerunds Only with Prepositions!

Hey, would you look at that! Finally, something that's concrete regarding ***infinitives*** and ***gerunds***! <u>When a **preposition** appears after a **verb**, we must always use a **gerund**</u> rather than an ***infinitive***. There's actually a pretty simple reason for this. In addition to being an ***infinitive*** marker, "**to**" is a ***preposition***. So, if we place "**to**" after a ***verb*** and then follow it with an ***infinitive***, we end up with "**to**" twice in a row (i.e., "… to to …")—the resulting sentence would be rather awkward. Hence, <u>after a **preposition**, we always use a **gerund**</u> rather than an ***infinitive***.

e.g.

What was the President's reaction <u>on</u> ***hearing*** the news?
No food must be consumed <u>before</u> ***getting*** up in the morning.

As a side-note, several words in English can appear twice in a row, e.g., "**in**", "**had**", "**this**", and "**that**." This type of word repetition occurs most often when we use phrasal verbs (e.g., "came **in**", "**had** to"). (If you'd like to learn more on this, try searching "using the same word twice in a row" on Google.)

11.5.2 Verb, Object, Preposition, and Gerund

Yep, in that exact order. When we use a *transitive verb* with a *preposition*, we can use only a *gerund* (not an *infinitive*), and you must follow the exact order shown in the title of this section.

I	asked	my mother	about	getting	a new dog, but she said no.
Subject	*Verb*	*Object*	*Preposition*	*Gerund*	*Rest of sentence*

I asked my mother <u>about</u> **getting** a new dog, but she said no.
He read the news <u>without</u> **laughing.**

Verb Patterns with Prepositions Exercises

✓ **Use the preposition and the verb given in the bracket to complete the sentences. If there's a noun in the bracket, use it as an object.**

1) He didn't give up _____ (in spite of, fail) many times.
2) _____ (after, finish) her studies, she moved to the big city.
3) Check _____ (facts, before, repost) news or stories from shady websites.
4) What was _____ (the President's reaction, on, learn) about this issue?
5) They won _____ (the award, by, work) hard as a team.
6) After his teacher pointed it out, Jack apologized _____ (for, tell) a lie.

A room without books is like a body without a soul.

- Marcus Tullius Cicero -

CHAPTER 12

Pronouns

words that are used to stand-in for nouns or noun phrases

12.1 English vs. Repetition

12.1.1 English Hates Repetition!

Have I ever mentioned how much English hates repetition? In English, it's considered clumsy to repeat the same (or even similar) vocabulary in two back-to-back sentences. In particular, you need to use extra caution with *proper nouns* and *adjectives/adverbs*. For example, consider the following situations.

1. Sally is 27 years old. Sally works at a hospital as a nurse. → *Bad!*
   Sally is 27 years old. She works at a hospital as a nurse. → *Good!*

2. Sally is a smart girl. She gets her smarts from her mother. → *Okay, but could be better!*
   Sally is a smart girl. She gets her intelligence from her mother. → *Good!*

In the first example, a *proper noun* is repeated. "**Sally**" is the name of a person, i.e., a *proper noun*. "**Sally**" as the *subject* of two sentences in a row makes the writing awkward (and if it doesn't seem awkward to you, then you should start noticing/realizing the awkwardness now). To fix this, we can use the *pronoun* "**she**" to replace "**Sally**" in the second sentence. As you'll see in the following sections of this chapter, *pronouns* are effective at replacing *proper nouns*.

The second situation illustrates a case where two words with the same root are used back-to-back. The *adjective* "**smart**" and the *noun* "**smarts**" have the same root, "**smart.**" As such, the writing could be considered low-level and effortless. In contrast, when you employ a completely different *noun*, "**intelligence**" (as in the second sentence) your writing will be perceived as more interesting and professional.

To take this further, if you really want to achieve high-level writing, you should avoid such repetitions within short passages as well. Continuous encounter of varied vocabulary while working through a paragraph helps keep the reader interested enough to finish it. If you keep repeating the same word, eventually even the most patient of readers can become annoyed.

12.1.2 Repeating For Emphasis

Here's a fun fact: that sense of awkwardness or annoyance can be applied to create emphasis in your writing. Think of a real life case—if you see something out of place, it stands out; it's very conspicuous. You can use the same psychology in English to direct your reader's focus to a certain aspect of your writing. Consider the following situation.

1. **Tom is able to quickly predict the defenders' movements. That's why he has an edge over other footballers worldwide.**

2. **Tom is able to quickly predict the defenders' movements. His quick predictions are what give him the edge over other footballers worldwide.**

3. **Tom is able to quickly predict the defenders' movements. This ability is what gives him the edge over other footballers worldwide.**

In #1, the entire idea in the first sentence: "**Tom is able to quickly predict the defenders' movements**" is condensed into the single *relative pronoun* "**that**" in the second sentence. Hence, among the three options above, #1 is the simplest, but there is no emphasis placed on any aspect, and so the statement sounds a bit weak.

In #2, the *verb phrase*, "**quickly predict**" in the first sentence is repeated as the *noun phrase* "**quick predictions**" in the second sentence. I intentionally used repetition to direct the reader's focus. As a result, the reader will probably concentrate on Tom's ability to "**quickly predict.**" In other words, I used repetition to emphasize the aspect of the sentence that I most want the reader to quickly and easily take note of.

In #3, the *auxiliary verb* "**able**" is repeated in the second sentence in its *noun* form "**ability.**" Again, this creates a slight sense of awkwardness which, in turn, guides the reader's attention. This version is more concise than the second case, but "**ability**" is not very specific. Therefore, if the "**ability**" in question was described in great detail or at length, your reader might actually forget it before they reach the point of repetition. In my opinion, "**to quickly predict the defenders' movements**" in #3 above is too long for use with this technique. Hence, I'd say that #2 is the best choice here.

12.1.3 The Takeaway

Here's the takeaway about English and repetition. Under general circumstances, you should strive to avoid repetition and aim for a varied vocabulary. And, even though directing the reader's focus through repetition is a brilliant writing technique, it may become ineffective or rather annoying if you use it too frequently. As I always say, there's a limit to everything, and with great power (i.e., writing skill, in this case) comes great responsibility. Don't overuse the special writing techniques you learn; you and your writing will look cooler when you only use such techniques once in a while.

12.2 What are Pronouns?

12.2.1 Why We Need Pronouns

As I mentioned above, *pronouns* are words that help us avoid repetition. More specifically, *pronouns* replace *nouns*, especially *proper nouns*. I think you have enough information about why to avoid repetition that you understand how important *pronouns* are for making your writing natural and interesting.

12.2.2 Types of Pronouns

Pronouns are categorized based on the type of *noun* (i.e., what part of the sentence) they replace. So, where can a *noun* appear in a sentence? Fundamentally, a *noun* can be the *subject* or the *object* of a sentence. The *pronouns* that replace *subjects* and *objects* are called *personal pronouns*, and they include *subject pronouns* and *object pronouns*.

But, **personal pronouns** are only a small part of **pronouns**. **Pronouns** can also be used to reflect back on the **subject** of a sentence. The reason you'd reflect back on the **subject** is simple: to emphasize it. <u>**Pronouns** that help us reflect back are called **reflexive pronouns**</u>.

Next, <u>you can use **pronouns** to express possession</u>, i.e., to indicate that something belongs to someone. <u>Such pronouns are called **possessive pronouns**</u>. One interesting thing about **possessive pronouns** is that **possessive determiners**, which are not technically **pronouns**, are usually associated with them. We'll look at both of these in this chapter, and continue our discussion of **determiners** in the next chapter. In simple terms, **determiners** are words placed in front of a **target noun** to describe and contextualize it.

Finally, **indefinite pronouns** are a very interesting variety of **pronouns**. <u>An **indefinite pronoun** can refer to either an unspecified entity, an entire group of people or objects, or to none of the people or objects in a certain group</u>. They are words like "**anyone**," "**someone**," "**everybody**," and "**nobody**." **Indefinite pronouns** prove themselves useful in making general statements or calling for random member(s) from a certain group.

Although there are other types of **pronouns** in English, our coverage in this chapter is limited to the above types. Later on in the book, we'll cover one more **pronoun** type: **relative pronouns**, which we are saving for later because they are reserved for **relative clauses**.

Personal Pronouns	Personal pronouns represent specific people or things. They can replace the subject or the object of a sentence.	
	subject pronouns I, you, he, she, it, we, they	**object pronouns** me, you, him, her, it, us, them
Reflexive Pronouns	We use a reflexive pronoun when we want to refer back to the subject of the sentence or clause to emphasize it.	
	"-self" (singular) myself, yourself himself, herself, itself	**"-selves" (plural)** ourselves, yourselves themselves
Possessive Pronouns	We use possessive pronouns to indicate to whom a particular thing belongs, to describe ownership.	
	mine, yours, his, hers, its, ours, theirs	
Indefinite Pronouns	An indefinite pronoun does not refer to any specific person, thing or amount. Instead, it's used to talk about a group of people or things. It can either represent the entire group, some entities in the group, or no one/nothing in the group.	
	anyone/anybody & someone/somebody, everyone/everybody & no one/nobody something & anything, nothing & everything	

12.2.3 Pronouns Depend on the Perspective

Every type of *pronouns* (except the *indefinite pronouns*) is further distinguished into <u>six</u> categories as shown in the illustration below. These six categories are based on <u>two criteria</u>.

1) **Whether the *target noun* is *singular* or *plural*.**
   The first criterion focuses on <u>how many people/objects</u> make up the *target noun*.

   A. *Target noun* = *singular* → use **<u>singular</u>** pronoun

   B. *Target noun* = *plural* → use **<u>plural</u>** pronoun.

2) **The relationship between the *target noun* and the narrator.**
   The second criterion focuses on the *target noun* in relation to the speaker.

   A. If *target noun* = <u>narrator</u> → use **1ˢᵗ *person*** pronoun

   B. If *target noun* = <u>direct audience</u> → use **2ⁿᵈ *person*** pronoun

   C. If *target noun* = <u>neither the narrator nor the direct audience</u> → use **3ʳᵈ *person*** pronoun

Based on these criteria, the six categories are formed as illustrated below. I've used **subject pronouns** as examples, as they are the most easily intuited.

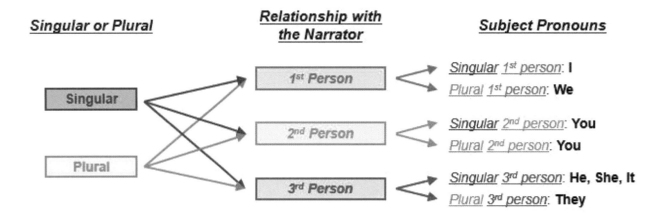

12.3.1 Subject Pronouns

A **subject pronoun** replaces the **subject** of a sentence. Recall when we talked about the **present simple**. I told you that there are <u>seven</u> **subject pronouns**: **I**, **you**, **he**, **she**, **it**, **we**, and **they**. We can sort them according to the six detailed categories above as follows.

Subject Pronouns	1ˢᵗ Person	2ⁿᵈ Person	3ʳᵈ Person
Singular	I	you	he, she, it
Plural	we	you	they

Though it's probably very obvious, I'll still briefly explain the three *3rd person singular subject pronouns*. We use "**he**" for one male, "**she**" for a one female, and "**it**" for a one object or idea.

The following is an example of how to use a *subject pronoun*.

- **That's <u>Andy</u>. <u>Andy</u> is a policeman.**
  → **That's <u>Andy</u>. <u>He</u> is a policeman.**

Instead of repeating "**Andy**" in the second sentence, we can use the appropriate *subject pronoun*, "**he**," to make the writing smoother.

12.3.2 Object Pronouns

An *object pronoun* replaces the *object* in a sentence. The following are the <u>seven</u> *object pronouns*.

Object Pronouns	1st Person	2nd Person	3rd Person
Singular	me	you	him, her, it
Plural	us	you	them

The following shows an example of how we use an *object pronoun*.

- **I met <u>Lizzy</u> yesterday. I gave <u>Lizzy</u> a puppy.**
  → **I met <u>Lizzy</u> yesterday. I gave <u>her</u> a puppy.**

12.3.3 Common Mistake 1: Made When Including Yourself in a List of People

A common mistake associated with *personal pronouns* occurs <u>when you're including yourself as a *subject* in a list of people</u>. Consider the following sentences.

1. **<u>Me and Joe</u> are going to play soccer this afternoon.**
2. **<u>Joe and me</u> are going to play soccer this afternoon.**
3. **<u>I and Joe</u> are going to play soccer this afternoon.**
4. **<u>Joe and I</u> are going to play soccer this afternoon.**

Of the four sentences, only one is grammatically correct. Can you spot which one? That's right! <u>Sentence #4 is the only correct one</u>. First of all, "**me**" is an *object pronoun*, so you can't use it as the *subject* of a sentence; knowing this, we can rule out the first two. The third option is wrong because <u>it's conventional in English to place yourself last when including yourself in a list of people</u>. Hence, only the final sentence is correct. Be careful in cases like this.

12.3.4 Using Personal Pronouns Correctly

One of the most common mistakes a novice English writer or speaker can make is <u>to use a *3rd person pronoun* without specifying a *target noun* beforehand</u>. Remember: a *pronoun* replaces a *noun* that was mentioned in the previous sentence or clause, so as to avoid repetition. When there is no *target noun* or when the *target noun* is unclear, using a *pronoun* is pointless and will likely cause confusion. <u>Whenever you use a *3rd person pronoun* in your sentence, make sure you are replacing a clear *target noun*</u>. This applies to all other *pronoun* types as well, but *3rd person pronouns* are especially tricky in the regard.

In particular, <u>many sentences include more than one **noun** that can accept the same **3rd person pronoun**</u>. Worst case scenario, when there are precisely two **nouns** that can accept the same **3rd person pronoun**, your audience is left to make a guess on which one the **pronoun** stands for. Take the following example.

● **Jack met Michael yesterday. <u>He</u> told <u>him</u> that <u>he's</u> getting married in a couple of weeks.**

Jack and **Michael** are both males and they are both **singular subjects**. Therefore, they can both be "**he/him**." As such, based on the information in this sentence alone, we can't tell who's who, i.e., who is "**he**" and who is "**him**." We can't tell which man is getting married!

That said, you can use the **1st person singular pronouns** (i.e., **I** and **me**) without specifying the **target noun** because only one person is involved: the narrator. Nevertheless, you can't use the **1st person plural pronoun** (i.e., **we**) like this, because other than the narrator, all the people in the group are unknown. Also, you can usually use the **2nd person pronoun** (i.e., **you**, both **singular** and **plural**) without referring back to a **target noun**, because "**you**" always points to the direct audience. But you need to be careful when using "**you**" in the **plural** sense, as who's being directly addressed might not be obvious, just like the **1st person plural** case.

Personal Pronouns Exercises 01

✓ **Put appropriate subject pronouns in the blanks to complete the sentences.**

1) My name is Sue. _____ am 24 years-old.
2) My mom's name is Angie. _____ is from Germany.
3) Bob is my dad. _____ works as a chiropractor.
4) I still have two friends back in my hometown. _____ are both in the police force.
5) My favorite activity is running. _____ makes me feel energetic.
6) To all of the students in the class, have _____ ever been to Greenland?
7) Today is Jack's 70th birthday. _____ used to be my high school teacher.
8) Isabelle is my dog. _____ is a girl.
9) I have 13 colleagues at work. _____ all love playing tennis; that's why everyone's in the tennis group.

Personal Pronouns Exercises 02

✓ **Put appropriate object pronouns in the blanks to complete the sentences.**

1) My sister Jane loves books. This novel is for _____.
2) My children like Disney films. The video is for _____.
3) My brother Matt collects picture postcards. These postcards are for _____.
4) We had to bring one dish each to the party. I brought casseroles for _____.
5) I like watches. This new watch is for _____.
6) Here is another souvenir. I don't know what to do with _____.
7) I bought these flowers for _____ to celebrate your graduation.
8) My dream is to become a police officer. I enrolled into a police school for _____.
9) Since you told me you wanted to watch a sad movie, I borrowed this one for _____ tonight.

12.4 Reflexive Pronouns

12.4.1 What are They?

As briefly mentioned previously, we use **reflexive pronouns** to refer back or toward the **subject** in the same sentence; that is the **pronoun** reflects (or mirrors) the **subject**. **Reflexive pronouns** usually end in "-self" or "-selves." The following are the eight **reflexive pronouns** in English. Notice that the **2nd person plural** form is different than the **2nd person singular** form here, unlike the cases we've handled so far.

Reflexive Pronouns	1st Person	2nd Person	3rd Person
Singular	myself	yourself	himself, herself, itself
Plural	ourselves	yourselves	themselves

12.4.2 Where Do We Use Them?

So, when would you actually use a **reflexive pronoun**? Here again we take our cue from avoiding repetition. We established that a **reflexive pronoun** reflects the **subject** of the same sentence in which it appears. In other words, the **subject** is referred to again in the same sentence. Recall the first section of this chapter. I told you that while English generally hates repetition, we can use repetition to emphasize a certain aspect of a sentence. That is, we use a **reflexive pronoun** to direct focus to (and remind the audience of) the **subject** of a sentence.

There are two places for a **reflexive pronoun** in a sentence—at the end of the clause or right after the **subject**. Where you place the **reflexive pronoun** depends on which aspect you want to highlight.

1. Placing the *reflexive pronoun* **at the end of the clause**:
   You're emphasizing that the *subject* (*not* someone else) performed the action

2. Placing the *reflexive pronoun* **immediately after the** *subject*:
   You're emphasizing that the *subject* is a very important entity

Consider the following situations.

1. **The company director gave the talk** himself.

2. **The company director** himself **gave the talk.**

In #1, the **reflexive pronoun** is placed at the end of the sentence to highlight that the **subject** is the one who gave the talk, not someone else in the organization. In other words, #1 could be expanded as follows: "**The company director gave the talk instead of making someone else do it.**"

In #2, the **reflexive pronoun** is placed directly after the **subject**. This suggests that the **subject** is an important person. Accordingly, we could rewrite #2 as follows: "**The company director, who is a very important person, gave the talk.**"

Can you see the difference between the two cases?

One important thing to remember here is that the second usage is not that common. If you think about it, there aren't too many situations where you need to emphasize the **subject's** high status. Rather, the **reflexive pronoun** is most frequently used to emphasize that a certain person is performing the action. A very common expression using a **reflexive pronoun** is: "**I did it** myself.**"**

12.4.3 Where Reflexive Pronouns Can't Be Used

Another important thing about **reflexive pronouns** is that they can't be used for all activities. In other words, some **verbs** cannot be used with **reflexive pronouns**. Though there's no concrete rule that identifies these **verbs**, a rule of thumb is: *don't use a reflexive pronoun if you don't have to*. In situations where the **verb** itself refers back to the **subject** (i.e., something you always do to yourself or by yourself), you shouldn't use a **reflexive pronoun** because doing so would involve unnecessary repetition. Here are some **verbs** that you should not use **reflexive pronouns** with.

relax	concentrate	feel	meet
get up	shave	go to bed	hurry

Consider the following.

- I can't concentrate <u>myself</u> with all the loud noises in the background. → *Wrong!*

- I can't concentrate with all the loud noises in the background. → *Correct!*

"**Concentrate**" is to direct all your attention to one particular thing, which obviously requires your own effort. If you wanted to be excessively complete, you could rewrite the first sentence as: "**I can't [focus all my attention on one thing myself] myself with all the loud noises in the background,**" whereby the bracketed ("[...]") part is equal to "**concentrate.**" As you can see, using the **reflexive pronoun** "**myself**" in this way creates unnecessary repetition. Hence, you should not use a **reflexive pronoun** in this sentence.

12.4.4 Reflexive Collocations

"**Collocations**" are common phrases—words that go together like bread and butter (or jam, if you prefer—I'm not here to judge). **Reflexive pronouns** are often used to give orders and make suggestions, and in many such cases, we can omit the **subject**. Recall the four basic sentence types. Remember the **imperative sentence**? That's the one you use to order someone around, and, interestingly, an **imperative sentence** starts with a **verb** instead of a **noun**. Now, combine what you know about **reflexive pronouns** and **imperative sentences**. The situation is similar here with **reflexive collocations**.

This type of writing or speaking, however, is only available with certain **verbs**. As I said, **collocations** are things that go together, and not all things do. Here, I denote the **verbs** that can appear in **reflexive collocations** by "**pattern verbs**". Using the **pattern verbs**, we can form **reflexive collocations** that take the following structure.

- ✓ **Pattern verb** + **reflexive pronoun** (+ **preposition**)

Consider the following examples.

1. (You) <u>Enjoy</u> *yourself*!

2. (You need to) <u>Familiarize</u> *yourself* with the company's policies.

3. (You should) **Try to** <u>tear</u> *yourself* **away from your smartphones as often as possible.**

While you can include the **subject** (shown in parentheses) for each sentence, we use these expressions more often without them.

12.4.5 "Each Other"

"**Each other**" is a **reflexive pronoun** that we use to describe two or more people who are performing the same action together at the same time. The action involved usually has a certain directionality, and each person performs the action on everyone else in the group. In other words, everyone involved in the group benefits from or is affected by the action. "**Each other**" is equivalent to "**one another.**" Consider the following examples.

1. Ralph and April looked at <u>each other</u>.

2. They exchanged gifts with <u>each other</u>.

3. The construction workers are shouting at <u>one another</u> over the loud machinery.

Reflexive Pronouns Exercises 01

✓ **Use reflexive pronouns to complete the sentences. For some sentences, you should not use one.**

1) He decided to fix the fence _____.
2) Calm _____ down. You shouldn't be so loud in an airplane.
3) I didn't believe in him until I saw the UFO _____.
4) Sally looked at _____ in the mirror.
5) He went to bed _____ at 10 PM yesterday.
6) You should do your homework _____.
7) Boys, can you make your beds _____?
8) We can move the table _____.
9) What does a cat think when it sees _____ in the mirror?

Reflexive Pronouns Exercises 02

✓ **Pick the correct location to put the reflexive pronoun.**

A. Upon calling the company, he heard that he'd have to wait at least a month for a technician to be arranged for him. Therefore, _____.
   1) he himself decided to fix the fence.   2) he decided to fix the fence himself.
B. Church was awesome yesterday! _____.
   1) The priest himself gave a speech to us.   2) The priest gave a speech to us himself.
C. _____ to address the new project.
   1) The CEO himself will give a speech today   2) The CEO will give a speech today himself
D. As his employee, Tyler is absent today, _____.
   1) Jack himself will have to man the counter.   2) Jack will have to man the counter himself.

Reflexive Pronouns Exercises 03

✓ **Complete the sentences by putting in a reflexive pronoun, "each other", or nothing.**

1) John hurt _____ while climbing the tree.
2) Peter and Sue helped _____ with the homework.
3) My parents helped _____ to some soup first at the buffet.
4) The wild monkey looked at _____ in the mirror.
5) I feel _____ much better today.
6) Bridget and Billy smiled at _____.
7) I don't remember _____ where we spent our holiday last year.
8) Did you make that _____?

12.5 Possession

12.5.1 How to Express Possession

In English, you can signal possession by modifying a *noun* in two ways: by placing a *possessive determiner* before the *noun* or by placing a *possessive pronoun* after the *noun*. As I mentioned above, *possessive determiners* (as the name suggests) are *determiners*, not *pronouns*. However, since they serve a crucial role in expressing possession, we'll cover them here along with *possessive pronouns*.

12.5.2 Possessive Determiners

A *possessive determiner* is placed directly before the *target noun* it possesses. There are seven *possessive determiners* in English.

Possessive Determiners	1st Person	2nd Person	3rd Person
Singular	my	your	his, her, its
Plural	our	your	their

We use them like this.

1.   Garfield is <u>my</u> *cat.*
2.   Tyler is <u>her</u> *dog.*

12.5.3 Possessive Pronouns

A *possessive pronoun* appears after a *target noun* and is usually equated with the *target noun* using a form of "be." Like *possessive determiners*, there are seven *possessive pronouns* in English.

Possessive Pronouns	1st Person	2nd Person	3rd Person
Singular	mine	yours	his, hers, its
Plural	ours	yours	theirs

Note that we usually avoid using the *possessive pronoun* "its" as it can cause confusion between the *possessive adjective* as well as the contraction "it's."

In a sentence, we would use them like so.

1.   This *house* is <u>mine</u>. (= This is <u>my</u> *house.*)
2.   These *toys* are <u>hers</u>. (= These are <u>her</u> *toys.*)

12.5.4 Possession for Other Nouns

When a single owner is involved, we use "**apostrophe + s**" ("**-'s**") to express possession. Consider the following examples.

1. This is <u>Yvonne's</u> *mother*.

2. This is <u>Trisha's</u> *dog*.

3. This is the <u>cat's</u> *bed*.

Next, we know that many **plural nouns** already end with "**-s**." <u>To express possession of a **plural** owner that end with "**-s**," we simply add an **apostrophe** to the end of the word</u> (i.e., <u>no extra "**s**"</u>). Consider the following examples.

1. Lucy is my <u>parents'</u> *cat*.

2. That is my <u>grandparents'</u> *yacht*.

However, not all **plural nouns** end with an "**-s**." <u>For those that do not, we follow the same rule as with **singular** owners</u> (i.e., <u>we add "**-'s**"</u>), as in the following examples.

1. Isabelle is our <u>children's</u> *caretaker*.

2. This is the <u>women's</u> *changing room*.

12.5.5 Possession and the Verb "Have"

The **verb** "**have**" is frequently associated with expressing possession. It is an **irregular verb** and when used in the **present simple tense** with **3rd person singular subject pronouns** (i.e., **he**, **she**, and **it**), it changes to "**has**". As we've seen, we use "**do not (don't)**" or "**does not (doesn't)**" to write in the negative, and we place "**do**" or "**does**" at the front of the sentence to form questions. Now, take all that together and consider the following examples.

1. I <u>have</u> a small pear tree in my yard.

2. Jake <u>doesn't have</u> a garage in his house.

3. <u>Do you have</u> a spare toothbrush?

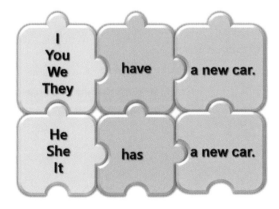

✓ **Common Mistake 1: Pronouns vs. Contractions**

Some <u>contractions</u> are pronounced the same as some *possessive determiners* or *possessive pronouns*. Consider the differences between the two (or more) words in each of the following examples.

1. **its vs. it's**
2. **your vs. you're**
3. **their vs. they're vs. there**
4. **his vs. he's**

Consider the following case.

1. **The dog is playing with <u>it's</u> ball. → *Wrong!***
2. **The dog is playing with <u>its</u> ball. → *Correct!***

They sound the same when spoken loud, but in writing, only one is ever clearly correct.

People get these mixed up to the point that the "**your**" vs. "**you're**" debate became a big internet joke. When you speak, it doesn't matter which one you use because they sound the same, but when you write, you should take care to use the right one.

As a side-note, there is a noun (that's also a verb) spelled the same way as the possessive "**mine**." In fact, "mine" has <u>multiple other meanings</u>, including 1) excavating the earth to extract minerals and 2) a type of bomb placed on the ground or in the water that detonates when stepped on or touched.

✓ **Common Mistake 2: Years and Apostrophes:**

We <u>don't</u> use apostrophes to express decades or centuries.

1. I was born in the 1990's. → *Wrong!*
2. I was born in the 1990s. → *Correct!*

Possession Exercises 01

✓ **Use possessive determiners to complete the sentences.**

1) Here's a postcard that I received from _____ friend, Peggy.
2) She lives in Australia, but the rest of _____ family lives in Japan.
3) Mark works at a fashion company. _____ company is located in Sydney.
4) Meg and Mohammed live in Newcastle. _____ children both go to a school 15 minutes away from their house.
5) We decided to sell _____ car because we moved closer to our workplace.
6) Yesterday, I lost _____ purse in the metro. Thankfully, I picked it up today at Bryant Park station.
7) We mowed _____ lawn last weekend but it already looks like it needs another mowing.

Possession Exercises 02

✓ **Use possessive pronouns to complete the sentences.**

1) I bought this book for you. The book is all _____.
2) This games console is _____. We take turns using it.
3) We met Paul and Jane last night. That house across the street is _____.
4) Mr. Smith has requested us to hold his luggage for him until he leaves tonight. These bags are all _____.
5) I just bought this car yesterday. I still can't believe that it's _____!
6) There's a bird in our garden. That nest is _____.
7) I just finished processing Mrs. Bellini's photos. Those ones on my desk are all _____.
8) This was not my fault. It was _____, so you should fix it.

Possession Exercises 03

✓ **Use the "apostrophe + s" ("-'s") to express possessions.**

1) _____ (Lizzie) cat
2) _____ (Thomas) car
3) Our _____ (parents) house
4) _____ (men) rooms
5) _____ (America) favorite singer
6) _____ (my father) tools

Possession Exercises 04

✓ **Use appropriate expressions of possessions to fill in the blanks.**

It's so nice to be visiting my hometown. That house across the street used to be _____. I've lived there for nine years, right until I left this town. _____ parents also grew up in this town. I don't remember _____ house though. I have a friend who still lives in this town – Mark; that house over there is _____. We went to the same elementary school, and we used to use the playground like it was _____. That's not _____ ("Mark") car though – I know _____ car. It must be _____ ("his wife") car. That pool is _____ too – I heard he installed it just last year.

Possession Exercises 05

✓ **Find what's wrong with the following sentences and correct the mistakes. Some sentences may not have any mistakes.**

1) Wait, that's Sarah's dog! I know its her! Why is it by itself?
2) Up until the late 2000's, men usually wore his ties long, but now, they usually wear them short.
3) Hey, that's Tom's and Sarah's house! They moved in together after they got married.
4) That's his new car. I know it's his because I've seen it on Thanksgiving Day.
5) That's their childrens' toy. They get really mad if you touch it.
6) Happy birthday Gary! What's you're first thought of entering your 30's?
7) Wait, isn't that Chris's watch? Why is it on my desk?

12.6.1 What are They?

Indefinite pronouns are some of the most interesting and useful *pronouns*. They are used frequently in both formal and informal speech and writing, and they prove especially handy to discuss general facts. *Indefinite pronouns* refer to either 1) an unspecified person/object, 2) an entire group of people/objects, or 3) none of the people/objects in a group. The following are the *indefinite pronouns* of English.

Indefinite Pronouns	Unspecified	The Entirety	None
People	anyone, someone, anybody, somebody	everyone, everybody	no one, nobody
Objects	anything, something	everything	nothing

As you can see, for people, we use either "**-one**" or "**-body**," while for objects, we use "**-thing**."

12.6.2 "Any" vs "Some": People

To refer to the entire group or to no entity in the group, there's only one *indefinite pronoun* option each. However, there are two options available to refer to an unspecified entity in the group: "**any**" and "**some**." Which one you choose depends on the tone of your sentence (i.e., positive, negative, or question). Also, the rules are different for people than for objects.

With people, we use "**any**" for negative statements and questions, while we use "**some**" for positive statements and questions. Consider the following examples.

1. "Any": There isn't anybody in this town. / Did anyone visit this morning?

2. "Some": Someone came by at 10 o'clock. / Would you like to talk to somebody?

Let's look at the questions in more detail. As you can see, we can use both "**any**" and "**some**" for questions. Is there a difference between them? Yes, there is. When you use "**any**," it can mean that you're genuinely curious or that you don't expect the thing to be true. When you use "**some**," it suggests that you've noticed a clue or had a hunch. For example, consider the following case.

1. Did anyone call me this morning?

2. Did someone call me this morning?

You might use the first version after you've just arrived at your office. Perhaps you have no idea whether someone might have called you, and you're asking in general whether you received any calls while you were away. In contrast, you might use the second version if you noticed that a message was left on your phone. In that case, you are almost certain that someone had called you, and you're asking for confirmation.

Also, here's some brief information about "**-one**" vs. "**-body**"—they basically mean the same thing, but "**one**" is more formal than "**body**." In other words, you use "**one**" more often when you write than when you speak.

12.6.3 "Any" vs. "Some": Objects

The situation is slightly different for objects. While "**some**" is still used for only positive statements and questions, we can use "**any**" for all of the cases (i.e., positive, negative, and questions) with objects. Consider the following examples.

1. "<u>Any</u>": Is there <u>anything</u> I can do for you? / No, there isn't <u>anything</u> I need help with. / <u>Anything</u> my father builds is awesome.

2. "<u>Some</u>": Do you have <u>something</u> to eat? / Yes, take <u>something</u> from my bag.

Similar to above, "**any**" has more of a general tone, while "**some**" usually aims at something a bit more specific.

12.6.4 "Every" vs. "No": People and Objects

For people and objects alike, "**every-**" means the entirety of the group while "**no-**" means none of the elements (people or things) in the group. What's important is that we use <u>both of these in positive statements and questions only</u>. In other words, <u>you cannot use them in negative statements</u>. Consider the following examples.

1. "<u>Every</u>": Where is <u>everyone</u>? / <u>Everybody</u> has gone to the big dance party.

2. "<u>No</u>": Why is there <u>nobody</u> in the house? /There is <u>no one</u> here.

Notice that there is no negative sentence here (i.e., no "**not**"), even with "**no**."

Recall when we looked at *countable* and *uncountable nouns*. We saw that there are two ways to express the negative (i.e., when there's nothing): "**not any**" and "**no**." The case is similar here in that "<u>any</u>" and "<u>no</u>" are exchangeable in terms of conveying the negative sense. Consider the following examples.

1. There <u>is nothing</u> I anticipated seeing in this exhibition.

2. There <u>isn't anything</u> I anticipated seeing in this exhibition.

Both sentences mean the same thing, but in the first sentence, we're using "**no**" while in the second sentence, we're using "**any**." The same applies when discussing people.

12.6.5 More Indefinite Pronouns

In addition to *indefinite pronouns* for people and objects, there are also *indefinite pronouns* for places, numbers, and to designate particular entities from within a group. Here are some examples.

Places	anywhere, somewhere, everywhere, nowhere, someplace
Specific quantities	few, many, several, enough, little, much, one
Designative	each, either, less, more, neither, another, others

✓ **Common Mistake 1: Always Singular**

A very common mistake made with indefinite pronouns, especially "**every**," involves the fact that most of them are <u>singular</u>. Even when you're referring to the entire group at once (using "**every**") such pronouns are considered <u>singular nouns</u>. You can think of them as similar to collective nouns (e.g., **team**, **group**). However, in the case of singular indefinite pronouns, you are referring (collectively) to the individuals or things in the group, i.e., "each and every" person in the group or "every single" thing in the group. Consider the following examples.
1. **Everyone <u>are</u> at the big meeting.** → *Wrong!*
2. **Everyone <u>is</u> at the big meeting.** → *Correct!*

Note that not all indefinite pronouns are singular. Consider the following table.

Singular	another, anybody/anyone, anything, each, other somebody/someone, either, enough, one, less everybody/everyone, everything, something little, much, neither, nobody/no one, nothing
Plural	both, few, fewer, many, others, several
Both singular & plural	all, any, more/most, none, such, some

✓ **Common Mistake 2: "No" vs. "Any"**

Another common mistake associated with indefinite pronouns involves the uses of "**no**" and "**any**." The important takeaway here is that "**no**" is used for <u>positive</u> statements, while "**any**" is used for <u>negative</u> statements. Consider the following examples. As a reminder, <u>negative statements include the word "**not**"</u>; positive statements do not.
1. **There <u>isn't no one</u> here.** → *Wrong!*
2. **There <u>is anyone</u> here.** → *Wrong!*
3. **There <u>isn't anyone</u> here.** → *Correct!*
4. **There <u>is no one</u> here.** → *Correct!*

<u>Indefinite Pronouns Exercises 01</u>

✓ **Put indefinite pronouns in the blanks to complete the sentences.**

1) She wants to live _____ by the sea one day.
2) She put _____ in the box; literally all that she had.
3) Does _____ have a phone charger?
4) We went _____ this weekend. We stayed at home.
5) You didn't bring _____! You knew it was Britany's birthday party today, right?
6) Is there _____ in this bathroom stall?
7) Q: What's wrong? / A: _____, I'm fine.
8) Would you like to go _____ this weekend? We've stayed in the house for the entire week.
9) _____ was really friendly, including all the managers and even the CEO.

✓ **Find what's wrong with the following sentences and correct the errors. Some may not have any mistakes.**

1) You can have anything you want!
2) There is anybody here.
3) Everybody are here for Christmas – even my grandparents!
4) There really isn't nothing you can do under his surveillance.
5) Does anybody need help?
6) Why is anybody here?
7) Can someone teach me how to play this game?

12.7 Table of Designative Pronouns

Here's a handy table for you. It includes the *pronouns* that point to a specific person, thing, or group of people or things (i.e., all the *pronouns* we've covered in this chapter <u>except</u> the *indefinite pronouns*)—we call these the *designative pronouns*. Note that all *designative pronouns* can be distinguished by the point of view of the sentence (i.e., first-, second-, or third-person), as we've seen.

	Subject Pronouns	Object Pronouns	Possessive Adjectives	Possessive Pronouns	Reflexive Pronouns
1st person	I	me	my	mine	myself
2nd person	you	you	your	yours	yourself
3rd person (male)	he	him	his	his	himself
3rd person (female)	she	her	her	hers	herself
3rd thing (object)	it	it	its	its	itself
1st person (plural)	we	us	our	ours	ourselves
2nd person (plural)	you	you	your	yours	yourselves
3rd person & thing (plural)	they	them	their	theirs	themselves

CHAPTER 13

Determiners

words that come before and describe nouns/put nouns into context

13.1 Introduction

13.1.1 "Level 2" Sentences

At the start of the *verbs* chapter, I mentioned that the shortest sentences in English consist of single *verbs*. For example: "**Run**," "**Stop**," and "**Clean**." What do you think is <u>the next simplest type of sentences</u>? Such sentences can be defined as follows.

✓ "<u>Level 2</u>" sentences <u>combine an *action verb* with an *object*</u> to form the most basic *imperative sentence*.

Recall when we looked at the four fundamental sentence types. We saw that *imperative sentences* begin with *verbs* and are used to give orders: e.g., "**Clean your room.**" "**Do your homework.**"

Let's return to "single-verb sentences" for just a moment. You know that these types of sentences only work with an *action verb*. Recall that we distinguish two categories of *action verbs*: *transitive verbs* and *intransitive verbs*. *Transitive verbs* require an *object*, while *intransitive verbs* do not. When we use an *intransitive verb* as a single-verb sentence, it makes complete sense. For example, "**Run**." "**Stop**." and "**Smile**." But, <u>when we use a *transitive verb*</u> in this way, it often creates a confusing situation. For example, "**Paint**," "**Read**," and "**Clean**." Sure, these single-verb sentences make sense on their own, but <u>if they were delivered without additional context, they could be confusing</u>. What are you supposed to **paint**? <u>What</u> are you supposed to **read**? And <u>where</u> are you supposed to **clean**?

Granted, most of the time, in most real-life situations, the context would be clear enough. If your boss handed you a paintbrush and said "**Paint**," you're probably facing a wall. Or if you were in class and your teacher said "**Read**," you probably have a book on your desk. Nevertheless, <u>hearing these single-verb sentences without any visual assistance makes them incomplete in terms of meaning</u>. <u>What you need to complete each of these sentences is an *object*</u> (after all, by definition, *transitive verbs* require *objects*). For example, when you say: "**Paint that wall**" or "**Read this book**" the sentences are complete and grammatically sound. But wait, if all we needed was an *object*, <u>why add the extra words</u>? <u>What's with "**that**" and "**this**,"</u> and why do we need them? Let's break down each sentence in more detail.

1. <u>Paint that wall.</u> → <u>Paint</u> = *verb*, <u>wall</u> = object (*noun*), <u>that</u> = ?

2. <u>Read this book.</u> → <u>Read</u> = *verb*, <u>book</u> = object (*noun*), <u>this</u> = ?

Okay, now it's probably a little easier to understand. In #1, the **verb** "**paint**" denotes the activity you're being ordered to undertake, while "**wall**" is the **object** that you are to perform the activity on. But what **part of speech** is "**that**"? How about in #2? The activity you've been ordered to perform is "**read,**" and the **object** you'll perform it on is a "**book**." But what about "**this**"? Well, "**that**" and "**this**" are exactly what we're covering in this chapter: *determiners*.

13.1.2 What Exactly Are You?

Hopefully you're already familiar with the vocabulary word "**determine**." Unlike the other three **parts of speech** we've looked at so far—**verb**, **noun**, and **pronoun**—the name of this **part of speech** is not a term reserved solely for grammar. **Determiners**, as the name suggests, are literally agents ("**-er**") that perform the act of "**determining**." To "**determine**" means to "ascertain or establish exactly," often the identity or quantity of something or someone. Accordingly, in English, **determiners** are the grammatical agents that clarify the identity or quantity of other words in a sentence.

To explain this precisely, **determiners** are words that provide additional context to **nouns** with regards to their identity, quality, possession, quantity, and relationships with other **nouns**. They describe **nouns** and often appear in front of **nouns** in a sentence. We use **determiners** to say that a **noun** is a particular **noun** out of all the others of its kind. In a sentence, **determiners** hold similar grammatical positions to **adjectives**. Though we haven't covered **adjectives** yet, if you have an idea of what they are and how to use them, then you already have a good idea of how we use **determiners**.

13.1.3 Types of Determiners

Determiners are interesting because we borrow lots of them from other **parts of speech**. And many of the word used as **determiners** are used for other purposes as well. We find a wide variety of **determiners** in English; as such we will traverse a wide range of vocabulary words in this chapter. But that's not because **determiners** are all that complex in and of themselves. Rather, it's because I explain other uses of words that can be used as **determiners** too. You'll be encountering many new words here, and I intend to provide you with all their main uses, on top of their role as **determiners**. Hence, while this chapter is titled "**Determiners**," it actually covers many different aspects of English grammar.

Since many different kinds of words can be used as **determiners** in English, there are many different ways to categorize such words. In this book, I divide them into six different types.

Articles	a, an, the
Quantifiers	much, a little, a few
Demonstratives	this, that, these, those
Numbers	one, two, first, second
Distributives	both, each, every, either
Possessives	my, your, his, her

13.2 Articles

13.2.1 The Indefinite Articles: A & An

This should evoke a relatively recent memory—recall our discussion of **countable** and **uncountable nouns**. We saw that for **singular countable nouns**, we must place "**a**" or "**an**" in front of them in a sentence. But, back then we didn't talk about why we need to put them there or how they affect the meaning of the sentence. We'll talk about these things right now.

Fundamentally, "**a**" and "**an**" are considered **indefinite articles**, and they are placed in front of **singular nouns**. The **noun** an **indefinite article** describes represents a general idea rather than a particular thing. When you're not pointing to one specific thing but rather to a typical example or general idea, you use "**a**" or "**an**." The following are some specific cases for using **indefinite articles**.

a group, class or category	a doctor, an Indian, a Hindu
an example of something	a large nose, a thick beard
to mean exactly "one" of something	a necklace, a portrait
for something mentioned for the first time	There was a book on the desk.

13.2.2 A vs. An: Which One to Use?

As previously mentioned, we use "**a**" before a **noun** that begins with a consonant sound, while we use "**an**" before a **noun** that begins with a vowel sound. Again, remember that the sound is the important factor, not the letter itself. While you'd usually use "**a**" in front of words that start with a consonant (e.g., **a clock**, **a cat**) and use "**an**" in front of words that start with a vowel (e.g., **an egg**, **an apple**), there are counterexamples as well. For example, "**hour**" starts with the consonant "**h**" but is pronounced "*our,*" which begins with a vowel. Therefore, "**an hour**" is correct. Conversely, "**united**" starts with the vowel "**u**," but is pronounced "*yew-nie-tid,*" which begins with a consonant. Therefore, "**a United States senator**" is correct.

✓ Words that begin with a consonant sound but are spelled with a vowel		
a use	a euro	a unit
a union	a university	a uniform
✓ Words that begin with a vowel sound but are spelled with a consonant		
an heir	an honest man	an X-ray
an hour before	an honorable woman	

The same applies when an **adjective** precedes the **noun**. What's important is the sound that comes directly after "**a**" or "**an**"; it doesn't matter if that sound belongs to an **adjective** or a **noun**. In other words, if there is an **adjective** before the **noun**, we focus on the starting sound of the **adjective**. If the **adjective** starts with a consonant sound, we use "**a**," and if it starts with a vowel sound, we use "**an**." For example, "**an intelligent girl**," "**a fast car**," and "**a rotten egg**."

13.2.3 Indefinite Articles: Uncountable and Plural Nouns

You cannot use "**a**" or "**an**" in front of *uncountable* or *plural nouns*. When we want to discuss an indefinite quantity with *uncountable* or *plural nouns*, we use "**some**" (for positive statements) and "**any**" (for negative statements and questions). *Indefinite articles* for *uncountable nouns* can be especially tricky as they are often grammatically *singular*. Consider the following examples.

> There are <u>a hospitals</u> in this town. → *Wrong!*
> There are <u>some</u> hospitals in this town. → *Correct!*

> We don't have <u>an</u> information. → *Wrong!*
> We don't have <u>any</u> information. → *Correct!*

Note that the *indefinite articles* "**some**" and "**any**" do not modify *uncountable* and *plural nouns* in the general sense. Rather, they indicate that an *uncountable* or a *plural noun* is indefinite in quantity. When we use an *uncountable* or *plural noun* in the general sense, we use the *zero article*, as you'll see later.

13.2.4 The Definite Article: The

If you ask me what the trickiest grammar component in English is, "**the**" will always be near the top of my list. While using "**the**" as a *determiner* is pretty straightforward, things get really confusing when using it with *proper nouns*. As I said, I'll cover all the main uses of "**the**" in English here, not only its role as a *determiner*.

First though, let's start by looking at "**the**" as a *determiner*. As you can probably guess, "**the**" is used in situations that are opposite the ones in which "**a**" or "**an**" are used (*indefinite articles* vs. *definite article*). In other words, we use "**the**" to talk about a specific person or thing. As a *determiner*, "**the**" holds three major functions.

1. To refer to something/someone that has been already mentioned:
I saw a pretty girl at the mall today.   **The** pretty girl, however, did not see me.
2. To talk specifically about a particular thing (+ *further description*):
The pictures *on the wall* are beautiful.   **The** dog *that I saw earlier* was adorable
3. When both parties to the conversation are clearly aware of what is being discussed:
I went on a tour and **the** guide was excellent.   Where is **the** bathroom?

Notice that in all these situations, the *noun* that follows "**the**" always points to a particular entity, not a general kind of entity. Even in #3 above, the "**bathroom**" is not pointing to the general idea of a bathroom but rather to a bathroom in your vicinity, because you need to use it now.

13.2.5 General Uses of "The"

"The" has many more uses than just as a *determiner*. In particular, "the" often appears in front of *proper nouns*. Here are most of the "dos and do-nots" with regards to "the." While I cannot say that this list is complete, it's pretty close. If you're a novice English speaker, it'll be almost impossible for you to memorize all of this in one sitting. Instead, from now on, try to keep your ears and eyes open to where people place "the" in English sentences. Eventually, you'll become familiar enough to intuit all these rules.

Where to use "the":

Where to use "the"	Examples	
Superlatives and ordinals	the most interesting thing …	
	the first person to …	
Unique objects	the Colosseum	the Eiffel Tower
	the Capitol	the White House
Unique titles	the President	the Pope
Groups of people	the Americans	the Koreans
Groups of years (decades & centuries)	the sixties	the 1930s
	the 2000s	the twentieth century
Someone's ability to play a musical instrument	Can you play the piano?	
	I can play the violin.	
Plural or grouped country names	the United States	the Netherlands
	the Philippines	
Geographic Areas	the South Pole	the West
	the South	the Asia Pacific
Oceans, rivers, seas, deserts, forests & canals	the Pacific Ocean	the Potomac River
	the Mediterranean Sea	
Names of schools that include "of" or "for"	the University of Maryland,	
	the Maryland School for the deaf.	
Names of some places	the library	the cafeteria
	the hospital	the post office
Acronyms where each letter is pronounced	the UN	the US
	the CIA	the FBI
Groups of people described by Adjectives (the + adjective)	the rich	the young
	the elderly	

Where NOT to use "the":

Where NOT to use "the"	Examples	
Names of people	~~the~~ John	~~the~~ Dr. Yang
	~~the~~ President Kennedy	
Names of countries without "of"	~~the~~ South Korea	~~the~~ Great Britain
	~~the~~ Russia	
Names of continents	~~the~~ Africa	~~the~~ Asia
	~~the~~ Europe	~~the~~ Australia
Names of some geographical areas	~~the~~ Western Europe	
Names of cities and states	~~the~~ New York	~~the~~ Paris
	~~the~~ Washington State	
Names of streets	~~the~~ Park Avenue	~~the~~ Fourth Street
Names of lakes	~~the~~ Lake Ontario	~~the~~ Lake Geneva
Names of universities and schools without "of" or "for"	~~the~~ Harvard University	
	~~the~~ Maryland University	
Names of landmarks	~~the~~ Pete Hall	~~the~~ Kendal School
	~~the~~ Merrill Learning Center	
Names of companies	~~the~~ Twitter	~~the~~ Facebook
	~~the~~ Microsoft	
Names of languages	~~the~~ Russian	~~the~~ French
	~~the~~ English	~~the~~ Spanish
Names of sports	~~the~~ skiing	~~the~~ football
	~~the~~ yoga	~~the~~ hockey
Noun + number	~~the~~ room 221	~~the~~ platform 2
Acronyms pronounced as a word	~~the~~ NATO	~~the~~ UNESCO
	~~the~~ UNICEF	~~the~~ NASA
Acronyms for university degrees	~~the~~ MBA	~~the~~ UCLA
	~~the~~ Ph.D.	~~the~~ MIT

13.2.6 The Zero Article

Earlier in this chapter, we looked at the *indefinite articles* "a" and "an." As established, we use these only for general, rather than specific, *singular countable nouns*. Then, what kind of *article* do we use for general *plural countable nouns* and general *uncountable nouns*? In these situations, we no use no article at all. Alternatively, we say that we place the *zero article* in front of general *plural* and general *uncountable nouns*.

We also saw that while the *indefinite articles* "a" and "an" point to general *nouns*, the *definite article* "the" points to specific *singular nouns*. The situation is similar here—we place the *zero article* in front of general *plural* and *uncountable nouns*, whereas we place "the" in front of specific *plural* and *uncountable nouns*. To help you keep this straight, I've prepared a table that compares the uses of the *zero article* and the uses of the article "the." Note that whether a *noun* is general or specific is not the only way to decide whether to use the *zero article* or "the."

The Zero Article	The Definite Article, "The"
General uncountable & plural nouns	**Specific uncountable & plural nouns**
You should wash yourself. You've got sand everywhere! You can see famous sights all over New York City.	The meal was terrible. Especially, **the** coffee tasted too bitter. Don't get in the shower yet. **The** water is too cold.
Proper nouns (names)	**Some proper nouns need "the"**
My mother's name is Rose. I gave her a rose on Mother's Day. I received that doll on Christmas two years ago.	Jack graduated from **the** University of Maryland. *(See section 13.2.5 for more examples.)*
Places and institutions when their purpose is clear	**Specific places and institutions**
The students start school this fall. College provides opportunities for students to learn and meet new people.	Thomas goes to **the** school on Park Street. **The** college in our town is currently renovating their gym.
General classes of things	
Body gestures are often key in effective communication.	**The** body gesture is often the key tool for effective communication.

Before we move on, let's talk a little about the final entry in the table: "**General classes of things**." In this situation, we discuss the general role or function of a given class of things. For this purpose, we can use either of the following two expressions: [the *zero article* + a *plural noun*] or ["the" + a *singular noun*]. Carefully note which type of *noun* is used with each such *article*. The meanings of a sentence using either expression would be identical.

13.2.7 Articles with Names: Special Situations

When someone happens to have the same name as a well-known person, we use the *definite article* "**the**" to resolve the ambiguity. Consider the following example.

- Come meet my uncle, Neil Armstrong. → He's not **the** Neil Armstrong, is he?

Also, when the name is an entry on a list, we use the *indefinite article* "**a**" or "**an**." Consider the following example.

- I'm certain that I was invited to this party! Check the list again. → Nope, I'm afraid there isn't **a** "John Doe" on this list.

13.2.8 Articles Overview

Here's an overview of *articles* from the perspective of the types of *nouns* they can precede.

- *Singular Nouns*

    1. *Indefinite Articles* ("**a**" & "**an**") → **For things in general,**
       e.g., He wants to buy **a** car. / I've got **a** beautiful green coat.

    2. *Definite Article* ("**the**") → **For specific things,**
       e.g., Is **the** red car outside yours?
       I want to buy **the** green coat hanging in the window.

    3. *Zero Article* → **Never used with singular nouns!**

- *Plural Nouns*

    1. "**Some**" → **For things in indefinite quantities,**
       e.g., I just planted **some** roses. / I bought **some** clothes today.

    2. *Definite Article* ("**the**") → **For specific things,**
       e.g., **The** shoes Sam bought were very expensive.
       The roses you planted outside are beautiful.

    3. *Zero Article* → **For general classes of things,**
       e.g., Sam is always buying shoes. / Roses come in various colors.

- *Uncountable Nouns*

    1. "**Some**" → **For indefinite quantities of things,**
       e.g., I left **some** money on the table. / There is **some** milk in the fridge.

    2. *Definite Article* ("**the**") → **For specific things,**
       e.g., I left **the** money on the table. / **The** milk is expired; don't drink it.

    3. *Zero Article* → **For general ideas,**
       e.g., She earns a lot of money. / Children should drink milk.

Articles Exercises 01

✓ **Put "a", "an", or nothing in the blanks to complete the sentences.**

1) This is _____ book.
2) I bought _____ interesting book yesterday.
3) I like to read _____ books.
4) He is _____ engineer at a small company.
5) Do you have _____ computer at home?
6) Do you like _____ chocolates?
7) Could you give me _____ pen, please?
8) People need _____ food.
9) He will arrive here in _____ hour.
10) She teaches _____ mathematics.

Articles Exercises 02

✓ **Put "a", "an", or "the" in the blanks to complete the sentences.**

1) Does Tom have _____ car?
2) He was not very successful as _____ actor.
3) I went to _____ supermarket to buy some bread.
4) _____ story that he told me was interesting.
5) There is _____ old man at the door.
6) Would you like _____ sandwich?
7) Madrid is _____ capital of Spain.
8) My son is at _____ airport now.
9) It's going to rain. Take _____ umbrella.
10) Maria is wearing _____ nice gray suit today.

Articles Exercises 03

✓ **Put "the" or nothing in the blanks to complete the sentences.**

1) Welcome to _____ United States!
2) I mostly use _____ Facebook to communicate with my friends.
3) Although Jack was born in _____ Canada, his mother language is _____ Russian.
4) _____ FBI headquarters is located in _____ Washington, D.C.
5) I heard that _____ University of Pennsylvania is collaborating with _____ Stanford University to find the cure to the disease.
6) _____ Pope delivered a speech about the gender minorities at _____ Vatican Palace.
7) _____ 1910s was an agonizing period for _____ Koreans as the country was under control by _____ Japan.
8) There's a huge hotel under construction on _____ Brighton Avenue.

Articles Exercises 04

✓ **Put "a", "an", "the", or nothing to complete the following paragraph.**

And so even though we face _____ difficulties of _____ today and _____ tomorrow, I still have a dream. It is _____ dream deeply rotted in _____ American dream. I have a dream that one day this nation will rise up and live out _____ true meanings of its creed: "We hold these truths to be self-evident, that all _____ men are created equal." I have a dream that one day on _____ red hills of Georgia, _____ sons of former slaves and _____ sons of former slave owners will be able to sit down together at _____ table of brotherhood. I have a dream that one day even _____ state of Mississippi, _____ state sweltering with _____ heat of _____ injustice, sweltering with _____ heat of _____ oppression, will be transformed into _____ oasis of _____ freedom and _____ justice. I have a dream that my four little children will one day live in _____ nation where they will not be judged by _____ color of their skin, but by _____ content of their character.
(Taken from Martin Luther King, Jr.'s famous speech, "I Have a Dream.")

13.3 Quantifiers

13.3.1 The Basics

"Quantifier" is another straightforward, easily understandable term—it's a combination of "**quantify**" and "**-er.**" In other words, a *quantifier* is a type of *determiners* that gives us information about the quantity of *nouns*. While using any language, we must often describe amounts of things. In English, we use *quantifiers* to express ideas about quantities. Note that *quantifiers* do not give us the exact quantities of things—we use *numbers* to do that. (*Numbers* are another type of *determiner* that we'll cover later.) Rather, *quantifiers* give us a rough estimate of how much of thing there is—e.g., whether there's a lot of something or just a little or whether there are many items or just few.

What crucially distinguishes a *quantifier* in English is whether it can modify *countable nouns*, *uncountable nouns*, or **both**. As we've talked about, with *countable nouns* we can count the individual components, while with *uncountable nouns* that's often impossible. Accordingly, *quantifiers* that can be used with *countable nouns* allow for counting, while those that can only be used with *uncountable nouns* only give a general sense of quantity. The *quantifiers* that can modify **both** neither imply a clear a countability nor a sense of strict proportionality. The table below summarizes the different kinds of *quantifiers* in English.

Type(s) of Nouns	Quantifiers
Countable Nouns	a majority of, a number of, several, many, a few, few
Uncountable Nouns	much, a bit, a little, little, a great deal of, a large quantity of, a large amount of,
Both	enough, least, some, all, no, plenty of, more, none, lots of, a lot of, most, any, less, not any

As with most other *determiners*, *quantifiers* are placed before the *noun* in a sentence. If there's an *adjective* modifying the *noun*, the *quantifier* is before the *adjective*. Consider the following examples.

1. There are only <u>a few</u> eggs left in the fridge.

2. There are <u>lots of</u> tall skyscrapers in New York City.

3. There is <u>not enough</u> flour in this recipe.

4. I have <u>little</u> money left; I can't afford to go out tonight.

13.3.2 Making Comparisons with Quantifiers

Although we mostly use _quantifiers_ to signal definite amounts, some can also be used to compare the quantities of different objects. The _quantifiers_ used for such comparisons include "**more**," "**less**," and "**fewer**." "**More**" indicates that there is a greater amount of the object in focus than a certain standard, and it's used for **both _countable_ and _uncountable nouns_**. On the other hand, "**less**" and "**fewer**" both mark that there is a lesser amount of the object in focus than a certain standard. "**Less**" is only used for _**uncountable nouns**_, while "**fewer**" is only used for _**countable nouns**_. Consider the following examples.

1. **I have <u>less</u> sugar than I need.**

2. **I have <u>fewer</u> onions than I need.**

3. **We need <u>more</u> rice.**

4. **I'll bring <u>more</u> cookies.**

We use "**than**" with these comparative _quantifiers_ to compare the quantity of certain _noun_ with a given quantity. Consider the following examples.

1. **Tigers eat <u>more than</u> 20 pounds of _meat_ each day.**

2. **There are <u>fewer than</u> 15,000 _manatees_ in the wild.**

3. **The Georgia Zoo costs <u>less than</u> $10 to visit.**

As a side-note, the _noun_ (**money**) is not explicitly stated in the last example, but we can all understand that **money** is being referred to, based on the symbol "**$**."

more than	Used to compare amounts of uncountable nouns or numbers of countable nouns.
fewer than	Used to compare the exact numbers of people or things.
less than	Used to compare the quantities of uncountable nouns, like amounts, distances, time, and money

13.3.3 The Quantifier Line

Here's how we order _quantifiers_. In the illustration below, the more to the left you go, the less you have of something, and the more to the right you go, the more you have of something.

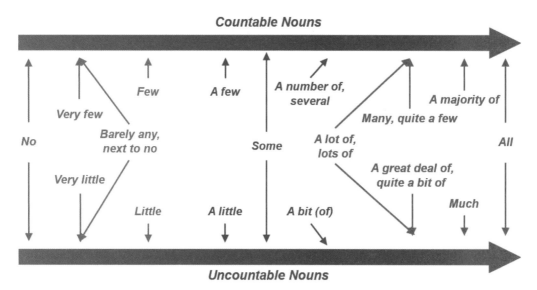

One interesting thing about the *quantifiers* in the lower range is that <u>if you place "a" in front of one of them, it indicates a relatively larger amount</u>. For example, "**little**" means a small amount, while "**a little**" means a small but notable amount. See the table below for more.

● a large quantity of something	
a lot of	- commonly used informally
lots of	- before uncountable and plural countable nouns

● for small amounts: used with uncountable nouns	
little = not much	Focuses on the fact that there is a very small amount something, e.g., We have **little** time left; we must hurry.
a little = some	Focuses on the fact that there is definitely a certain amount of something although generally a small amount, e.g., We have **a little** time left. Why don't we quickly grab something to eat?

● for small quantities: used with plural countable nouns	
few = not many	Focuses on the fact that there is a very small number of something, e.g., **Few** people are on the streets at this time of the day.
a few = some	Focuses on the fact that there is definitely a certain number of something, though generally, a small number, e.g., There are **a few** people on the streets even at this time of the day.

● for large quantities	
quite a few = many	Though "a few" and "a bit" are used to indicate small amounts or quantities,
quite a bit (of) = a lot of	if we place "quite" in front of them, it indicates large amounts or quantities.

The next diagram describes *quantifiers* for evaluating an amount against a certain satisfactory standard. A prime example of these is "**enough**."

enough / not enough / too many	with countable nouns
enough / not enough / too much	with uncountable nouns

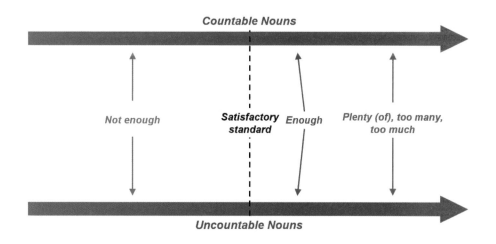

13.3.4 Other Expressions of Quantity

Here are some other *quantifiers* that are less commonly used than the ones listed above.

Countable Nouns Only	a couple of, hundreds of, thousands of...
Uncountable Nouns Only	a good/great deal of, a large/small amount of...
For Both	heaps of, a load of, loads of, tons of...

One additional thing about "**a couple of**"—the phrase can either mean exactly two of something or "just a few" of something.

We use *quantifiers* a lot when we report on statistics. Here are some common expressions we use to talk about stats.

1. Approximate Quantities: **We use *quantifiers* to indicate the general number of cases,**
   e.g., in some cases, in a few cases, in most cases, in a number of cases;
   e.g., In most cases, students live on campus in dormitories.

For approximate quantities, we use the word "**case**" in conjunction with *quantifiers*. By including such an expression in your sentence (usually at the start), you can hedge your statement so that it does not provide the full picture, which is sometimes desirable as statistics can mean different things in different situations.

2. Approximating Statistics: **We use *quantifiers* along with a rounded number or percentage to approximate a stat,**
   e.g., about/approximately half, just under a third, well over fifty percent, almost all;
   e.g., Approximately half of the employees are from Asia.

For approximate statistics, we often write a close-enough whole number or percentage and then use *quantifiers* to modify their meanings. The reason we do this is because a close approximation (like **half**, **a third**, and **three quarters**) may be more intuitable than the specific stat. For example, if your results indicate that **48%** of people do a certain thing, readers may more easily understand "**almost half**." That's why reports on statistics use these expressions a lot.

3. Surprising Numbers: **We use "as [*quantifier*] as,"**
   e.g., as much as, as little as, as many as, as few as, ...;
   e.g., As many as 13,000 people has lost their lives due to the plague.

As you can see, for a surprising large or small number, we use the expression "**as [*quantifier*] as.**" In reality, the expression "**as [*adjective*] as**" is used to compare two things with similar qualities, as described by the *adjective*. However, by using a *quantifier* instead of a general *adjective*, we can compare two things of similar quantities. In this way, using *quantifiers* to describe extremes, like "**much**," "**little**," "**many**," and "**few**," we can emphasize the largeness or smallness of a quantity.

✓ **Common Mistake 1:**
   Exclusivity of Quantifiers

As mentioned above, a lot of quantifiers are exclusively available for either countable or uncountable nouns. You need to carefully consider which one is available for the type of noun you're using before you decide.

Only <u>a little</u> people understand this concept correctly. → *Wrong!*
Only <u>a few</u> people understand this concept correctly. → *Correct!*

✓ **Common Mistake 2:**
   Only Plurals with Quantifiers

Quantifiers discuss an approximate <u>number</u> of countable nouns. In other words, <u>they're meaningless for use with singular countable nouns</u>. Therefore, we <u>only</u> use quantifiers with plural countable nouns.

I have several <u>friend</u> in LA. → *Wrong!*
I have several <u>friends</u> in LA. → *Correct!*

✓ **Common Mistake 3:**
   Even If a Quantifier Starts with "A," the Noun is Still Plural

Some quantifiers start with "a," and so you might confuse them with singular entities. However, when we use a quantifier with a countable noun, the noun itself is <u>always plural</u>.

There <u>is</u> a lot of rooms in this hotel. → *Wrong!*
There <u>are</u> a lot of rooms in this hotel. → *Correct!*

Quantifiers Exercises 01

✓ **Put either "little" or "few" in the blanks.**

1) Julia ate _____ rice; she wasn't very hungry.
2) Mike ate _____ chips; he wasn't very hungry.
3) I have _____ cousins that speak French; the rest of them only speak English.
4) She found _____ cookies under her bed.
5) I need _____ water to feel better, that's all.
6) I want to save _____ money to buy a present for my mother.
7) Robert gave me _____ coins to buy a sweater; it is not enough!
8) Ashley needs _____ sugar for the cake!
9) My dad says that I should learn _____ words in German before leaving for Germany this weekend.

Quantifiers Exercises 02

✓ **Put either "much" or "many" in the blanks.**

1) There are _____ students who want to work in our school.
2) Claire has _____ brothers but only one sister.
3) I don't have _____ time; I can't wait for you.
4) Tom works _____ hours every day—that is why he is always tired.
5) Lisa doesn't drink _____ water when she eats.
6) They have _____ rooms in their house; it is very big.
7) How _____ apples did you buy?
8) How _____ money do you need to have to buy the TV?
9) People don't write _____ letters nowadays—they use the email instead.
10) I think it's too _____ salt for my taste.

Quantifiers Exercises 03

✓ **Put appropriate quantifiers in the blanks to <u>describe yourself</u>.**

1) I have _____ friends at school.
2) I have _____ members in my family.
3) I get _____ money for my weekly/monthly allowances.
4) I spend _____ time for my studies during the weekdays.
5) I spend _____ time to relax during the weekends.
6) I have _____ books in my house.
7) I have _____ toys in my house.
8) I eat _____ snacks between meals.
9) I drink _____ water during meals.

13.4 Demonstratives

13.4.1 Physical Distance

Demonstratives might be a little difficult to understand based solely on the name. If you're a quick study, you might have realized that the term originates from the word "**demonstrate.**" In case you aren't familiar with the word, and because it has a few different meanings, I'll explain *demonstratives* for you.

A *demonstrative* is a type of *determiner* that points to a *noun*, usually to express its physical location. Unlike other types of *determiners* that include many words, there are only four words that can be considered *demonstratives*.

Demonstratives	Singular & Uncountable Nouns	Plural Nouns
Near	this	these
Far	that	those

In a sentence, you can use *demonstratives* as follows.

1. Bella bought me <u>this</u> book.
2. My parents brought me <u>those</u> flowers for my birthday.

13.4.2 Other Distances

In addition to physical distances, you can use *demonstratives* to describe psychological distances and distances in time. Consider the following examples.

1. <u>This</u> job is great. / <u>That</u> job was boring.
2. <u>This</u> play is awesome. / I'd like to see <u>that</u> play.

In #1, "**this** job" is the job you have currently, while "**that** job" means your previous job. In #2, you're currently watching "**this** play," while you haven't experienced "**that** play" yet.

13.4.3 Demonstratives as Pronouns

Demonstratives can be used as *pronouns* as well. Recall that *pronouns* replace *nouns*. Consider the following examples.

1. <u>This</u> is my dog.
2. <u>That</u> is my car.
3. <u>These</u> are my bags.
4. <u>Those</u> are awesome books.

Demonstratives Exercises

✓ **Put "this", "that", "these", or "those" in the blanks.**

1) _____ books are mine. (close to you)
2) _____ toys are broken. (far away from you)
3) _____ program was planned to boost your health.
4) It seems like _____ course didn't end up helping you much.
5) I went on a 4-hour hike yesterday. _____ was exhausting.
6) Thanks for inviting me to the party. _____ is so much more fun than I expected.
7) The books on this table are staying but _____ by the fireplace are going.
8) _____ are the cookies that I baked. Try them—they turned out great.

13.5 Numbers

13.5.1. Introduction

Time for some math! Not a big fan? Well, don't worry; I won't make you do any arithmetic or perform any sort of calculation. However, we will look into *numbers* in this section. As with the other *determiners* we've covered in this chapter, I won't limit the section solely to *numbers* as *determiners*. Instead, I'll talk about general uses for *numbers* as well.

In English, as with most languages, there are two main types of *numbers*: *cardinals* and *ordinals*. *Cardinals* are numbers used for counting—**1 (one)**, **2 (two)**, **3 (three)**, and so on. These are probably what first come to your mind when someone says "*numbers*." On the other hand, *ordinals* are numbers used to order items in a list—**1st (first)**, **2nd (second)**, **3rd (third)**, and so on. *Ordinals* are often used in competitive settings with the word "place" to convey the order of the winning contestants, e.g., 1st place, 2nd place (like in the Olympic Games).

13.5.2 Using Numbers as Determiners

Cardinals and *ordinals* are used as *determiners* for different types of *nouns* in English. *Cardinals* are used as *determiners* for *plural countable nouns* to express an exact number or quantity (e.g., *two* **apples**). On the other hand, *ordinals* are used as *determiners* to point to a certain *noun* in a list or to order certain *nouns* into a list (e.g., the *fifth* **place**, the *second* **exam**).

When using *numbers* as *determiners*, we follow the same rule we've used for all the other *determiner* types we've handled so far—the *number* is placed directly before the *target noun*. Consider the following sentences.

1. **I ordered two *cakes*.**

2. **Three hundred angry *people* were present.**

3. **Jane won the first *prize* and Jo won the third *prize*.**

4. **They have just produced their one millionth *sports car*.**

Before we move on, I'd like to redirect your attention to #2 above. Think back to our look at *articles*. We saw that the *indefinite articles* "**a**" and "**an**" are placed before any and all *adjectives* that appear in front of the *target noun*. The same applies to *numbers* and all other *determiners*—the *determiner* always comes first, then the *adjective(s)*, and then the *target noun*.

In cases where you use *ordinals* and *cardinals* together, the *ordinals* usually come first. Consider the following example.

1. The <u>first</u> <u>three</u> *prizes* **went to the same family.**

13.5.3 Ordinals and "The"

<u>*Ordinals* are usually required to follow the</u> ***definite article*** <u>"the."</u> Recall our look at "**the**"—we said that we use "**the**" as a *determiner* to refer to a specific *noun* rather than to its general type. If you think about it, for each *ordinal*, <u>there's usually only a single entity in that position on a given list.</u> In any competition, there's usually only one **1st place**, one **2nd place**, and so on. Therefore, it makes sense to highlight that uniqueness by placing "**the**" in front of the *ordinal*. Consider the following examples.

1. **John won** *the* <u>first</u> **prize.**

2. **It's** *the* <u>first</u> **time she's trying it.**

<u>*Possessive determiners* are commonly used with</u> *ordinals*<u>, instead of "the."</u> Consider the following examples.

1. **It's** *my* <u>first</u> **time driving on the highway.**

2. **This is** *their* <u>first</u> **house.**

As a brief extension of this topic, note that <u>two or more</u> ***determiners*** <u>can be used in a row</u>. Consider the following cases.

1. **It's** <u>her</u> <u>twenty-first</u> **birthday today.**

2. **His car is** <u>twice</u> <u>the</u> **price of mine.**

3. <u>All</u> <u>six</u> of <u>the</u> **children started crying hysterically.**

As you can see above, *numbers* usually appear last in a list of *determiners*. Hence, they are sometimes referred as "*post-determiners*." However, the exact order of *determiners* in any given multi-determiner noun phrase depends on the *determiner* types involved.

I will skip any further explanation here as the order of *determiners* is a very complicated topic. All you need to know for now is that 1) *determiners* can be used in succession, 2) the order of *determiners* depends on the given variety of *determiners*, and 3) *numbers* usually come last.

13.5.4 More on Numbers

As I said previously, we now shall look at *numbers* beyond their role as *determiners*. From this point on (in this chapter), we'll cover the basics of *numbers* in English. However, the numbers will simply be matched with their spellings, and no further explanation will be provided. If you're confused on any of these, you should look them up and study them yourself.

The ones
1 (one), 2 (two), 3 (three), 4 (four), 5 (five), 6 (six), 7 (seven), 8 (eight), 9 (nine)

The tens

10 (ten), 20 (twenty), 30 (thirty), 40 (forty), 50 (fifty),
60 (sixty), 70 (seventy), 80 (eighty), 90 (ninety)

11-19

11 (eleven), 12 (twelve), 13 (thirteen), 14 (fourteen), 15 (fifteen),
16 (sixteen), 17 (seventeen), 18 (eighteen), 19 (nineteen)

Two Digits, 20 ↑

(the tens are listed first, then the ones) = 22 (twenty-two), 45 (forty-five)

Higher units

100 (a/one hundred), 1,000 (a/one thousand), 10,000 (ten thousand),
100,000 (a/one hundred thousand), 1,000,000 (a/one million)
- **Don't add 's' to 'hundred,' 'thousand,' 'million'**

300(three hundred), 2,000(two thousand), 2,300(two thousand, three hundred)

Three-Digit Numbers

- *[(number of hundreds) + "hundred" + "and" + (two-digit number)]*
  315 (three hundred and fifteen), 473 (four hundred and seventy-three)

Major units

1,000 (a/one thousand), 1,000,000 (a/one million), 1,000,000,000 (a/one billion)

More complicated numbers

- *You pronounce them "three-digits by three-digits" (see examples below)*
  1,958 (one thousand nine hundred and fifty-eight)
  296,308 (two hundred and ninety-six thousand three hundred and eight)

Ordinals

1st (first), 2nd (second), 3rd (third), 4th (fourth),
5th (fifth), 6th (sixth), 7th (seventh), 8th (eighth), 9th (ninth), 10th (tenth),
11th (eleventh), 12th (twelfth), 13th (thirteen) …, 19th (nineteenth), 20th (twentieth),
21st (twenty-first), 22nd (twenty-second), 23rd (twenty-third), 24th (twenty-fourth),
25th (twenty-fifth) …, 30th (thirtieth) …, 40th (fortieth) …, 100th (one hundredth),
101st (one hundred and first) …, 142nd (one hundred and forty-second) …,
1000th (one thousandth) …, 2,575th (two thousand five hundred and seventy-fifth) …

Years

- ***You pronounce them "two-digits by two-digits" (see examples below)***
  1998 (nineteen ninety-eight), 1592 (fifteen ninety-two), 2020 (twenty twenty),
  2022 (twenty twenty-two)
- <u>**Exceptions:**</u> ***2000-2009***
  2000 (two thousand), 2006 (***US:*** two thousand six; ***UK:*** two thousand and six)

Dates

- ***(US) "month + cardinal" or "month + ordinal"***
  July 18 (July eighteenth), July the 18th (July the eighteenth), the 18th of July (the eighteenth of July)
- ***(UK) usually ordinals only***
  July the 18th (July the eighteenth) / the 18th of July (the eighteenth of July)

Dates with years

- ***(US) "month + day, + year,"***
  On May 13, 2007 (May thirteenth, two thousand seven), Dan was born.
- ***(UK) "day + month + year,"***
  On 13 May 2007, (the thirteenth of May, two thousand and seven), Dan was born.

Dates as numerals

- ***(US) "month/day/year"***
  July 2, 2021 = 7/2/2021
- ***(UK) "day/month/year"***
  2 July 2021 = 2/7/2021

Centuries

- ***(century start) + "-s" = (first two-digit + 1) ordinal + "century"***
  1800s (the eighteen hundreds) = 1800 to 1899 = the nineteenth century

Decades

- ***(decade start) + "-s" = Apostrophe + (last two digits) + "-s"***
  = the last two digits in plural
  1980s (the nineteen eighties) = 1980 to 1989 = '80s = the eighties

Age

- ***Cardinal + "years old"***
  24 years old (twenty-four years old)

- **for 1-12 (not used); for 12-19 (teens); for all others (plural tens).**
  He is in his 20s (twenties).
  He's still in his teens. = He's still a teenager.

Time

- **(hour) + (minute)**
  8:38 PM = eight thirty-eight PM = eight thirty-eight in the evening.
  (Regular use: morning = 00:00-11:59 AM; afternoon = 12:00 PM-11:59 PM;
  evening* = 18:00-21:59; night = 22:00-23:59)
  *only used in the military in the US

Fractions

- **(cardinal for numerator) + (ordinal for denominator),**
  e.g., 1/5 (one fifth), 2/7 (two seventh), 2/3 (two thirds)
- **Irregularly named fractions:**
  1/2 (a half), 1/4 (a quarter), 3/4 (three quarters)

Decimals

- **(number before the decimal place) + "point" + (each number after the decimal place)**
  1.63 (one point six three), 32.67 (thirty-two point six seven), 0.3 ((zero) point three)

Percentage

- **(number) + "percent"**
  12% (twelve percent), 55.5% (fifty-five point five percent)

Isn't it interesting that we use *numbers* in so many different situations?

13.5.5 To Spell or To Write?

In most cases, you write out *numbers* using symbols like 1, 2, 3, and so on. However, in some situations, it's better to spell out the *numbers* in full. Here are some situations where you'd spell out *numbers* instead of writing them.

1. *Cardinals* under 100:
   e.g.) She is *twenty-two* years old.

2. **Those with irregular names: a half, a quarter,**
   e.g., More than *half* of the people agreed that the issue was important.
   It's currently *quarter* past nine.

3. **Starting a sentence with a number: you should write it out, in most cases.**
   e.g.) *Seventeen seventy-six* was the year America became a nation.

Numbers Exercises 01

✓ **Spell out the following expressions as how you'd *say* them.**

1) 294
2) 0.67
3) 1776 (year)
4) 7:30 PM
5) 22 (age)
6) 1/5
7) 1500s (century)
8) '70s (decade)

9) Jul 14
10) Sep 11, 2009
11) 24360 (number)
12) 56%
13) 37th
14) 5.282

Numbers Exercises 02

✓ **Convert the expressions in bold as numbers.**

We welcome you to the **seventh** annual meeting of the Green Energy Society (GES)! It's being held on **June sixteenth, twenty twenty-one,** and our main focus this time is renewable energy. Over **a thousand** members have already expressed their will to attend this meeting, with roughly **one fifth** of them being professors from all over the world! Regarding your stay, we regret to inform you that, due to the overflow of participants, we must allocate at least **thirty percent** of the attendees to a hotel that's not on the site. We hope you would understand the situation. Finally, don't forget to attend the dinner party on the day, which is held in the main hall at **half past six**! We're looking forward to meeting every single one of you!

13.6   Distributives

13.6.1 Introduction

Distributives are a class of *determiners* used to talk about how something is shared or divided among multiple owners. Though many words can be used for this purpose, we'll focus on the following five in this section.

- Each, every, either, neither, & both

Among these, the following four: "**each**," "**every**," "**either**," and "**neither**" can be used only as *distributives* and not as other types of *determiners*.

13.6.2 Each vs. Every

"**Each**" and "**every**" have very similar meanings: "all the separate entities in a group." In fact, they're often interchangeable. That said, there are two very important fundamental rules for using them.

1. **We always use a *singular noun* after "each" and after "every." *Noun phrases* containing "each" and/or "every" are always considered *singular.***
   e.g., **Each/every *child*** got a medal.
   Each/every *time* I go shopping, I spend more money.

We've discussed this a little already in the chapter on *nouns*. Any *noun phrase* that contains either "**each**" or "**every**" is considered *singular*. Fittingly, we place only *singular nouns* after "**each**" and after "**every**."

> 2. <u>We cannot use "every" for just two things.</u>
> e.g., She had mittens on **every** hand. → *Wrong!*
> She had mittens on **each** hand. → *Correct!*

When there are exactly two of something, we cannot use "**every**"; the word is reserved for cases of three or more things. In cases of two things, we can only use "**each**."

The biggest difference between "**each**" and "**every**" lies in how each one refers to the entities comprising a group. Although both words refer to "all the separate entities in a group," "<u>**each**</u>" emphasizes the uniqueness of the individual entities in a given group, while "<u>**every**</u>" emphasizes all the entities as being part of a single group.

- "**Each**" can be used to talk about <u>**every member of a group separately**</u>.

- "**Every**" can be used to talk about <u>**all the separate members of a group at once**</u>.

Consider the following sentences.

> 1. **Four girls came, and <u>each</u> *one* sang a different song.**

> 2. **<u>Every</u> *teacher* has a key to the building.**

Can you tell the difference between these sentences? In #1, the four girls each sang a different song. However, in #2, every individual teacher in the specific group of teachers has a copy of the same key. In other words, "<u>**each**</u>" involves individual group members' unique positions, while "<u>**every**</u>" places all individual members in the same position. Consider the following examples as well.

> 3. **<u>Each</u> *ticket* should have a number on the back.**

> 4. **Katrina danced with <u>every</u> *boy* at the party.**

Try to spot the difference between these two on your own.

Now, I'll briefly introduce to you some expressions related to "**each**" and "**every**."

- **Everyone, everybody, and everything**

Since we looked at these expressions in the previous chapter on *pronouns*, under the *indefinite pronouns* section, I'll skip any further explanation here.

- **Each of (the) + *[plural noun]***

This is an interesting expression because you use a *plural noun* instead of a *singular noun* after "**each**." This is similar to "**each + *[singular noun]***" but <u>it allows us to precisely express the size of the group</u>. The "**the**" in the expression can be replaced with any other *determiner*, especially *numbers*. <u>*Numbers* allow us to discuss how many members are in the group we're referring to</u>. For example, "**each of 45 students**" is more informative than "**each student**." Also, this expression is still considered *singular,* and so a *singular verb* like "**is**," "**has**," or "**does**" must be placed after it.

> 1. <u>**Each of the 45 students**</u> **has to hand in their own assignment.**

> 2. <u>**Each of the 12 people**</u> **is going to bring their own dish to the party.**

- **Each and every**

The expression "**each and every**" has the same principal meaning as "**every**," but <u>it puts a bit more emphasis on the individual entities in the group</u>. This expression is <u>used to indicate respect for the members of the group</u> (e.g., in business settings), especially when the responsibility each member of the group holds involves something crucial.

> 1. <u>**Each and every member**</u> **of this company must keep their own work record.**

As a quick side-note, "**each and every**" is always considered *singular*. (You can tell above from the *singular noun* "member" placed after "**each and every**.") However, "**their**," a *plural pronoun*, was used to represent "**member**" in the example. Although this may seem awkward, the above sentence is grammatically sound. We use *plural pronouns* such as "they" and "their" to ensure the gender inclusivity of a *singular noun*. The *singular noun* in such cases is often a *collective noun* that embodies a group of people or animals. In the above sentence, to say "**... his own work record**" or "**... her own work record**" would not account for all the genders of the employees (which would include males, females, and other genders). As such, remember that you can use a *plural pronoun* to represent a *singular noun* to acknowledge all the genders that may comprise a group.

13.6.3 Both, Either, and Neither

These *distributives* are used in situations where there are two (or more) options. "**Both**" indicates two at the same time, while "**either**" indicates only one or the other of two (or more) things, and "**neither**" indicates none of the things. Note that "**both**" can only be used in situations where there are exactly two options, whereas "**either**" and "**neither**" can be used for situations where there are more than two options.

Though less common, you can also use these words as direct *determiners* with *countable nouns*. We use a *plural noun* after "**both**," while we use a *singular noun* after "**either**" and "**neither**." Consider the following examples.

1. I participated in <u>both</u> *events*.

2. You can enter <u>either</u> *tournament*.

3. <u>Neither</u> *event* **is being aired on TV.**

Since "**both**" refers to two things at the same time, and "**either**" refers to one of two things, these two cases should be straightforward. On the other hand, zero/none is always the confusing case, because "zero" is considered *plural* (isn't that peculiar?). However, "**neither**" only agrees with a *singular noun* when it's used as a direct *determiner*.

All three words can also be used along with the *preposition* "of." The *nouns* that follow the expressions "**both of**," "**either of**," and "**neither of**" must be *plural*. The *plural noun* points to two equivalent things: "**both of**" means two things, "**either of**" means one of two things, and "**neither of**" indicates zero of two things. Consider the following examples.

1. We love <u>both of</u> *our teachers*. They are proud of <u>both of</u> *us*.

2. I could buy <u>either of</u> *these cars*, but I don't really need <u>either of</u> *them*.

3. We won <u>neither of</u> *the competitions*. <u>Neither of</u> *us* prepared hard enough.

The most common way of using these words is by <u>listing items one by one using appropriate *conjunctions*</u>. The exact expressions that we use are: "**both ... and**," "**either ... or**," and "**neither ... nor**." For each of these three expressions, <u>the first item comes before the *conjunction*</u> and the second item comes after. Consider the following examples.

1. I want <u>both</u> the pork <u>and</u> the chicken.

2. I will buy <u>either</u> the pork <u>or</u> the chicken.

3. <u>Neither</u> the pork <u>nor</u> the chicken tasted good.

An interesting thing about these expressions is that <u>you can use either *singular* or *plural nouns* with any of the three expressions shown—you can even mix and match *singular* and *plural nouns*</u>! This raises an important question: <u>which **_noun_** do we look to for subject-verb agreement</u>? There's a set of peculiar rules for this.

- If the **_first noun_** is **_singular_**, the **_verb_** must agree with the **_second noun_**.

- If the **_first noun_** is **_plural_** and the **_second noun_** is **_singular_**, the **_verb_** can agree with either one.

Consider the following examples.

1. **Either _a mobile phone_ or _a tablet PC_ <u>is</u> needed for the course.**

2. **Neither _the child_ nor _his parents_ <u>were</u> happy.**

3. **Neither _the classrooms_ nor _the office_ <u>has/have</u> internet access.**

Extraordinary, isn't it?

<u>Distributives Exercises</u>

✓ **Put in appropriate distributives in the blanks.**

1) The train leaves _____ four hours.
2) There are two towels in the bathroom. You can take _____ them. (only one)
3) I have two sisters. _____ them are teachers. (all of them)
4) _____ child wants to win the prize but only one of them can win it.
5) Eva and Julie are _____ students.
6) I like _____ the films you've recommended. (none)
7) _____ Susie _____ Eva are nice and friendly. I like them.
8) Everybody gets one meal during the flight. You can order _____ the beef _____ the chicken meal.
9) _____ the children _____ the teachers found the principal's speech interesting.

13.7 Possessives

As the name suggests, <u>the **_possessive determiners_**</u> we looked at in the previous chapter are also used as **_determiners_**. Since a detailed explanation of them was provided there, I'll omit it here. Instead, I'll just remind you of the <u>seven</u> **_possessive determiners_** in English.

Possessive Determiners	1st Person	2nd Person	3rd Person
Singular	my	your	his, her, its
Plural	our	your	their

Consider the following examples.

1. **This is <u>my</u> book.**

2. **Alfred is <u>his</u> cat's name.**

3. **This is <u>their</u> car.**

Adjectives

words that describe nouns or pronouns

14.1 Introduction

Say that you're in a car with your friends. While you're cruising the streets, an incredibly sexy red Ferrari appears out of nowhere. You look around to see if anyone else has spotted it, but it seems you're the only one who's noticed the stallion. You then go to point it out to your buddies saying, "**Look at that car!**" One of your friends asks, "**Which one?**" Of course, the road is filled with cars, and you're the only one who's noticed the Ferrari; your friend will not be able to pinpoint the car you're talking about at first glance. To help them, you answer, "**The <u>red</u> one.**" Here, "**<u>red</u>**" is an *adjective*. You need to <u>describe the car in further detail</u> so that the other person can identify the one you're talking about—and that, <u>providing details, is precisely what *adjectives* do</u>.

<u>Adjectives</u> are words that describe or modify <u>nouns</u> (and <u>pronouns</u>); they give more information about <u>nouns</u> (and <u>pronouns</u>). Sometimes, they're essential to your sentence, like in the Ferrari case above—without using the *adjective* "<u>red</u>," your friend might have a hard time spotting the car you're talking about. As such, <u>*adjectives* serve the important function of pinpointing the exact thing your *noun* represents</u>. But, <u>more generally, *adjectives* provide interesting additional details about *nouns*; they give *nouns* more context</u>. Though that level of description may not be wholly necessary, it makes your writing a lot juicier and more flavorful. Without *adjectives*, your sentences might sound dry and dull.

However, that doesn't mean that you should use as many *adjectives* as you wish. As with most things, it's never a good idea to overuse *adjectives*. Most of the time, one is enough. And to find the perfect *adjective*, you need to know a lot of them, which is why you need a great vocabulary. While this is, unfortunately, not something I can directly help you with in this book, I will give you some tips on how to improve your vocabulary near the end of this chapter. For now, just remember this: <u>try to limit yourself to a single *adjective* per clause</u>.

14.2 Using Adjectives

14.2.1 The Positioning

There are mainly <u>two positions</u> that an *adjective* can take in a sentence with respect to the ***target noun***—<u>before the **noun**</u> or <u>after the **noun**</u>. Consider the following.

1. <u>Before the **noun**</u>:

He is a <u>busy</u> *man*.

These are <u>busy</u> *streets*.

2. <u>After the **noun**</u>:

This *man* is <u>busy</u>.

These *streets* are <u>busy</u>.

In #1, the *adjectives* are placed before the ***target nouns***. <u>In such cases, the *adjective* usually appears directly before the ***target noun***</u>. On the other hand, in #2, the *adjectives* are placed after the ***target nouns***. <u>In such cases, an appropriate *'be'-verb*</u> must appear between the *adjective* and the ***target noun***. Which *'be'-verb* you choose depends entirely on the ***target noun***.

Are there differences in meaning between the two versions? Not usually. For example, the sentence "**He is a busy man**," conveys a similar idea as "**This man is busy**." However, you'd use each version under different situations.

<u>Adjectives</u> <u>that appear before the **noun** are usually not crucial to the entire sentence. Rather, they provide additional information about the **noun**</u> to assist the reader in understanding the situation better. In some cases, the *adjective* might have nothing to do with the situation itself. What then would be the focus of this type of sentence? <u>When you place the *adjective* before the **noun** in a sentence, it shifts the main focus to the **verb**</u>. We might place an *adjective* before a **noun** in a sentence to divert the reader's attention away from the *adjective* or the **noun** <u>to emphasize the action or the state described by the **verb**</u>. Consider the following examples.

1. **The busy man <u>is running to work</u>.**

2. **These busy streets <u>are always loud</u>.**

In both sentences, the underlined parts that indicate the action of the "**busy man**" and the state of the "**busy streets**," respectively, are the focus. The *adjective* "**busy**" in each sentence just provides additional detail about the *nouns* "**man**" and "**streets**"; the word "**busy**" doesn't hold much importance in either sentence. In fact, you can remove "**busy**" from both sentences, and they will still make perfect sense.

On the other hand, <u>when an *adjective* appears after the **noun** in a sentence, the focus is on the *adjective*</u>. <u>The additional information provided by the *adjective* is critical to the sentence</u>, which would not make sense if you removed the *adjective*. Since the *adjective* is in focus in such cases, <u>we often pair it with an *adverb* to fine-tune the degree or magnitude of the *adjective*</u>. Consider the following examples.

1. **This man is <u>always busy</u>.**

2. **These streets are <u>usually busy</u>.**

The underlined parts in both sentences are formed by pairing an *adverb* with an *adjective*. The most important aspect in both sentences is that the *subject* of the sentence is "**busy**." Furthermore, in both examples, the *adjective* "**busy**" is paired with a *frequency adverb* to indicate how often the *subject* is "**busy**." We'll talk more about *adverbs* in the next chapter.

Next, I'll give you some common *adjectives* that are *antonym* pairs. At the end of *tenses*, I talked about the importance of knowing *antonyms*—recall that in general we rarely use the word "**not**" but instead use an *antonym*. Use the following table as a reference.

- **Common adjective antonym pairs**

Adjective	Antonym	Adjective	Antonym	Adjective	Antonym
alive	dead	early	late	nice	nasty
backward	forward	fast	slow	patient	impatient
beautiful	ugly	fat/thick	thin	polite	rude/impolite
big/large	small	friendly	unfriendly	poor	rich
bitter	sweet	full	empty	quiet	noisy
blunt	sharp	funny	unfunny	right	wrong
boring	interesting	good	bad	safe	dangerous
bottom	top	happy	sad/unhappy	selfish	unselfish
brave	cowardly	hardworking	lazy	short	long
broad/wide	narrow	healthy	sick/ill	single	married
careful	careless	high	low	smart	stupid
cheap	expensive	hot	cold	soft	hard
clean	dirty	intelligent	stupid	sour	sweet
curly	straight	interesting	boring	strong	weak
dark	bright	light	heavy	true	false
deep	shallow	loose	tight	warm	cool
delicious	awful	modern	traditional	well	ill/unwell
difficult	easy	near	far	white	black
dry	wet	new	old	young	old

Using Adjectives Exercises 01

✓ **Rewrite** the sentences while using the adjective in the brackets to describe the noun in bold. Use the adjective <u>before</u> the noun.

1) He is a **basketball player**. (skillful)
2) The **dog** returned to her owner with her toy. (intelligent)
3) The **presentation** took an hour to finish. (boring)
4) He is the **runner** who won the race. (fast)

Using Adjectives Exercises 02

✓ **Rewrite** the sentences while using the adjective in the brackets to describe the noun in bold. Use the adjective <u>after</u> the noun.

1) This is a **train**. (long)
2) This is a **car**. (blue)
3) This is a **chair**. (broken)
4) This is a **tree**. (tall)

Live always in the best company when you read.

- Sydney Smith (1771-1845) –

14.2.2 Types of Adjectives

Adjectives in English can be distinguished into <u>two</u> major categories: **fact adjectives** and **opinion adjectives**. Hopefully those category names speak for themselves.

<u>**Fact adjectives**</u> <u>convey a particular fact about a</u> **noun**. In particular, there are <u>seven types</u> of **fact adjectives**. The table below presents the seven types and numerous examples of each.

● **Common Fact Adjectives**

Size and weight	heavy	light	big	small	little
	tiny	tall	short	fat	thin
	wide	high	large	long	low
	narrow	huge	vast	enormous	great
	gigantic	jumbo	weighty	hefty	giant
Age	old	new	young	childlike	teenage
	pubescent	aged	elderly	senior	ancient
	mature	junior	senescent	older	antique
	aging	youthful	recent	modern	age-old
	ten-year-old		old-fashioned		long-lived
Shape	circular	rectangular	triangular	round	oval/elliptical
	flat	straight	cylindrical	zigzag	wavy
Color	orange	green	yellowish	purple	white
	tanned	pastel	metallic	silver	colorless
	dark-green		transparent		translucent
Origin/Nationality *(only the words in **bold** are adjectives)*	**Australian** (apples)		a **Balinese** (dancer)		the **French** (flag)
	Thai (boxing)		a **Scottish** (kilt)		an **Italian** (car)
	Chinese (kung fu)		an **Indian** (temple)		a **Mexican** (hat)
Material	glass	wooden	concrete	fabric	cotton
	plastic	leather	ceramic	metal	steel
	silicon	woolen	silk	paper	gold
	copper	polyester	nylon	stone	diamond
Purpose *(only the words in **bold** are adjectives)*	**running** (shoes)		a **sleeping** (bag)		a **calculable**(problem)
	a **frying** (pan)		a **tennis** (racket)		**writing** (paper)
	school (shoes)		**gardening** (gloves)		a **shopping** (bag)

Opinion adjectives tell you what someone thinks about the ***noun***. In particular, there are two types of *opinion adjectives*. *General opinion adjectives* can describe lots of different things while ***specific opinion adjectives*** can only describe set types of ***nouns***. The first table below presents commonly used ***opinion adjectives*** and the second table sorts common ***opinion adjectives*** under the two categories (i.e., ***general*** and ***specific***).

- **Common Opinion Adjectives**

amazing	clean	fantastic	important	pretty	ugly
antique	clever	fashionable	intelligent	rich	uncomfortable
awful	comfortable	favorite	interesting	scarce	unusual
bad	dangerous	friendly	jealous	sexy	useful
beautiful	delicious	funny	kind	spicy	usual
best	difficult	generous	lovely	strange	valuable
better	dirty	good	nasty	strong	wasteful
boring	disgusting	great	nice	surprising	wonderful
brilliant	excellent	happy	pointless	tasty	worthless
casual	expensive	honest	poor	terrible	worthy

General opinion	nice	lovely	good	bad
	strange	unusual	amazing	brilliant
	excellent	wonderful	nasty	awful
Specific opinion	**food**: spicy, delicious, tasty			
	clothes: fashionable, casual			
	furniture: antique, comfortable, uncomfortable			
	people: clever, intelligent, generous, friendly			

Let's consider the difference between *general opinion adjectives* and *specific opinion adjectives* a little further. Take the *general opinion adjectives* "**nice**" and "**lovely**" for example—they can describe many different things, including the weather, people, pets, and food. However, the *specific opinion adjective* "**friendly**" can usually only modify people or pets, and "**delicious**" can usually only modify food items. Yet, "poetic license," i.e., literary freedom allows us to use *specific opinion adjectives* for other types of *nouns* as well—for example, you can say "**a set of friendly instructions**" or "**a delicious book.**"

14.2.3 Ordering Adjectives

When we use several *adjectives* to describe a single *noun*, they must often be placed in a specific order. Note that when you use several *adjectives* at once, you can usually only place them before the *noun*; placing them after the *noun* doesn't generally work. The following table presents the order of *adjectives*. To use this table, read across each row from left to right to see the full phrase.

Opinion	Size	Shape	Age	Color	Origin Nationality	Material	purpose	noun
dirty			old					flannel
	tall			red		plastic		cups
handsome			new		Italian			teacher
			old	blue	German			car
beautiful			young		Korean			woman
wonderful			new		French			movie
	big			brown		wooden		desk
		round	antique					table
			old			leather	gardening	gloves

Now, consider the following sentences.

1. I used to drive an **old blue German** car.
2. He recently married a **beautiful young Korean** woman.
3. We bought this **big brown wooden** desk last week.

For each of the underlined parts, placing the *adjectives* in any other order would be grammatically incorrect. Confusing? Too much to remember? Well, if you think those were bad, consider the following case.

- Look at this **beautiful small old brown Greek bronze** coin.

That's six *adjectives* for a single *noun*! In no case whatsoever would this much detail be necessary! Here's some food for thought: just use one. I've already said this, but one *adjective* should be enough in most situations. You'd usually only use multiple *adjectives* when describing physical objects; but even in such cases, keep it under three. Compare the following sentence with the one above.

- Look at this **Greek bronze** coin.

If you think about it, the rest of the *adjectives* describe very obvious features of the coin—the instant you look at it, you'll see that it's "**beautiful**," that it's "**small**," that it's "**old**," and that it's "**brown**." On the other hand, it might be difficult to realize that the coin is "**Greek**" and that it's made out of "**bronze**." Hence, you'd want to keep those two, while you can safely erase the other four. In other words, only use *adjectives* that clarify obscure information about a *noun* (i.e., omit *adjectives* that describe obvious features of a *noun*).

Using Adjectives Exercises 03

✓ **Rewrite** the sentences while using the adjectives in the brackets to describe the noun in bold. Be careful of the <u>order</u> in which you use the adjectives.

1) Look at that **dog**. (brown, small)
2) A **man** told me how to get to here. (kind, old)
3) He seems to really like that **jacket**. (black, leather)
4) She just bought that **truck**. (big, red, American)
5) He is a **basketball player**. (young, agile, tall)
6) This is a **dress** I bought yesterday. (new, comfortable, velvet)
7) That's a **coffee mug**. (lovely, ceramic, old)
8) What a **skirt**! (white, nice, cotton)

14.2.4 Participles as Adjectives

This one's another big throwback to a previous chapter. When we first started looking at *perfect tenses*, we discussed how we can form *adjectives* by modifying *verbs*—we called them "*participles*." Specifically, there were two types of *participles*: the *present participle* and the *past participle*. We saw that the *present participle* is formed by adding "**-ing**" to the end of a *verb*, such as when forming *continuous tenses*. Next, we saw that the *past participle* is formed by adding "**-ed**" to the end of a *verb*, and we also established that there are lots of irregular *past participles*. Most importantly, <u>we defined *participles* as *adjectives* derived from *verbs*</u>.

So, how do we use *participles* as *adjectives*? As you can probably imagine, *present participles* and *past participles* have different uses. First, <u>we use *present participles* to describe the effect something has</u>. In other words, <u>the focus is on the effect of the *noun*</u>. Consider the following examples.

1. **His speech was <u>inspiring</u>.**

2. **Your video was <u>intriguing</u>.**

On the other hand, <u>we use *past participles* to describe how something or someone is affected</u>. In other words, <u>the focus is on the *noun* being affected by something else</u>. Consider the following examples.

1. **Everyone was <u>inspired</u> by his speech.**

2. **I was <u>intrigued</u> by your video.**

Hopefully these contrasting examples clearly illustrate the difference between the two types of *participles*.

Not using the correct type of *participle* is one of the most common mistakes made by intermediate English writers. In particular, English learners with extensive reading experience but who have never seriously studied grammar often make mistakes in this area. If you're one of these people, you need to be careful here.

-ing adjectives	-ed adjectives
alarming What an **alarming** noise!	**alarmed** I was **alarmed** by the loud bang.
boring I've never seen such a **boring** film!	**bored** The students looked **bored** as the teacher talked and talked.
confusing Could you come and help me? I find these instructions very **confusing**!	**confused** I was **confused** because I asked two people, and they told me two different things.
embarrassing That is the most **embarrassing** photo! I look terrible!	**embarrassed** John was really **embarrassed** when he fell over in front of his new girlfriend.
exciting It was a really **exciting** book. I couldn't wait to find out what happened at the end.	**excited** I'm so **excited**! I'm going on vacation tomorrow!
interesting That was a very **interesting** book.	**interested** She's **interested** in animals, so she's thinking of studying to become a vet.
shocking What a **shocking** crime! It's terrible.	**shocked** I was **shocked** when my co-worker admitted to stealing money from the cash register.
surprising It's **surprising** how many people don't want to travel to another country.	**surprised** She was **surprised** when she arrived at her destination.

Using Adjectives Exercises 04

✓ **Find what's wrong with the following sentences and fix them. Some sentences may not have anything wrong with them.**

1) The lightning and thunder really frightening my dog last night.
2) The movie you recommended to me was very entertaining.
3) This song has very interested lyrics.
4) I was really boring during the flight.
5) I was alarming by the loud sound.
6) The weather in UK is always so depressing!
7) John was really embarrassing when he fell over in front of his friends.
8) Thanks for introducing me to this very excited book.
9) I hate doing chores because it's exhausting.

14.2.5 Coordinate Adjectives

We saw before that when there are several *adjectives* that modify a single *noun*, we need to order them in a certain way. In such cases we don't need to add any *punctuation* between them. Nevertheless, there are certain pairs or groups of *adjectives* that we must separate with a *comma* (",") or with the word "**and**." We call these *coordinate adjectives*.

Usually, two or more *adjectives* are considered *coordinate* when they hold similar importance or describe the same aspect of the *noun*. Accordingly, two *adjectives* in the same category ("category" = *general opinion adjectives*, *specific opinion adjectives*, *size adjectives*, *color adjectives*, etc.) are often *coordinate*. Consider the following examples.

1.   **This is going to be a <u>long, cold</u> winter.**

2.   **Isabel's <u>dedicated and tireless</u> efforts made all the difference.**

3.   **My grandmother knitted this <u>red and black</u> sweater for me.**

However, as we have seen, not all pairs or groups of *adjectives* are *coordinate*. Again, when two *adjectives* are in different categories, they're usually not *coordinate*. Consider the following examples.

1.   **My cat, Goober, loves sleeping on this <u>tattered woolen</u> sweater.**

2.   **No one could open the <u>old silver</u> locket.**

3.   **I received this <u>little china</u> mug from Jack on my last birthday.**

If you think about it, it's very difficult for two *fact adjectives* to be *coordinate*. For two *fact adjectives* to be *coordinate*, they would both have to come from the same one of the seven categories. However, this would often lead to rather nonsensical phrases. Consider the following examples.

A.   **That is an <u>enormous and tiny</u> house.**

B.   **This is an <u>old and new</u> table.**

As you can see, using two *coordinate fact adjectives* may lead to ridiculous situations. A "**house**" can either be "**enormous**" or "**tiny**," but never both at the same time; similarly, a "**table**" can be either "**old**" or "**new**," but never both at the same time. As such, we typically encounter *coordinate adjectives* when using multiple opinion adjectives, not *fact adjectives*.

Whenever you're confused about a particular pair, there are two effective ways to check if they're *coordinate*.

● <u>The "and" check</u>: **Try putting "and" between the two** *adjectives*.
   e.g.) tattered woolen sweater → tattered **and** woolen sweater = *Awkward!*

● <u>The reversal check</u>: **Try reversing the order of the** *adjectives*.
   e.g.) old silver locket → **silver old** locket = *Awkward!*

Basically, with both tests, you're assuming that the pair is *coordinate* and checking if that assumption makes sense. If two *adjectives* are *coordinate*, they should sound natural together with "**and**" between them or when their order is reversed. Accordingly, if two *adjectives* are not *coordinate*, then, adding "**and**" between them or reversing their order will result in awkwardness. So, these are good tests for checking if two *adjectives* are *coordinate* or not.

Using Adjectives Exercises 05

✓ **Use the two adjectives in the brackets to describe the noun in bold. Think carefully about which sets are <u>coordinate</u> and which are not.**

1) It's a **puppy**. (happy, lively)
2) Who put this **sticker** here? (red, big)
3) What a **day**. (gratifying, productive)
4) This is a **book**. (thrilling, suspenseful)
5) Thanks for this **gift**. (lovely, little)
6) His **house** has three rooms. (large, brick)
7) **Jamie** quickly advanced as a class leader. (smart, funny)
8) Your son is a **boy**. (nice, intelligent)
9) Your daughter is a **girl**. (athletic, young)

14.2.6 Gradable & Non-gradable Adjectives

We'll see in the next chapter that *adverbs* can be used to modify the meaning of *adjectives*. However, certain *adjectives* can only be used with certain *adverbs*. Depending on their meanings, *adjectives* fall into one of <u>two</u> groups: *gradable adjectives* and *non-gradable adjectives*. Similarly, you'll see later that we can also distinguish *adverbs* into *gradable adverbs* and *non-gradable adverbs*. Intuitively, *gradable adjectives* can only receive *gradable adverbs*, while *non-gradable adjectives* can only receive *non-gradable adverbs*.

<u>Gradable adjectives</u>, as the name suggests, can be ranked. In other words, <u>they can be modified to indicate varying degrees of strength</u>. Such modifications are made using *gradable adverbs* like "**very**," "**less**," "**a bit**," "**really**," "**extremely**," and "**quite**." For example, "**difficult**" is a *gradable adjective*, and so we can modify its strength as follows.

- **The test was <u>difficult</u>.**

  The test was *a little* <u>difficult</u>.

  The test was *rather* <u>difficult</u>.

  The test was *very* <u>difficult</u>.

  The test was *extremely* <u>difficult</u>.

Notice how the level of difficulty of the test is different in each sentence. More information about *gradable adverbs* can be found in the next chapter.

Furthermore, as you'll see later, <u>only the *gradable adjectives* can be used for comparisons</u> (i.e., as *comparatives* and *superlatives*). We'll talk about *comparatives* and *superlatives* in the following sections, but here are some examples to get you started.

- <u>Normal</u>: Hotel A is <u>cheap</u>.

- <u>Comparative</u>: Hotel B is <u>cheaper</u> than Hotel A.

- <u>Superlative</u>: Hotel C is the <u>cheapest</u> of them all.

On the other hand, *<u>non-gradable adjectives</u>* are those that <u>cannot be ranked</u>; <u>their level of strength cannot be modified</u>. This is because <u>their inherent meaning already indicates an extreme</u>. For example, "**finished**" and "**dead**" are both *non-gradable adjectives*. You cannot be "**a little finished**" or "**very finished**," just like you can't be "**a little dead**" or "**very dead**."

However, that doesn't mean there are no *adverbs* that can be used with *non-gradable adjectives*. We refer to *adverbs* that can modify *non-gradable adjectives* as *non-gradable adverbs*. Consider the following cases.

- **His lecture was *absolutely* <u>awful</u>.**

- **This question is *virtually* <u>impossible</u>.**

Though the *adjectives* "<u>awful</u>" and "<u>impossible</u>" are *non-gradable*, adverbs like "*absolutely*" and "*virtually*" can be used to modify them.

In addition, unlike the *gradable adjectives* above, <u>*non-gradable adjectives* cannot be used for comparisons</u>. In other words, *non-gradable adjectives* do not have *comparative* or *superlative* forms.

Non-gradable adverbs can be further distinguished into two categories: those that mean "**entirely**" and those that mean "**almost entirely**." Examples of *non-gradable adverbs* include "**totally**," "**absolutely**," and "**practically**." More information about *non-gradable adverbs* can be found in the next chapter.

Interestingly, there are numerous pairs of *gradable* and *non-gradable adjectives*. In other words, <u>there's usually a *gradable* word and a *non-gradable* word for a single description/idea</u>. The following table presents common *gradable* and *non-gradable adjective* pairs.

Gradable adjectives	Extreme adjectives	Gradable adjectives	Extreme adjectives
angry	**furious**	hungry	**starving**
bad	**awful, terrible**	old	**ancient**
big	**huge, gigantic**	tasty	**delicious**
pretty	**gorgeous**	sad	**miserable**
clean	**spotless**	scary	**terrifying**
cold	**freezing**	happy	**elated**
crowded	**packed**	small	**tiny**
nice	**lovely**	surprising	**astounding**
dirty	**filthy**	tired	**exhausted**
funny	**hilarious**	ugly	**hideous**
good	**fantastic, excellent**	long	**endless**
disappointed	**gutted**	expensive	**exorbitant**
hot	**scorching, roasting, boiling**		

14.3 Comparatives

14.3.1 Where to Use Comparative Adjectives & "Than"

Comparative adjectives are used to compare two *nouns* based on the context provided by the basal *adjective*. This is also called the *comparative form* of an *adjective*. Consider the following example.

- **This is Noah. This is William. They are both tall, but Noah is <u>taller</u>.**

Here, "**<u>taller</u>**" is the *comparative form* of the *adjective* "**tall**." "**Noah is <u>taller</u>**" indicates that Noah has reached a greater height than William. In this way, we can use *comparatives* to compare two things.

The word "**than**" is used to compare two things directly. "**Than**" comes directly after the *comparative*. Consider the following example.

- **Noah is <u>taller</u> *than* William.**

A very common mistake is to use "**then**" instead of "**than**." They sound similar—"then" rhymes with "men"; "than" rhymes with "man"—but they mean completely different things; be careful not to make this mistake in your writing or speaking.

Before moving on, make a good mental note that only *'be'-verbs* should be used before *comparatives*. Whenever we use a *comparative*, we're comparing the states of two entities, and all the context is provided by the *comparative* itself. Therefore, we don't need a *verb* that's any more complex than a *'be'-verb*.

14.3.2 Syllables

If you're confused about what *syllables* is doing here, I understand. You're probably surprised to see this in our section on *comparatives*. However, in order to discuss how to form *comparatives*, we must cover the concept of *syllables*. This is because forming *comparatives* depends heavily on the number of *syllables* the basal adjective contains.

The dictionary definition of a *syllable* is: "a unit of pronunciation having one vowel sound, with or without surrounding consonants." Following this definition, it's important to notice that *syllables* are only relevant in spoken English. We briefly talked about vowel sounds back when we looked at *indefinite articles*. To explain this in a bit more detail here, a vowel sound is a unit of sound that you make with a relatively open vocal tract. In contrast, consonant sounds are created by altering the structure of your vocal tract and then flowing air through the gap(s). There are numerous vowel sounds in English, and it'd be tedious for us both if I listed them all here. So, I'll explain with examples instead.

- Water = "wa" + "ter" → **two *syllables***

- Inferno = "in" + "fer" + "no" → **three *syllables***

With these two words, the concept should be quite straightforward. "Water" has two *syllables*, "wa" and "ter"; "inferno" has three, "in," "fer," and "no." As you can see, the number of *syllables* a word has is pretty much equal to the number of different sounds you must make when pronouncing it. However, it's important to note that the number of *syllables* is not the same as the number of vowels. Consider the following words.

- Lean = "lean" → **one *syllable*, two <u>vowels</u>**

- Office = "o" + "ffice" → **two *syllables*, three <u>vowels</u>**

- Rhythm = "rhy" + "thm" → **two *syllables*, no <u>vowels</u>**

As you can see, the number of *syllables* and the number of vowels in many words don't match. In some extreme cases, you might not have any vowels in your word (though all words in English must have either a vowel or "y"), but it'll still have *syllables*.

14.3.3 How to Form Comparative Adjectives

Now that we've covered **syllables**, we can discuss how to form **comparatives**. As I mentioned before, their formation depends entirely on the number of **syllables** the basal **adjective** has. Keep this in mind as you go through this section.

Basically, there are two ways to form the **comparative** of a particular **adjective**: 1) adding "**-er**" to the end of the **adjective** or 2) placing the word "**more**" in front of the base form of the **adjective**. Most of the time, only one version is grammatically correct. The following are the specific rules for forming the **comparative** form of all **adjectives** in English.

1. One-syllable adjectives		
A. General one-syllable adjectives: add "-er" at the end		
tall → taller	near → nearer	weak → weaker
B. Those ending in "-e": just add "-r" at the end.		
close → closer	large → larger	
C: Those ending with [vowel + consonant]: double the last consonant and add "-er".		
big → bigger	fat → fatter	
D. Exceptions: Some need "more":		
fun → more fun	lost → more lost	
buff → more buff	burnt → more burnt	

2. Two-syllable adjectives		
A. Those ending in "-y": remove "-y" and add "-ier"		
happy → happier	funny → funnier	
B. Other two-syllable adjectives: use "more"		
bizarre → more bizarre	careful → more careful	
C. Exceptions: Some can take both forms:		
narrow → narrower/more narrow	simple → simpler/more simple	
quiet → quieter/more quiet	clever → cleverer/more clever	

3. Three-or-more-syllable adjectives		
always use "more"		
exciting → more exciting	interesting → more interesting	

4. Irregular adjectives		
bad → worse	good → better	little → less
much → more	far → farther or further	

Observe how every rule is based on the number of *syllables* the original *adjective* has. Also, notice that there are several exceptions to these rules. To explain a bit more about the exceptions, I'd like you to focus on **1-D** first. Some *one-syllable adjectives* require "**more**" instead of the standard "**-er**" modification. An easy way to check for these exceptions is to try forming the "**-er**" version and to see if it sounds like another pre-existing word. For example, the "**-er**" version of "**fun**" would be "**funner**," but that sounds too close to "**funnel**". Furthermore, "**loster**" ("**lost + er**") sounds too much like "**lobster**." In addition, "**buffer**" ("**buff + er**") is actually an existing word. As such, it makes sense to avoid such expressions to avoid confusion.

Now let's look at **2-C**. With *two-syllable adjectives*, *participles* (i.e., the ones ending in "**-ing**" or "**-ed**") always take the "**more**" form. On the other hand, as you can see from **2-A**, *two-syllable adjectives* ending in "**-y**" always take the "**-er**" form. However, several of the in-between *adjectives* (i.e., *two-syllable adjectives* that are neither *participles* nor end with "**-y**") can take both forms. That's where this exception comes from.

The table below summarizes the general rules from the perspective of the forms used.

The "-er" Form	The "more" Form
One-syllable adjectives Two syllable adjectives ending in "-y"	Two syllable adjectives <u>not</u> ending in "-y" Three-or-more syllable adjectives

14.3.4 Comparatives with Modifiers

You can use modifiers with most *comparatives*. "Modifiers" refers to words like "**much**," "**a lot**," "**far**," "**a little**," "**a bit**," and "**slightly**." These words can be placed before *comparatives* to signify the magnitude of difference between the two things in question. Consider the following examples.

1. His girlfriend is <u>far</u> *older* than him.

2. Arabic is <u>much</u> *more difficult* than Chinese.

3. My sister's hair is <u>slightly</u> *longer* than mine.

Comparatives & As... As Exercises 01

✓ **Combine** the two sentences into one by using an appropriate comparative to compare the two nouns in bold.

1) Tom is 172 cm tall. Jack is 181 cm tall.
2) A cheetah can run as fast as 74.6 mph. A coyote can run as fast as 42.9 mph.
3) A Ragdoll cat usually weighs around 15 lbs. An American Shorthair cat usually weighs around 10 lbs.
4) Fireworks are usually as loud as 140 dBs. Car horns are usually as loud as 110 dBs.
5) A 1.5-L bottle of Coca Cola costs $3.10. A 1.5-L bottle of Pepsi costs $2.50.
6) The sun rises at around 5:30 AM during the summer. The sun rises at around 7:30 during the winter.
7) *Wonder* is 310 pages. *The House of the Scorpion* is 380 pages

---

14.3.5 Two Comparatives Together

We can use two *comparatives* in the same sentence to show the effect of an action, to show a cause-result relationship. Consider the following examples.

1. The <u>harder</u> you study, the <u>higher</u> your test scores will be.

2. The <u>higher</u> you climb, the <u>harder</u> it is to breathe.

An interesting type of expression arising from the use of two comparatives in one sentence is the double *comparative* that involves using "**better**" (or other similar *comparatives* that generally mean "good"). This type of expression is often contracted because its meaning is still obvious when we omit words. This is especially true when answering a question with a double *comparative*. Consider the following situations.

1. **How would you like your coffee?** → The <u>stronger</u> the <u>better</u>.
   = *The <u>stronger</u> (the coffee is,) the <u>better</u> (it tastes to me).*

2. **When do you want the package delivered?** → The <u>sooner</u> the <u>better</u>.
   = *The <u>sooner</u> (the package is delivered,) the <u>better</u> (it is for me).*

Comparatives & As... As Exercises 02

✓   **Rewrite** the sentences using the <u>double comparative</u> expression.

1) Your body gets stronger as you train harder.
2) You learn more as you study harder.
3) It is more dangerous to drive a faster car.
4) You feel less relaxed if you think about your problems more.
5) If a person is richer, he enjoys more privilege.
6) If you study for a test more, your score will be higher.
7) A crazier idea is more fun to try.
8) If a task is more difficult, it is sweeter to succeed in it.

14.3.6 Using the Same Comparative Twice to Emphasize a Change

We can use the same *comparative* twice in a row to emphasize that a change is taking place. The exact expression takes the following form: "*[comparative]* + and + *[the same comparative]*." Consider the following examples.

1. **These exams *get* <u>worse and worse</u> every year.**

2. **She *gets* <u>more and more beautiful</u> every time I see her.**

3. **That child *is getting* <u>taller and taller</u>.**

4. **The climate *is getting* <u>hotter and hotter</u>.**

5. **This city *is becoming* <u>more and more crowded.</u>**

Notice that <u>the *verbs* that appear directly before each expression (like "**get**" and "**become**") refer to change</u>.

14.3.7 "As... as"

So far, we have seen that a *comparative* is a modified form of an *adjective* and that it compares two things with different values or magnitudes. But <u>what if you want to say that two things have the same value or magnitude</u>? Then, we can use the expression "**as... as**." To be precise, the expression is: "**as** + *[adjective]* + **as**." Note carefully that <u>we do not use the *comparative* here but rather the base *adjective*</u>. Consider the following examples.

1. **The blue car is <u>as fast as</u> the red car.**

2. **The onion soup was <u>as delicious as</u> the tomato soup.**

3. **Her hands were <u>as cold as</u> ice.**

4. **Silver is <u>not as heavy as</u> gold.**

5. **Today it's <u>not as windy as</u> yesterday.**

Note that <u>you can form the negative of this expression by placing "**not**" in front of it</u>, as shown in #4 and #5 above.

Like with *comparatives*, <u>you can use modifiers with "**as… as**."</u> Consider the following examples.

1.   **This race was <u>just</u> *as easy as* the previous one.**

2.   **This new dress is <u>nearly</u> *as comfortable as* my old one.**

Notice how <u>we always put a *'be'-verb*</u> before the "**as… as**" expression. I've mentioned that the *'be'-verb* is a placeholder verb that equates whatever's before it with whatever's after it. We just talked about how "**as… as**" is used to indicate that two things are of the same value or magnitude. Can you see why we use the *'be'-verb* now?

<u>Comparatives & As… As Exercises 03</u>

✓   **Express the following similarities and differences using the "as… as" expression.**

1)   Both Ralph and Craig are 171 cm tall.
2)   Domestic cats are as fast as 29.8 mph, while the Galapagos tortoises are as fast as 0.2 mph.
3)   Both Ragdoll cats and Maine Coon cats weigh around 15 lbs.
4)   Both traffic and vacuum cleaner sounds are around 70 dBs.
5)   The sun rises at around 5:30 AM during the summer. The sun rises at around 7:30 during the winter.
6)   Sitting for too long is bad for your health like smoking.
7)   *Wonder* is 310 pages. *The House of the Scorpion* is 380 pages.

14.4   Superlatives

14.4.1 Where to Use Superlative Adjectives

You just saw that we use *comparatives* to compare two things. When comparing more than two things, we use *superlatives*. But that doesn't mean that we compare each entity in the group to all the others when we use *superlatives*—that could be tedious with large groups. Instead, <u>we use *superlatives* to talk about an extreme case—the best or the worst case in a group.</u>

Like with *comparatives*, <u>we can only use *'be'-verbs* before *superlatives*</u>. Once again, we're comparing the states of two things, and <u>all the extra context is provided by the *superlative* itself</u>. Therefore, <u>we don't need a verb</u> that's any more complex than a *'be'-verb*.

1.   **Mount Everest *is* <u>the highest</u> mountain in the world.**

2.   **Peter *is* <u>the tallest</u> boy in his class.**

3.   **This *is* <u>the most expensive</u> shop in town.**

4.   **Where *are* <u>the tallest</u> buildings in the world?**

5.   **She*'s* <u>the most beautiful</u> girl I've ever seen.**

6.   **Jack and Jenny *are* <u>the most intelligent</u> students in my class.**

7.   **This cup *is* <u>the biggest</u> one.**

8.   **Joe *is* <u>the most intelligent</u> person I've ever met.**

9.   **Of all the people I know, Joe *is* <u>the most important</u>.**

14.4.2 How to Form Superlative Adjectives

Similar to *comparatives*, there are two ways to form the *superlative form* of an *adjective* in English: 1) by adding "**-est**" to the end of the *adjective* or 2) by placing the word "**most**" in front of the base *adjective*. The specific rules for forming *superlatives* are exactly the same as for forming *comparatives*—even the exceptions are the same.

1. One-syllable adjectives

A. General one-syllable adjectives: add "*-est*" to the end.

tall → tall<u>est</u>	near → near<u>est</u>	weak → weak<u>est</u>

B. For those ending in "*-e*": just add "*-st*" at the end.

close → clos<u>est</u>	large → larg<u>est</u>

C: For those ending with [vowel + consonant]: double the last consonant and add "*-est.*"

big → big<u>gest</u>	fat → fat<u>test</u>

D. Exceptions: Some need "*most*":

fun → <u>most</u> fun	lost → <u>most</u> lost
buff → <u>most</u> buff	burnt → <u>most</u> burnt

2. Two-syllable adjectives

A. For those ending in "*-y*": remove "*-y*" and add "*-iest.*"

happy → happ<u>iest</u>	funny → funn<u>iest</u>

B. For other two-syllable adjectives: use "*most.*"

bizarre → <u>most</u> bizarre	careful → <u>most</u> careful

C. Exceptions: Some can take both forms.

narrow → narrow<u>est</u>/<u>most</u> narrow	simple → simpl<u>est</u>/<u>most</u> simple
quiet → quiet<u>est</u>/<u>most</u> quiet	clever → clever<u>est</u>/<u>most</u> clever

3. Three-or-more-syllable adjectives

Always use "*most.*"

exciting → <u>most</u> exciting	interesting → <u>most</u> interesting

4. Irregular adjectives

bad → worst	good → best	little → least
much → most	far → farthest or furthest	

- **Irregular and confusing adjectives**

adjectives	comparative form	superlative form
bad	worse	worst
good	better	best
far (place)	farther	farthest
far (place or time)	further	furthest
late (time)	later	latest
late (order)	latter	last
little (size)	littler	littlest
little (amount)	less	least
many/much/some	more	most
old (people)	elder	eldest
old (people or thing)	older	oldest

Again, the table below summarizes the general rules from the perspective of the form used.

The "-est" form	The "most" form
One-syllable adjectives Two syllable adjectives ending in "-y"	Two syllable adjectives not ending in "-y" Three-or-more syllable adjectives

Importantly, when using a *superlative* in a sentence, the *definite article* "the" must always be placed in front of it. Recall the definition of *definite article*; it's used when there's only a single unique entity in the group. There is usually only one extreme of a group. Therefore, it makes sense to place "the" in front of most *superlatives*.

14.4.3 Superlatives with Modifiers

Like *comparatives*, *superlatives* can be adjusted with modifiers. We do this to express the magnitude of difference between the extreme case and the runner-up (i.e., the 2nd-place entity). However, unlike *comparatives*, where many different types of modifiers can be used, only "**easily**," "**by far**," and "**nearly**" are generally used with *superlatives*. Consider the following examples.

1. She is <u>by far</u> *the oldest* person in the congregation.

2. Bellini's is <u>by far</u> *the best* restaurant in town

3. *Parasite* is <u>easily</u> *the best* movie I have seen this year.

4. I'm <u>nearly</u> *the tallest* in the class.

14.4.4 "One of"

In spoken English, there's a commonly used form of expression that involves *superlatives*. The exact expression is: "**one of + [superlative] + plural noun.**" This form is used to say that something is among the extreme cases (i.e., near the top) in a particular group of things, i.e., the "**plural noun**" at the end. Consider the following examples.

1. Ireland is one of *the richest* countries in the world.

2. Watermelon is one of *the best* things about summer.

We use this expression a lot in conversations because we don't want to sound condescending. When we use the *superlative* without modification, we're indicating that something is the one and only extreme case in a group, and that might not always be true. Especially, in a sentence where you're expressing your opinion, using a bare *superlative* could aggravate people who don't share your opinion. To avoid that, you can use the expression "**one of...**" to hedge your opinion and sound humble. Consider the following cases.

1. *Parasite* is *the best* movie ever made!

2. *Parasite* is one of *the best* movies ever made!

Sure, you might think that *Parasite* is the best movie that you've ever seen, but that may not hold true for all people. It could sound like you're suppressing or ignoring the opinions of others if you say #1. However, if you say #2, you're conveying respect for others' opinions and reinforcing your own opinion at the same time. So, it's usually better to say something like #2 than something like #1.

A final note about "**one of...**": remember to always place a *plural noun* at the end of the expression. You're not referring to a single extreme but rather to one extreme among multiple extremes within a larger group of things.

Superlatives Exercises 01

> ✓ Use superlatives to write two sentences for each given group to express both extremes.

1) Tom is 172 cm tall; Jake is 181 cm tall; Carl is 174 cm tall; Brooke is 168 cm tall.
2) ITX trains speed up to 180 km/h. Nuriro trains speed up to 150 km/h. KTX trains speed up to 305 km/h. Subway trains speed up to 90 km/h.
3) Leopards weigh up to 80 kg, cheetahs weigh up to 45 kg, tigers weigh up to 305 kg, and jaguars weigh up to 100 kg.
4) A whisper is as loud as 30 dBs, a firework 140 dBs, an alarm clock 80 dBs, and a jet plane 120 dBs.
5) *The House of the Scorpions* is 380 pages; *Wonder* is 310 pages; *Hoot* is 292 pages; *A Wrinkle in Time* is 256 pages.

14.4.5 Adjectives with Specific Endings

The functions and meanings of some *adjectives* can be identified based on their endings. In fact, we refer to the recurring ending patterns of words as "*suffixes*." We'll look at *suffixes* exclusively in a later chapter in the book. The following table summarizes some common *adjective suffixes* and their functions.

-ful	Means having a lot of something, e.g., painful = having a lot of pain / hopeful = having a lot of hope.			
	a **beautiful** dress		a **faithful** dog	
	a **useful** tool		**playful** puppies	
	awful	cheerful	doubtful	forceful

-less	e.g.	Means "without."			
		a **careless** driver		a **harmless** insect	
		homeless people		**useless** knowledge	
		doubtless	fearless	breathless	colorless
		endless	helpless	groundless	restless

Some adjectives have forms that end in both -less and -ful. The form that ends in -less has the opposite meaning of the form that ends in -ful.

e.g.	careful – careless	colorful – colorless
	harmful – harmless	useful – useless

-y	Usually added to the end of a noun i.e., "noun + y" to state that the target noun is characterized by or imbued with the meaning of the noun.	
	e.g.	a **dirty** street	a **muddy** path
		a **noisy** room	a **sleepy** passenger
		a **stormy** sea	an **oily** pot

-y	e.g.	a **dirty** street	a **muddy** path
		a **noisy** room	a **sleepy** passenger
		a **stormy** sea	an **oily** pot

-ive	Usually added to the end of a verb , i.e., "verb + ive" to describe situations characterized by the meaning of the verb.	
	e.g.	a **creative** toy	an **active** child
		an **attractive** hat	**talkative** pupils

-ing	Usually added to the end of a verb, i.e., verb + ing, and placed in front of a noun to indicate that the noun is in the process of performing the activity indicated by the verb.	
	e.g.	a **caring** nurse	a **cunning** fox
		a **smiling** face	an **interesting** book
		dazzling sunshine	**matching** clothes

-ly	Adjectives ending in -ly can have multiple functions. Some indicate certain intervals involving the target noun, while others are mostly related to emotion or personality.** ** Many adverbs also end in –ly	
	e.g.	a **costly** diamond ring	a **friendly** police officer
		lively kittens	an **elderly** woman
		a **daily** newspaper	a **weekly** magazine

-able	To describe a certain capability of the target noun or its usefulness.	
	e.g.	a **comfortable** chair	**reasonable** prices
		available facilities	a **valuable** experience

-al	Usually added to the end of a noun, i.e., noun + al, and placed in front of another noun to indicate that the target noun is related to or characterized by the root noun from which the adjective is formed.	
	e.g.	a **musical** instrument	a **national** costume

	To describe the state of the target noun or the material it is made of.		
-en	e.g.	a **broken** chair	a **wooden** table
		a **woolen** sweater	
-ible	To describe a certain characteristic or quality of the noun.		
	e.g.	a **horrible** smell	a **terrible** mess

	Another way to describe a characteristic of the target noun: use noun + ish.		
-ish	e.g.	a **foolish** act	**childish** behavior
-ous	Similar to -ful. These adjectives indicate that the target noun is imbued with a certain characteristic.		
	e.g.	a **dangerous** place	a **famous** pop singer
		a **poisonous** snake	

14.4.6 "Very" and "Too" In Front of Adjectives

We can place "**very**" or "**too**" in front of *adjectives* to signify that a certain quality attributed to them is excessive. The interesting difference between these two words in this scenario is that "<u>very</u>" means "<u>difficult but possible</u>" while "<u>too</u>" means "<u>impossible.</u>" Consider the following cases.

1.   **The box is <u>very heavy</u>, but Tom can lift it.**
     The box is <u>too heavy</u>; Bob can't lift it.

2.   **The coffee is <u>very hot</u>, but I can drink it.**
     The coffee is <u>too hot</u>; I can't drink it.

3.   **The weather is <u>very cold</u>, but we can still go to the beach, if you wish.**
     The weather is <u>too cold</u>; we can't go to the beach.

"**Very**" can also be used in more general situations in addition to these "difficult situations." Again, "**very**" is only associated with positive/possible situations. Consider the following sentences.

1.   **Wow, that concert was <u>very good</u>!**

2.   **Compared to a human, a mouse is <u>very small</u>.**

Complete the sentences using too or very.

1)   The tea is _____ hot, but I can drink it.
2)   The tea is _____ hot. I can't drink it.
3)   I can't sleep. It's _____ noisy in the dorm at night.
4)   You can't lift a car. A car is _____ heavy.
5)   An elephant is big. A mouse is _____ small.
6)   I lost your dictionary. I'm _____ sorry. I'll buy you a new one.
7)   I can't put my dictionary in my pocket. My dictionary _____ is big.
8)   Did you enjoy your dinner last night? / Yes. The food was _____ good!
9)   Can you read that sign across the street? / No, I can't. It's _____ far away
10) A sports car is _____ expensive, but Anita can buy one if she wants to.

14.5 Outlook on Adjectives

An *adjective* is like a double-edged sword. While it's an incredible tool that can upgrade your English writing substantially, *adjective* overuse can unnecessarily complicate your writing. Hence, it's important to always remember to use the least number of *adjectives* needed in order to effectively clarify a *noun*. This brings me to what I mentioned at the start of this chapter.

- **Try to limit yourself to <u>one *adjective* per clause</u>; one should be enough.**

This is especially true for *opinion adjectives*. It's true that, sometimes, "**the red cup**" is not enough; you might need to be more specific, like "**the little red plastic cup**." But, instead of saying "**the nice, kind, and intelligent young man**," it's enough to say "**the brilliant man**." Yeah, it's true that you sacrifice some precision, but you will still get your point across.

Writing the longest piece or the most descriptive one won't make you the best writer ever. In English, <u>the most effective writings are often the shortest ones</u>. Being able to convey a plethora of messages within a paragraph or two clearly indicates your skill as a writer. That's why your teachers consistently enforce word limits in your assignments—the shorter the better. Besides, you wouldn't want to read through an essay that's fifty pages long if twenty-five pages would do, would you? Your teachers probably don't want to either.

As such, to be honest, vocabulary is more important than grammar with regards to *adjectives*. And as I said, formally expanding your vocabulary isn't something that I can directly help you with here—learning and using new vocabulary is purely your job to do. I will tell you that it'd be foolish to simply memorize words and their definitions from a dictionary. <u>Many *adjectives* have sophisticated undertones that dictionaries cannot provide</u>. The only way to truly acquire new vocabulary is through reading. You need to read sentences that use *adjectives* effectively, and you can find such sentences in good books and newspaper articles. Books are great places to start, but newspapers provide something books do not—incredibly useful phrasal expressions. While the authors of books generally use uncommon single-word *adjectives* to describe situations, the authors of newspaper articles prefer multi-word phrases consisting mostly of very easy words. Reading an appropriate mix of both media types will substantially help you with your vocabulary.

A book that is shut is but a block.

- Thomas Fuller (1608-1661) -

CHAPTER 15

Adverbs

words or groups of words that describe or add to the meaning of a verb, an adjective, another adverb, or a whole sentence

15.1 Introduction

15.1.1 "How?" and "How Much?"

An *adjective* answers the question "**What?**"; an *adverb* answers the questions "**How**" and "**How much?**" For example, consider the following simple sentence.

- **Thomas is *fast*.**

Okay, so that sentence tells us that Thomas is fast (probably referring to his running skills), but exactly how fast is he? To answer that "**How much?**" question in our sentence, we need to include an *adverb*.

- **Thomas is <u>very</u> *fast*.**

- **Thomas is <u>fairly</u> *fast*.**

- **Thomas is <u>not particularly</u> *fast*.**

- **Thomas is <u>slightly</u> *fast*.**

In the above sentences, all the underlined words are *adverbs*. They all answer the question "**How fast is Thomas?**" To see this explicitly, consider the following conversation.

> A: Thomas is *fast*.
>
> B: <u>How fast</u> is he?
>
> A: Thomas is <u>very</u> *fast*.

Returning to the four sentences above, notice that every one of them feels different—in each one, Thomas is said to have a different speed. As you can see, <u>*adverbs* can modify the strengths of *adjectives*</u>.

But, that's not all they can do—<u>*adverbs* can also modify *verbs* and even other *adverbs* in similar ways</u>. Consider the following example.

- **Thomas *speaks* <u>very</u> <u>softly</u>.**

In this sentence, there are two *adverbs*, "**very**" and "**softly**." The *adverb* "**very**" modifies the other *adverb*, "**softly**," and, in turn, "**softly**" modifies the *verb* "*speaks*." Again, the *adverb* "**softly**" specifically indicates the strength of the *verb* "*speaks*."

- **How does Thomas *speak*?** → **He *speaks* softly.**

Next, the *adverb* "**very**" specifically indicates the strength of the *adverb* "**softly**."

- **How softly does Thomas *speak*?** → **He *speaks* very softly.**

In this way, *adverbs* can modify the strengths of *verbs*, *adjectives*, and other *adverbs*. However, that's not the only type of change an *adverb* can make to these types of words. *Adverbs* can also provide additional information about *manner*, *degree*, *time*, *frequency*, *place*, and *affirmation* for *verbs*, *adjectives*, and other *adverbs*. Some *adverbs* can also modify entire sentences. We'll cover all these types of *adverbs* in the following sections in this chapter.

15.1.2 Adverb Positioning

The most important grammatical aspect of *adverbs* is where to put them. In any sentence, an *adverb* can appear in up to four different positions. Consider the following.

1. **Patiently, he *waited* for his mother to arrive.**

2. **He patiently *waited* for his mother to arrive.**

3. **He *waited* patiently for his mother to arrive.**

4. **He *waited* for his mother to arrive, patiently.**

In all of four sentences, the *adverb* "**patiently**" modifies the *verb* "*waited*." As you can see, it can be placed in four different spots—at the start of the sentence, just before the *verb*, right after the *verb*, and at the end of the sentence. Interestingly, in this case, all four locations are available (i.e., grammatically correct), and the meaning of the sentence remains unchanged regardless of which position is selected. However, this is not true in most cases.

For a lot of *adverbs*, not all four slots are available, and the emphasis or meaning of the sentence changes depending on where you place the *adverb*. Hence, you should focus on the positioning of the *adverbs* you encounter as you proceed through this chapter. To be frank, as with *adjectives*, with *adverbs* vocabulary is more important than the grammar. If you are looking for ways to formally expand your vocabulary, revisit the advice I gave you at the end of the previous chapter. For now, as we question the grammatical aspects of *adverbs* in this chapter, you should pay attention to where they can be used and how their positions influence the meaning of the sentences we look at.

15.1.3 The Seven Types of Adverbs

Here's a summary of the <u>seven</u> types of *adverbs* that we'll cover in this chapter.

Adverbs of Manner	Adverbs of manner answer the question "How?" They describe the manner or way in which an action occurs. They usually modify verbs. *e.g.* He speaks **slowly**. They **gladly** helped us. James Bond drives his cars **dangerously**.
Adverbs of Degree	Adverbs of degree answer the question "How much?" They modify the strengths of adjectives and other adverbs. You can also use these for verbs. *e.g.* She **completely** agrees with him. Ashley is **incredibly** beautiful. He drove **quite** fast
Adverbs of Time	Adverbs of time answer the question "When?" They clarify the time of an event or prospective event. They usually modify verbs. *e.g.* He came here **yesterday**. I want it done **now**.
Adverbs of Place	Adverbs of place answer the question "Where?" They indicate the place an event happens. They usually modify verbs. *e.g.* Please sit **over there**. I've looked **everywhere** for you! Three cars were parked **in front**.
Adverbs of Frequency	Adverbs of frequency answer the question "How often?" They indicate how often an event occurs. They usually modify verbs. *e.g.* We get newspapers delivered **daily**. We **sometimes** watch a movie on the weekends.
Adverbs of Affirmation & Negation	Adverbs of affirmation & negation answer the question "How certain are you?" They tell us how sure someone is about an idea. They can modify either a verb, an adjective, or another adverb. *e.g.* I can **probably** be there. I **never** see him anymore.
Adverbs for Full Sentences	Adverbs for full sentences modify entire sentences. They are often placed at the start of sentences or after the subject *e.g.* The roads, **thankfully**, were free of snow and ice by noon. **Unfortunately**, I won't be able to make it to your birthday party.

15.2 Adverbs of Manner

15.2.1 Where to Use Adverbs of Manner

Adverbs of manner answer questions of "**How?**" They only modify *verbs*. Consider the following sentence.

- **Paul** *sings*.

Okay, so he sings, but how? *Adverbs of manner* can provide answers.

- **Paul** *sings* <u>loudly</u> **in the shower.**

- **Paul** *sings* <u>softly</u> **to his son in bed.**

- **Paul** *sings* <u>skillfully</u>**; that's why he won the singing competition.**

- **Paul** *sings* <u>terribly</u>**; nobody wants to hear him sing.**

As you can see, *adverbs of manner* describe the quality of an action.

15.2.2 How to Form Adverbs of Manner

Notice that all the underlined *adverbs of manner* above end with "**-ly**." As such, *adverbs of manner* are semi-consistent in form. However, note that <u>most *adverbs* do not have fixed forms and cannot be identified based on their spelling</u>.

That said, <u>only *adverbs of manner* are semi-consistently formed by adding "**-ly**" to the end of an *adjective*</u>. Consider the following examples.

- **Many adverbs of manner are made by adding –ly to adjectives**

Adjective	Adverb	Adjective	Adverb
beautiful	beautifully	heavy	heavily
brave	bravely	loud	loudly
bright	brightly	peaceful	peacefully
careless	carelessly	playful	playfully
cheap	cheaply	safe	safely
clear	clearly	selfish	selfishly
close	closely	skillful	skillfully
correct	correctly	slow	slowly
different	differently	smart	smartly
fierce	fiercely	sound	soundly
happy	happily	sweet	sweetly

However, this is not true for all **adverbs of manner**—some take the exact same form as the corresponding *adjective*.

- **Adverbs of manner that take the same forms as their respective adjective forms**

Adjective	Irregular Adverb	Adjective	Irregular Adverb
fast	fast	straight	straight
far	far	wrong	wrong/ wrongly
early	early	lively	lively
daily	daily		

How do you think we distinguish whether the modifiers above are **adjectives** or **adverbs**? Well, it depends on the kind of word being modified. Remember: **adjectives** can only modify **nouns**, whereas **adverbs** can modify **verbs**, **adjectives**, and other **adverbs**. Put another way, if a **noun** is being modified, then the modifier is an **adjective**; if any other word is being modified, then the modifier is an **adverb**. Consider the following situations.

hard	**adj.** solid, rigid, or difficult	This chocolate is **hard**. The test was **hard**.
	adv. done with a lot of effort	She studies **hard**.
hardly	**adv.** barely any often used with "any"	She **hardly** trains. I **hardly** have any free time.

late	**adj.** past an acceptable time	You're **late**.
	adv. past an acceptable time	You've arrived **late**.
lately	**adv.** in recent times	I've been waking up early **lately**.

Some even take a completely different form than the base **adjective**.

- **Good → well**

well	**adj.** in good status (often related to health)	My parents are **well**.
	adv. in a satisfactory manner	He does the job **well**.

15.2.3 Comparative and Superlative Adverbs of Manner

Another unique characteristic of **adverbs of manner**: they are the only type of **adverb** that can be used for comparisons. As with **adjectives**, we can add "**more**" or "**most**" before **adverbs of manner** to compare quality. Note that there's no way to alter the **adverb of manner** itself to signify comparison, unlike with **adjectives**. Consider the following situation.

1. **He smiled *warmly*.**

2. **He smiled <u>more</u> *warmly* than the others.**

3. **He smiled the <u>most</u> *warmly* of all.**

Notice how #2 uses "**more**" to compare the warmth of his smile to the warmth of the smiles of all the others, while #3 uses "**most**" to express that the warmth of his smile is the extreme case.

Just because *adverbs of manner* can be used in this way doesn't mean that it's common to do so. In fact, we rarely use *adverbs of manner* for direct comparisons. Instead, we turn the activity (i.e., *verb*) into a *noun* and then use a *comparative* or *superlative adjective*. (Remember that *adjectives* can only modify *nouns*.) In other words, we'd rather say something like the following instead of # 3 above.

- He *smiled* the <u>most warmly</u> of all. → His *smile* was the <u>warmest of all</u>.

Notice that we transformed the *verb* "*smiled*" into to the *noun* "*smile*" in the second sentence. In this way, we used the *superlative adjective* "<u>warmest</u>" instead, which is shorter than the other form, "**most warmly**." As mentioned in the previous chapter, <u>the shorter your writing is, the better</u>.

Interestingly, with this form of expression <u>you can use a *comparative adjective* directly with the *verb*</u>. Note that this is technically incorrect grammar, but it's generally allowed, especially in spoken English. Consider the following situation.

- My dog *moves* <u>more slowly</u> than my cat. → My dog *moves* <u>slower</u> than my cat.

Again, the second sentence is technically wrong, but it sounds more natural when spoken, and the other person won't feel like they're talking to a grammar book. However, what's even more common is to <u>skip the *verb*</u> entirely. We can do this, especially in spoken English, when the situation is clear enough. Let's reconsider our dog and cat sentence.

- My dog *moves* <u>more slowly</u> than my cat. → My dog is <u>slower</u> than my cat.

In this way, the second sentence is now both concise and grammatically sound.

15.2.4 Linking Verbs Take Adjectives, Not Adverbs

Only *action verbs* take *adverbs*; *linking verbs* take *adjectives* instead. This leads to a pretty common mistake among intermediate English writers. Consider the following situation.

- I *feel* <u>badly</u> about what happened. → *Wrong!*

- I *feel* <u>bad</u> about what happened. → *Correct!*

In the above two sentences, the *verb* "*feel*" is used as a *linking verb* meaning "to experience a particular emotion." Hence, you need to use the *adjective* "<u>bad</u>" to modify it, not the *adverb* "<u>badly</u>." Note that "*feel*" can also be used as an *action verb* meaning "to touch something with your hand in order to identify it." In other words, saying you "**feel badly**," could imply that you are having problems with your sense of touch. Be careful not to make this mistake in your writing.

Remember that some *verbs* can be *linking verbs* or *action verbs* depending on the context. One example we looked at was the *verb* "**look**." When we use "**look**" in the sense of "to observe a certain scene," it's an *action verb*, whereas if we use it in the sense of "resemble," it's a *linking verb*. Consider the following sentences.

1. He <u>looked</u> *tiredly* at his dirty room.

2. She <u>looks</u> *beautiful* today.

In #1, "**looked**" is an *action verb*—he's scanning his room with his eyes. Hence, an *adverb* ("*tiredly*") must follow the *verb*. However, in #2, "**looks**" is a *linking verb*—the sentence is describing someone's appearance. Hence, an *adjective* ("*beautiful*") must follow the *verb*. If you're unsure about this, revisit *Chapter 4*.

15.2.5 Positioning an Adverb of Manner with an Intransitive Verb

We have now arrived at the most important part of this section. As mentioned, the crucial thing about **adverb** grammar is placement. **Adverbs of manner** can take various positions in a sentence, and different positions emphasize different aspects of a sentence. The correct position depends on whether the **target verb** is **transitive** or **intransitive**. Recall that **transitive verbs** always require an **object**, while **intransitive verbs** do not.

When an **adverb of manner** modifies an **intransitive verb** that does not have an **object**, it can appear in any of the four available locations. This is the only case where an **adverb** can be placed in any of the four spots. The table below summarizes the locations and their functions. In each sentence example, the **adverb** was underlined, and the **emphasis** was **bolded**.

Positioning Adverbs of Manner with Intransitive Verbs		
Position	**Emphasis**	**Example**
Before the Verb	Adverb (i.e., "how")	He **patiently** waited for his mother to arrive.
After the Verb	Verb (i.e., "what")	He **waited** patiently for his mother to arrive.
Start of the Sentence	Spark reader's curiosity *(literary use)*	Patiently, he waited for his mother to arrive.
End of the Sentence	Verb (i.e., "what")	He **waited** for his mother to arrive, patiently.

Placing the **adverb of manner** before the **verb** focuses the reader on the **adverb** rather than the **verb**. In other words, the emphasis is on **"how"** the **subject** performed the activity, not on the activity they performed. On the other hand, putting the **adverb of manner** either after the **verb** or at the end of the sentence emphasizes the activity itself. Finally, you can spark your reader's curiosity by starting a sentence with an **adverb of manner**. However, note that this last position is mostly reserved for literary uses; in other words, you'd generally only use this structure if you were writing a book or a poem.

15.2.6 Positioning Adverbs of Manner with a Transitive Verb

Next, when an **adverb of manner** modifies a **transitive verb** that takes an **object**, the **adverb of manner** can only be placed in three of the four positions. When there's an **object** in the sentence, the **adverb of manner** cannot be placed after the **verb**. In other words, the **adverb of manner** cannot be placed between the **verb** and its **object**. The points of emphasis are the same as for **intransitive verbs** above, so I'll skip further explanation here. The table below summarizes the locations and their functions.

Positioning Adverb of Manner With Transitive Verbs		
Position	**Emphasis**	**Example**
Before the Verb	Adverb (i.e., "how")	He **greedily** ate the chocolate cake.
After the Verb	*GENERALLY IMPOSSIBLE!*	
Start of the Sentence	Spark reader's curiosity *(literary use)*	Greedily, he ate the chocolate cake.
End of the Sentence	Verb (i.e., "what")	He **ate** the chocolate cake greedily.

15.2.7 Positioning Adverbs of Manner when there are Two Verbs

An interesting situation arises when you have two *verbs* in the same sentence. In such cases, you can place the *adverb of manner* in two different positions. By placing the *adverb of manner* before the *first verb*, you modify the *first verb*. Conversely, by placing the *adverb of manner* at the end of the sentence, you modify the *second verb*. Consider the following situation.

1. The teacher <u>quietly</u> *asked* the children to finish their game.

2. The teacher asked the children to *finish* their game <u>quietly</u>.

In #1, the *adverb of manner* "<u>quietly</u>" modifies the *first verb*, "*asked*." In other words, #1 means that "the teacher's voice was not loud when she asked the children to finish their game." On the other hand, in #2, the same *adverb of manner* "<u>quietly</u>" modifies the *second verb*, "*finish*." In other words, in #2 "the teacher asked the children to lower their voices while playing their game and urged them to finish it soon." Can you see the difference?

The table below summarizes the possible locations and their functions.

Positioning an Adverb of Manner When There are Two Verbs		
Position	**Target**	**Example**
Before the First Verb	**First verb**	The teacher <u>quietly</u> **asked** the children to finish their game.
End of the Sentence	**Second verb**	The teacher asked the children to **finish** their game <u>quietly</u>.

15.2.8 More Adverbs of Manner

Here are some common *adverbs of manner* sorted by their functions. Note again that studying vocabulary is your job.

Function	Adverbs of Manner
Intention	accidentally, thoughtfully, wisely
Strength	hard, gently, tightly, weakly, wearily, tenderly, violently
Movement	gracefully, swiftly, sleepily, recklessly
Emotion	angrily, anxiously, awkwardly, cheerfully, frantically, generously, greedily, joyously, kindly, rudely, sadly, shyly, sharply, stupidly, truthfully
Speed	hastily, quickly, rapidly, suddenly
Opinions	frankly, honestly, inadequately, suspiciously

Adverbs of Manner Exercises 01

   ✓   **Add the adverb given in brackets into each sentence.**

1) James coughed to attract her attention. (loudly)
2) He plays the flute. (beautifully)
3) We dress on Fridays. (casually)
4) She finished her dinner. (quickly)
5) He opened the door. (quietly)
6) It rained through the entire night. (heavily)
7) You should close the lid. (tightly)
8) The nurse picked up the baby. (gently)
9) You performed in the concert yesterday. (fantastically)
10) She opened the present. (hurriedly)

Adverbs of Manner Exercises 02

   ✓   **Fix the errors in the following sentences. Some may not have any errors.**

1) I slept badly last night.
2) You speak fluently English.
3) He hard worked to get a promotion.
4) Try to do it carefully so we don't have to redo it.
5) Julie tearfully said goodbye to her boyfriend.
6) They ate happily the food.
7) The ball fast flew past them.
8) They missed unfortunately the train.
9) The cat skillfully caught the mouse.
10) The dog quickly ran after the ball.

Adverbs of Manner Exercises 03

   ✓   **Put <u>either</u> the adverb or the adjective in the blanks. Pay attention to the type of verb being used in the sentence.**

1) Peter _____ walked toward the door. (quick or quickly)
2) The wine tastes _____. (fine or finely)
3) Sarah felt _____ about shouting to her mother. (terrible or terribly)
4) The sommelier tasted the wine _____. (careful or carefully)
5) The food all went _____. (bad or badly)
6) She slammed the door _____. (angry or angrily)
7) He _____ woke the sleeping woman. (gentle or gently)
8) Though she was scared stiff, she remained _____. (calm or calmly)
9) I knew that giving a good impression would become _____ later. (important or importantly)

Adverbs of Manner Exercises 04

✓ **You're combining the two sentences into one. Choose between A or B where to put the adverb in bold.**

1) He told me that everyone in the house was asleep. So, he asked me to be quiet while leaving the house.
   → He asked me **A** to leave the house **B**. (**quietly**)

2) Upon arrival, she soon realized that she didn't like the party. So, she decided to leave as soon as possible.
   → She **A** decided to leave the party **B**. (**quickly**)

3) She had to leave the party, but she didn't want anyone to notice. So, she decided to act fast.
   → She **A** decided to leave the party **B**. (**quickly**)

4) The children were being so loud. So, the teacher asked them to be quiet and finish their game.
   → The teacher **A** asked the children to finish their game **B**. (**quietly**)

5) The children were taking too long finishing the game. So, the teacher gently asked them to finish it.
   → The teacher **A** asked the children to finish their game **B**. (**quietly**)

15.3 Adverbs of Degree

15.3.1 Where to Use Adverbs of Degree

Adverbs of degree usually modify *adjectives* and other *adverbs* (unlike *adverbs of manner*, which only modify *verbs*). As the name suggests, *adverbs of degree* work to answer the question of "**How much?**"; they clarify the strengths of *adjectives* and other *adverbs*. Consider the following situations.

1. **Adverb of Degree → *Adjective***

   ● **The woman is quite *pretty*.**

      ➢ *(quite [**adv.**] → pretty [**adj.**] → the woman [**noun**])*

   ● **We will be slightly *late* to the meeting.**

      ➢ *(slightly [**adv.**] → late [**adj.**] → we [**pronoun**])*

   ● **My cat was incredibly *happy* to see me.**

      ➢ *(incredibly [**adv.**] → happy [**adj.**] → my cat [**noun**])*

2. **Adverb of Degree → *Another Adverb***

   ● **The weather report is almost *always* accurate.**

      ➢ *(almost [**adv.**] → always [**adv.**] → accurate [**adj.**] → the weather report [**noun**])*

   ● **You talk too *softly* for me to understand you well.**

      ➢ *(too [**adv.**] → softly [**adv.**] → talk [**verb**])*

Remember that *adjectives* and *adverbs* both modify other words themselves as well; they cannot stand alone. Hence, whenever you use an *adverb of degree*, a sort of chain reaction occurs. To make this clear, I've highlighted the chain of modifications in the sentences above. Remember that *adjectives* only modify *nouns*, whereas *adverbs* can modify *verbs*, *adjectives*, and other *adverbs*.

15.3.2 How Many is Too Many?

As the examples above suggest, the chain reaction can easily make things too complicated. As always, there's a limit to how many **adverbs** we should use. If you use too many **adverbs** in a row, your sentence will sound weak and clunky, as in the following sentence.

- **Paul** *sings* <u>rather</u> <u>extremely</u> <u>too</u> <u>loudly</u>.

    ➢ *(rather [**adv.**] → extremely [**adv.**] → too [**adv.**] → loudly [**adv.**] → sings [**verb**])*

As you can see, there are <u>four</u> **adverbs** involved in the chain of modifications of the single **verb** "**sings**." This makes the entire sentence unnecessarily long.

So, how many is too many? In terms of **adverbs**, <u>anything more than two is usually too many</u>. Up to two **adverbs** per sentence is generally alright, but if you use any more than that, your sentence is likely to become too complex. <u>Though a max of one is recommended, there are some situations where you need two.</u> Also, when you must use two, at least try to use two different types rather than two from the same category. Let's fix the sentence above as an example.

- **Paul** *sings* <u>too</u> <u>loudly</u>.

    ➢ *(too [**adv.**] → loudly [**adv.**] → sings [**verb**])*

The two **adverbs** "<u>too</u>" and "<u>loudly</u>," are sufficient to convey how annoying Paul's singing is, without including the unnecessary **adverbs** "<u>rather</u>" and "<u>extremely</u>."

15.3.3 Gradable and Non-Gradable Adverbs of Degree

We looked at this briefly in the previous chapter with **adjectives**—we saw that **gradable adjectives** only agree with **gradable adverbs**, while **non-gradable adjectives** only agree with **non-gradable adverbs**. **Gradable adverbs** can be ordered based on their magnitudes, while **non-gradable adverbs** cannot be ordered. Rather, **non-gradable adverbs** usually mean either "entirely" or "almost entirely."

First, let's focus on **gradable adverbs**. As I said, <u>they can be used to adjust the strengths of **gradable**</u> **<u>adjectives</u>**. Consider the following examples.

1. **This book is <u>very</u> *interesting*.**
2. **This book is <u>fairly</u> *interesting*.**

In these sentences, the **gradable adjective** "*interesting*" is being modified by the **gradable adverbs** "<u>very</u>" and "<u>fairly</u>."

The following diagram presents <u>some common **gradable adverbs** and their strengths</u>.

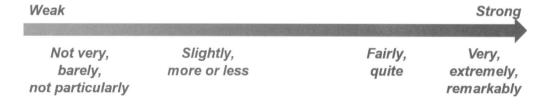

Weak			*Strong*
Not very, *barely,* *not particularly*	*Slightly,* *more or less*	*Fairly,* *quite*	*Very,* *extremely,* *remarkably*

Now, on to **non-gradable adverbs**. <u>They can be used to modify **non-gradable adjectives**</u>. Consider the following examples.

1. **Our trip was <u>totally</u> *awesome*.**
2. **Her presentation was <u>absolutely</u> *awful*.**
3. **This test is <u>practically</u> *impossible*.**

The words "**totally**," "**absolutely**," and "**practically**" are all *non-gradable adverbs*.

In the previous chapter, I said that *non-gradable adjectives* already have strong meanings, so they usually don't require further modification by an *adverb*—that idea still holds true here. There are two types of *non-gradable adverbs*: those that mean "entirely" and those that mean "almost entirely." Usually, placing an *adverb* that means "entirely" in front of a *non-gradable adjective* is redundant. Take a look at sentences #1 and #2 above. Even if you remove the *non-gradable adverbs* "**totally**" and "**absolutely**," each sentence would convey a similar degree of strength. In other words, the *non-gradable adjectives* "*awesome*" and "*awful*" are strong enough by themselves to convey ideas of the extremes.

On the other hand, the *non-gradable adverbs* that mean "almost entirely" are quite useful, as you can apply them in order to hedge the meanings of extreme *non-gradable adjectives*. In other words, you can soften *non-gradable adjectives* that are too intense. Take a look at sentence #3 above. If the sentence didn't include the *non-gradable adverb* "**practically**," the sentence would indicate that the test is 100% unsolvable. But, with "**practically**," the test sounds around 95% unsolvable. As I've mentioned, speeches and sentences that include absolute extremes (described by *non-gradable adjectives* or *superlatives*) are usually neither friendly nor convincing. Even when you want to convey a very strong idea, you should usually hedge at least a bit.

The following table provides some examples of the two types of *non-gradable adverbs*. Again, this list is not exhaustive, and you should study vocabulary on your own to learn other *non-gradable adverbs*.

Non-Gradable Adverbs	
Non-Gradable Adverbs That Mean "Entirely"	**Non-Gradable Adverbs That Mean "Almost Entirely"**
absolutely, utterly, completely, totally, entirely, fully, perfectly, exclusively	nearly, practically, virtually, essentially, mainly, almost, largely, primarily

Note that some *non-gradable adverbs* work in pairs with *non-gradable adjectives*. In many cases, certain *non-gradable adjective* can only agree with one *non-gradable adverb*.

15.3.4 Positioning Adverbs of Degree with Adjectives and Adverbs

Again, the most important thing about any type of *adverb* is where to place it. As mentioned, virtually all *adverbs of degree* modify either an *adjective* or an *adverb*. In both cases, practically the only available spot for an *adverb of degree* is directly before the *adjective*/*adverb*. The emphasis is almost always on the *adverb of degree* itself.

Positioning an Adverb of Degree With an Adjective or an Adverb		
Position	**Emphasis**	**Example**
Before the Target	**Adverb of degree**	I've had a **very** good day today.
After the Target	*GENERALLY IMPOSSIBLE!*	
Start of the Sentence	*GENERALLY IMPOSSIBLE!*	
End of the Sentence	*GENERALLY IMPOSSIBLE!*	

An exception to this rule is "**enough**." "**Enough**" always appears after the *adjective* or the *adverb*, as in the following example.

- **This room is *big* <u>enough</u> for eight people.**

15.3.5 Positioning Adverbs of Degree with Verbs

This has not been specifically mentioned previously in this section, but ***adverbs of degree*** can also modify ***verbs***. Consider the following sentences.

- I <u>quite</u> *enjoy* cycling.

- I <u>really</u> *don't like* cooking.

- She <u>absolutely</u> *hates* waking up early.

- I've <u>virtually</u> *finished* my work.

Even when an ***adverb of degree*** is modifying a ***verb***, it can only be placed directly before the ***target verb***.

Positioning an Adverb of Degree with a Verb		
Position	**Emphasis**	**Example**
Before the Target	Adverb of degree	I <u>quite</u> enjoy cycling.
After the Target	*GENERALLY IMPOSSIBLE!*	
Start of the Sentence	*GENERALLY IMPOSSIBLE!*	
End of the Sentence	*GENERALLY IMPOSSIBLE!*	

15.3.6 More Adverbs of Degree

Here are some common ***adverbs of degree*** sorted by their functions.

Function	Adverb of Degree
Gradable	very, extremely, really, remarkably, fairly, quite, slightly, more or less, just about, not very, barely, not particularly
Non-Gradable (Entirely)	absolutely, completely, utterly, perfectly, totally
Non-Gradable (Almost Entirely)	nearly, essentially, practically, mainly, pretty much, largely, almost, mostly, virtually
Both	really, fairly, pretty

Adverbs of Degree Exercises 01

✓ **Add the adverb given in brackets into each sentence.**

1) The water was cold. (extremely)
2) The movie is interesting. (quite)
3) She is running fast. (very)
4) You are walking slowly. (too)
5) You are running fast. (enough)
6) You seem exhausted. (absolutely)
7) I am starving. (totally)
8) This cake is wonderful. (absolutely)
9) The temperature was above freezing. (barely)
10) Our driveway is frozen. (completely)

Adverbs of Degree Exercises 02

✓ **Add the appropriate word in the blank between the two given in brackets. Think about whether the adjective/adverb is gradable or non-gradable.**

1) Let's stay in tonight; it's _____ freezing outside. (very or absolutely)
2) I was _____ devastated when I heard the news. (absolutely or very)
3) This work of art is _____ unique. (a bit or totally)
4) It's _____ important to have good friends. (totally or very)
5) Peter is _____ angry with Sarah today. (extremely or absolutely)
6) The documentary is extremely _____. (fascinating or interesting)
7) These photographs are very _____. (excellent or good).
8) David's new house is absolutely _____. (big or enormous).
9) I'm _____ starving. What's for dinner? (totally or very)

15.4 Adverbs of Time

15.4.1 The Four Types of Adverbs of Time

Adverbs of time offer more precise information about exactly when something happens. Hence, as you can imagine, you use *adverbs of time* mostly for *verbs*. There are four main types of *adverbs of time*.

1. Adverbs of Absolute Time,
   e.g., today, tomorrow, yesterday, last year ...

   A. Edmund *went* to Charlie's house yesterday.

   B. I'm going to *tidy up* my room tomorrow.

2. Adverbs of Relative Time—Right Now,
   e.g., now, just, about to ...

   A. I have to *leave* now.

   B. The plane is about to *land*.

3. Adverbs of Relative Time—Not Right Now,
   e.g., already, yet, later ...

   A. I'll *call* you later.

   B. I haven't *left* work yet.

4. Adverbs of Duration,
   e.g., still, all [period of time], for [period of time], since [absolute time]

   A. He*'s* still *watering* the flowers. He*'s been doing* that all day!

   B. She *lived* in France for a year.

Note that *adverbs of absolute time* can also be used as *nouns*. Consider the following cases.

1. Today is hot. → *noun*

2. I saw Sally today. → *adverb*

In the first sentence, "**today**" is used as a *noun*, while in the second sentence, it's used as an *adverb*.

15.4.2 Positioning Adverbs of Time

The position of an *adverb of time* depends largely on the *adverb* itself. That said, *adverbs of time* often appear at the ends of sentences. When used in this position, there's no particular emphasis; you're simply signaling the sense of time of the event in the sentence, as in the following examples.

- I *saw* that movie last year.

- Mary *went* to Chris's house yesterday.

Next, an *adverb of time* can be placed at the start of a sentence that emphasizes time; in this type of sentences, the time is more important than the action. Consider the following examples.

- Later on, Frank *ate* some porridge.

- Tomorrow, I*'m leaving* for Italy.

Less commonly, *adverbs of time* can be placed before the *verb*. They appear in this position in formal reports, like a police report. Consider the following.

- **Thomas <u>later</u> *visited* the grocery store.**

<u>Since this position is not generally used, we consider it unavailable</u>.

Finally, <u>you cannot place an **adverb of time**</u> after the **verb**; that position is always impossible.

Positioning Adverbs of Time		
Position	**Emphasis**	**Example**
Before the Target	*GENERALLY IMPOSSIBLE! (Only in formal reports)*	
After the Target	*GENERALLY IMPOSSIBLE!*	
Start of the Sentence	**Time (i.e., on the adverb)**	<u>Later</u>, Frank ate some porridge.
End of the Sentence	**No particular emphasis**	Mary went to Chris's house <u>yesterday</u>.

Nevertheless, as mentioned above, <u>many **adverbs of time** occupy unique positions in the sentence</u>, as in the following examples.

- **<u>Adverbs of Time with Set Positions</u>**

    1. **<u>About to</u>**
       → Must be placed <u>before the **verb**</u>.

       ◆ **Look, he's <u>about to</u> *jump*!**

    2. **<u>Just</u>**
       → Must be placed <u>before the **verb**</u>.

       ◆ **I've <u>just</u> *arrived* home.**

    3. **<u>Now</u>**
       → Usually placed at the <u>end of the sentence</u>. <u>Changes the meaning</u> of the sentence depending on its position.

       ◆ **We have to *go* <u>now</u>.**

       ◆ **We <u>now</u> have to *go*.**

    4. **<u>All [period of time]</u>**
       → Must be placed at the <u>end of the sentence</u>.

       ◆ **My cat's been *sleeping* <u>all day</u>.**

15.4.3 More Adverbs of Time

Here are some common *adverbs of time* sorted by their functions.

Function	Adverbs of Time
Points	tomorrow, tonight, yesterday, today, then, now
Relationships	already, before, early, earlier, eventually, finally, first, last, late, later, lately, formerly, previously, recently, now, just, next, yet, soon
Durations	still, all [period of time], for [period of time], since [absolute time]

Adverbs of Time Exercises

✓ **Add the adverb given in brackets into each sentence.**

1) Robin Hood swindled the Sheriff of Nottingham. (yesterday)
2) I'm sick of living in chaos, so I'm going to clean my house. (today)
3) She stayed at her grandmother's house. (all day)
4) My father was up with the heartburn. (for hours)
5) She was born. (in 1978)
6) They're tired because they've arrived home. (just)
7) There was a storm. (during the night)
8) They have lived here. (since 2004)
9) My mother lived in France. (for a year)
10) We should leave. (now)

15.5 Adverbs of Frequency

15.5.1 Where to Use Adverbs of Frequency

Adverbs of frequency show how often something happens. Again, these commonly modify **verbs**. Consider the following examples.

- I **regularly** *go* fishing.

- I **always** *watch* TV after I've finished my work.

The diagram below ranks **adverbs of frequency** by how regularly they occur.

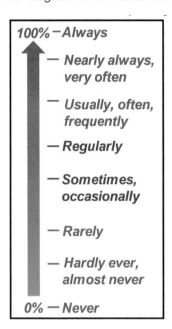

Here are a couple of interesting expressions involving frequency. Both "**every now and then**" and "**from time to time**" express the same magnitude of frequency as "**sometimes**" or "**occasionally**" (i.e., 50-60%). However, these should only be used at the start or the end of a sentence; they cannot be placed in the middle of a sentence. Consider these examples.

- She *drinks* wine <u>every now and then</u>.

- <u>From time to time</u>, I *visit* my mother.

Instead of using general expressions, you can also use precise expressions about the frequency of an activity. One type of precise expression is <u>to use the word "**every**" with a period of time</u> (i.e., "**every [period of time]**"), as in the following examples.

- I *go* fishing <u>every Tuesday</u>.

- I *visit* my parents <u>every week</u>.

- I *exercise* <u>every day</u>.

An alternative for the expression "**every [day of the week]**" is "**on [day of the week]+s**." Note carefully that you need to add an extra "**-s**" to the end of the day of the week. The expression "**on [day of the week]+s**" is <u>equal</u> to "**every [day of the week]**." Consider the following sentences.

- I take a yoga class <u>on Wednesdays</u>. = I take a yoga class <u>every Wednesday</u>.

- I relax <u>on Sundays</u>. = I relax <u>every Sunday</u>.

Another common type of precise expression involves using <u>a **number** followed by the word "**times**" followed by a period of time</u> (i.e., "**[number] times a [period of time]**"). This indicates that you repeat the activity a certain **[number]** of times during a single **[period of time]**. Consider the following sentences.

- I *cycle* to work <u>five times a week</u>.

- She needs to *take* these pills <u>three times a day</u>.

In addition to using specific numbers, you can also use <u>indefinite numeral adjectives</u> like "**several**" or "**a few**."

- I only *meet* him <u>a few times a year</u>.

- I *take* showers <u>several times a day</u> during the summer.

Note that instead of the expression "one time," we often use "**once,**" and instead of "two times," we often use "**twice.**" Though there are more expressions like this, such as "thrice," they are rarely used. Consider the following sentences.

- I *visit* my grandparents <u>once a month</u>.

- I *brush* my teeth <u>twice a day</u>.

<u>You can ask about frequency using the *question phrase* "**how often**.</u>" Consider the following cases.

- <u>**How often**</u> do you *visit* the dentist?

- <u>**How often**</u> do you *go* to the beach?

15.5.2 Positioning Adverbs of Frequency

<u>*Adverbs of frequency*</u> usually appear before the ***target verb***, as in the following sentences.

- I <u>often</u> *eat* vegetarian food.

- He <u>never</u> *drinks* milk.

However, remember that <u>they appear after ***auxiliary verbs*** and *'be'-verbs*</u>.

- You *must* <u>always</u> fasten your seat belt.

- I *am* <u>seldom</u> late.

Some ***adverbs of frequency*** can take one of two positions (stronger or weaker), and <u>their strengths change depending on which position is selected</u>. The following table includes some examples of these kinds of ***adverbs of frequency***. <u>When in the stronger position, the emphasis is on the frequency; when in the weaker position, the emphasis is on the action.</u>

Generally	Stronger Position	<u>**Generally**</u>, I don't like spicy foods.
	Weaker Position	I <u>generally</u> **don't like** spicy foods.
Occasionally	Stronger Position	I go to the opera **<u>occasionally</u>**.
	Weaker Position	I <u>occasionally</u> **go** to the opera.
Often	Stronger Position	**<u>Often</u>**, I jog in the morning.
	Weaker Position	I <u>often</u> **jog** in the morning.
Sometimes	Stronger Position	I get up early **<u>sometimes</u>**.
	Weaker Position	I <u>sometimes</u> **get up** early.

Lastly, <u>precise expressions usually appear at the end of the sentence</u>. However, note that precise expressions are technically not ***adverbs of frequency***. That said, consider the following sentences.

- **This magazine *is published* <u>monthly</u>.**

- I *work* <u>five days a week</u>.

Hence, we can summarize the positions of *adverbs of frequency* as follows.

Positioning Adverbs of Frequency		
Position	**Emphasis**	**Example**
Before the Target	**Frequency (i.e., adverb)** *(general position)*	I **often** eat vegetarian food.
After the Target	**Frequency (i.e., adverb)** *(if auxiliary or "be")*	You must **always** fasten your seatbelt.
Start of the Sentence	*GENERALLY IMPOSSIBLE!*	
End of the Sentence	*GENERALLY IMPOSSIBLE!*	

15.5.3 More Adverbs of Frequency

Here are some common *adverbs of frequency* sorted by their functions.

Function	Adverbs of Frequency
100%	always
90%	usually, almost always
80%	generally, normally
70%	often, frequently
50%	sometimes
30%	occasionally
15%	seldom
5%	rarely, almost never
0%	never

Adverbs of Frequency Exercises

✓ **Add the adverb given in brackets into each sentence.**

1) I remember to do my homework. (always)
2) He gets good marks in exams. (normally)
3) They are pleased to see me. (never)
4) She isn't bad tempered. (usually)
5) She can beat me in a race. (sometimes)
6) I would be unkind to someone. (hardly ever)
7) They might see each other again. (never)
8) They could be heard laughing. (occasionally)
9) I walk to work. (normally)
10) I put pepper on my food. (seldom)

15.6 Adverbs of Place

15.6.1 The Five Types of Adverbs of Place

Adverbs of place show where something happens. Hence, *adverbs of place* are also often associated with verbs. There are largely five *adverbs of place* types.

1. Prepositions
   You'll see in the next chapter that *prepositions* are words that describe locations. Some *prepositions* can be used as *adverbs* too,
   e.g., around, behind, down, about, in.

   A. The marble *rolled* around in my hand.

   B. Hurry! You are *getting* behind!

2. Prepositions + "here" or "there"
   "**Here**" is to say toward or with the speaker. "**There**" is to say away from or not with the speaker,
   e.g., up here/there, down here/there, in here/there, out of here/there.

   A. *Come* over here, and look what I found!

   B. What are you *doing* up there?

3. Words ending in "-where"
   These describe general ideas about location rather than specific locations,
   e.g., somewhere, nowhere, everywhere, anywhere, elsewhere.

   A. I'd like to *go* somewhere warm for my vacation.

   B. I *have* nowhere to go.

4. Words ending in "-wards"
   They signal directions of movement,
   e.g., backwards, forwards, upwards, downwards, eastwards, westwards.

   A. Cats don't usually *walk* backwards.

   B. The ship *sailed* westwards.

5. Adverbs for both movement & location,
   e.g., indoors, abroad, uphill, downhill, sideways, downstairs, upstairs.

   A. The child *went* indoors.

   B. He *lived* and *worked* abroad.

15.6.2 Positioning Adverbs of Place

Adverbs of place usually appear after the *verb* or at the end of the sentence. Consider the following examples.

- John *looked* around the house.

- I've *searched* everywhere for you!

- They *built* a house nearby.

- She *took* the child outside.

The table below summarizes the positions and the corresponding functions of *adverbs of place*.

Positioning Adverbs of Place		
Position	**Emphasis**	**Example**
Before the Target	*GENERALLY IMPOSSIBLE!*	
After the Target	Place (i.e., adverb)	I have **nowhere** to go.
Start of the Sentence	*GENERALLY IMPOSSIBLE!*	
End of the Sentence	Place (i.e., adverb)	She took the child **outside**.

15.6.3 More Adverbs of Place

Here are some common *adverbs of place* sorted by their functions.

Function	Adverbs of Place
Prepositions	about, down, in, near, on, over, under, above, behind, out, up, below, inside
"-where"	anywhere, everywhere, elsewhere, somewhere, nowhere
"-wards"	backwards, upwards, downwards, north/south/east/westwards
Movement & Location	abroad, downstairs, upstairs, indoors, downhill, uphill, sideways

---

Adverbs of Place Exercises

✓ **Add the adverb given in brackets into each sentence.**

1) You have to go for the men's bathroom. (upstairs)
2) I could find him. (nowhere)
3) She took the child. (outside)
4) I'm going to school in September. (back)
5) Maya looked to the sky. (upwards)
6) Don't go in. There's someone. (inside)
7) Oscar travelled to Los Angeles. (onward)
8) The parents searched for their child. (far and near)
9) The school is walking distance of my house. (within)
10) Tina dropped the ball, and it rolled the hill. (down)

15.7 Adverbs of Affirmation & Negation

15.7.1 Where to Use Adverbs of Affirmation & Negation

Adverbs of affirmation and negation show how certain an idea is, or if it's positive or negative. **Adverbs of affirmation** have positive tones and stand for truths while **adverbs of negation** have negative tones or stand for things that are absent or stated in the negative. These *adverbs* can modify all the three target types—**verbs**, **adjectives**, and other **adverbs**. Consider the following examples.

1. *Adverbs of affirmation*

    A. I can <u>probably</u> *go* there.

    B. He will <u>surely</u> *give* you money.

2. *Adverbs of negation*

    A. I have <u>never</u> *seen* him.

    B. He is <u>not very</u> *active*.

15.7.2 Positioning Adverbs of Affirmation & Negation

Adverbs of affirmation and negation are usually placed before the *main verb*.

- He <u>surely</u> *won't forget* your birthday.

- She <u>definitely</u> *left* the school before 11 o'clock.

However, when there's an *auxiliary verb* or a *'be'-verb*, the *adverb* goes after the *verb*.

- Raj *is* <u>certainty</u> a smart man.

- He *has* <u>definitely</u> forgotten her birthday.

You can also use these at the start of sentences.

- <u>Certainly</u>, I *will be* there.

- <u>Probably</u>, she *has forgotten* the meeting.

The table below summarizes the positions and the corresponding functions of *adverbs of affirmation* and *negation*.

Positions of Adverbs of Affirmation and Negation		
Position	**Emphasis**	**Example**
Before the Target	Opinion (i.e., adverb) *(general position)*	He <u>surely</u> won't forget your birthday.
After the Target	Opinion (i.e., adverb) *(if auxiliary or "be")*	He has <u>certainly</u> forgotten her birthday.
Start of the Sentence	Opinion (i.e., adverb)	<u>Certainly</u>, I will be there.
End of the Sentence	*GENERALLY IMPOSSIBLE!*	

An interesting thing about <u>using "**surely**" at the start of a sentence</u> is that <u>it actually suggests that you're not so sure</u>. It suggests that while you think something might be true, <u>you are looking for confirmation</u>. Consider the following examples.

- <u>**Surely**</u>**, you have a mobile phone.**

- <u>**Surely**</u>**, you're not going to bring your child to the office.**

15.7.3 More Adverbs of Affirmation & Negation

Here are some common *adverbs of affirmation* and *negation* sorted by their functions.

Function	Adverbs of Affirmation & Negation
Positive	surely, clearly, definitely, doubtlessly, exactly, truly, really, obviously, certainly, by all means, verily, indeed, undoubtedly
Mostly Positive	probably, possibly, likely, apparently
Mostly Negative	scarcely, rarely, not very, almost, hardly ever
Negative	never, no longer, contradictorily, invalidly, any

<u>**Adverbs of Affirmation & Negation Exercises**</u>

✓ **Add the adverb given in brackets into each sentence.**

1) I would feel awesome about your comment. (obviously)
2) The family embraces the Western culture. (truly)
3) The soldier should get an award for bravery. (certainly)
4) Ryan knows the right thing to do. (exactly)
5) They are leaving tomorrow. (definitely)
6) Mark agrees on his side. (doubtlessly)
7) He is active. (not very)
8) Simon visits his mom on weekends. (rarely)
9) I talk to him this way. (never)
10) Narendra Modi is a great politician. (undoubtedly)

15.8 Adverbs for Full Sentences

<u>*Adverbs for full sentences*</u> <u>usually appear at the start of sentences</u> and <u>modify the entire sentence</u>. Consider the following examples.

- <u>**Thankfully**</u>**, the lower roads were free of snow and ice on our drive over.**

- <u>**Unfortunately**</u>**, that was only the first of the bad things that happened.**

Here are some common **adverbs for full sentences**.

actually	curiously	interestingly	strangely
apparently	evidently	ironically	surprisingly
basically	fortunately	naturally	theoretically
certainly	hopefully	predictably	truthfully
clearly	ideally	presumably	ultimately
conceivably	incidentally	regrettably	unfortunately
confidentially	indeed	seriously	wisely

15.9 Outlook on Adverbs

15.9.1 Positioning All Types of Adverbs

The table below summarizes where you can position the different types of **adverbs**.

Adverb Positions Review

Y = Common/Correct
N = Rare/Wrong

Adverb Type	Before the Target	After the Target	At the Start	At the End	Exceptions
Adverbs of Manner	Y (in literature)	Y (most common N for objects)	Y (in literature)	Y	Well, badly hard, fast
Adverbs of Degree	Y	N (Y if target = verb; N for objects)	N (Y if target = verb)	N (Y if target = verb)	Enough
Adverbs of Time	N (Y for formal docs)	N	Y (emphasis = time)	Y	About to, just, now
Adverbs of Frequency	Y (N for aux. & be)	N (Y for aux. & be)	N (few Y & stronger)	N (few Y & stronger)	
Adverbs of Place	N	Y	N	Y	
Adverbs of Affirm./Neg.	Y (N for aux. & be)	N (Y for aux. & be)	Y	N	Surely
Adverbs for Full Sentences	N	N	Y	N	

15.9.2 Max of Two per Sentence

Ernest Hemingway once said, "**Adverbs** are useless!" Well, maybe not in those exact words, but he did despise **adverbs** and discouraged fellow authors from using them. I can tell you with confidence that Hemingway was <u>wrong</u>. The **adverb** is an essential part of the English language, and it's impossible to form fascinating sentences without **adverbs**. However, as you surely know by now, <u>you shouldn't use too many</u>; the use of unnecessary **adverbs** should always be avoided.

When using English, you will sometimes feel that your sentence is not strong enough. In such situations, <u>try using a stronger **verb** or an **adjective** before you resort to using an **adverb**</u>. Within the **verb** and **adjective** categories, you'll find many words with similar meanings but that infer different levels of emphasis. For example, when you're trying to say something is <u>good</u>, any of the following **adjectives** can be used.

1. <u>**Somewhat good**</u>: above average, satisfactory, adequate, decent, fair, sufficient, acceptable …

2. <u>**Very good**</u>: excellent, exceptional, great, incredible, marvelous, superb, superior, fantastic …

As you can see, <u>there's probably a stronger **verb** or an **adjective** you can use instead of adding an extra **adverb**</u>. In fact, in some cases, replacing the **verbs** or the **adjectives** may lead to more powerful statements than adding **adverbs**. As I always say—the fewer words you use, the more powerful your writing will be. Again, that's why you need a good vocabulary.

To learn to read is to light a fire;
every syllable that is spelled out is a spark.

- Victor Hugo (1802-1885) -

Prepositions

words used before nouns, pronouns, and gerunds to show a connection to another word

16.1 Introduction

16.1.1 Go Get My Wallet!

Hey, it seems your mom's doing some shopping online. You're in the living room, just chilling on the couch, while your mom is at the dinner table, immersed in her laptop screen. Then, suddenly, she calls out your name and tells you to fetch her wallet from upstairs. Grudgingly, you get up from the couch and ask her the following question: "**Where did you leave it?**" She answers: "**The bedroom dresser!**"

You go upstairs, into the bedroom. Thankfully there's only one dresser, so you don't have to guess which one. But then you realize you still have no idea where the wallet actually is. This, however, is not your fault—your mom should have provided more information about the wallet's location in relation to the dresser. What do I mean by that? Well, consider the following sentences.

1. "**On top of** the bedroom dresser."

2. "**In** the top drawer **of** the bedroom dresser."

3. "**Beside** the bedroom dresser."

4. "**In front of** the bedroom dresser."

It would've been very helpful if your mom had answered you with one of the above instead of just "**The bedroom drawer!**" In #1-#4, the each of the underlined expressions provides a clearer idea of where you might find your mother's wallet. Without those words, you would have to search everywhere—in each drawer and all around the dresser—in order to find the wallet. Imagine if it was actually **under** the dresser because she had dropped it—you could be looking for that wallet for hours!

16.1.2 Where? And When?

The underlined words in #1-#4 in the above section are called **prepositions**. By definition, **prepositions** are words that show relationships such as time, place, ownership, reason, mode of operation, between different parts of a clause. However, **prepositions of place** and **prepositions of time** are the two most common **preposition** types. That is, **prepositions** are most often used to point out a particular location or an instance in time.

In a sentence, the **preposition** usually appears near the end, and it always precedes a **noun**. With **prepositions of place**, this **noun** represents a certain location, whereas with **preposition of time**, this **noun** represents a certain time. Consider the following examples.

1. **They will meet in the cafeteria.**

2. **There's a hospital next to my house.**

3. **My math test is on Tuesday.**

4. **The show starts at 7 o'clock.**

Sentences #1 and #2 each contain a **preposition of place** and a **location noun**. In contrast, #3 and #4 each contain a **preposition of time** and a **time noun**.

Interestingly, there's a lot of freedom in terms of what can be placed before a **preposition**—it can be a **noun** (i.e., an **object**), a **verb**, or an **adjective**. Relatedly, the chunk of words that appear before a **preposition** can be either a complete stand-alone sentence or a fragment. But, whatever's placed prior to a **preposition** must be closely related to either the location or the time stated after the **preposition**.

By the way, you can also use **prepositions** at the start of sentences, but this is less common and mostly reserved for **prepositions of time**. The following are some cases wherein a **preposition** appears at the start of the sentence.

1. **Before 1950, only the rich had TVs in their homes.**

2. **By 11 o'clock, I had only read five pages.**

As a side-note, if you already have some knowledge of **prefixes**, maybe you noticed that the word **preposition** is formed by adding the **prefix** "**pre-**" to the word "**position**." In other words, a **preposition** is a word that appears before (i.e., "**pre-**") a "**position**."

16.1.3 Prepositions are Very Specific

Way back at the start of the book, when I was introducing the nine **parts of speech**, I said that the most common grammatical mistakes occur with **prepositions**, **conjunctions**, and **determiners**. The reason people make a lot of mistakes with **prepositions** is because they have very specific uses.

As you'll see throughout this chapter, there are numerous **prepositions** in English. In turn, any particular **preposition** has very limited use. In other words, a certain **preposition** usually has just a few functions, or even just one. This also means the converse, i.e., that in any given situation, only a single **preposition** usually fits. Hence, you should familiarize yourself with the functions of each **preposition** in English (or at least the common ones).

But, "familiarize" does not mean "memorize"; unlike some other **parts of speech** we've looked at, **prepositions** are fairly intuitive. They usually consist of easy words that you are already familiar with, and the meanings of these easy words are big hints as to where a given **preposition** should be used.

For example, you probably know the **preposition** "**in**." How do you define "**in**"? It's a word used to describe something that's inside a certain space, right? As per its definition, "**in**" is used mostly with **subjects** contained in large areas or three-dimensional spaces. More specifically, the following are some situations wherein you'd use "**in**."

1. **They will meet in the cafeteria.**

2. **They live in South Korea.**

3. **I'm in a taxi right now.**

4.   **Look up the word <u>in</u> the dictionary.**

5.   **You can see how I looked nine years ago <u>in</u> this picture.**

Most of these uses make sense, don't they? Either physically or metaphorically, what comes before "**in**" is contained within the space designated by the *location noun* that appears after it in each sentence. It gets a bit more confusing with *prepositions of time*, but that situation is not too difficult either.

The point is, don't pressure yourself to memorize every single use of each *preposition* shown in this chapter. Try to understand their uses and link them to the fundamental meanings of the *prepositions* themselves. Even without memorizing each use, you'll be virtually mistake-free in no time.

16.1.4 There are Just Too Many!

With so many *prepositions*, it feels inefficient to explain each one in detail. Hence, <u>I'll only focus on the three major ones: "**in**," "**at**," and "**on**."</u> These three *prepositions* are the most diversely used; for each, the definition does not do all the available functions justice. In other words, <u>it's difficult to figure out the full range of uses based on their definitions only</u>. Hence, detailed descriptions will be provided for this trio. Regarding the other *prepositions*, I'll only provide simple summaries of the uses in tables without further explanation. Most *prepositions* other than "**in**," "**at**," and "**on**" have limited uses that are strongly hinted by their definitions.

16.2   Prepositions of Place

16.2.1 "In"

As mentioned briefly above, <u>"**in**," when used as a *preposition of place*, precedes words denoting large areas or three-dimensional spaces</u>. <u>"**In**" is used to indicate that something is contained within a given space</u>. More specifically, we use "**in**" to indicate that something is contained in locations such as the following.

1	**rooms, buildings, cities, towns, & countries**	<u>in</u> the cafeteria, <u>in</u> the kitchen, <u>in</u> London
2	**books & other publications**	<u>in</u> the book, <u>in</u> the dictionary, <u>in</u> the newspaper
3	**vehicles**	<u>in</u> the car, <u>in</u> the taxi
4	**"picture/photograph" & "the world"**	<u>in</u> the picture, <u>in</u> the world

Reconsider the sentences we saw in *Section 16.1.3*.

- **They will meet <u>in</u> *the cafeteria*.**

- **They live <u>in</u> *South Korea*.**

- **I'm <u>in</u> *a taxi* right now.**

- **Look up the word <u>in</u> *the dictionary*.**

- **You can see how I looked nine years ago <u>in</u> *this picture*.**

Once again, pay attention to the *location noun* that follows "**in**" in each sentence.

16.2.2 "At"

"**At**," used as a **_preposition of place_**, precedes a word that pinpoints an exact location. Compared to "**in**," which indicates that some object is contained anywhere inside a certain large space, "**at**" indicates that some object is located at an exact place. In other words, "**at**" is more precise than "**in**"; it provides more accurate information about where something is. But, like "**in**," this is not the only situation wherein we use "**at**." The following **_location nouns_** all accept "**at**."

1	exact locations	<u>at</u> the door, <u>at</u> the station
2	events	<u>at</u> the concert, <u>at</u> the party
3	"table"	<u>at</u> the table
4	places where something typical is done	<u>at</u> the cinema, <u>at</u> school, <u>at</u> work

Perhaps #3 and #4 are a little interesting. We use "**at**" in front of the word "**table**" to indicate that a person is sitting in a chair in front of a table. To be exact, we'd have to say "**sitting in a chair in front of a certain spot at the table**," but no one ever really says that; "**at the table**" or "**sitting at the table**" are used almost exclusively to describe that situation. As for #4, when the place in question has a clear purpose, we usually use "**at**." For example, a "**cinema**" is a place specifically for watching movies, a "**school**" is a place for studying, and "**work**" implies the place you go to do your job. In most situations, the primary activity you're performing at these locations need not be explained; hence, "**at**" can be used.

Consider the following sentences.

- Hey, we have a guest <u>at</u> *the front door*.

- I'll meet you at 12 o'clock <u>at</u> *Town Hall station*.

- Sally is <u>at</u> *a concert* right now.

- Don't use your phone <u>at</u> *the dinner table*.

- I'm currently <u>at</u> *work*; I can't pick up the package, sorry.

16.2.3 "On"

"**On**," used as a **_preposition of place_**, indicates that something is located above a certain surface, is directly touching a surface, or is attached to a surface. An important thing about "**on**" is that the object in focus must be touching a surface, either by being located above it or by being attached to it. Like the other two above, "**on**" has many other uses as well.

1	attached	<u>on</u> the wall, <u>on</u> the fridge
2	places near rivers or other bodies of water	<u>on</u> the Thames; <u>on</u> the waterfront; <u>on</u> the ocean
3	above a surface	<u>on</u> the table, <u>on</u> the couch, <u>on</u> the beach
4	sides (left or right)	<u>on</u> your left, <u>on</u> your right
5	floors (stories)	<u>on</u> the first floor, <u>on</u> floor 15
6	public transport	<u>on</u> the bus, <u>on</u> the train
7	"TV" and "radio"	<u>on</u> TV, <u>on</u> television, <u>on</u> the radio

Again, to pick out some interesting ones, maybe you haven't really thought about #4, #6, and #7. They are all common expressions that we use with "**on**." When you want to indicate that something is on one of your sides, you use "**on**," as in "**on your left**" or "**on your right**." Also, we use "**on**" for the use of public transport, as in "**on the bus**" and "**on the train**." Finally, we use "**on**" with the words "**TV**" and "**radio**." To talk about programming for these two types of media, we only use the *preposition* "**on**."

Consider the following sentences.

- **There's a nice picture <u>on</u> *this wall*.**

- **London is <u>on</u> *the Thames*.**

- **You left your car keys <u>on</u> *the table*.**

- **Your destination is <u>on</u> *your left*.**

- **The men's bathrooms are <u>on</u> *the first* and *third floors* only.**

- **I'm <u>on</u> *the bus* right now; I can't speak loudly.**

- **I heard that song <u>on</u> *the radio* yesterday.**

Some books should be tasted, some devoured,
but only a few should be chewed and digested thoroughly.

- Francis Bacon (1561-1626) -

16.2.4 The Big Tables of Prepositions of Place

Here's a table that summarizes the uses of "**in**," "**on**," and "**at**" as *prepositions of place*.

- **"In," "On," and "At" as Prepositions of Place**

in	If something is **contained inside a given space**, we use "in":				
	e.g.	in a house	in a cup	in my stomach	in a bottle
		in bed	in a book	in the classroom	in the sea
		in a river	in class	in the hospital	in the kitchen
		in a drawer	in a field	in the newspaper	in the bedroom
	For **vehicles** that we **usually sit inside of**, we use "in":				
	e.g.	in a car	in a helicopter	in a truck	in a rowboat
on	If something is **on top of a surface**, we use "on"				
	e.g.	on the table	on the wall	on the floor	on the **window**
		on my face	on a plate	on the page	on the sofa
		on a chair	on the river	on a t-shirt	on the ceiling
	For **vehicles** you **can stand or walk inside of** or that you **sit on top of**, we use "on":				
	e.g.	on a plane	on a bus / on a train	on a bicycle	on a ship
at	If something is **at a specific location,** we use "at":				
	e.g.	at the airport	at the door	at the table	at the bus stop
		at the theater	at the top	at the bottom	at the pub
		at the front	at the back	at the window	at the hospital
		at the piano	at the park	at the bank	at the library
		at the bookstore	at the post office	at the football stadium	
		at the traffic lights	at the restaurant	at university	
	"At" is also used **with home, work, and school**. Since these are generic rather than specific places, we don't need to place "the" in front of them.				
	e.g.	at home	at work	at school	

We use all the three *prepositions* when we describe where somebody lives. Note which information is linked with which *preposition*.

- **"In," "On," and "At" to Describe Where Somebody Lives**

in a country or city	Jenny lives **in** the United States. / She lives **in** New York City.
on a street, avenue, road	She lives **on** Hill Street.
at a street address	She lives **at** 987 Hill Street.

Here are some other common *prepositions of place*. Pay particular attention to the positions of the *prepositions* as you go through the table; notice that they always appear near the end of the sentences.

- **Other Common Prepositions of Place**

above	something **at a higher position than something else**
	e.g. The helicopter hovered **above** the house. Birds wheeled **above** us in the sky. There's a nice path **above** the lake.
behind	something located **at the back of something**
	e.g. He put his hands **behind** his back. The man is **behind** the bus. Jack is hiding **behind** the tree
below	something **at a lower position than something else**
	e.g. A small stream runs **below** that bridge. The fish are **below** the surface. Basements are dug **below** the ground.
between	something located **in the middle of two other things**
	e.g. There are many differences **between** them. It weighed **between** nine and ten kilos. The dog usually sits **between** Ed and Ben.
far from	something located **a long distance from something else**
	e.g. The restaurant is **far from** here. The hotel (where I stayed) was not **far from** the airport
in front of	something **at the face or the front of something else**
	e.g. I can't see because of the person **in front of** me. He sat nodding **in front of** the fire. The basket is **in front of** the cat.
near **and** **close to**	something **within a short distance of something else**. Usually, "near" and "close to" indicate further distances than "next to"
	e.g. The school is **near** the park. Our house is **near** the supermarket. Jack is **near** the tree. Keep **close to** my side. Our new house is **close to** the school.
next to **and** **beside**	something located **right beside something else**
	e.g. There was a little girl sitting **next to** him. There is a calendar **next to** the refrigerator. There's a hospital **next to** my house. I'm standing **beside** my father in this picture
under	something **below or covered by something else**
	e.g. She was hiding **under** the table. The box is **under** the grammar book. My cat is hiding **under** the blanket.

We also use **prepositions** to discuss <u>the movement and direction of objects</u>. These **prepositions** often appear after **verbs** of motion in a sentence. Here are some commonly used **prepositions of movement**. Recall that we've already covered these in *Section 15.6 Adverbs of Place*.

- **Prepositions of Movement**

across	expresses movement **from one side of something to the other**
	(e.g.) You must walk **across** the street at the crosswalk. She wheeled her bicycle **across** the road. The post office is **across** the street from the grocery store. Be careful when you walk **across**.
along	expresses movement **following a line**
	(e.g.) He's walking **along** the path. The jeep bumped **along** on the dirt track.
around	expresses movement **along the boundaries of a certain space**
	(e.g.) You must drive **around** the city center to reach the cinema. There is a fence **around** the house.
away	expresses movement **in the opposite direction of a specific space or object**
	(e.g.) She turned **away** and stared out of the window. He jerked the phone **away** from her.
down	expresses movement **from a higher position to a lower position**
	(e.g.) It came **down** the stairs. It's kind of creepy **down** in the cellar!
into	expresses movement **from the outside to the inside** of space
	(e.g.) We went **into** the shop on the corner. Jane is jumping **into** the pool. Can you go **into** the kitchen and grab me a cup of water?
off	expresses movement **away from something**
	(e.g.) We get **off** the train at the next stop. The books fell **off** the shelf.
onto	expresses movement that results **in an object ending up on top of a target**, or **stuck to the surface of a target**
	(e.g.) The cat jumped **onto** the roof. She glued the label **onto** the box. My cat jumped **onto** my bed as I was getting ready to sleep.
out of	expresses movement **from the inside to the outside** of a space
	(e.g.) He swung himself **out of** the car. She crept silently **out of** the room.
over	expresses movement **above the height of a certain object**
	(e.g.) The cat jumped **over** the wall. The horse jumped **over** the hurdle.

past	expresses movement that **goes beyond a certain space or object**	
	e.g.	Walk **past** the theater on the right, and the bank is on the left. The roses are **past** their prime now.
through	expresses movement **from one side to the other** of something that has a different entrance & exit, like a tunnel	
	e.g.	The car went **through** the tunnel. This train goes straight **through** to Busan. Go slow when you're driving **through** the border crossing.
toward	expresses movement **in the direction of a specific space or object**	
	e.g.	He was standing with his back **toward** me. She walked **toward** the door in the dark. Turn left **toward** the subway station.
up	expresses movement **from a lower position to a higher position**	
	e.g.	It went **up** the stairs. The dog ran **up**, wagging its tail.

Prepositions of Place Exercises 01

✓ **Put appropriate prepositions in the blanks.**

1) I'm currently _____ a cab right now; I'll be with you in a couple of minutes.
2) Have you seen my car keys? I swear I left them _____ the table yesterday.
3) Right _____ my house, there's a nice park. I go there for strolls every day.
4) It's so hot; I need some air conditioning. Let's go _____ that building.
5) I've just arrived _____ the train station. Where are you?
6) Walk 300 meters down this way; the building you're looking for should be _____ your right.
7) Sally's _____ the hospital right now. I'll have her call you back when she returns home.
8) Here's a present I brought for you all the way _____ my hometown.
9) I'm travelling _____ Switzerland next week for a family trip.
10) Whoa! A seagull just flew _____ my head!

Prepositions of Place Exercises 02

✓ **Put appropriate prepositions in the blanks (cont'd).**

1) No, there isn't a monster _____ your bed. There's not enough space for one in the first place.
2) Be careful when you jump _____ that gap. Your foot might get stuck in there.
3) What's that loud sound? / There's a plane flying right _____ our house right now.
4) A butterfly just landed _____ the dog's nose! Look how still he's being not to disturb it!
5) Come sit _____ me. I purposefully left this seat empty for you.
6) Oh, it's raining! Quickly, let's go _____ that awning.
7) There's a convenience store _____ my house and my school. I always visit it after school.
8) I know you're hiding _____ that tree; I can see your hair sticking out!
9) The police arrested the person who parked _____ the fire station, blocking the garage.
10) There's no department store _____ my home! I have to take the bus every time I need food.

16.3 Prepositions of Time

16.3.1 "In"

"**In**," when used as a *preposition of time*, is placed before months, seasons, times of day, and years.

- **My birthday is** <u>in</u> *July*.

- **Everybody gets a two-week leave** <u>in</u> *the summer*.

- **I usually take showers** <u>in</u> *the morning*.

- **I was born** <u>in</u> *1998*.

Also, <u>we use "**in**" to say that an event will occur after a certain period of time</u>. We most often use this expression to discuss the arrival of someone or something, including a mode of public transport.

- **I'll be there** <u>in</u> *half an hour*.

- **The bus will arrive** <u>in</u> *five minutes*.

16.3.2 "At"

"**At**," used as a *preposition of time*, is placed in front of certain points of time. As we saw with *prepositions of place*, "**at**" indicates preciseness; an exact point in time must follow "**at**." Consider the following sentences.

- **The show's starting** <u>at</u> *7 o'clock*.

- **My classes end** <u>at</u> *5:30 PM*.

We also use "**at**" in front of the word "**night**." While <u>we mostly use "**in**" in front of the times of days</u> (e.g., **in** the morning), only "**at**" can be used directly with "**night**."

- **I usually watch movies** <u>at</u> *night*.

- **I sometimes eat snacks** <u>at</u> *night*.

16.3.3 "On"

"**On**," used as a *preposition of time*, is placed in front of days of the week and <u>the word "**weekend**"</u>; in other words, "**on**" is related to time expressions involving the week. Consider the following sentences.

- **My math test is** <u>on</u> *Tuesday*.

- **I play football** <u>on</u> *the weekend*.

16.3.4 The Big Tables of Prepositions of Time

Here's a table that contains many of the **prepositions of time**, their uses, and corresponding example sentences. Though they mostly appear near the ends of sentences, **prepositions of time** can also appear at the very beginnings of sentences. You'll see some examples of this in the table below. Also, <u>the uses of "in," "at," and "on" are quite counterintuitive</u>, as you can see. That is, <u>it's difficult to predict their uses solely based on their respective definitions</u>. Hence, here, it will be helpful for you to memorize the uses of "**in**," "**at**," and "**on**."

- ## "In," "On," and "At" as Prepositions of Time

at	**at + a specific time on the clock**	We have class **at** 9 o'clock. I have an appointment with the dentist **at** 11 A.M. Breakfast is served **at** seven o'clock.
	at + night	I sleep **at** night. We go to bed **at** night.
in	**in + a specific month**	My birthday is **in** July. Autumn begins **in** September.
	in + a specific year	I was born **in** 2001. They were married **in** 1990.
	in + the morning	We go to class **in** the morning. We get up **in** the morning.
	in + the afternoon	My father takes a nap **in** the afternoon. The movie starts at two **in** the afternoon.
	in + the evening	I often watch TV **in** the evening.
	in + seasons	It's always hot **in** the summer.
	in + centuries	**in** the 19th century
	In + decades	**in** the sixties, **in** the 1790s
on	**on + a specific day of the week**	The post office isn't open **on** Sundays. Many shops close early **on** Saturdays. I have class **on** Thursday.
	on + a specific date or day	I was born **on** August 25, 2001. **on** the 20th of June, **on** my birthday, **on** Christmas, **on** Easter

- **Other Common Prepositions of Time**

from x to y	**From** (a specific time) **to** (a specific time)	We have class **from** 9:00 AM **to** 3:00 PM. Breakfast is served **from** 6:30 **to** 8:00. I have a business trip **from** Monday **to** Friday of next week.
since	From a certain point of time (until now)	That pizza place has been there **since** 1975.
for	Over a certain period of time (until now)	He's been in jail **for** the last two years for theft.
ago	A certain time in the past	I visited Australia two years **ago**.
before	Earlier than a certain point of time	**Before** 1950, only the rich had TVs in their homes.
to	Telling the time	It's currently quarter **to** five (4:45).
past	Telling the time	It's currently half **past** eleven (11:30).
till, until	Marks the end of a period of time	He is on leave **until** Friday.
by	Up to a certain time At the latest	**By** 11 o'clock, I had read five pages. I will be back **by** 6 o'clock.
during	Expresses when something is happening (not how long)	I relaxed **during** my break.

Prepositions of Time Exercises 01

✓ **Put appropriate prepositions in the blanks.**

1) This place has been under renovation _____ last year. I have no idea when they'll finish.
2) Smith has been working here _____ ten years already! Today's party is to honor him!
3) I need to get a haircut _____ this Saturday. I have to attend a wedding then.
4) Wow, I had no idea that "naïve" came from French _____ you just told me now.
5) Jack worked in this school _____ Jan 2019 _____ Dec 2020.
6) _____ last year alone, Peter has lost fifty pounds!
7) You must arrive _____ half _____ seven (7:30), or you won't be allowed to enter the show.
8) It's currently quarter _____ nine (8:45), and I still haven't had my dinner!
9) _____ next Sunday, the winner of the contest will have been decided.

Prepositions of Time Exercises 02

✓ **Put either "on", "in", or "at" in the blanks.**

1) He always jogs _____ the morning; I meet him every day while I'm going to work.
2) I have a doctor's appointment _____ Monday, so I won't be able to pick you up from school.
3) It never gets cold in Los Angeles – even _____ the winter!
4) _____ lunchtime today, a fire started in the cafeteria, so the teachers ordered lunch in for us.
5) Back _____ the '70s, Daejeon was nothing but farms.
6) My father and I always go hiking _____ the weekends.
7) We left our house an hour ago. We'll be there _____ half an hour.
8) There was a robbery here _____ 7 o'clock yesterday.
9) In the Gangwon province, it sometimes snows even _____ March

16.4 Other Prepositions

We don't only use *prepositions* for *place* and *time*; here are some other uses.

- **Other Uses of Common Prepositions**

from	Who gave it	I got this present **from** Jane.
of	Who/what it belongs to What does it show	This is Jack, a good friend **of** mine. This is a picture **of** my family.
by	Who made it Rise or fall of something Travelling	*The Giver* was written **by** Lois Lowry. The prices have risen **by** 10%. I'm getting there **by** bus.
on	Walking or riding a horse Entering a public transport vehicle	I can get there in 15 minutes **on** foot. I'm getting **on** the bus right now.
off	Leaving a public transport vehicle	I just got **off** the train.
in	Entering a car/taxi	Let's get **in** the car; we must go now.
out of	Leaving a car/taxi	He got **out of** his car.
at	Ages	She learned Russian **at** 45.
about	For topics	We were just talking **about** you.
with	"Accompanied by"	I went to a restaurant **with** my wife.
without	The absence of something	Vera came to the party **without** a gift.

The **preposition** "by" is very commonly used in English; it fits in various different situations. In fact, under some circumstances, "by" can be used as an **adverb** as well. The following table illustrates some of the many uses of "by."

- **The Many Uses of "By"**

1. by + place: In this context, "by" has the same meaning as the prepositions "beside," "next to," and "near."

The train station is **by** *a lake.*
Philip lives **by** *a police station.*
I wish I could live somewhere **by** *the sea.*

2. by + method of transport: such as train, car, boat, plane, taxi, bus, and coach.
By adding a general form of transportation, you can explain how you arrived somewhere.

Regina went to Manhattan **by** *train.*
I go to school **by** *car.*
My grandparents sometimes travel to France **by** *boat.*
Jack has never travelled **by** *plane* before.

3. by + method of communication: such as phone, fax, email, and mail.
By adding the general mode of communication, you can explain how you communicated with someone.

I spoke to her **by** *telephone.*
I will send you the invoice **by** *mail.*
Please confirm the order **by** *email.*

4. by + method of payment: such as credit card or check.
This structure is used to describe how you pay for something.

We paid for the computer **by** *check.*
Can I pay **by** *credit card?*

Note that we do not use "by" for cash payments. We use the preposition "in" or "with" interchangeably for that purpose e.g., David paid **in** *cash* for the newspaper. / He paid for the newspaper **with** cash.
It is also common to omit the preposition completely, particularly in spoken English: e.g., David paid *cash* for the newspaper.

5. by and the passive With the passive voice, "by" indicates who is performing the action.

1. David is cleaning the kitchen. (active)
   The kitchen is being cleaned **by** *David.* **(passive)**
2. Sarah wrote the book. (active)
   The book was written **by** *Sarah.* **(passive)**
3. Our school organized the concert. (active)
   The concert was organized **by** *our school.* **(passive)**

6. by + reflexive pronoun such as myself, yourself, himself, itself, yourselves.
By adding a reflexive pronoun, you clarify that only the person/people included in the pronoun is/are doing the activity.

I enjoy reading **by** *myself.*
Sarah is studying **by** *herself.*
Let's do something **by** *ourselves.*
My parents often go on holiday **by** *themselves.*

7. by + -ING verb This structure describes how to do something. It gives us more information about how to achieve a particular result.

You can turn on the radio **by** *pressing that button.*
Question: How can I turn on the radio?
Answer: By *pressing the button.*
The phrase "*pressing the button*" describes how to do something (i.e., how to turn on the radio).

8. by + time expression: The meaning of this structure is "not later than," i.e., before or at a particular time. We use this structure to describe deadlines. A deadline is the time by which something must be done.

Guests must vacate their hotel rooms **by** *11 am.*
Please send us the payment **by** *tomorrow.*
Students must enroll **by** *the end of June.*

Other Prepositions Exercises

✓ **Put appropriate prepositions in the blanks.**

1) This book is a present _____ Yvonne. It's written _____ my favorite author, Charles Dickens.
2) The suspect escaped the scene _____ foot.
3) I just got _____ the train. I'll be there in twenty minutes.
4) Sean Connery passed away _____ the age of 90, _____ 2020.
5) I got _____ my car _____ my umbrella, and I got soaked.
6) It only takes six minutes to get there _____ car; we can probably walk.
7) Come join us! We were just about to have a discussion _____ the book *The Giver.*
8) I arrived at her birthday party _____ just minutes to spare.

16.5 Dependent Prepositions

You know how I told you that a lot of mistakes are made with **prepositions**? And sure, we've seen this with **prepositions of place** and **time**, but here with **dependent prepositions** is really where such mistakes are most likely.

Many **nouns**, **verbs**, and **adjectives** must each be followed by a particular **preposition**; you can't just use whichever **preposition** you want. We call these **dependent prepositions**. Fun fact: if you Google "**dependent prepositions**," the first result directs you to a blog about the IELTS exam that gives you the mere 200 **dependent prepositions** that you need to remember for the test. You can go look at that webpage yourself, as I definitely won't give you 200 in this book.

Nevertheless, I will give you some important and common **dependent prepositions**. Have a look at the table below.

Dependent Prepositions with Adjectives

Adjective	Dependent Preposition	Sentence Example
according	to	**According to** reports, the criminal has been caught.
afraid	of	I'm **afraid of** clowns.
ashamed	of	You should be **ashamed of** yourself for failing such an easy test.
aware	of	I'm **aware of** Mary and Tom's divorce.
busy	with	He's still **busy with** his assignment.
capable	of	I'm **capable of** learning all these languages.
careful	with	Be **careful with** the china plates.
curious	about	Dogs are **curious about** everything around them.
different	from	The caffeine in coffee is **different from** the caffeine in tea.
excited	about	I'm very **excited about** this Thanksgiving.
famous	for	Los Angeles is **famous for** its warm weather.
fed up	with	He got **fed up with** having to do all the dishes.
fond	of	My brother is **fond of** imitating my speech.
good	at	Richard Feynman was very **good at** physics.
guilty	of	The suspect was found **guilty of** vehicle theft.
interested	in	Sammy is very **interested in** biology.
pleased	with	Peter is very **pleased with** his new house.
proud	of	He is very **proud of** his son for hitting a homerun in little league today.
responsible	for	Michael is **responsible for** the broken vase.
sensitive	to	Her attitude showed that she was very **sensitive to** others' perceptions of her.
sick	of	I am so **sick of** cooking every day.
similar	to	Baseball is **similar to** softball.
surprised	at/by	I was **surprised at/by** the scene of the crime.

• Dependent Prepositions with Nouns

Noun	Dependent Preposition	Sentence Example
attack	on	Some view the new law as an **attack on** freedom of speech.
comparison	between	A sophisticated **comparison between** American football and Australian football is provided in Jack's thesis.
decrease	in	A **decrease in** interest rates indicates that the economy is struggling.
delay	in	There appears to have been a **delay in** our flight.
focus	on	His **focus on** his goals has influenced his social life.
difficulty	in/with	I have no **difficulty in/with** making new friends.
information	about	Do you have any **information about** the timetable changes?
intention	of	Did you have any **intention of** hurting the child?
knowledge	of	Timothy's **knowledge of** hockey is incredible.
lack	of	The police had to free him due to a **lack of** evidence.
need	for	The **need for** food is a basic human condition.
reaction	to	The president's **reaction to** the incident was viewed as inappropriate by many.
reason	for	You can always find a **reason for** change.
change	in	Scientists have recently been noticing subtle **changes in** the atmosphere.
room	for	There's **room for** one more person on this couch.
possibility	of	My coach was the first to understand the **possibilities of** the strategy.
problem	with	I noticed a small **problem with** the essay you've submitted.
cause	of	Her sister is the **cause of** all her problems.
relationship	with	My **relationship with** John is becoming rockier by the day.

- **Dependent Prepositions with Verbs**

Verb	Dependent Preposition	Sentence Example
agree	with	I don't **agree with** the popular opinion here.
apologize	for	Harry always **apologizes for** his mistakes.
argue	about	They **argued about** which route to take.
ask	for	The student **asked for** a new pencil, as his broke.
believe	in	Christians **believe in** Jesus Christ.
belong	to	The house **belongs to** a renowned businessman.
care	about/for	He didn't **care for** the sweetness of the sauce.
comment	on	I can't **comment on** their decision; it's their choice.
compare	with	How does the restaurant's pasta **compare with** mine?
complain	about	The boy **complained about** his bedtime.
concentrate	on	He's trying to **concentrate on** his book; don't bother him.
deal	with	I can't **deal with** such a heavy load.
depend	on/upon	You can't **depend on** your parents forever.
disappear	from	I can't find my car keys; they seem to have **disappeared from** my desk.
escape	from	The prisoners **escaped from** their cells during the night.
forget	about	I **forgot about** the homework.
involve	in	My mother was **involved in** a car accident last month.
provide	for	Parents are expected to **provide for** their children; in turn, children are expected to **provide for** their aging parents.
search	for	Have you **searched for** your dog yet?

Again, there are many more of these. If you have extensive reading experience, you should already be familiar with most of them, but beware that knowing them doesn't mean that you'll be free from making mistakes. Try to memorize some of the common ones, like those listed in the tables above.

✓ **Put appropriate prepositions in the blanks.**

The police have just announced that they have apprehended the criminal **responsible** _____ the jewelry shop theft last week. **According** _____ the spokesperson, the investigators noticed that the burglary was very **similar** _____ the one that happened in the neighboring town several weeks ago, following their inspection of the crime scene. From this, they theorized that the suspect could be particularly **interested** _____ diamond sellers. **Based** _____ their hypothesis, they **advised** nearby police departments _____ **keep their eyes out** _____ suspicious people **hovering** _____ diamond-bearing jewelry stores. Around 8 o'clock today, a policeman noticed a suspicious person in front of the Zales store on 5th Ave. He seemed to be **hooked** _____ a diamond necklace on display, **unaware** _____ the policeman approaching him. When he finally noticed the policeman, he tried to **escape** _____ him, but the policeman soon **caught up** _____ him. When questioned, the suspect **insisted** _____ his innocence for a long time, stating that he has never **heard** _____ the robbery. But he eventually **gave** _____ and **admitted** _____ his actions. Despite the criminal **begging** _____ mercy, the police **intend** _____ **sentence** him _____ at least five years in prison.

16.6 Outlook on Prepositions

Prepositions are relatively easy compared to other *parts of speech*, as *prepositions* follow their root definitions very closely in terms of usage. This is especially true for *prepositions of place*, but also holds true for *prepositions of time* and other miscellaneous types of *prepositions*. That said, "**in**," "**at**," and "**on**" are particularly tricky as each of them has many uses; and further, since they are very simple words, their root definitions don't give many hints about their uses. Hence, it would be helpful to at least memorize the uses of these three troublemakers.

Prepositions are one of those word types best learned through reading. Are you really going to try to memorize each and every use of all those words? That's virtually impossible. You need to take *prepositions* nice and slow. After you read enough good books and articles, you'll unconsciously acquire a vast database of *prepositions*. By then, you'll be able to use the correct one with the correct word in most situations. It's like muscle memory; like riding a bicycle, once you repeat it enough times, your body will remember for the rest of your life. As such, once you've seen enough *prepositions*, you'll be able to use them automatically. It may take a long time before you reach that expert-level, but hang in there—you'll get there eventually.

CHAPTER 17

Conjunctions

words such as "but," "and," and "while" that connect parts of sentences, phrases, or clauses

17.1 Introduction

17.1.1 Cooking, Eating, and Doing the Dishes

Let's say you've joined a local social circle. You are sitting in a circle with the others, and it's time to share your hobbies. You enjoy cooking and eating your own food, but you hate doing the dishes afterwards. Your turn arrives, so you say the following.

1. **I like cooking. I like eating. I don't like washing dishes afterward.**

Well, that doesn't sound terribly natural, does it? Why might the above statement be considered awkward? Maybe there's a better way to say it. What do you think we can do to improve it? Not quite sure yet? How about version #2 below?

2. **I like cooking <u>and</u> eating, <u>but</u> I don't like washing dishes afterward.**

Now we have a <u>single sentence</u> that coherently summarizes your ideas. Notice how version #1 consists of <u>three short sentences</u> instead of one longer one. Which version sounds better? The second one, right? Why do you think that's so?

You probably already know that whenever there's a ***period*** ("."), you need to briefly stop reading (or speaking). When you have multiple short sentences, you stop too frequently. Stopping interferes with understanding the ideas contained in sentences. This becomes especially problematic when multiple related ideas are being conveyed simultaneously.

Take a look at #1 again. Each sentence contains a single idea only, and each idea is closely related to the other two. However, <u>when the three linked ideas are presented in separate sentences, it's difficult to understand their relationships and get the entire picture</u>. On the other hand, in #2, all three ideas are compiled into a single sentence. <u>Expressed like so, it's a lot easier to understand the individual relationships as well as the entire complex thought</u>.

To weave multiple ideas into a single sentence, we need an important grammatical tool, the ***conjunction***. In #2, the underlined words "<u>**and**</u>" and "<u>**but**</u>" are ***conjunctions***. ***<u>Conjunctions</u>*** <u>are words that link other words, phrases, or clauses together</u>, allowing us to <u>express complex ideas in just a single sentence</u>. Using ***conjunctions***, we can express sophisticated ideas concisely and also unveil relationships between sub-classes of ideas clearly.

17.1.2 Three Types of Conjunctions

Largely, there are three types of *conjunctions*: *coordinating conjunctions*, *subordinating conjunctions*, and *correlative conjunctions*.

Coordinating conjunctions	join two words, phrases, or clauses that are grammatically equal.	for, and, nor, but, or, yet, so.
Subordinating Conjunctions	join a dependent (subordinate) clause to an independent (main) clause.	although, because, since, unless, until, even though, etc.
Correlative Conjunctions	pairs of conjunctions that work together to relate two specific items. These two items are often grammatically equal.	either ... or, both ... and, neither ... nor, as ... as, rather ... than, etc.

17.2 Coordinating Conjunctions

17.2.1 The FANBOYS

Coordinating conjunctions join words, phrases, or clauses of equal importance. Grammatically, "equal importance" means of equal grammatical rank. Specifically, this means that *coordinating conjunctions* can join two or more *verbs*, *nouns*, *adjectives*, phrases, or *independent clauses* with each other. But here's the important thing: you can't mix them up. In other words, when you use a *coordinating conjunction*, a *verb* must only be joined with another *verb*, a *noun* only with another *noun*, and so on.

We often refer to the *coordinating conjunctions* in English as the *FANBOYS*. That's because the acronym stands for the seven common *coordinating conjunctions*.

1. *F – for*
2. *A – and*
3. *N – nor*
4. *B – but*
5. *O – or*
6. *Y – yet*
7. *S – so*

Now, let's look at each and every one of them in more detail.

17.2.2 "For"

We use "**for**" to discuss the reason a certain action occurred. In other words, in a sentence with "**for**," an action is presented first, followed by its cause. A sentence with "**for**" can take the following form.

- *[action]* + *for* + *[reason for/cause of the action]*.

"**For**" has a similar meaning as "**because**," "**since**," and "**as**," which, as you'll see later, are all *subordinating conjunctions*.

"**For**" is a ***coordinating conjunction***, which means that it must link two words, phrases, or clauses of the same grammatical rank. However, "**for**" generally links two ***independent clauses***. As above, "**for**" links an ***[action]*** with the ***[reason for/cause of the action]***. Both of these ideas are rather difficult to express in simple phrases, let alone single words. Hence, you'll often find yourself linking two clauses with "**for**." Consider the following examples.

1. *I go to the park every Sunday to meet him, <u>for</u> I long to see his face.*

2. *My husband sent me flowers, <u>for</u> he loves me.*

Notice that in each sentence, the parts before and after "**for**" are both clauses; more specifically, they are both ***independent clauses***. In other words, each part can stand alone as a complete sentence. For example, in #1, "**I go to the park every Sunday to meet him**" is a complete sentence, and "**I long to see his face**" is also a complete sentence.

Also notice that <u>the first **independent clause** introduces a certain action</u>, which is then supplemented by <u>the second **independent clause**, which states the reason for the action</u>. However, again, the "reason" clause is also an ***independent clause*** and can stand alone as a sentence. Have this in mind when you look at the ***subordinating conjunctions*** "**because**," "**since**," and "**as**" later, as the case will be different there.

17.2.3 "And"

<u>We use "**and**" to link similar ideas or to form lists of things.</u> "**And**" acts like the "**+**" sign; it simply adds different ideas together without modifying or relating them to one another. Unlike "**for**," <u>"**and**" is equally frequently used to link ***verbs***, ***nouns***, ***adjectives***, phrases, and clauses.</u> Consider the following examples.

1. Jazmin *lives* <u>and</u> *works* in Paris.

2. There's *a library* <u>and</u> *a restaurant* near my house.

3. Taylor is *beautiful* <u>and</u> *intelligent*.

4. Paul exercises every morning *to stay fit* <u>and</u> *to become stronger*.

5. *The hippopotamus is huge, <u>and</u> it drinks water from the river.*

In the examples above, five different types of grammatical components are linked—in #1, two ***verbs*** are linked, in #2, two ***nouns*** are linked, in #3, two ***adjectives*** are linked, in #4, two phrases are linked, and in #5, two ***independent clauses*** are linked.

As you can see in the above examples, <u>the ideas before and after "**and**" are two separate, (previously) independent ideas.</u> For example, #1 links the following two distinct ideas.

A. Jazmin lives in Paris.

B. Jazmin works in Paris.

But, as per our discussion at the start of this chapter, writing these two sentences in succession would be awkward and inefficient. Hence, we can use "**and**" to combine these ideas in the concise form presented in #1.

To be precise, <u>when we use "**and**" to combine two sentences, we erase overlapping parts and link only the parts that are different</u>. Coming back to sentences A & B, "**Jazmin … in Paris**" are the overlapping parts and the ***verbs*** "**lives**" and "**works**" are the parts that are different. Hence, when we combine these two sentences using "**and**," we only need to add the ***verbs***, as in #1.

1. Jazmin *lives* <u>and</u> *works* in Paris.

The case is exactly the same when you're adding two ***nouns***, two ***adjectives***, and two phrases. On your own, try to figure out the two respective base sentences that were combined to form #2, #3, and #4.

When you're linking two *independent clauses* using "**and**," they're often two (previously) unrelated ideas. For example, #5 above is formed by linking the following ideas.

C. The hippopotamus is huge

D. The hippopotamus drinks water from the river.

Again, the clauses before and after "**and**" can stand alone as complete sentences. The only thing to be cautious about when linking two *independent clauses* is avoiding repetition. We use *pronouns* for that purpose. Linking C and D could lead to the undesirable repetition of "**the hippopotamus.**" Hence, we use the *pronoun* "**it**" to replace the second *subject*, as seen in #5.

5. *The hippopotamus is huge, <u>and</u> it drinks water from the river.*

Finally, <u>you can link more than two ideas using "**and**." In such a case, you use *commas* ("**,**") to separate the items in the list, and you place "**and**" right after the final *comma*, just before the last item in the list.</u> Consider the following example.

● **I need *eggs, flour, <u>and</u> milk.***

Carefully note the positions of the *commas* as well as the position of "**and**."

17.2.4 *"Nor"*

<u>We use "**nor**" to link two ideas that are in the negative.</u> Similar to "**for**," when we use "**nor**," we often need to evaluate each linked idea in terms of validity. Hence, <u>both the parts before and after "**nor**" are usually *independent clauses*</u>. Nevertheless, "**nor**" can effectively link two *verbs*, *nouns*, phrases, and *adjectives* also.

Additionally, note that the above only holds true when we use the *coordinating conjunction* "**nor**" (on its own)—when we use the *correlative conjunction* "**neither … nor**," two *verbs*, *nouns*, phrases, and *adjectives* are commonly linked as well.

What's important about "**nor**" is that <u>the word already denotes the negative</u> (i.e., an <u>absence</u>). <u>Hence, the first *independent clause* appearing before "**nor**" must be in the negative, whereas the second *independent clause*, which appears after "**nor**," must be in the positive. Together, both clauses will ultimately denote the negative.</u> This is because "**nor**" signals a negative on behalf of the second *independent clause* despite it being in the positive.

Another important thing about "**nor**" is that <u>you need to flip the order of the *verb* and the *subject* in the second clause</u>. Consider the following examples.

1. *I've never eaten lobster, <u>nor</u> <u>do I</u> want to.*

2. *He can't play the guitar, <u>nor</u> <u>can he</u> sing.*

First, notice how the *verb* is swapped with the *subject* in the second *independent clause*. There isn't a clear reason for this; it's probably a rule created to reflect standard usage.

Next, notice how the second *independent clause* is actually in the positive. However, if we break #2 down, it becomes the following two negative sentences.

A. He can't play the guitar.

B. He can't sing.

But, when we combine these two sentences using "**nor**," we have to flip the tone in the second sentence. That is, we must adjust the second sentence as follows.

C. He can sing.

Then, we flip the order of the *verb* and the *subject*.

D. Can he sing

Finally, we can combine A and D using "**nor**," resulting in #2.

2. *He can't play the guitar,* <u>nor</u> *can he sing.*

17.2.5 "But"

<u>We use "**but**" in the middle of the sentence to flip the tone.</u> In other words, <u>a positive statement comes before</u> "**but**," <u>while a negative one comes after it.</u> Again, "**but**" often links two *independent clauses*, but it also efficiently links two *verbs*, *nouns*, phrases, and *adjectives*. A sentence with "**but**" would normally look like the following.

- *[a positive statement] +* <u>but</u> *+ [a related negative statement]*

The negative statement, or the second *independent clause*, is often related to the positive statement, or the first *independent clause*. Consider the following examples.

1. *There's a hotel,* <u>but</u> *there isn't a convenience store.*

2. *I went to the grocery store,* <u>but</u> *I forgot my purse.*

As you can see in #2, <u>the negative statement doesn't necessarily contain the word "**not**."</u> Rather, <u>it must present a conflict with the first *independent clause*</u> that appears before "**but**." Notice that in #1 and #2, both parts are *independent clauses* that can stand alone as complete sentences.

Now let me introduce you a case where two *nouns* are linked by "**but**."

3. **There is a** *hotel,* <u>but</u> **no** *convenience store.*

In sentence #3, the *nouns* "**hotel**" and "**convenience store**" are linked together. As such, "**but**" is also occasionally used to link grammatical components other than clauses. As a side-point, in #3, "**no**" placed after "**but**" simply signifies the conflict; "**no**" is not considered as a part of the component being linked (i.e., "**convenience store**").

"**But**" has a more or less identical meaning as some other *conjunctions* like "**however**," "**though**," "**although**," and "**whereas**." But, every one of these *conjunctions* are *subordinating conjunctions*; only "**but**" is a *coordinating conjunction*.

17.2.6 "Or"

<u>We use "**or**" to present alternatives or choices.</u> In this case, any of the five grammatical components (*verbs*, *nouns*, *adjectives*, phrases, and *independent clauses*) are frequently linked by "**or**." An example is as follows.

1. <u>Alternatives</u>: **Do you want to go to** *Germany* <u>or</u> *France*?

In #1, the two *nouns* "**Germany**" and "**France**" are linked by "**or**." These two *nouns* represent two alternatives being offered—you can choose to go to either **Germany** or **France**.

<u>We also use "**or**" to explain the consequence of an action.</u> More specifically, "**or**" <u>is used to give advice to help someone avoid performing an unfavorable act.</u> In line with this, the first part of this kind of sentence is in the negative. In this case, you often link two *independent clauses*. An example of such a situation is as follows.

2. <u>Consequences</u>: *Don't be late, <u>or</u> you'll miss the train.*

In #2, the part after "**or**" explains the consequence if you do what the part before "**or**" says not to do. For this purpose, you can use the expression "**or else**" or "otherwise" instead of "**or**."

17.2.7 "Yet"

<u>We use "**yet**" to talk about two conflicting facts or actions</u>. "**Yet**" has a similar feel as "**but**," but rather than linking two events that are opposite in tone, "<u>yet</u>" links two events that are conflicting, which creates a sense of irony. "**Yet**" is sometimes similar to "**in spite of**." Again, "**yet**" often links two *independent clauses*, but that doesn't always have to be the case. Consider the following examples.

1. *It's a warm day, <u>yet</u> Raymond's wearing a coat.*

2. *George lives in the countryside, <u>yet</u> he works in a nearby city.*

Can you tell how this usage is subtly different from the usage of "**but**"? The two events linked by "**yet**" just don't go together. Including them in one sentence creates a sense of irony and confusion. Remember that "**yet**" can only be used in such situations; "**yet**" is more specific than "**but**."

17.2.8 "So"

Finally, <u>we use "**so**"</u> (the last of our *FANBOYS*) <u>to handle cause-effect relationships</u>. Following this, "**so**" also often links two *independent clauses*. An important aspect of using "**so**" is that <u>the "cause" is always a fact or an observation</u>, while <u>the "effect" (or result) is always an action</u>. Consider the following examples.

1. *It was lovely day, <u>so</u> we went for a walk.*

2. *My house was a mess, <u>so</u> I spent the weekend cleaning.*

Notice that the first *independent clause* denotes a fact or an observation, which then provokes the action described in the second *independent clause*.

We saw that "**or**" can be used to talk about consequences as well. How then is "**or**" different? "<u>Or</u>" is used to talk about the consequence of an action. That is, <u>when you use "**or**," the "cause" is always an action</u>, and the "<u>result" is always a fact</u>. Let's look at the previous example again.

3. *Don't be late, <u>or</u> you'll miss the train.*

Here, the first *independent clause* denotes an action (in the negative), which will cause the result described in the second *independent clause*, which is a fact. This is the opposite of using "**so**."

Here's another interesting thing about "**so**": <u>out of the seven *coordinating conjunctions*, "**so**" is the only one that can also be used as a *subordinating conjunction*</u>. As explained above, "**so**" as a *coordinating conjunction* holds a meaning of "**therefore**," while "<u>so</u>" as a *subordinating conjunction* holds a meaning of "<u>so that</u>." You'll see later that a *subordinating conjunction* often links an *independent clause* with a *dependent clause*. Since a detailed explanation on *subordinating conjunctions* will be provided later, I will only leave you with some examples of using "**so**" as a *subordinating conjunction* for now.

4. *Thomas is saving money <u>so</u> he can afford a Ferrari 911.*

5. *I left a message <u>so</u> he would know I had called.*

17.2.9 Comma Rules

As we discussed briefly above, when you use a *coordinating conjunction*, you sometimes need a *comma* ("."). Largely, there are two situations wherein you need *commas* with *coordinating conjunctions*.

1. <u>Two *Independent Clauses*</u>
   When the *coordinating conjunction* links two *independent clauses*, <u>we need to place a *comma*</u> <u>before the *coordinating conjunction*</u> (<u>to separate the two *independent clauses*</u>). Consider the following sentence.

   - *It was raining,* <u>and</u> *there was lightening.*

2. <u>A List of More Than Two Items</u>
   As mentioned above, <u>whenever you're listing more than two items</u> (i.e., a <u>series</u>) <u>using "**and**" or "**or**,"</u> <u>you need "series" *commas* to separate the entries in the series</u>. For the final item on the list, a *coordinating conjunction* is placed after the comma. Consider the following sentences.

   - **I need** *eggs, flour,* <u>and</u> *milk.*

   - **Would you like** *tea, coffee,* <u>or</u> *juice*?

17.2.10 More examples

for	Regina eats healthy, <u>**for**</u> she wants to stay fit. Let's not linger on the past, <u>**for**</u> every day is a new day. We listened carefully, <u>**for**</u> each of us aimed for top of the class. I woke up early today, <u>**for**</u> I have a flight to catch.
and	I like to read, <u>**and**</u> I write my own stories every night. You should invite Frank <u>**and**</u> Terry to the party. Bella looks beautiful <u>**and**</u> mature in her new dress. The puppies bark <u>**and**</u> jump when a stranger comes to visit.
nor	My sister doesn't take notes in class, <u>**nor**</u> does she listen to the teacher. Our family hasn't been to America, <u>**nor**</u> have we been to Mexico. George didn't do the dishes, <u>**nor**</u> did he do the laundry. King Henry was not the ruler of France, <u>**nor**</u> was he alive in 1430.
but	Playing video games is a wonderful escape, <u>**but**</u> it interferes with my studies. We would love to attend the wedding, <u>**but**</u> we have plans that day. I was going to get my driver's license, <u>**but**</u> I failed the final test. My grandfather was awarded the Pulitzer Prize, <u>**but**</u> he never got to accept it.
or	Would you rather read a book <u>**or**</u> watch the movie? I can't decide if I should study physics <u>**or**</u> chemistry. We could have breakfast, <u>**or**</u> we could wait for the wedding buffet. Do you prefer beef <u>**or**</u> pork?
yet	I always have a book in my bag for my commute, <u>**yet**</u> I never seem to turn a single page. I really want a kitten, <u>**yet**</u> my mom says our dog won't get along with it. The students like their teacher, <u>**yet**</u> they wish he was more lenient with his grading. Wallace would like to make pasta, <u>**yet**</u> he's too tired from his work.

so	I like to write, **so** I didn't mind the long essay assignment. The clothing store was closed, **so** we went to the mall instead. Our stove won't work, **so** we called an appliance repair specialist. We found an abandoned kitten on the street, **so** we decided to buy a can of tuna.

 You can start a sentence with a coordinating conjunction, and you can put a comma after it if you want to introduce a pause. But, don't start a sentence with a coordinating conjunction too often. It can get annoying. In addition, it's discouraged to start a sentence with a coordinating conjunction in formal writings.

Coordinating Conjunctions Exercises 01

✓ **Put in the appropriate coordinating conjunction in each blank.**

1) We were out of milk, _____ I went to the store to buy some.
2) The children ran _____ jumped all over the playground.
3) Would you like cereal _____ toast for breakfast? *(either one)*
4) The old castle seemed grand _____ haunting.
5) Slowly _____ surely, the turtled finished the race.
6) This bowl of French onion soup is hot _____ delicious.
7) Rocky refuses to eat dry cat food, _____ will he touch a can of tuna.
8) They next bus was scheduled too late, _____ I decided to take the taxi.
9) Juanita eats healthy, _____ she wants to stay in shape.
10) I really want a kitten, _____ my mom says we have too many cats already.

17.3 Subordinating Conjunctions

17.3.1 Hierarchy

Subordinating conjunctions are often considered as the opposite of *coordinating conjunctions*, i.e., as words that join two grammatical components of unequal grammatical rank. In *Section 17.2*, we established that *conjunctions* can link words, phrases, or clauses. In most situations, it's difficult to grade words and phrases based on their grammatical rank. Following this, *subordinating conjunctions* are often said to connect an *independent clause* with a *dependent clause*. Recall that a *dependent clause*, also called a *subordinating clause*, is a clause that cannot stand alone as a sentence; instead, such clauses are included in other sentences to provide more information about another clause in the sentence.

However, there is an important difference between *coordinating conjunctions* and *subordinating conjunctions*. A *coordinating conjunction* acts similar to a mathematical symbol (e.g., "+", "-"); it is an agent that joins two grammatical components, and is not considered a part of either component. However, a *subordinating conjunction* is considered a part of the grammatical component it joins. More specifically, a *subordinating conjunction* is considered a part of the *dependent clause*. In other words, a sentence containing a *subordinating conjunction* would take the following form.

- *[independent clause] + [dependent clause]*
  = [independent clause] + [(subordinating conjunction) + rest of the dependent clause]

Observe how the *(subordinating conjunction)* is formally a part of the *[dependent clause]*. The *[dependent clause]* provides extra information about the *[independent clause]*, and how that information relates to the *[independent clause]* is determined by the function of the *(subordinating conjunction)* in use.

As such, it is more correct to say that a *subordinating conjunction* links two ideas rather than grammatical components; it links an *independent clause* to an idea that is related to the *independent clause*. (Here, the "idea" = "*rest of the dependent clause*.") The sum of this "idea" and the *subordinating conjunction* is equal to the *dependent clause*.

Subordinating conjunctions can be distinguished based on their roles or by the information they relay. The following are eight common types of *subordinating conjunctions* sorted by their functions.

Purpose	so that, in order to
Reason	because, since, as
Concession	although, even though, though
Comparison	(rather) than, whether ... or, as much as, whereas
Time	after, as soon as, as long as, before, by the time, until, now that, once, since, till, when, whenever, while, when
Place	where, wherever
Condition	if, in case, unless, provided that, assuming that, only if, even if, lest
Manner	how, as though, as if

Now, let's look at these one by one.

17.3.2 Purpose

Subordinating conjunctions of purpose are used to talk about the purpose of an action. In sentences that use them, the *independent clause* states a certain action, and the *dependent clause* explains why the *subject* performed such an act or the intention(s) of the *subject*. The following are the common *subordinating conjunctions of purpose* in English.

- **So that, in order to**

An important difference between these two common *subordinating conjunctions of purpose* is that "**so that**" is always followed by a clause, whereas "**in order to**" is always followed by an *infinitive verb* (i.e., a *verb* in its base form). Consider the following examples. (In each example, the *dependent clause* was *italicized*.)

1. **He trained hard *so that* *he'd get first place*.**

2. **He dropped out of school *in order to* *focus on his training*.**

As you can see, in each sentence the part that appears after the *subordinating conjunction* describes why the *subject* performed the act. Also, notice that each sentence is formed by the addition of an *independent clause* and a *dependent clause*. For example, sentence #1 is formed by the addition of the following two clauses.

A. **he trained hard**

B. **so that he'd get first place**

Here, A is an *independent clause*, while B is a *dependent clause*. Recall that when a *subordinating conjunction* is used in a sentence, <u>the *subordinating conjunction* itself marks the beginning of a *dependent clause*</u>.

As was hinted in *Section 17.2.8*, the "**that**" in "**so that**" can be omitted. That's why we established that "**so**" can be used as either a *coordinating conjunction* or a *subordinating conjunction*. As mentioned previously, "**so**" as a *coordinating conjunction* holds a meaning similar to "**therefore**," while "**so**" as a *subordinating conjunction* is equivalent to erasing "**that**" from "**so that**," which is a *subordinating conjunction* in and of itself.

17.3.3 Reason

<u>*Subordinating conjunctions of reason*</u> are used to discuss the reason that something has happened. In sentences that use them, an *independent clause* describes <u>a certain action</u>, and a *dependent clause* tells us <u>why that action occurred</u>. The following are common *subordinating conjunctions of reason* in English.

- **Because, since, as**

<u>The difference between *purpose* and *reason* is whether the action was planned</u>. When you use a *subordinating conjunction of purpose*, it suggests that the action was planned beforehand (by the *subject*) based on the intention described in the *dependent clause* in that sentence. However, when you use a *subordinating conjunction of reason*, the action might not have been planned (by the *subject*) in advance—it might have been spontaneous or unexpected. On top of that, there may not even be any action in a sentence with a *subordinating conjunction of reason*—some sentences handle particular situations or facts and why they are so. Consider the following examples. (In each example, the *dependent clause* was *italicized*.)

1. **He got first place *<u>because</u> he trained hard*.**

2. **The washing machine is making so much noise *<u>since</u> one of its screws is missing*.**

3. **I decided to move to Switzerland *<u>as</u> it's beautiful there*.**

Notice that #2 is handling a fact or an observation, rather than an action. And again, realize that each segment that begins with the *subordinating conjunction* is a *dependent clause*.

17.3.4 Concession

This one might be a bit difficult to figure out from the title itself; "*concession*" is a fairly big word. <u>*Subordinating conjunctions of concession*</u> are used to talk about things that are unexpectedly true. Usually, in sentences using such *conjunctions*, the *independent clause* states the <u>unexpected fact</u>, while the *dependent clause* provides evidence for <u>why the fact is unexpected</u>. The following are common *subordinating conjunctions of concession* in English.

- **Although, even though, though**

Consider the following sentences. (In each example, the *dependent clause* was *italicized*.)

1. ***<u>Although</u> I left my home early*, I was late to work.**

2. ***<u>Though</u> my nephew is already five*, I've never met him.**

3. **I'm going to be at the baseball match this weekend, *<u>even though</u> I don't understand it fully*.**

Like in #1 and #2, you can start a sentence with a *subordinating conjunction* by swapping the positions of the *independent* and the *dependent clauses*. However, note that some *subordinating conjunctions* sound more natural when used in the middle of a sentence.

17.3.5 Comparison

Subordinating conjunctions of comparison are used to compare and contrast two things. These do not necessarily have to link two clauses; some can link two **_verbs_**, **_nouns_**, or phrases as well. The following are common **_subordinating conjunctions of comparison_** in English. Note that we can further distinguish these by whether they compare or contrast the two things ("compare" means the two things are similar; "contrast" means they are different).

- **Comparing**: as much as

- **Contrasting**: (rather) than, whereas

Consider the following sentences. (The **_dependent clauses_** were not _italicized_ here, as one example involves the linkage of two **_nouns_**.)

1. **<u>As much as</u> I love cooking, I love eating more.**

2. **Sam is more skilled at computer programming <u>than</u> Frank.**

3. **Tim likes chocolate <u>whereas</u> Sally prefers candy.**

As mentioned, **_subordinating conjunctions of comparison_** do not necessarily have to link two clauses. You can see this in #2, where the **_conjunction_** "**than**" links two **_nouns_**: "**Sam**" and "**Frank**." Comparing and contrasting (especially comparing) often involves two entities of equal importance or rank. Hence, despite being a **_subordinating conjunction_**, a sentence containing a **_subordinating conjunction of comparison_** may not include a **_dependent clause_**.

17.3.6 Time

Subordinating conjunctions of time are used to provide a time sense for an action. In sentences that use them, the **_independent clause_** mentions <u>a certain action</u>, while the **_dependent clause_** describes <u>when it happened, happens, or will happen</u>. The following are common **_subordinating conjunctions_** of **_time_** in English.

- **After, as soon as, until, when, while, now that**

Consider the following sentences. (In each example, the **_dependent clause_** was _italicized_.)

1. **_<u>After</u> Valentine's Day is over_, we'll go out to eat.**

2. **_<u>Now that</u> your tests are over_, you may play video games again.**

3. **We'll go outside _<u>when</u> it has stopped raining_.**

4. **I'll pick you up _<u>as soon as</u> your class finishes_.**

5. **I watered the plants _<u>while</u> my husband mowed the lawn_.**

17.3.7 Place

Subordinating conjunctions of place are used to provide a sense of location for an action. In sentences that use them, an **_independent clause_** introduces <u>a certain action</u>, while a **_dependent clause_** states <u>where it happened, happens, or will happen</u>. The following are common **_subordinating conjunctions_** of **_place_** in English.

- **Where, wherever**

Consider the following sentences. (In each example, the **_dependent clause_** was _italicized_.)

1. **The pirate hid the gold _<u>where</u> nobody could ever find it_.**

2. **_<u>Wherever</u> possible_, you should swap unhealthy foods for healthier options.**

17.3.8 Condition

Subordinating conjunctions of condition are used to discuss the condition of an action. In sentences that use them, an **independent clause** states an action that can only occur if the demand in the **dependent clause** is satisfied. The following are common **subordinating conjunctions of condition** in English. Note that some of them describe negative conditions; in other words, if the condition is fulfilled, then the action in the **independent clause** will not occur.

- **If, in case, unless, provided that, assuming that**

Consider the following sentences. (In each example, the **dependent clause** was _italicized_.)

1. _Unless you can convince her to be nice_, I'm not coming to dinner.

2. Tim wasn't willing to work extra hours _if it meant missing the big game_.

3. _Assuming that you've done your homework_, you can go out and play.

17.3.9 Manner

Finally, _subordinating conjunctions of manner_ are used to discuss the manner in which an action unfolds. In sentences using them, an **independent clause** introduces an action, while the **dependent clause** describes the manner in which the action occurs. The following are the common **subordinating conjunctions** of _manner_ in English.

- **How, as though, as if**

Using these has a very similar effect to using **adverbs of manner**, but sometimes such **adverbs** are not enough to describe exactly how an action occurs. In those cases, we can explain the situation in more detail by using **subordinating conjunctions of manner**.

Consider the following sentences.

1. Tim started to dig _as if his life depended on it_.

2. Sally cried _as though she were a baby_.

3. Tell me _how you persuaded Danny to see that film_.

The **conjunctions** "as if" and "as though" are mostly used for exaggeration, rather than explanation. Hence, we often intentionally use unusual/awkward grammar in the **dependent clause** to further emphasize the manner, as shown in #2.

Subordinating Conjunctions Exercises

✓ **Identify inappropriate subordinating conjunctions and fix them.**

1) Although my mom told me to come home early, I stayed out late.
2) She didn't know she was a talented singer after she sang in the school concert.
3) You will not pass the exam unless you work harder.
4) Everyone looked at me when I came in the room.
5) Robin wasn't allowed in the car anymore so that he wouldn't wear a seatbelt.
6) As if his father got home, Jack took a secret ride in his father's car.
7) Since Fei refused to pay her electric bills, electricity was cut from her house.
8) Even though the semester is over, I can focus more on my health.
9) I'll start working on Mr. Finch's homework while his class finishes.
10) He took off for the traffic light as if someone was chasing after him.

17.4.1 Double-Team

Correlative conjunctions <u>join words, phrases, or clauses of equal importance</u>, similar to **coordinating conjunctions**, <u>but they work in pairs</u>. In English, there are <u>five common</u> **correlative conjunctions**.

- **Both … and, either … or, whether … or, neither … nor, not only … but also**

Recall that we've looked at many of these already in the **determiners** chapter.

<u>They mostly handle situations that involve two items</u> (but <u>they can involve more than two items too</u>). We can further distinguish them based on what you decide to do with or kind of choice you make between the two items. See the following.

1. <u>Item 1 ✓, Item 2 ✓</u>

    - **Both … and & not only … but also**

2. <u>Item 1 ✓, Item 2 ✗ (or Item 1 ✗, Item 2 ✓)</u>

    - **Either … or, whether … or**

3. <u>Item 1 ✗, Item 2 ✗</u>

    - **Neither … nor**

Now let's look at each situation in detail with examples.

17.4.2 Both of Them

<u>When two options were already selected at some point in the **past**, you either use "**both … and**" or "**not only … but also.**"</u> "**Both … and**" simply says that both items are included, while "**not only … but also**" emphasizes that the 2nd item is surprising or notable in that context. Consider the following examples.

1. <u>**Both**</u> _my brother_ <u>**and**</u> _I_ play golf.

2. Tay loves <u>**not only**</u> _chemistry_ <u>**but also**</u> _physics_.

A peculiar thing about "**not only … but also**" is that the **subject** and **verb** placements sometimes need to be switched up when you include two clauses. Consider the following.

3. <u>**Not only**</u> _have I finished_ my homework, <u>**but**</u> _I have_ <u>**also**</u> _finished_ preparing for the next class.

Notice how in the first clause, the position of the **auxiliary verb** "**have**" and that of the **subject** "**I**" have been swapped. Furthermore, in the second clause, the **subject** "**I**" and the **auxiliary verb** "**have**" have been placed in between "**but**" and "**also**."

17.4.3 One or the Other

<u>When you can choose only one of two options, you can use "**either … or**" or "**whether … or.**"</u> You won't necessarily select the first option; the second option is also available. Consider the following sentences.

1. <u>**Either**</u> _I drive to the airport_, <u>**or**</u> _I get a taxi_.

2. You can stay <u>**either**</u> _with me_ <u>**or**</u> _with Janet_.

3. Someone has to speak in the public, <u>**whether**</u> it's _you_ <u>**or**</u> _me_ doesn't matter.

Preposition placement is a bit interesting with *correlative conjunctions*. Taking #2 above as an example, note that it's okay to rewrite the sentence as follows.

> **4.   You can stay *with* <u>either</u> *me* <u>or</u> *Janet*.**

As you can see, you can also place the ***preposition*** in front of the expression containing "**either … or**"; sentences #2 and #4 mean exactly the same thing.

17.4.4 None of The Above

When you want to make a negative statement about two items, you use "**neither … nor.**" Consider the following sentences.

> **1.   We got so wet. We had <u>neither</u> *umbrellas* <u>nor</u> *raincoats* with us.**

> **2.   <u>Neither</u> *our families* <u>nor</u> *our friends* know that we are getting married.**

Now is a good time to talk about "double negatives." Some words and expressions are negative by definition (e.g., "no," "neither," "nor," "neither … nor"). The words and expressions are used to convey that something is absent or that it does not exist. Adding an extra "not" leads to a double negative, which turns the negative expression into a positive one and often results in a grammatically incorrect, confusing, or misleading statement.

e. g.) We got so wet. We <u>didn't not have</u> <u>neither</u> umbrellas <u>nor</u> raincoats with us. → *Incorrect!*

17.5   Outlook on Conjunctions

Conjunctions are very useful tools that allow you to effectively relay complicated ideas. Though most of the ***conjunctions*** that we use in English are provided in this chapter, some interesting ones were left out. But, studying vocabulary is your job, as I'm sure you know by now.

The main thing to watch out for when using ***conjunctions*** is grammar, especially that relating to the placement of the ***subject*** and the ***auxiliary verb***. As you've seen throughout this chapter, some ***conjunctions*** have peculiar grammar rules that could be considered incorrect in some other situations. If you don't remember this, back up and have another look at "**nor**," "**as if**," "**as though**," and "**not only … but also**." Not only for ***conjunctions*** but also for all the other stuff we've looked at so far, whenever you're unsure about grammar, look it up. The thing is, not everybody will be completely grammar savvy, especially considering all the exceptions floating around in English grammar. The internet is a great place to find resources to consult when you're stuck on English grammar.

CHAPTER 18

Dummy Subjects

Clauses that are not imperative must have a subject. As such, sometimes we need to use what's known as a "dummy" or "empty" subject when no subject is attached to the verb and where the real subject is somewhere else in the clause.

18.1 Introduction   18.3 "There"

18.2 "It"   18.4 Outlook on Dummy Subjects

18.1 Introduction

18.1.1 What Now?

So, we've finally made it through the nine **parts of speech**. Does that mean you've conquered English grammar? Not quite yet. Sure, now that you have a good idea about the different **parts of speech** in English, you'll be able to write simple sentences without making serious mistakes. But, to go beyond simple sentences, what you need are some **sentence techniques**.

Sentence techniques involve skills you can develop to write fancier, more complex sentences. Transitioning from **parts of speech** to **sentence techniques** means that you're moving on to a higher level of English grammar. This means that the concepts will get more complicated and more diverse. This also means that you can no longer expect my book to be complete; there is no way I can cover all the English **sentence techniques** out there within this single book. However, worry not, as I'll tell you all about some essential ones.

Four essential **sentence techniques** in English are: **dummy subjects**, **relative clauses**, the **passive voice**, and **conditionals**. They are what we'll be focusing on in this book. Here's a short preview for each.

1. **The Dummy Subject Technique**
   We use **dummy subjects** when the **actual subject** is too long or complicated. There are two words in English that you can use as a **dummy subject**: "it" and "there." When used as a **dummy subject**, "it" usually precedes an **adjective**, while "there" is used to indicate that something or someone is at a particular location or in a particular situation.

2. **The Relative Clauses Technique**
   We use **relative clauses** to provide more information about something in our sentence. Essentially, **relative clauses** allow us to combine two sentences into one, similar to **conjunctions**. However, **relative clauses** can involve much more diverse and sophisticated ways of combining sentences than **conjunctions**.

3. **The Passive Voice Technique**
   In "normal" sentences (i.e., those using the **active voice**), the focus is on the **subject** of the sentence. We use the **passive voice** to shift the focus to the **object** or to the action itself, as denoted by the **verb**. We can also use the **passive voice** when we don't know who or what the **subject** is, or when it is unimportant or better left unstated.

4. **Conditionals Technique**

   We use ***conditionals*** to propose hypotheses, i.e., to make educated guesses. Simply put, ***conditionals*** are sentences that contain the word "**if**." In a ***conditional*** sentence, a hypothetical situation in the ***present*** or the ***past*** is first introduced. The situation may either be positive or negative. Then, the result of the proposition is presented in the second part of the sentence.

After we look at all these ***sentence techniques***, we'll finish up the book by looking briefly at some miscellaneous topics, specifically, ***capitalization rules***, ***prefixes*** and ***suffixes***, ***question words***, and ***punctuation***.

18.1.2 Too Long!

While you write in English, sometimes your ***subject*** will end up being way too long. Whenever your ***subject*** is too long, your reader can get lost reading it. This is very problematic as the most important part of your sentence is the ***verb***; if the ***subject*** is too long, the reader might get lost before they find out what the ***subject*** is doing (described by the ***action verb***) or what the ***subject*** is like (described by the ***linking verb***).

So, when do we encounter long ***subjects***? There are two main situations that involve complex ***subjects***.

   A. **When either an *infinitive* or a *gerund* is the *subject*.**

   B. **When the *subject* contains at least one *prepositional phrase*.**

The following are examples of the respective situations.

   1. **To wear a helmet when you engage in any dangerous sport is important.**

   2. **A woman who wants to talk to you is waiting outside.**

In the two sentences, the underlined parts are the respective ***subjects***. Notice how long they are. With such long ***subjects***, your sentences are difficult to read.

Interestingly, when that long ***subject*** is moved to the end of the sentence, the sentence suddenly becomes easier to read. Consider the following sentences.

   3. *It* is important **to wear a helmet when you engage in any dangerous sport.**

   4. *There* is **a woman waiting outside who wants to talk to you.**

Can you see that #3 and #4 are much easier to read than #1 and #2? Hence, whenever you have a long ***subject***, it's a lot better to place it at the end of the sentence. And a great way to do this is by using ***dummy subjects***. In fact, #3 and #4 are already using ***dummy subjects***—"**it**" and "**there**."

18.1.3 The Duo

The two ***dummy subjects*** at your disposal are "**it**" and "**there**." When used as ***dummy subjects***, they take the role of the ***subject*** of the sentence and hence appear at the very start of the sentence (see #3 and #4 in the previous section). What's important is that these ***dummy subjects***, as their name suggests, don't hold any significance; they don't mean anything. They're just placeholders and do not represent the main idea of the sentence. The main idea comes after, usually in the form of a complex ***noun***. However, a long ***subject*** is not the only case where we'd use ***dummy subjects***. Watch out for some of their other specific uses as you go through this chapter.

18.2.1 The General Use of "It" as a Dummy Subject

When describing an activity, we can use an *infinitive* or a *gerund* as the *subject*. Then, we can follow it up with an *adjective* to describe how we feel about the activity. The following are examples of such a construction.

1. <u>*Having* your passport number written down</u> is useful in case you lose your passport.

2. <u>*To find out* about your family history</u> is always interesting.

You can see that in sentences of this kind, the *subject* tends to be long. This is because you need to include extra bits of detail to precisely designate the activity. In the above examples, "**having**" and "**to find out**" alone are not enough to define the activities you're discussing. And as I said above, when the *subject* is too long, it's difficult to read your sentence.

In this case, we can use "**it**" as the *dummy subject* to resolve this issue. <u>To use "it" as a *dummy subject* we place it in front of the *adjective*</u>. Here's how to transform this kind of sentences using "**it**."

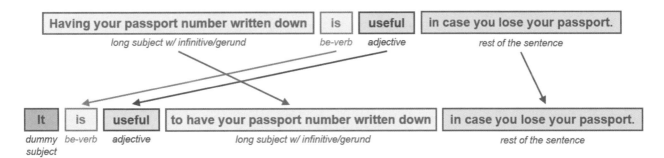

3. <u>It is</u> useful to have your passport number written down in case you lose your passport.

Here's a little side-point about #3: <u>many "*'be'-verb* + *adjective*" constructions only allow a *'to'-infinitive* to follow them</u>; that's why the *gerund* "having" in #1 was changed to the *'to'-infinitive* "to have" in #3 (as we transformed the original sentence to include the *dummy subject*, "**it**"). We already established that the *'to'-infinitive* form and the *gerund* form of a *verb* hold the same meaning. Therefore, switching from one to the other does not alter the meaning of the sentence. A related construction to this is: "*'be'-verb* + *adjective* + *preposition* + *gerund*" (e.g., "**Jeremy** <u>is scared of flying</u>," "**Taylor** <u>is committed to improving</u> her swimming skills."). Recall that we can only use a *gerund* after a *preposition*.

Similarly, we can change #2 to the following.

4. <u>It is</u> always interesting *to find out about your family history*.

First, notice how #3 and #4 start in exactly the same way with "**it is**." Then, compare #1 with #3 and compare #2 with #4—in each case, which one's easier to read? As you can see, #3 and #4 are much easier to read than #1 and #2. <u>This is because the long *subject* has been moved toward the end of the sentence.</u>

18.2.2 Be Careful, "It" is Originally a Pronoun!

Where have we seen the word "**it**" before? In our discussion of **pronouns**. We know that "it" can be used to replace a singular, genderless thing, be it the **subject** or the **object** of a sentence. We also know that a **pronoun** usually refers back to a **noun** mentioned in the previous clause or sentence.

That said, a confusing situation can arise if you use the **dummy subject** "it" directly after mentioning a **singular**, genderless thing. For example, consider the following.

1. My mom just pulled out <u>an old family photo album</u>. *It* is full of memories from her childhood.

2. My mom just pulled out <u>an old family photo album</u>. *It* is always interesting to find out about your family history.

In #1, "**it**" is used as a **pronoun** to point back to the **singular**, genderless thing, "**an old family photo album**," in the previous sentence. In #2, "**it**" is used as a **dummy subject** to allow the long **actual subject**, "**to find out about your family history**," to the end. Here, "**it**" is not pointing to a **noun** but rather is just acting as a meaningless placeholder for that long **subject**. However, as you can see, the second sentence in #1 and #2 start out exactly the same, i.e., with "**it is**" followed by an **adjective** ("**full**" in #1; "**interesting**" in #2).

The thing is, "it" is way more commonly used as a **pronoun** than as a **dummy subject**. Hence, in #2, before the reader reaches the end of the second sentence, they will naturally think that "it" is pointing to "**an old family photo album**." Consequently, they will likely experience initial confusion, even after reaching the end. To avoid confusing the reader, you must be careful not to create such situations. For the above case, maybe you can change the second sentence to the following.

3. My mom just pulled out an old family photo album. I always love finding out about my family history.

By replacing "**it**" with a different **subject**, "**I**," there is no possibility of confusion.

18.2.3 Specific Uses of "It" as a Dummy Subject

In addition to dealing with **infinitive** and **gerund** situations, the **dummy subject**, "it" has <u>two</u> other very important uses.

1. **To talk about time, dates, and distances**

   I. <u>It's</u> nearly one o'clock.

   II. <u>It's</u> my birthday.

   III. <u>Is it</u> Friday already?

   IV. How far <u>is it</u> to the hospital?

   V. <u>It's</u> two miles that way.

2. **To talk about the weather**

   I. <u>It's</u> raining.

   II. <u>It's</u> a lovely day.

   III. <u>It was</u> getting really cold.

Again, "**it**" is used as a **dummy subject** in each sentence above and holds no particular meaning.

"It" Exercises

✓ **Rewrite the following sentences using the dummy subject, "it".**

1) To be honest with each other in a relationship is important.
2) To know when to give up is essential for a happy life.
3) Reading articles from respected news agencies is helpful to improve your vocabulary.
4) Learning about your country's recent history from your parents is always fascinating because they've actually lived through that era.

18.3 "There"

18.3.1 The General Use of "There" as a Dummy Subject

We use "**there**" as a ***dummy subject*** to talk about something or someone that exists at a particular place, time, or a combination of two (i.e., a particular situation). Whenever we discuss such ***subjects***, we need to add extra information to precisely designate the thing or person we're talking about. Hence, the ***subject*** can end up being too long in such situations. Consider the following sentences.

1.   **An eclipse of the moon will happen tonight.**

2.   **A woman who wants to talk to you is waiting outside.**

But, a more serious problem arises when we're talking about something that happens at some place, time, or in some situation. When we try to simply say that something exists or happens, the ***verb*** becomes rather redundant. Just by mentioning the thing, person, or event, we can convey the idea that it exists or happens. Hence, the ***verb*** can feel unnecessary, which can interfere with the precise description. Consider the following situations.

3.   **Two shops exist in the village.**

4.   **An interesting book lies on the shelf.**

5.   **A car accident occurred yesterday in front of my school.**

6.   **A nasty fight happened last week in the shop.**

In the examples #3-#6, all the ***verbs*** mean to either **exist** or **happen**. However, some of these ***verbs*** are not really needed—it's obvious that the things **exist** and that the events **happen(ed)**. What's important are the details about the thing or the event—the locations of the things and the times the events occurred. You can see that such details appear after the ***verb*** in each sentence above. In other words, the thing/event/person and the details are split up by the unnecessary ***verb***; the ***verb*** just gets in the way of describing the thing/event/person.

Below is a list of some such "***unimportant verbs***."

●   "**Exist**": exist, lie, stay, be

●   "**Happen**": happen, occur, take place, come about

Also, notice that #1 and #2 above have the same problem as #3-#6—the thing/event/person ("**eclipse**" and "**woman**") and the details ("**tonight**" and "**waiting outside**") are split up by placeholder ***verbs*** ("**happen**" and "**is**"). Conversely, the ***subject*** would become too long if you place such details before the placeholder ***verb***.

Using "**there**" as a *dummy subject* allows us to group the thing/event/person with the details, ultimately resolving this issue. Here's how we change this kind of sentence using "**there**."

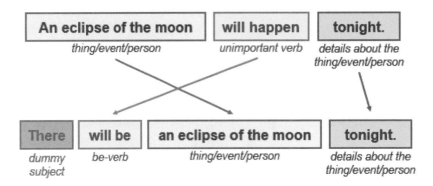

Notice how using "**there**" allowed us to group the thing/event/person with the important details. This makes it a lot easier to identify the thing/event/person we're talking about.

Using this technique, you'd change the rest of the sentences (#2-#6) as follows.

7. <u>There is</u> *a woman waiting outside who wants to talk to you*.

8. <u>There is</u> *an interesting book on the shelf*.

9. <u>There are</u> *two shops in the village*.

10. <u>There was</u> *a car accident yesterday in front of my school*.

11. <u>There was</u> *a nasty fight last week in the shop*.

First, notice how all the sentences now start in the exact same format: "**there**" followed by a *'be'-verb*. Next, notice how grouping the thing/event/person with the important details makes it a lot easier to pinpoint the *subject* (i.e., get the whole picture).

18.3.2 Specific Uses of "There" as a Dummy Subject

The specific uses of "**there**" more or less stem from its general use. Despite overlapping with the general uses, I mention each for your convenience.

1. <u>To talk about the where or when of something</u>

    I. <u>There's</u> **an interesting book on the shelf.**

    II. <u>There'll</u> **be an eclipse of the moon tonight.**

2. <u>To talk about the quantity or amount of something</u>

    I. <u>There is</u> **plenty of bread left.**

    II. <u>There were</u> **twenty people at the meeting.**

3. <u>To talk about existence or occurrence</u>

    I. <u>There's</u> **a small problem.**

    II. <u>There was</u> **a power outage.**

"There" Exercises

✓ **Rewrite the following sentences using the dummy subject, "there".**

1) A big argument between my parents broke out during dinner yesterday.
2) More than 3,000 deadly sick patients are present in this hospital right now because of the pandemic.
3) A construction of what is to be the biggest mall in this city is taking place just two kilometers away from my house.
4) Only two professional electricians live in this town.

18.4 Outlook on Dummy Subjects

Dummy subjects are excellent tools for making your writing clearer. We use them when our *subject* is too long or when an unimportant *verb* interferes with providing a full description of a thing/event/person. By using *dummy subjects*, you can place the long *subject* at the end of the sentence or omit unimportant *verbs* and group your full description. Both methods can make your writing much clearer. Using these techniques wisely can improve your writing skills immensely. Just be careful when using "**it**"—you know why.

Read much, but not many books.

- Benjamin Franklin (1706-1790) -

The Relative Clause

a part of a sentence that includes a verb and is joined to the rest of the sentence with "who," "where," etc...

19.1 Introduction

Relative clauses act quite similarly to *conjunctions*. Like *conjunctions*, relative clauses join two sentences. However, *relative clauses* are often more concise and effective than *conjunctions*. Consider the following situation.

1. **She lives in New York. She likes living in New York.**

Having explored *conjunctions*, you likely identified #1 as one of the worst ways to express two related ideas. The main reason this sounds so awkward is because of the repetition of the long phrase: "**live in New York**"

How can we shorten this using a *conjunction*? Which one should we use? Since both sentences are *independent clauses* and two separate, but related ideas, the best *conjunction* to use would be "**and**." So, let's try to make this sound better using "**and**."

2. **She lives in New York, and she likes living in New York.**

Okay, a little better. Although we still have the same repeated phrase issue, at least we now have a single sentence. As I said before, back-to-back sentences that relay linked ideas are undesirable because they interfere with readability by making you stop, which may hinder your understanding. But, we can still do better.

3. **She lives in New York, and she likes living there.**

Still a bit better, yeah? We've removed the repetition of the location "**New York**" with the appropriate *pronoun*, "**there**." But, the *verb* "**live**" still appears twice (as "**lives**" and "**living**"). Okay, so how about this?

4. **She lives in New York, and she likes it.**

Wow, that's short. Between #2 and #4, we've swapped the entire *gerund phrase* "**living in New York**" with the *pronoun* "**it**" resulting in a very concise sentence. However, here, "**it**" can be a source of confusion for the readers. While some may understand that "**it**" = "**living in New York**," others might misunderstand this as "**it**" = "**New York**," as in, she likes the place itself, rather than the act of living there. In this case, thankfully, the original message isn't disrupted too badly—if she likes "**New York**," she probably likes "**living in New York**" too. However, this type of thing could result in catastrophic misunderstandings in some situations.

Hmm, it seems we've hit at a dead end. None of the simplifications we've made using the **conjunction** "**and**" (i.e., #2-#4) feel satisfactory. What if we use a **relative clause** instead? Watch this.

5.   She lives in New York, _which_ she likes.

Hey, that sounds nice! We've finally gotten rid of the entire long repeating bit, "**live in New York**"! In fact, #5 is even shorter than #4, which was the shortest sentence you could make using the **conjunction** "**and**." You might argue that "_**which**_" can still refer to either "**living in New York**" or simply "**New York**." But you'll see later in this chapter that we don't use "_**which**_" to refer to places in that way. In addition, you'll see that "_**which**_" is often used to refer to the entire clause that appears before it. In other words, there's not much room for confusion in #5.

So, what do you think? Can you now see the power of **relative clauses**? Using them is probably the most effective way of linking two ideas together concisely in English.

19.2   Relative Pronouns & Their Uses

19.2.1 Five Common Relative Pronouns

A **relative clause** always opens with a **relative pronoun**. (In #5 in the previous section, the **relative pronoun** "**which**" was used.) Five **relative pronouns** are commonly used in English. Think of them as flags that signal the use of a **relative clause** within a sentence. The table below summarizes all five **relative pronouns** based on their uses.

	Subject	Object	Prepositional	Possessive	Entire Sentence
Who	People only	People only	People only	X	X
Whom	X	People only	People only	X	X
Whose	X	X	X	People or Things	X
Which	Things only	Things only	Things only	X	Y
That	People or Things	People or Things	People or Things	X	X

19.2.2 Uses of the Five Relative Pronouns

The headers (i.e., the top row) in the above table denote how the **relative pronouns** beneath them are used. In this section, we'll look at each use in detail. As you go through them, recall our look at **pronouns** (e.g., I, you, he, she, and it) and how they can be used.

A.   Subject
We can replace the **subject** with a **relative pronoun**. When the **relative pronoun** replaces the **subject**, it is always followed by a **verb**. Here's an example.

I.   I told you about a woman. The woman lives next door.
→ **I told you about the woman who _lives_ next door.**

B. Object

We can replace the *object* with a *relative pronoun*. When the *relative pronoun* replaces the *object*, it is always followed by a *noun*. Here's an example.

   I.   This is a house. Jack built <u>this house</u>.
        → **This is the house <u>that</u> *Jack* built.**

C. Prepositional

We can replace the *object of a preposition* with a *relative pronoun*. The *object of a preposition* is a *noun* that appears directly after a *preposition*. <u>The *preposition* can appear in two different places, except for "that,"</u> in which case the *preposition* must always come at the end (i.e., <u>the #II case only</u>).

   I.   We bought a chainsaw. We cut up all the wood *with* <u>the chainsaw</u>.
        → **We bought a chainsaw, *with* <u>which</u> we cut up all the wood.**

   II. We bought a chainsaw. We cut up all the wood *with* <u>the chainsaw</u>.
        → **We bought a chainsaw, <u>which</u> we cut up all the wood *with*.**

D. Possessive

We can replace an expression of possession with a *relative pronoun*. Only "**whose**" is available for this use. Here's an example.

   I.   The dog is over there. <u>The dog's</u> owner lives next door.
        → **The dog, <u>whose</u> owner lives next door, is over there.**

E. Entire Sentence

We can replace an entire sentence with a *relative pronoun*. Only "**which**" is available for this use. Here's an example.

   I.   He couldn't read. The fact that <u>he couldn't read</u> surprised me.
        → **He couldn't read, <u>which</u> surprised me.**

19.2.3 What Can Relative Pronouns Stand In for?

Now let's look at this from a different angle. As you can see in the table in *Section 19.2.1* above, some *relative pronouns* can only be used for people, while others can only be used for things. <u>Let's distinguish the *relative pronouns* based on what they can stand in for</u>.

1. **PEOPLE ONLY: Who & Whom**

   <u>We use "**who**" and "**whom**" for people only</u>. "**Who**" can stand for the *subject*, the *object*, or the *prepositional* use, while "**whom**" can stand for the *object* or the *prepositional* use (i.e., it <u>cannot</u> stand for the *subject*).

   ### A. Subject

   ● **Marie Curie is the woman <u>who</u> *discovered* radium.**
     *(notice the **verb** after "**who**")*

   ### B. Object

   ● **This is George, <u>who(m)</u> *you* met at our house last year.**
     *(notice the **noun** after "**who(m)**")*

   ### C. Prepositional

   ● **I had an uncle in Germany, *from* <u>who(m)</u> I inherited a bit of money.**

   ● **I had an uncle in Germany, <u>who(m)</u> I inherited a bit of money *from*.**

2. **THINGS ONLY: Which**
   We use "**which**" for things only. "**Which**" can stand for the *subject*, the *object*, or the *prepositional* use.

   A. **Subject**

   - Do you see the cat <u>which</u> *is* sitting on the roof?
     (notice the **verb** *after "*which*")*

   B. **Object**

   - We had fish and chips, <u>which</u> *I* always enjoy.
     (notice the **noun** *after "*which*")*

   C. **Prepositional**

   - We bought a chainsaw, *with* <u>which</u> we cut up all the wood.

   - We bought a chainsaw, <u>which</u> we cut up all the wood *with*.

3. **BOTH PEOPLE & THINGS: Whose & That**
   We use "**whose**" and "**that**" for both people and things. "**Whose**" can only be used for the *possessive*. "**That**" can be stand for the *subject*, the *object*, or the *prepositional* use. "**That**" can only be used in *defining relative clauses*.

   A. **Subject**

   - Marie Curie is the woman <u>that</u> *discovered* radium.
     (notice the **verb** *after "*that*")*

   B. **Object**

   - This is the house <u>that</u> *Jack* built.
     (notice the **noun** *after "*that*")*

   C. **Prepositional**

   - I didn't know the uncle <u>that</u> I inherited the money *from*.
     *(with "*that*", the* **preposition** *must appear at the* <u>end</u>*)*

   D. **Possessive**

   - This is Chris, <u>whose</u> sister went to school with me.

4. **ENTIRE SENTENCE: Which**
   Only "**which**" can stand for entire sentences.

   E. **Entire Sentence**

   - He couldn't read, <u>which</u> surprised me.

Relative Pronouns & Their Uses Exercises

✓ **Put appropriate relative pronouns in the blanks.**

1) I need a television _____ works!
2) Her necklace, _____ she'd just bought, was stolen.
3) Jay, _____ I used to live with, came to stay with us for a few days.
4) I'm looking for a job _____ I'll enjoy.
5) Do you know anyone _____ knows how to fix a bike?
6) He's the actor _____ we saw last week.
7) The suspect, _____ we had been following for many days, was arrested.
8) The book _____ I just read is excellent.
9) We spoke to Linda, _____ had recently been mugged.
10) Our new house, _____ is by the beach, is beautiful.

19.3 Defining & Non-Defining Relative Clauses

19.3.1 Defining Relative Clauses

I hinted at these above when I was talking about "**that**"—I said that we can only use "**that**" for *defining relative clauses*. So, what are *defining relative clauses*, and what about *non-defining relative clauses*?

Defining relative clauses provide information that defines the *target noun* (reflected by the *relative pronoun*). The information provided by a *defining relative clause* is necessary for the complete identification of the *target noun*. In other words, without the *defining relative clause*, the sentence wouldn't make sense. A very important rule for using *defining relative clauses* is to never use *commas* (","). Consider the following examples.

1. I like the *paintings* that hang in the SASB North lobby.

2. *Students* who study hard will do well in my class.

3. I hope I hear from the *person* with whom I spent hours talking last night.

In #1–#3, the underlined parts are *defining relative clauses*. First, notice that no *commas* are used.

Next, let's try rewriting the sentences by omitting each *defining relative clause*.

4. I like the *paintings*.

5. *Students* will do well in my class.

6. I hope I hear from the *person* last night.

Without the respective *defining relative clauses*, the *target nouns* lack description. Which "*paintings*" do you like? What kind of "*students*" will do well in your class? And, which "*person*" do you wish to hear from? Notice how each *defining relative clause* is an essential part of the sentence; without it, we are left confused about the *noun*.

19.3.2 Non-Defining Relative Clauses

On the other hand, ***non-defining relative clauses*** provide extra information about the ***target noun*** that is not essential for precise identification of the ***noun***. In other words, even without the ***non-defining relative clause***, the sentence will make sense. In this case, the very important rule is to always use ***commas*** (",") to set off the ***non-defining relative clauses***. Consider the following examples.

7. *My mother*, who is an excellent cook, is thinking of opening a restaurant.

8. I'm planning to grow *roses*, which I find quite beautiful.

9. *Lord Thompson*, who is 76, has just retired.

In #7-#9, the underlined parts are ***non-defining relative clauses***. First, notice that the ***non-defining relative clauses*** are set off by ***commas***.

Next, let's try rewriting the sentences by erasing the ***non-defining relative clauses***.

10. *My mother* is thinking of opening a restaurant.

11. I'm planning to grow *roses*.

12. *Lord Thompson* has just retired.

Even without the ***non-defining relative clauses***, the sentences make sense. The information that's provided in the respective ***non-defining relative clauses*** is not essential for defining the ***target nouns***. However, #7-#9 are more interesting and logical than #10-#12. The ***non-defining relative clauses*** help us better understand the actions denoted in those sentences.

19.3.3 "That" and Defining Relative Clauses

You can only use "**that**" with ***defining relative clauses***. Consider the following examples.

1. Children <u>who</u> hate chocolate are uncommon.
   → **Children <u>that</u> hate chocolate are uncommon.** → *Okay!*

2. An elephant is an animal <u>which</u> lives in hot countries.
   → **An elephant is an animal <u>that</u> lives in hot countries.** → *Okay!*

Look at the original sentences in #1 and #2, which contain "**who**" and "**which**," respectively. Are the ***relative clauses*** essential to the identification of the ***target nouns*** "**children**" and "**an elephant**"? Yes. What if we remove the ***relative clauses***; do the sentences become awkward? Yes. Hence, the ***relative clauses*** in #1 and #2 are both ***defining***, and we can use "**that**" instead.

Now, consider the following examples.

3. He gave me a letter, <u>which</u> was in a blue envelope.
   → **He gave me a letter, <u>that</u> was in a blue envelope.** → *Wrong!*

4. John's mother, <u>who</u> lives in Scotland, has six grandchildren.
   → **John's mother, <u>that</u> lives in Scotland, has six grandchildren.** → *Wrong!*

Again, look at the original sentences in #3 and #4. Are the ***relative clauses*** essential to the identification of the ***target nouns***? No. What if we removed the ***relative clauses***; would the sentences still make sense? Yes. Hence, the ***relative clauses*** in #3 and #4 are both ***non-defining***, and we cannot use "**that**" instead.

As a side-note, go back to each of the sentences and look for ***commas*** (","). Which ones include ***relative clauses*** set off by ***commas***, and which ones do not?

19.3.4 "Which" and Defining Relative Clauses (American vs. British English)

So far, we've never considered the difference between American and British English with regards to any of the topics we covered. In reality, there are a considerable amount of variation between the grammar rules for American and British English. However, none of the discrepancies that we could have discussed has been particularly striking, and that's why I never mentioned any. But there is a very important difference between the two language styles that I must acknowledge here.

In American English, we never use "**which**" in a *defining relative clause*; whenever we write or say a *defining relative clause* in American English, we always use "**that**." In contrast, British English allows "**which**" to be included in both a *defining relative clause* and a *non-defining relative clause*. Consider the following sentence.

- **A "garnish" is an item** <u>which</u> **is added to a prepared food dish or drink as a decoration.**

Notice how the *relative clause* that begins with "**which**" is *defining*; without it, the sentence would lack too much information. The above sentence would be considered incorrect (or rather awkward) in American English, whereas perfectly fine in British English. Can you understand the difference now?

Defining & Non-Defining Relative Clauses Exercises

   ✓   **Identify the relative clause in each sentence as either defining (D) or non-defining (ND).**

1) ____ I'm writing about people who commit crimes.
2) ____ I saw the car which the criminal stole.
3) ____ All the burglars were arrested, which was a great relief.
4) ____ They live in a house whose roof is full of holes.
5) ____ We stopped at the museum, which we had never visited before.
6) ____ Yesterday I met a woman named Susan, whose husband works in London.
7) ____ The dish that I ordered was delicious.
8) ____ Stratford-on-Avon, which many people have written about, is Shakespeare's birthplace.
9) ____ There's something that you should know.

19.4   Relative Adverbs

19.4.1 The Dropouts

Relative adverbs are words that can be used like *relative pronouns* but are not formally considered *relative pronouns*. Maybe it's a bit unfair that they can't be placed in the same group as "**who**," "**whom**," "**whose**," "**which**," and "**that**," but at least we can still use them in similar ways. There are <u>four</u> main *relative adverbs* in English.

1. **When**
   We use "**when**" to refer to an expression about time.

   - **He's looking forward to** *the day* <u>when</u> **he'll be released from prison.**

2. **Where**
   We use "**where**" to refer to an expression about a place.

- This is *the place* <u>where</u> the judge sits.

3. <u>Whereby</u>
<u>We use "**whereby**" to refer to an expression about a process.</u>

- A trial is *a process* <u>whereby</u> a person is found guilty or innocent of a crime.

4. <u>Why</u>
<u>We use "**why**" to refer to a reason.</u>

- *The assignment due in two weeks* is <u>why</u> we met today.

19.4.2 Quantifiers or Numbers with Relative Pronouns

Other expressions that can be used as *relative pronouns* come in the form of a *quantifier* or a *number* followed by a *relative pronoun*.

- *[quantifier] + "of" + [relative pronoun]* OR *[number] + "of" + [relative pronoun]*

Here are some common expressions formed through this method.

- all of which/whom

- most of which/whom

- many of which/whom

- a few of which/whom

- none of which/whom

- one of which/whom

Consider the following examples.

1. She has three *brothers*, <u>two of whom</u> are in the army.

2. I read three *books* last week, <u>one of which</u> I really enjoyed.

3. There were some good *programs* on the radio, <u>none of which</u> I listened to.

<u>Relative Adverbs Exercises</u>

✓ **Put in appropriate relative adverbs in the blanks.**

1) I've just come back from London, _____ John lives.
2) The reason _____ I came here today is not important.
3) Let's go to a country _____ the sun always shines.
4) I remember my twentieth birthday. It was the day _____ the tsunami hit.
5) Do you remember the place _____ we caught the train?
6) There's a new system _____ students submit their work online.
7) I still remember the day _____ I met him.
8) 1821 is the year _____ Napoleon Bonaparte died.
9) This is exactly the reason _____ they don't let you run in museums.

19.5 Shortening Relative Clauses

You can drop the ***relative pronoun*** in a single, very specific case. The case must satisfy both of the following conditions.

    A. The ***relative pronoun*** must stand for an ***object***.

    B. The ***relative pronoun*** must be part of a ***defining relative clause***.

In this case and only in this case, you can omit the ***relative pronoun***. Consider the following examples.

    1. She loves the *chocolate* that I bought.
       → **She loves the *chocolate* I bought.**

    2. The *bike* which I loved was stolen.
       → **The *bike* I loved was stolen.**

Shortening Relative Clauses Exercises

    ✓   **Shorten the following sentences, if possible.**

1) My grandmother, who is dead now, came from the North of England.
2) He gave me the letter that was in a blue envelope.
3) Everything that you say seems silly to me.
4) The doctor whom I was hoping to see wasn't on duty.
5) This is the best film that I've ever seen.
6) I'm sorry, but that is all that I saw.
7) He sent me the email, which I read immediately.
8) Ralph's father, who lives in Australia, has four grandchildren.
9) Nothing that anyone does can make me happy right now.
10) Do you have anything that will help my throat?

19.6 Common Mistakes

19.6.1 Mistake 1: Repeating the Subject/Object

Recall our definition of ***pronouns***—we said that they are words that replace ***nouns***. So are ***relative pronouns***; they replace the ***target nouns***. Hence, it's wrong to rewrite the ***subject*** or the ***object*** that's being replaced by the ***relative pronoun***. It would be the same as writing the ***subject*** or the ***object*** twice in a row. The ***relative pronoun*** is already the ***subject*** or the ***object*** of the ***relative clause***.

    1. Marie Curie is the woman who she discovered radium. → *Wrong!*

    2. Marie Curie is the woman who discovered radium. → *Correct!*

19.6.2 Mistake 2: "That" and Defining Relative Clauses

Here it comes again: "**that**" is only used for **defining relative clauses**. Whenever you use a **non-defining relative clause**, you cannot use "**that**." Reconsider the definitions of the two types of **relative clauses**.

1. **I met Rebecca in town yesterday, <u>that</u> was a nice surprise.** → *Wrong!*

2. **I met Rebecca in town yesterday, <u>which</u> was a nice surprise.** → *Correct!*

3. **This is the house <u>that</u> Jack built.** → *Correct!*

4. **This is the house <u>which</u> Jack built.** → *Correct!*

As mentioned, it's fine to use "**which**" for **defining relative clauses** in British English (and it's not devastating to do this in American English either). However, many people prefer to use "**that**" in **defining relative clauses** because it foreshadows that the information to follow will define the **target noun**. Nevertheless, you can still use "**which**" in **defining relative clauses**.

19.6.3 Mistake 3: "That" and the Preposition Position

Another one about "**that**," huh? Damn troublemaker. Again, this was stated above: "**that**" can only accept a **preposition** at the end of the **relative clause**. Note that, on the other hand, all the other **relative pronouns** can accept the **preposition** in either one of two possible locations.

1. **We can't find the chainsaw <u>with</u> *that* we cut all the wood.** → *Wrong!*

2. **We can't find the chainsaw *that* we cut all the wood <u>with</u>.** → *Correct!*

3. **We can't find the chainsaw <u>with</u> *which* we cut all the wood.** → *Correct!*

4. **We can't find the chainsaw *which* we cut all the wood <u>with</u>.** → *Correct!*

Notice how both locations are available for the **preposition** "**with**" when we use "**which**" instead (#3 & #4).

19.6.4 Mistake 4: You Can't Always Drop Relative Pronouns

As mentioned in the preceding section, you can only drop the **relative pronoun** under a single, specific situation: when it replaces an **object** and is part of a **defining relative clause**.

1. She has a son <u>who</u> is a doctor.
   → **She has a son is a doctor.** → *Wrong!*

2. We had fish and chips, <u>which</u> I always enjoy.
   → **We had fish and chips, I always enjoy.** → *Wrong!*

3. The bike <u>which</u> I loved was stolen.
   → **The bike I loved was stolen.** → *Correct!*

In #1, the **relative pronoun** "**who**" is replacing a **subject**—notice how a **verb** directly follows "**who**." Therefore, you cannot omit the **relative pronoun** here. In #2, the **relative pronoun** "**which**" is part of a **non-defining relative clause**. Therefore, you cannot omit the **relative pronoun** here either. Only #3 satisfies both of the conditions under which the **relative pronoun** can be dropped.

Common Mistakes Exercises 01

✓ **Identify what's wrong with the following sentences and fix the errors. Some sentences may not have any errors in them.**

1) I don't know the person from that I received this package.
2) My boss, that is very nice, lives in Manchester.
3) Chris did awfully in his exams, which is quite a surprise.
4) Michael Faraday is the man invented the electric motor.

Common Mistakes Exercises 02

✓ **Identify what's wrong with the following sentences and fix the errors. Some sentences may not have any errors in them (cont'd).**

1) This is the fence that Tay painted it.
2) This is the textbook with which I studied math during my high school freshman year.
3) The woman my brother loves is from Mexico.
4) My sister, that I live with, knows a lot about computers.

Reading without reflection
is like eating without digesting.

- Edmund Burke (1729-1797) —

CHAPTER 20

The Passive Voice

passive: the form of a verb used when the subject is affected by the action of the verb.

active: the form of a verb in which the subject is the person or thing that performs the action

20.1 Introduction

20.1.1 What is the Passive Voice?

So far, all the example sentences we've seen in this book have been in the *active voice*. However, the *active voice* is not the only grammatical *voice* in English—we also have the *passive voice*. So, what are *voices*, and what's the difference between the *active voice* and the *passive voice*?

In English grammar, the *voice* of a sentence (or of a *verb*) is roughly defined as the relationship between the *verb* (i.e., the action) and the *subject*. The *active voice* is a type of grammatical *voice* in which the *subject* performs the action described by the *verb*. On the other hand, the *passive voice* is a *voice* in which the *subject* is acted upon; the *subject* is the direct receiver of the action described by the *verb*. In other words, the *subject* in the *passive voice* is equal to the *direct object* in the *active voice*.

Often, we can express the same idea in either one of the two *voices*. Consider the following case.

1. *Active Voice*: Students <u>take</u> the final exams in July.

2. *Passive Voice*: The final exams <u>are taken</u> by students in July.

In changing the *voice* of the sentence, the *direct object* in #1, "**the final exams**," has become the *subject* of #2, whereas the *subject* in #1, "**students**," is now a part of a *prepositional phrase* in #2.

However, the most important change between the *active voice* and the *passive voice* is the *verb form*. First, the *auxiliary verb* "**are**" has been added, and the original *main verb* "**take**" has been changed into its *past participle* form, "**taken**." As such, <u>whenever we write a sentence in the *passive voice*, we always add an auxiliary verb (or verbs) and then write the *main verb* in its *past participle* form.</u> Often, the *auxiliary verb* is simply "**be**.

> ➤ <u>Passive Voice:</u>

| Receiver of the action | be | main verb past participle | performer of the action |

- **Examples**

    A. Milk <u>is delivered</u> in the morning.

    B. This book <u>was written</u> in English by him.

    C. This castle <u>was built</u> in the 1800s.

    D. The telephone <u>was invented</u> more than 140 years ago (by A.G. Bell).

    E. All my friends <u>will be invited</u> to my birthday party.

Now, let's look at a good real-life example wherein the ***passive voice*** is used.

20.1.2 Today's News

Despite ever-evolving security, crime is still prevalent even in the safest of the world's countries. Every day on the news, you'll hear about at least a couple cases of your fellow citizens' big or small misbehaviors. Today's no exception. You turn on a news brief and hear the following.

- A 15-million-dollar mansion in Beverly Hills <u>was reportedly broken into</u> last night by an unknown perpetrator. A 5-million-dollar Bentley parked in the garage <u>was stolen</u>, along with several valuable objects from both the front and the back yard of the mansion. The Beverly Hills Police Department is currently undertaking an extensive examination of the security footage that <u>was captured</u> by the surveillance cameras around the property. The officer in charge triumphantly declared this morning that the perpetrator <u>shall be apprehended</u> in no time.

Thank God the homeowner was prepared with security cameras. Hopefully the criminal will be caught soon.

In the meantime, we should break this paragraph down in terms of its grammar. <u>The underlined parts indicate the usage of the **passive voice**</u>. In these sentences, the ***object*** and the ***verb*** (i.e., the <u>action</u>) take the spotlight rather than the ***subject***. In other words, whenever the ***passive voice*** is used, your attention is diverted to <u>1) what the action is (i.e., the **verb**)</u> and <u>2) who or what receives the action (i.e., the **object**)</u> rather than who performs the action (i.e., the ***subject***).

20.1.3 The Active Voice vs. The Passive Voice

As we have seen, there are two ***voices*** in English—the ***active voice*** and the ***passive voice***. Before we continue looking at these, let's expand our explanation of "***voice***." <u>The **voice** of a sentence concerns how the sentence is written</u>, especially with regards to <u>1) the **verb phrase** structure</u> and <u>2) the order of the **subject** and the **object**</u>. Ultimately, the ***voice*** of the sentence determines the focus of the sentence (i.e., the emphasis of the sentence).

The ***active voice*** is what we usually use in sentences. The ***active voice*** starts with the ***subject***, which is followed by a ***verb***, which is then followed by an ***object***. <u>The **active voice** puts the **subject** in focus</u>. On the other hand, the ***passive voice*** starts with an ***object*** and ends with a modified ***verb phrase***. <u>The **subject** is, in fact, optional when you use the **passive voice**</u>—you can drop it if you want. <u>The **passive voice** puts the **object** and/or the **verb** (i.e., the action) in focus</u>.

- <u>Active Voice:</u>

- <u>Passive Voice:</u>

Consider the following sentences.

1. <u>*Active Voice*</u>: **Chris has fed the cats.**

2. <u>*Passive Voice*</u>: **The cats have been fed (by Chris).**

Sentence #1, which is in the ***active voice***, starts with "**Chris**," the ***subject*** (i.e., the one performing the action). We understand that "**feeding**" is the action Chris is performing and that he's performing that action on "**the cats**," the ***object***. The important thing here is "**Chris**," the ***subject***. The crucial idea in #1 is that <u>**Chris** is the one who fed the cats</u>.

In contrast, sentence #2, which is in the ***passive voice***, starts with the "**the cats**," which is the ***object*** (i.e., receiver of the action). The ***modified verb phrase*** tells us that someone else performed the act of "**feeding**" "**the cats**," the ***object***. However, as you can see, the ***subject***, "**Chris**," is optional—you may omit it if you want. Hence, when we use the ***passive voice***, we might never learn who performs the action, i.e., in this case, who actually fed the cats. But, that's okay because the important thing here is "**the cats**," the ***object***, and "**feeding**," the action. The critical idea in #2 is that <u>**the cats received food**</u>, and <u>who actually fed them is irrelevant</u>.

The last part is a little hint as to why we'd use the ***passive voice***. Still unsure? How about we revisit that news report one more time. Consider the following sentences.

3. <u>*Active Voice*</u>: **Someone broke into a 15-million-dollar mansion in Beverly Hills.**

4. <u>*Passive Voice*</u>: **A 15-million-dollar mansion in Beverly Hills was broken into (by someone).**

Look at #3. The ***active voice*** used in the sentence puts focus on "**someone**," the ***subject***. However, that's not the important thing here, is it? The news is contained in the rest of the sentence, "**broke into a 15-million-dollar mansion in Beverly Hills**." Obviously, the <u>action</u> (i.e., the ***verb***) and the <u>target</u> (i.e., the ***object***) should be in focus here; those are the interesting parts of the sentence. On top of that, we don't even know who the "**someone**" in the sentence is yet.

Hence, the ***passive voice*** fits this situation a lot better. Look at #4 now. Using the ***passive voice***, we can put "**the 15-million-dollar mansion located in the Beverly Hills**," the ***object***, and "**breaking into**," the ***verb***, in the spotlight, where they deserve to be. Furthermore, the sentence sounds more natural without the ***subject*** "**someone**." This is because, again, the interesting information is that **the mansion was broken into**.

As such, <u>we often use the ***passive voice***</u> when the ***subject*** <u>is unknown and/or irrelevant</u>. In these situations, <u>the action</u> (i.e., the ***verb***) and <u>the target</u> (i.e., the ***object***) <u>are more important</u>. But there are many other situations where we'd opt for the ***passive voice***, and we'll cover most of them in this chapter.

20.2.1 The Basic Idea

Any idea in English can be expressed in either the *active voice* or the *passive voice*. In other words, there are at least two possible versions of any sentence in English. This also means that the two *voices* are interchangeable, grammatically speaking.

As I said, the basic sentence forms for the two *voices* are the following.

- *Active Voice*: **[subject] + [verb] + [object]**

- *Passive Voice*: **[object] + [modified verb phrase] + [subject]**

Let's make these structures more grammatically proper.

- *Active Voice*: **[subject] + [main verb] + [object]**

- *Passive Voice*: **[object] + [auxiliary verb(s)] + [past participle of main verb] (+ [preposition, usually "by"] + [subject])**

Doesn't it look a bit complicated when we explicitly express how to form the *passive voice*? Don't worry, it's not as scary as it looks.

First, if you are converting an *active* sentence to a *passive* one, the *original object* in the *active voice* becomes the *new subject* in the *passive voice*. Then, you place *auxiliary verb(s)* in front of the *main verb*, and the *main verb* is then presented in its *past participle* form. Finally, the *original subject* is optional, but if you so desire, you can include it in the form of a *prepositional phrase*. Note that while the *original object* becomes the *new subject*, the *original subject* does not become the *new object*. Instead, it becomes part of an optional *prepositional phrase*. Also note that in this *prepositional phrase* (that includes the *original subject*), the *preposition* "by" is used almost exclusively.

Let's try to identify the changes that take place when we convert #1 to #2, as follows.

1. *Active Voice*: **Jake is building a doghouse in our backyard.**

2. *Passive Voice*: **A doghouse is being built by Jake in our backyard.**

First off, the *active voice* (i.e., #1) is in the *present continuous tense*. Hence, the *main verb* "**build**" is in its *present participle form*, "**building**," and an *auxiliary verb*, "**is** (be)," already accompanies it. Furthermore, the *original subject* is "**Jake**," and the *original object* is "**a doghouse**."

In the *passive voice* (i.e., #2), we first notice that "**a doghouse**," the *original object*, has become the *new subject*. Next, "**being**," an additional *auxiliary verb*, has been added after "**is**," the preexisting *auxiliary verb*. "**Build**," the *main verb*, has also been changed to its *past participle form*, "**built**." Finally, "**Jake**," the *original subject*, has been placed after the *preposition* "**by**."

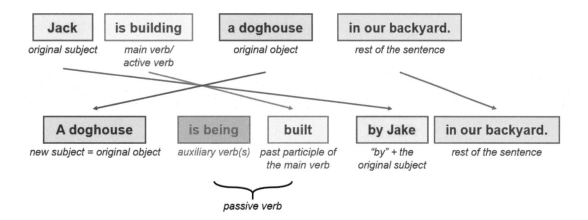

Hopefully you now have a basic idea of how to change the *active voice* into the *passive voice*.

Often, a *verb* in the *passive voice* is followed by one particular *preposition*. The table below shows examples of *verbs* in the *passive* that take *dependent prepositions*.

- **Verbs in the passive that are followed by dependent prepositions**

be associated with	be impressed with	be scared of
be based on	be interested in	be separated from
be concerned about	be involved in	be shocked at
be confused with	be known as	be surprised at
be connected to/with	be known to	be terrified of
be covered with	be limited to	be thrilled at/with
be disappointed with/at	be married to	be tired of
be excited about	be pleased about/with	be troubled with
be filled with	be related to	be used to
be finished with	be satisfied with	be worried about
be made from: if the raw material changes chemically as well as physically		
be made of: if there is only a physical change in the raw material		

20.2.2 All the 12 Tenses

The *passive voice* can be used for each of the twelve *tenses* in English. The following tables show you how to form the *passive voice* for each *tense*.

Tense	Voice	Subject	Aux. Verb(s)	Main Verb (Past Participle)	Object
Present Simple	*Active:*	Rita		writes	a letter.
	Passive:	A letter	is	written	by Rita.
Present Continuous	*Active:*	Rita		is writing	a letter.
	Passive	A letter	is being	written	by Rita.
Present Perfect Simple	*Active:*	Rita		has written	a letter.
	Passive:	A letter	has been	written	by Rita.
Present Perfect Continuous	*Active:*	Rita		has been writing	a letter.
	Passive:	A letter	has been being	written	by Rita.

Tense	Voice	Subject	Aux. Verb(s)	Main Verb (Past Participle)	Object
Past Simple	*Active:*	Rita		wrote	a letter.
	Passive:	A letter	was	written	by Rita.
Past Continuous	*Active:*	Rita		was writing	a letter.
	Passive	A letter	was being	written	by Rita.
Past Perfect Simple	*Active:*	Rita		had written	a letter.
	Passive:	A letter	had been	written	by Rita.
Past Perfect Continuous	*Active:*	Rita		had been writing	a letter.
	Passive:	A letter	had been being	written	by Rita.

Tense	Voice	Subject	Aux. Verb(s)	Main Verb (Past Participle)	Object
Future Simple	*Active:*	Rita		will write	a letter.
	Passive:	A letter	will be	written	by Rita.
Future Continuous	*Active:*	Rita		will be writing	a letter.
	Passive	A letter	will be being	written	by Rita.
Future Perfect Simple	*Active:*	Rita		will have written	a letter.
	Passive:	A letter	will have been	written	by Rita.
Future Perfect Continuous	*Active:*	Rita		will have been writing	a letter.
	Passive:	A letter	will have been being	written	by Rita.

20.2.3 Special Passives

In this section, we'll look at some special cases related to forming the *passive voice*.

A. **Two Objects**

- We know that sometimes, a single *verb* can take two *objects*—a *direct object* and an *indirect object*. As a reminder, the *subject* acts upon the *direct object*, while the *indirect object* benefits from the action.

- In this case, either one can become the **new subject** when converting the *active voice* to the *passive voice*. In other words, there are at least two *passive* forms that any such sentence can take. However, in many cases, taking the *indirect object* as the **new subject** is more natural than taking the *direct object*. Compare the examples below.

- **Examples:**

  I. *Active*: **He gave *me the book*.**

  II. *Passive*, Version 1 (*new subject = indirect object*):
  ***I* was given *the book* (by him).**

  III. *Passive*, Version 2 (*new subject = direct object*):
  ***The book* was given to *me* (by him).**

B. **Passive + 'To'-infinitive**

- When used in the *passive voice*, some *verbs* are frequently followed by a *'to'-infinitive*.

- **Examples:**

  I. **John *has been asked* to make a speech at the meeting.**

  II. **You *are supposed* to wear a uniform.**

  III. **The meeting *is scheduled* to start at seven.**

C. **Impersonal Passives**

- We said that the *original object* in the *active voice* becomes the *new subject* in the *passive voice*. If you think about this in reverse, this means that, <u>usually, only *transitive verbs* can be changed into the *passive* form</u>.

- But, there's still a way that we can speak in the *passive voice* using an *intransitive verb*. So, we know that *intransitive verbs* don't take an *object*. This means that when you try to form the *passive voice*, there's no *subject* to use. What do you think we can do then? Well, we can use a *dummy subject*.

- <u>With an *intransitive verb*, you can form the *impersonal passive* by using the *dummy subject*,</u> <u>"it."</u>

  I. *Active*: They *say* that women live longer than men.

  II. *Impersonal Passive*: <u>It</u> is *said* that women live longer than men.

- However, <u>when the *intransitive verb* takes a *subordinate clause*, the **subject of the** **subordinate clause** can be used to form the *personal passive* as well.</u>

  I. *Active*: They *say* that <u>women</u> live longer than men.

  II. *Personal Passive*: <u>Women</u> are *said* to live longer than men.

D. **Passives in Clauses**

- <u>Individual clauses (rather than entire sentences) in the *active voice* can also be changed into the</u> <u>*passive voice*</u>. The method is similar, except you change only the *subject* and the *object* of the clause, and you leave everything else alone.

- **Examples**:

  I. *Active*: He knew that *people* had built *the church* in 1915.

  II. *Passive*: He knew that *the church* had been built in 1915.

E. **Infinitives and Gerunds of Passives**

- Just like *active voice verbs*, <u>*passive voice verbs* can also be changed into the *'to'-infinitive* or</u> <u>the *gerund*. You use "**to be**" to form the *passive 'to'-infinitive*</u>, while <u>you use "**being**" to form the</u> <u>*passive gerund*</u>.

- **Examples**:

  I. *Passive infinitive*: She would like <u>to be</u> *promoted*.

  II. *Passive gerund*: The child loves <u>being</u> *cuddled*.

How to Form the Passive Exercises

✓ **Rewrite the following sentences in the passive voice; include the subject.**

1) The Beatles wrote "Hey Jude".
2) My father has been building this house for two years.
3) Chester is painting his fence.
4) The hunter had killed the lion already when he realized that it was off-season.

✓ **Rewrite the following sentences in the passive voice; drop the subject.**

1) The city disposes of waste materials in a variety of ways.
2) Someone has cleaned the windows.
3) Someone was serving lunch.
4) Someone will lock the doors at ten o'clock.

20.3 When to Use the Passive

20.3.1 The General Uses

We've already briefly talked about general uses of the *passive voice*. Principally, we use the *passive voice* to place the focus on the action (i.e., the *verb*) and/or its recipient (i.e., the *object*). Consider the following situation.

1. <u>*Active Voice*</u>: **George *offered* Philip the chance to take on a new role with the committee.**

2. <u>*Passive Voice*</u>: **Philip *was offered* the chance to take on a new role with the committee.**

In #1, what's important is that **George** offered something to Philip. In contrast, in #2, what's important is that **Philip was offered the role**. Depending on which information you want to emphasize, you pick either the *active voice* or the *passive voice*. If you want to highlight that George specifically asked Philip, then you'd use the *active voice*. However, if you want to focus on the fact that Philip was offered the role (that George offered it to him is not important here), then, you'd use the *passive voice*.

Next, another general use of the *passive voice* is when the *subject* is less important than the *object*. When you place the focus on the *object*, it naturally diminishes the significance of the *subject*. We can use this feature of the *passive voice* when the *subject* is unnecessary and we want to remove it completely from the sentence. The following are situations wherein the *subject* is better left out, and, hence, the *passive voice* is better to use.

1. **Unknown Subject**
   We use the *passive voice* when the *subject* is unknown. In such cases, you need to add a <u>placeholder</u> *subject* like "**someone**" or "**they**" when you use the *active voice*. The sentence usually sounds much better in the *passive voice*, as you <u>don't need</u> a placeholder for the *subject*.

   ● *Passive Voice*: **My bike has been stolen.**
     (*Active Voice*: *Someone* stole my bike.)

2. **Unimportant Subject**
   We use the *passive voice* when the *subject* is not important. In these cases, if the sentence or clause

is written in the **active voice**, the **subject** just <u>gets in the way</u> and makes the sentence <u>unnecessarily long</u>. As such, it's better to use the **passive voice** to remove the **subject**.

- *Passive Voice*: **The road is being repaired.**
  (*Active Voice*: *The construction workers* are repairing the road.)

3. **Obvious Subject**

   <u>We use the **passive voice**</u> when the **subject** is obvious. It can seem <u>redundant</u> if the **subject** is stated when you can guess it easily. Accordingly, it's better to use the **passive voice** in these cases.

   - *Passive Voice*: **The criminal was arrested.**
     (*Active Voice*: *The police* arrested the criminal.)

4. **General Subject**

   <u>We use the **passive voice**</u> when the **subject** is the general public. Just like in case #1, the **subject** in this situation is merely a <u>placeholder</u>; it holds <u>no value</u> and <u>no meaning</u>. It's better to remove the **subject** by using the **passive voice**.

   - *Passive Voice*: **The ticket can be purchased from the website.**
     (*Active Voice*: *People* can buy the ticket from the website.)

20.3.2 The Specific Uses

Now, here are some specific cases wherein you'd use the **passive voice**. Try to keep the general uses above in mind as you go through each of the following. Each of these specific uses result from the general uses.

1. **Reports of crimes & incidents**

   - The <u>incident</u> (i.e., the **direct object**), the <u>victim</u> (i.e., the **indirect object**), and <u>damage caused</u> (i.e., the **verb**) are important points. Also, the <u>perpetrator</u> (i.e., the **subject**) is often <u>unknown</u>.

   - **Examples:**

     I. **The buildings *were destroyed* by fire.**

     II. **The car *was stolen* yesterday (~~by someone~~).**

2. **Scientific contexts**

   - The person who performs the action (i.e., the **subject**) is <u>irrelevant</u> or <u>obvious</u>.

   - **Examples:**

     I. **The rat *was placed* in a T-shaped maze (~~by the scientists~~).**

     II. **The drug *was administered* to the test subjects (~~by the scientists~~).**

3. **Formal writings**

   - In formal writing, you should avoid using <u>idle placeholder</u> words like "someone," "we," "people," and "they."

   - **Examples:**

     I. **The brochure *will be finished* next month (~~by us~~).**

     II. **The project *will have been completed* by the end of next week (~~by us~~).**

4. **To place new information at the end of a sentence/clause**

- When a <u>new piece of information</u> appears <u>before</u> an <u>already-mentioned piece of information</u>, it can feel very <u>abrupt</u> and <u>distracting</u>.

- **Example:**

  I. **Three books are used in this class. <u>Dr. Bell</u> *wrote* the books.** → *Bad!*

  II. **Three books are used in this class. The books *were written* by <u>Dr. Bell</u>.** → *Good!*

5. **Very long subjects**

- When the ***subject*** is too long, the reader can get <u>lost</u> and/or <u>exhausted</u> while reading the ***subject*** and <u>not be able to understand</u> the sentence.

- **Example:**

  I. **<u>How well the students did on the test</u> *surprised* me.** → *Bad!*

  II. **I *was surprised* by <u>how well the students did on the test</u>.** → *Good!*

6. **Shift the blame**

- When you <u>don't want to blame anyone</u> for an event, or when <u>you don't want to take responsibility</u> for what you've done, you can use the ***passive voice*** to <u>shift or deflect the blame</u>.

- **Example:**

  I. **Mistakes *were* made.** (→ <u>*You* probably made the mistake, but you don't want to own up to it.)</u>

7. **Passive aggressiveness**

- A <u>literary use</u> of the ***passive voice*** is to <u>politely poke fun</u> at someone. Note that we <u>usually don't use</u> the ***passive voice*** in literature (i.e., books, poetry, etc.).

- **Example** from *Sense and Sensibility* by Jane Austen:

  I. **<u>Passive voice (from the book)</u>: "… Though [Mr. Middleton]'s entreaties *were carried* to a point of perseverance beyond civility, they could not give offense."**

  II. **<u>Transformed to the active voice</u>: Though Mr. Middleton *carried* his entreaties to a point of perseverance beyond civility, they could not give offense.**

- Notice how version II sounds less sincere than version I. By writing the sentence in the ***passive voice***, Austen expressed the harsh idea in a more polite way. Such contradictions make the book even more enjoyable.

20.3.3 So, It's a Good Thing, right?

Not usually. <u>Using the ***passive voice*** is, in fact, generally discouraged</u>. This is because expressions in the ***active voice*** are often more <u>intuitable</u>; <u>expressions in the ***passive voice*** can be confusing</u>. Furthermore, <u>expressions in the ***passive voice*** are usually longer</u> than those in the ***active voice***. This is obvious, because you need to add extra words (i.e., ***auxiliary verbs***) in order to form the ***passive voice***. As I said previously, the shorter your writing is, the better.

The most extreme case for the *passive voice* ruining your writing involves short *prepositional phrases*. Consider the following situation.

1. *Active voice*: I have *prepared* breakfast <u>for us</u>.

2. *Passive voice*: Breakfast *has been prepared* <u>for us by me</u>.

Sentence #1 in the *active voice* already includes a short *prepositional phrase*, i.e., "for us." You know that applying the *passive voice* to the sentence will create a new short *prepositional phrase*, i.e., "by [subject]." Hence, the *passive voice* in #2 has <u>two short, back-to-back *prepositional phrases*</u>, i.e., "for us by me." This kind of writing is very awkward and should be avoided. In addition, even if you didn't include "by me" in #2, the *passive voice* would still make the sentence unnecessarily complicated.

As such, it's not actually a good idea to use the *passive voice* everywhere. However, in some cases, the *passive voice* fits the sentence leagues better than the *active voice*, including the seven specific cases I described above. Nevertheless, always remember to <u>use the *passive voice* only when you really need to</u>.

When to Use the Passive Exercises 01

✓ **Between the active (A) and passive (P) voice, pick the more natural one.**

1) **A**: Someone broke into our house last night.
   P: Our house was broken into last night (by someone).
2) **A**: I am studying astrophysics.
   P: Astrophysics is being studied (by me).
3) **A**: The workers will have prepared the pamphlets by Sunday.
   P: The pamphlets will have been prepared (by the workers) by Sunday.
4) **A**: They have now removed the roadblock on 5th Avenue.
   P: The roadblock on 5th Avenue has been removed (by them).
5) **A**: I met Jane, my old friend, at the mall yesterday.
   P: Jane, my old friend, was met (by me) at the mall yesterday.

When to Use the Passive Exercises 02

✓ **The following sentences are all in the active voice. Rewrite the ones that you think the passive voice would fit better.**

1) Many people around the world speak English.
2) The judge has sentenced the criminal to six years in prison.
3) The train had left before we arrived at the station.
4) The scientists administered the rats with small doses of the test drug.
5) I bought this shirt yesterday at the thrift shop.
6) The fire engulfed the building.

20.4 Outlook on The Passive Voice

In English writing and speaking, the *passive voice* is an extremely powerful tool that can completely change the focus of your clause or sentence. When you wish to highlight the **object** or the **verb**, it's a lot more effective and direct to use the *passive voice* than the **active voice**. And as you saw in *Section 20.3.2*, there are actually many situations where the *passive voice* is a way better fit. Coming from a science background myself, I'm actually more comfortable writing in the *passive*.

However, the *passive voice* is generally not the best choice. If you aren't sure which voice to use, go with the *active voice*. The *active voice* is almost always more straightforward and easier to understand than the *passive voice*. Using the *passive voice* just to be fancy can lower your grades. Hence, always remember: only use the *passive voice* when you need it.

*If we encounter a man of rare intellect,
we should ask him what books he reads.*

- Ralph Waldo Emerson (1803- 1882) -

CHAPTER 21

Conditionals

a conditional sentence usually begins with "if" and expresses something that must be true or that must happen before something else can be true or happen

21.1 Introduction

21.1.1 Here Comes a New Challenger!

Near the very start of this book (*Chapter 3*), we handled the four basic **types of sentences** in English. Let's revisit the table I used in that chapter. Now take a good look at the four basic **types of sentences** and their functions.

Types of Sentences	Purpose & Punctuation	Example
Declarative Sentence	To state something Ends with a **period** (".")	I have a blue dress.
Interrogative Sentence	To ask something Ends with a **question mark** ("?")	When are we eating?
Imperative Sentence	To give an order Ends with a **period** (".")	Clean your room.
Exclamatory Sentence	To show strong feeling End with an **exclamation point** ("!")	The dog has fleas!

The **conditional sentence** is an advanced **type of sentence** in English. And just like the four basic types described above, **conditionals** have a particular purpose and accept only one type of **punctuation**, which is the **period** ("."). The purpose or function of **conditionals** is to present guesses, postulations, or hypotheses. So, we now can add the following extra row to our table of sentence types.

Types of Sentences	Purpose & Punctuation	Example
Conditional Sentence	To present a guess, postulation, or hypothesis. Ends with a **period** (".")	If you heat water to 100 °C, it boils.

21.1.2 "If" & the Structure of Conditionals

Characteristically, *conditionals* often feature the word "if." "If" is the opener; it's placed directly before a given *condition* (i.e., a hypothetical situation). In a *conditional sentence*, the given *condition* is followed by its possible *result*. All *conditionals* take the following structure.

- *Conditional sentence*: *[condition]* → *[result]*

The *[condition]* part contains "**if**." You can use "**when**" instead, but "**when**" is less common than "**if**." Furthermore, as you'll see, in terms of order, the *[condition]* and the *[result]* can be swapped. We'll talk more about these things later.

21.1.3 Five Types of Conditionals

There are five main types of *conditionals* in English. They are distinguished based on the following two factors.

    A. The respective time sense of the *[condition]* and the *[result]*.

        (※ They do not have to be in the same time period.)

    B. Whether the *[condition]* is likely/true or unlikely/false.

The following table summarizes five main types of *conditionals* in English.

Name	Uses Time Sense: *[condition]* → *[result]*		Example
Zero conditional	Truths, facts, habits.		If you heat water to 100 °C, it boils.
	present → future		
First conditional	To describe a realistic future circumstance.		If he needs help, he will call.
	likely present → future result		
Second conditional	To describe an unrealistic future circumstance.		If I had more time, I would exercise more.
	unlikely present → unlikely future		
Third conditional	To show regret about the past.		If we had left earlier, we would have arrived on time.
	unreal far past → unreal near past		
Mixed conditional	To describe an alternate present.		If you had studied harder, you'd be at a higher level now.
	unreal past → unreal present		

21.2 The Zero Conditional

The *zero conditional* is used to handle permanent truths, scientific facts, and general habits. A *zero conditional* sentence simply states that if you perform a certain act, a certain result will occur. The following are all *zero conditionals*.

1.   **If you eat a lot, you put on weight.** → *permanent truth*

2.   **If you heat water to 100 °C, it boils.** → *scientific fact*

3.   **When I'm tired, I go to bed early.** → *general habit*

In terms of time sense, the *[condition]* is in the *present*, while the *[result]* is in the *future*. However, note that the *tenses* for the *zero conditional* do not match the time sense exactly—you use the *present simple* for both parts. Hence, we can express the *zero conditional* form as follows.

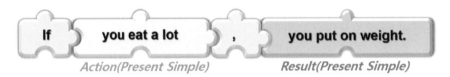

If | you eat a lot | , | you put on weight.

Action(Present Simple) | *Result(Present Simple)*

Next, in terms of the likelihood of the events in a *zero conditional* sentence, the *[condition]* involves a 50% possibility—you either take the action or you do not. The *[condition]* presented in a *zero conditional* is usually not a particularly difficult act to perform. The *[result]* involves a 100% possibility—if you satisfy the *[condition]*, the *[result]* will surely happen.

I summarize the *zero conditional* in the following table.

The Zero Conditional		
Uses	Permanent truths, scientific facts, & general habits	
Parts	*[Condition]*	*[Result]*
Time Sense	*present*	*future*
Possibility	50%	100%
Form/Tense	If + *[present simple]*	*[present simple]*

Basic Conditionals Exercises
(Watch your tenses!)

   ✓   **Convert each set of cause & result into a zero conditional sentence.**

1)   You heat ice. → Ice melts.
2)   I drink too much coffee. → I can't sleep at night.
3)   It rains. → The grass gets wet.
4)   Babies are hungry. → They cry.

The ***first conditional*** is used to explain the ***future*** result of an activity that can happen in the ***present***. In other words, the *[condition]* refers to a fairly likely ***present*** situation. The following are both ***first conditionals***.

1. **If it rains, I won't go to the park.**

2. **If you don't hurry, you will miss the train.**

Here, the *[condition]* is in the ***present***, while the *[result]* is in the ***future***. This time, the **tenses** are in line with the actual time sense—you use the ***present simple*** for the *[condition]* and the ***future simple*** for the *[result]*. Recall that there are two ways to express the ***future***: "**will**" and "**be going to**"; you can use either expression. Hence, we can express the form of the ***first conditional*** as follows.

We can also replace the ***future simple*** with the ***auxiliary verbs*** "**can**" and "**must**." "**Can**" presents an <u>offer</u> involving the ***future***, while "**must**" presents an <u>obligation</u> involving the ***future***. Consider the following sentences.

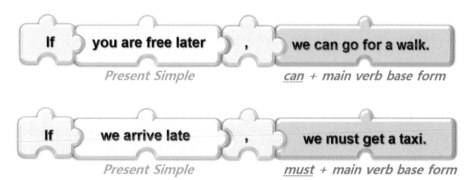

With regards to the likelihood of the events in a ***first conditional*** sentence, the *[condition]*, again, represents a 50% possibility—<u>it's not a difficult requirement to satisfy</u>. Even when you don't have the choice of setting up such a situation, the *[condition]* has a fair possibility of being satisfied. The *[result]* involves a 100% possibility as it's going to happen no matter what, that is, as long as the *[condition]* is satisfied.

I summarize the ***first conditional*** in the following table.

The First Conditional		
Uses	To explain the future result of an activity that <u>can/is likely to</u> happen in the present.	
Parts	*[Condition]*	*[Result]*
Time Sense	*present*	*future*
Possibility	50%	100%
Form/Tense	If + *[present simple]*	*[future simple]* or *[can/must + main verb base form]*

> **Basic Conditionals Exercises**
> *(Watch your tenses!)*
>
> ✓   **Convert each set of cause & result into a first conditional sentence.**
>
> 1) The train is delayed. → She is late.
> 2) She doesn't leave soon. → She misses the bus.
> 3) It doesn't rain tomorrow. → We go to the beach.
> 4) I have enough money. → I buy some new clothes.

21.4   The Second Conditional

The **_second conditional_** (a.k.a. the **_subjunctive past_**) is used to explain the **_future_** result of an activity that won't happen in the **_present_**, i.e., an activity that is unlikely to happen in the **_present_**. In other words, the _[condition]_ handles a situation that has almost no chance of occurring. The following are both **_second conditionals_**.

1.   **If I won the lottery, I would buy a big house.**

2.   **If I had his number, I would call him.**

Your chances of winning the lottery are slim to none, close to 0%, so it's natural to use the **_second conditional_** form here. On the other hand, the very fact that #2 is presented in the **_second conditional_** form indicates that you don't have his number (i.e., there's an absolutely 0% chance that you have his number now).

The time sense for **_second conditional_** sentences is exactly the same as for **_first conditional_** sentences—the _[condition]_ is in the **_present_**, while the _[result]_ is in the **_future_**. However, do note the use of **_tenses_** is completely messed up (i.e., contrary to the literal)—this is because we're signaling that the _[condition]_ is very unlikely to be satisfied. We use the **_past simple_** for the _[condition]_, while we use the **_auxiliary verb_** "**would**" for the _[result]_. Hence, we can express the **_second conditional_** in the following form.

| **If** | **I won the lottery** | **,** | **I would buy a big house.** |

Past Simple   *would + main verb base form*

Note that we can replace "**would**" with "**could**" or "**might**." "**Could**" signals that the challenging _[condition]_ is preventing the **subject** from performing the activity described in the _[result]_; the **subject** wishes to carry out the _[result]_, but the difficult _[condition]_ is stopping them from doing so. On the other hand, "**might**" signifies that even if the _[condition]_ is met, there's a chance the **subject** would not perform the activity noted in the _[result]_; the _[result]_ provides an option the **subject** can take, rather than a set plan.

| **If** | **he didn't have to work late** | **,** | **he could go out with his girlfriend.** |

Past Simple   *could + main verb base form*

If | I saved enough money | , | I might buy a new car.

Past Simple   *might* + *main verb base form*

We can add "**ever**" before the *past simple* to make the *[condition]* feel extra impossible. Consider the following.

3. If I <u>ever</u> *met* the Queen of England, I *would shake* her hand.
("If" + "ever" + [past simple] + ["would" + main verb infinitive].)

So, here's an interesting thing about *second conditionals*: <u>whenever the *[condition]* part includes a *'be'-verb*, we use "**were**" for all **subjects**</u>—even when it could be considered grammatically incorrect! When you intentionally use unusual grammar in the *[condition]* part, it highlights that the *[condition]* is difficult to meet. Consider the following sentence.

4. If <u>I *were*</u> rich, I *would spend* all my time travelling.
("If" + ["were"] + ["would" + main verb base form].)

Related to this, a very common expression in the *second conditional* is: "**If I were you …**".

5. If I *were* <u>you</u>, I *would ask* your teacher for help.
("If I were you" + ["would" + main verb base form].)

In terms of the likelihood, there is a 0-5% possibility that the *[condition]* will be met—<u>the *second conditional* handles requirements that are either difficult or impossible to be met</u>. However, the *[result]* still involves a 100% possibility—except when clearly impossible situations are involved; if the difficult *[condition]* is met, the *[result]* will surely occur. Nevertheless, the point of *second conditionals* is that <u>the *[condition]* can almost never be satisfied</u>.

I summarize the *second conditional* in the following table.

The Second Conditional		
Uses	To explain the future result of an activity that <u>won't/is unlikely to</u> happen in the present.	
Parts	*[Condition]*	*[Result]*
Time Sense	*present*	*future*
Possibility	0-5%	100%
Form/Tense	*If + [past simple*]* *(* "were" if 'be'-verb)*	*would/could/might + [main verb base form]*

<u>**Basic Conditionals Exercises**</u>
(Watch your <u>tenses!</u>)

✓ **Convert each set of cause & result into a second conditional sentence.**

1) She study. → She passes the exam.
2) I speak Italian. → I am working in Italy.
3) You go to bed early. → You are not tired.
4) I am you. → I don't worry.

The ***third conditional*** (a.k.a. the ***subjunctive past perfect***) is used to express a regret about a ***near past*** event by providing an alternative situation that should have happened in the ***far past***. In other words, the ***[condition]*** presents an alternate ***far past*** that would have led to the ***[result]***, i.e., an alternate ***nearer past*** result that should have happened instead of the actual result. The following are both ***third conditionals***.

1. **If we had left earlier, we would have arrived on time.**

2. **If you hadn't forgotten about her birthday, she wouldn't have been so upset.**

The use of ***third conditional*** form tells us that neither of the events above actually happened. For example, in #2, the reality is: you forgot her birthday, and because of that she got upset. However, if you hadn't forgotten it, then she wouldn't have been mad.

In terms of time sense, ***third conditional*** sentences stay within the limits of the ***past***; such sentences never reach the ***present*** or the ***future***. As mentioned above, the ***[condition]*** is in the ***far past***, while the ***[result]*** is in the ***near past***. As with the ***second conditional***, the ***tenses*** are all messed up—the ***[condition]*** part takes the ***past perfect***, while the ***[result]*** takes the following expression: "**would have + [main verb past participle].**" Hence, we can express the form of the ***third conditional*** as follows.

Here as well, we can replace "**would**" with "**could**" or "**might.**" "**Could**" suggests a missed opportunity for improvement. On the other hand, "**might**" suggest an option you could have selected under the alternative ***past [condition]***. Consider the following sentences.

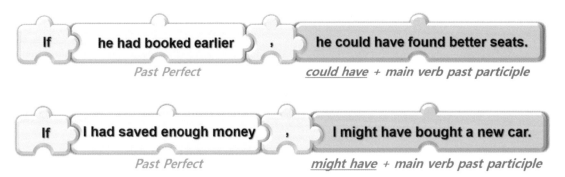

In terms of the likelihood, there is an absolute 0% possibility that the ***[condition]*** will occur—it's an alternative ***past***; you can't go back in time and meet the alternative ***[condition]***. However, here again, the ***[result]*** is 100% possible—the alternative ***near past*** would have been reality if you had satisfied the alternative ***[condition]*** in the ***far past***.

I summarize the **third conditional** in the following table.

The Third Conditional		
Uses	To express <u>regret about the near past</u> by presenting an <u>alternative far past</u>.	
Parts	*[Condition]*	*[Result]*
Time Sense	*far past*	*near past*
Possibility	0%	100%
Form/Tense	If + *[past perfect]*	*would/could/might + have + [main verb past participle]*

Basic Conditionals Exercises
(Watch your <u>tenses!</u>)

   ✓   **Convert each set of cause & result into a third conditional sentence.**

1) I don't eat so much. → I don't feel sick.
2) We take a taxi. → We don't miss the plane.
3) She goes to a university. → She becomes a teacher.
4) He leaves his house at nine. → He is on time for the interview.

21.6 The Mixed Conditional

The **mixed conditional** <u>is used to suggest an alternative **present** by proposing an alternative **past**</u>. In other words, the *[condition]* presents an alternative **past** that would have led to the *[result]* in the **present**. This form is called the **mixed conditional** because it's like a mash up of the **second** and the **third conditional** forms—the **second conditional** involves an unrealistic **present**, while the **third conditional** involves an alternate **past**. The following are both **mixed conditionals**.

1. **If we hadn't missed the plane, we would be lying on the beach right now.**

2. **If they hadn't lost so many matches, they would have much more confidence.**

The grammatical technicalities related to the **mixed conditional** also show the mixing of the **second** and the **third conditionals**. The *[condition]* is in the **past** (like the **third conditional**), while the *[result]* is in the **present** (like the **second conditional**). Furthermore, <u>the *[condition]* part takes the **past perfect tense**</u> (like the **third conditional**), while the *[result]* part takes "**would**" (like the **second conditional**). Hence, we can express the form of the **mixed conditional** as follows.

If)we hadn't missed the plane	,	we would be lying on the beach right now.
Past Perfect		*would + main verb base form*

Again, we can replace "**would**" with "**could**" or "**might**." "**Could**" suggests an alternate improved *present* if you had done something different in the *past*. "**Might**" offers an option that would have been available to you in the *present* if you had done something different in the *past*. Consider the following sentences.

In terms of likelihood, the *[condition]* again involves an absolute 0% possibility—you still cannot change the *past*. However, just like all other *conditionals*, the *[result]* is 100% possible—had that alternative *past* been true, then the *present* would (theoretically) exactly reflect the *[result]*.

I summarize the *mixed conditional* in the following table.

The Mixed Conditional		
Uses	To explain what could have happened in the present if the past was different (i.e., alternate past).	
Parts	*[Condition]*	*[Result]*
Time Sense	*past*	*present*
Possibility	0%	100%
Form/Tense	If + *[past perfect]*	*would/could/might + [main verb base form]*

Basic Conditionals Exercises
(Watch your tenses!)

✓   **Convert each set of cause & result into a mixed conditional sentence.**

1) We look at the map. → We are not lost.
2) I work harder at school. → I have a better job now.
3) I don't get the job in Tokyo. → I am not with my current partner.
4) You decide to study. → You are a professor now.

21.7 Swapping the Condition and the Result

By now, you know that any *conditional* sentence consists of two parts—the *[condition]* and the *[result]*. So far, in all the examples provided, we have placed the *[condition]* first and the *[result]* after it. In reality, you can place either one first.

However, a very important distinction between sentences where the *[condition]* is placed first versus where the *[result]* is placed first is whether to use a *comma* (",") in between the *[condition]* part and the *[result]* part. First, when you place the *[condition]* first, you need a *comma* after it. Consider the following examples.

1. **If you heat water to 100°C, it boils.**

2. **If I had practiced more, that song would have sounded better.**

But, if you write the *[result]* first, you do not use a *comma*. Consider the following examples.

3. **Ice forms if you chill water to 0°C**

4. **They wouldn't have hired you if you hadn't had some experience abroad.**

This is the same for all five types of *conditionals*.

Basic Conditionals Exercises
(Watch your tenses!)

✓ **Rewrite each conditional sentence by stating the result first.**

1) If you freeze water, ice forms.
2) If I go jogging, I will lose weight.
3) If I knew her number, I would call her.
4) If I had woken up on time, I would have done my hair.

21.8 Other Conditionals-Related Expressions

Here, we'll look at some leftover, bite-sized ideas about *conditionals*. These include some alternative words to "if," how to use different types of clauses, and how to add extra expressions for more specific messages.

1. **"If" vs. "When"**
   We use "**if**" when we're not sure if the *[condition]* will be met (i.e., 50%). We use "**when**" when we know for sure that the *[condition]* will be met eventually (i.e., 100%). This means that you can never use "**when**" for *second, third*, and *mixed conditionals*.

   I. **If you're unsure, ask me a question.**
      (→ *I don't know if you will be unsure, but if you are, then ask me a question.*)

   II. **You should call your parents when you get home.**
      (→ *I know you'll eventually get home later today. You should call your parents after you do.*)

2. **"Unless"**
   We can use "**unless**" for *first conditionals*. "**Unless**" = "**if… not.**"

    I.   **Unless** you study hard, you will fail your exams.
        (→ If you don't study hard, you will fail your exams.)

    II. **Unless** you get up now, you'll be late for work.
        (→ If you don't get up now, you'll be late for work.)

3. <u>Formal Third Conditional (i.e., "had")</u>
When using the ***third conditional***, instead of starting your sentence with "if," <u>you can start it with "**had**"</u> <u>(in the ***past perfect tense***) to form the formal version</u>.

    I.   *If you <u>had</u> attended the meeting, you would have met the manager.*
        → <u>Had</u> you attended the meeting, you would have met the manager.

4. <u>"What if" & "Suppose"</u>
We use **"what if"** and "**suppose**" to refer to ***<u>future</u>*** possibilities. "**What if**" can start a question, while "**suppose**" can start a sentence.

    A. When we talk about a <u>likely ***future***</u> situation, we use the ***present simple tense***.

        I.   <u>**What if**</u> I *fail* **my exams? I won't be able to go to college.**

    B. When we talk about an <u>unlikely ***future***</u> situation, we use the ***past simple tense***.

        I.   <u>**Suppose**</u> **our flight** *was canceled*. **We'd be stuck here!**

    C. When we talk about an <u>alternative ***past***</u>, we use the ***past perfect tense***.

        I.   **That was so dangerous!** <u>**What if**</u> **you** *had broken* **your leg?**

5. <u>"Wish" & "If only"</u>
We use "**wish (*verb*)**" or "**if only**" to talk about <u>wishes</u> and <u>regrets</u>.

    A. To talk about a <u>wish</u> or a <u>desire</u> in the ***present***, we use the ***past simple tense***.

        I.   **I** <u>**wish**</u> **I** *earned* **more money so I could live in a bigger house.**

        II. **These mountains are incredible!** <u>**If only**</u> **I** *knew* **how to ski.**

    B. To talk about a wish or a desire for the ***future***, we use "**would**" or "**could**."

        I.   **She** <u>**wishes**</u> **her teacher** *would give* **her less work.**

    C. To express <u>regret</u> for the ***past***, we use the ***past perfect tense***.

        I.   **I've failed my exams. I** <u>**wish**</u> **I** *had studied* **harder.**

        II. **I really wanted to take pictures.** <u>**If only**</u> **I** *had charged* **my phone.**

6. <u>"Should have" & "Ought to have"</u>
We use "**should have**" or "**ought to have**" to talk about <u>regrets</u> about the past. The ***verb*** that follows must be in its ***past participle*** form.

        I.   **This bill is so high. I** <u>**should have**</u> *used* **less electricity.**

        II. **I'm so full. I** <u>**ought to have**</u> *eaten* **less.**

7. <u>"(Just) in case"</u>
We use "**(just) in case**" with the ***present simple tense*** to talk about <u>planning for a possible ***future***</u> <u>situation</u>.

        I.   **Make sure the windows are shut** <u>**(just) in case**</u> **the cat** *tries* **to escape.**

8. **Using Imperatives**

The *[result]* part of a *zero conditional* sentence can take an *imperative* form (i.e., give an order).

I. **If you're cold, *put on a coat.***

II. **If you feel sick, *call a doctor.***

Basic Conditionals Exercises
(Watch your tenses!)

✓ **Identify the following conditionals as either zero ("0"), first ("1"), second ("2"), third ("3"), or mixed ("M")..**

1) ____ If you heat ice, it melts.
2) ____ If you'd been born a month earlier, you would be a Virgo like me.
3) ____ If you'd been wearing a coat, you might have stayed warm.
4) ____ If I had more time, I could take up karate.
5) ____ I'd call him if I had his number.
6) ____ Oil floats when you pour it onto water.
7) ____ If it snows, I'll go skiing.
8) ____ I could have been a doctor if I'd studied harder.
9) ____ If we go to Africa, we'll go on a safari.

21.9 Outlook on Conditionals

Out of all the *sentence techniques* that we've covered in this book, the *conditionals technique* is probably the most powerful. Through modification of basic sentence structures, it offers a completely new sentence structure. Being able to modify these basic sentence structures allows you to convey new sets of ideas, as you saw throughout this chapter. This is why there are more diverse uses of the *conditionals technique* compared to the other three *sentence techniques*—the *conditionals technique* can be used to state truths, facts, habits, plans, *future* predictions, hopes/wishes, regrets, and even alternate realities.

The biggest thing to watch out for when you use *conditionals* is the *tenses*. Each of the five *conditional* types is accompanied by a unique duo of *tenses* and/or *auxiliary verb(s)*. This means that if you mess up your *tenses*, you'll probably scramble the time sense and the likelihoods of the *[condition]* and the *[result]*. Be sure to pay extra attention to your word choice when you use *conditionals*.

CHAPTER 22

Prefixes and Suffixes

---

prefix: a group of letters added to the beginning of a word to change its meaning and create a new word

suffix: a letter or group of letters added to the end of a word to change its meaning and create a new word

---

22.1 Introduction to Prefixes and Suffixes   22.3 Suffixes

22.2 Prefixes

22.1 | Introduction to Prefixes and Suffixes

22.1.1 The Special Topics

Wow, we've gotten through over twenty chapters! As you can tell, the book is nearing the end. So, what have we looked at so far? We started out with an overview of the nine *parts of speech* in English, and we conceptualized phrases, clauses, and sentences. While we were looking at sentences, we also learned about the different components of a sentence, like the *subject* and the *object*, as well as the different structures and types of sentences.

Then, we continued to a detailed look at each of the nine *parts of speech*. We started with *verbs*, and the twelve *verb tenses* amounted to a hefty chunk of this book. Then, we looked at *nouns*, *pronouns*, *determiners*, *adjectives*, *adverbs*, *prepositions*, and *conjunctions*, in that order. And with that, we examined the most fundamental English word types.

Next, we covered four important *sentence techniques*: *dummy subjects*, *relative clauses*, the *passive voice*, and *conditionals*. Hopefully your memory's still fresh on these topics. You can apply those techniques when forming your sentences to make them more prolific and sophisticated.

Now, it's time to consider some *miscellaneous topics*. I've decided to save these topics for the end of the book and categorize them under "*miscellaneous*" because they do not require extensive explanation (unlike most of the other topics in the book!). This does not mean, however, that these topics are unimportant.

There are seven *miscellaneous topics* that we'll now consider: *prefixes* and *suffixes*, *punctuation*, *capitalization rules*, *contractions*, *question tags*, and *reported (indirect) quotation*. As mentioned, none of these topics bring about long, carefully unfolded stories like the other topics we've handled. However, they are all important and useful. Of the seven, *prefixes* and *suffixes* require the most explanation. Hence, we'll handle them separately in this chapter, while we'll look at all the others collectively in the next chapter.

22.1.2 Vocabulary Cheat Code

So, I've already talked to you several times about learning vocabulary being your job. But I never said it was an easy job. According to the Oxford English Dictionary, there are over 170,000 words currently in English and over 47,000 words no longer used. Does that mean you need to start with word number 1 and keep learning words until you eventually hit 170,000? Absolutely not. Not only is that horribly inefficient, but <u>once you learn about a third of the words, you'll be able to intuit many of the other two thirds</u> when you encounter them and <u>automatically add them to your head.</u>

How is that possible? To understand the concept, you first need to consider where English words come from. As I told you in the very first chapter, English has evolved through its passage through many different countries and through its use by the native speakers of many other languages. In this way, English borrows words from many different languages. On top of borrowing fully formed words, <u>English excels at borrowing **root words** from other languages to form new English words.</u>

English most frequently borrows **root words** from two languages: <u>Greek</u> and <u>Latin</u>. For example, "**pan**" is a **Greek root word** that means "**all**." It appears as a word segment at the start of many English words. Below are some examples of English words that include the **Greek root word** "pan."

1. <u>*Pan*demic (*noun*)</u>: **a disease that affects (almost) <u>all</u> people worldwide.**

2. <u>*Pan*acea (*noun*)</u>: **a solution to <u>all</u> difficulties; a cure for <u>all</u> diseases.**

3. <u>*Pan*orama (*noun*)</u>: **a view in <u>all</u> directions.**

4. <u>*Pan*theon (*noun*)</u>: **a temple of <u>all</u> gods.**

See how every word has a sense of complete inclusivity; the above definitions all include the word "**all**" because they start with the **Greek root word** "pan."

Here's another example—this one comes from <u>Latin</u>: "**ment**." It often appears as a word segment at the end of English words and is a tool for turning **verbs** into **nouns**. Below are some examples of English words that use the **Latin root word** "ment".

5. <u>Entertain*ment* (*noun*)</u>: **the act of providing or being provided with amusement or enjoyment (→ "entertain (*verb*)").**

6. <u>Amaze*ment* (*noun*)</u>: **a feeling of great surprise or wonder (→ "amaze (*verb*)").**

7. <u>State*ment* (*noun*)</u>: **something that is declared orally or in writing (→ "state (*verb*)").**

8. <u>Banish*ment* (*noun*)</u>: **being sent far away from home as a penalty for some action (→ "banish (*verb*)").**

Notice that for every **noun** above, there is a similar-looking **verb**. If you take the **verb** and attach the **Latin root word** "ment" to the end of it, you have the **noun**.

As you can see, <u>many English words include **root words** that hint at their meanings</u>. As above, the **root word** often appears at either the start or the end of the word. <u>When the **root word** appears at the start of an English word, we call it a **prefix**; when the **root word** appears at the end of an English word, we call it a **suffix**.</u>

Prefixes and **suffixes** are like a cheat code for broadening your vocabulary. That's because knowing **prefixes** and **suffixes** can allow you to gain multiple new words easily, sometimes just by learning one new word. For example, if you know that the **suffix** "-ment" turns **verbs** into **nouns**, once you learn the **verb** "entertain," you will automatically arrive at the **noun** "entertainment."

Furthermore, knowing **prefixes** and **suffixes** can allow you to decipher the meanings of new words when you encounter them. For example, if you know the meaning of the **prefix** "pan," on your first encounter with the word "**pandemic**" you will instantly notice that it means "**all**" of something. The context of the text will likely clue you that the word is related to diseases. Combining these two assumptions, you will glean that "**pandemic**" means "**a disease that affects all people**," even the first time you see it.

As such, both **prefixes** and **suffixes** are incredibly useful tools for improving and increasing your vocabulary. In the following sections, I'll provide the most commonly used **prefixes** and **suffixes** in English, along with definitions and example words.

Prefix	Meaning	Example Words
ab-	*not, away*	**ab**sent, **ab**normal, **ab**sorb
amb-/ambi-	*around, both*	**amb**ient, **ambi**guous, **ambi**dextrous
anti-	*against*	**anti**bacterial, **anti**body, **anti**biotics
co-	*together*	**co**worker, **co**pilot, **co**education
de-	*down, reverse*	**de**code, **de**crease, **de**-escalate
dis-	*not*	**dis**approve, **dis**appear, **dis**courage, **dis**able
ex-	*former*	**ex**-soldier, **ex**-boyfriend/girlfriend, **ex**-wife/husband
ex-	*out of, away from*	**ex**hale, **ex**plosion, **ex**clude, **ex**it
im-/in-/ir-	*not*	**im**possible, **ir**resistible, **in**correct, **ir**regular
inter-	*(implies) between*	**inter**national, **inter**rupt, **inter**cept, **inter**vene
mid-	*middle*	**mid**-sentence, **mid**-September, **mid**-1900s
mis-	*wrongly*	**mis**judge, **mis**understand, **mis**interpret
non-	*not*	**non**sense, **non**existent, **non**fiction
out-	*better*	**out**performing, **out**standing, **out**class
over-	*too much*	**over**work, **over**heat, **over**react, **over**cook
post-	*after*	**post**mortem, **post**-dated, **post**war
pre-	*before*	**pre**arrange, **pre**pare, **pre**cook
pro-	*for, forward*	**pro**active, **pro**cess, **pro**gram
re-	*again*	**re**gain, **re**assure, **re**apply, **re**grow
self-	*oneself*	**self**-confident, **self**ish, **self**-respect, **self**-cleaning
sub-	*under, smaller*	**sub**standard, **sub**set, **sub**marine, **sub**atomic
super-/sur-	*above, over*	**sur**charge, **super**sonic, **super**hero, **super**lative
un-	*reverse, not*	**un**lock, **un**chained, **un**able, **un**happy
under-	*beneath, below*	**under**charge, **under**cook, **under**-nourished

Suffix	Meaning	Example Words
-able/-ible	*possible*	accept**able**, enjoy**able**, convert**ible**, vis**ible**
-al/-ial	*characterized by or related to*	circumstant**ial**, aer**ial**, den**ial**, natur**al**
-ance/-ence	*of a state*	domin**ance**, brilli**ance**, depend**ence**, abs**ence**
-ate	*become*	activ**ate**, fortun**ate**, insul**ate**
-dom	*place or state*	free**dom**, king**dom**, star**dom**
-en	*become*	wid**en**, strength**en**, bright**en**, wood**en**
-er/-or	*person that takes a certain type of action*	writ**er**, perform**er**, act**or**, visit**or**
-ful	*full of, containing*	use**ful**, success**ful**, grate**ful**, pain**ful**
-graph	*write*	para**graph**, calli**graphy**, auto**graph**
-ic/-tic/-ical	*of character*	phys**ical**, dynam**ic**, scientif**ic**, domes**tic**
-ism	*action, state, system*	surreal**ism**, optim**ism**, ideal**ism**, commun**ism**
-ist/-ian	*person that takes a certain type of action*	pian**ist**, violin**ist**, electric**ian**, technic**ian**
-ity/-ty	*of quality*	equal**ity**, univers**ity**, secur**ity**, safe**ty**
-ize	*make*	maxim**ize**, minim**ize**, steril**ize**, fossil**ize**
-ject	*throw, away from*	e**ject**, re**ject**, inter**ject**
-less	*without*	limit**less**, power**less**, relent**less**, tire**less**
-ment	*condition, product (primarily used to turn a verb into a noun)*	invest**ment**, refresh**ment**, orna**ment**
-ness	*of a certain state*	fit**ness**, weak**ness**, ill**ness**, dark**ness**
-ous	*of quality*	venom**ous**, fam**ous**, seri**ous**, religi**ous**
-sion, -tion	*of state, act*	conclu**sion**, func**tion**, deci**sion**, addi**tion**
-y	*characterized by*	cloud**y**, sunn**y**, mess**y**, victor**y**

The Usual Suspects

23.1 Introduction

In this chapter, we'll handle some simple yet important topics in English grammar. While they are all crucial pieces of grammar, none are terribly complex; there won't be much to say about any of them. Hence, I'll only briefly introduce these topics and then summarize the rules that apply to them in tables and figures.

23.2 Capitalization Rules

The first of the usual suspects are the **capitalization rules**. In English, there are few cases where the first letter of a word is **capitalized**. It can depend on <u>where the word appears within the sentence</u> or <u>what kind of word is involved</u>. Recall that we touched on this very briefly in *Chapter 10*—I mentioned that the first letter of all **proper nouns** (i.e., <u>names</u> of a particular person, animal, or place) must be **capitalized**. Other than **proper nouns**, there are a few more situations wherein you must **capitalize** a word. The table below summarizes the rules accordingly.

● the first letter of the first word in a sentence			
	The dog jumped up when the man whistled. **L**et's go home before it rains. **W**hat sports do you like best?		

● the pronoun 'I' is always capitalized			
	I stayed here for five days. **I**'ll wait here till she comes. **I** was so hungry that **I** could not walk.		

● names of people			
e.g.	Bill Gates	Mark Twain	Huckleberry Finn	Pinocchio
	Snow White	Harry Potter	Albert Einstein	Pablo Picasso
	My favorite author is **Mark Twain**.			

- names of places: continents, countries, cities, and states/provinces

Asia	Europe	South America	Australia
Canada	Egypt	Germany	South Korea
Ottawa	Cairo	Frankfurt	Seoul
Wisconsin	California	New Jersey	Hawaii

The capital of **Australia** is **Canberra**.

1. He lives in the city.
2. He lives in **New York City**.

In the first sentence, the word "city" is used as a common noun. Therefore, it is not capitalized. However, in the second sentence, "city" is part of the name "New York City." Therefore, it must be capitalized.

- names of places: oceans, beaches, lakes, rivers, desserts, mountains, and mountain ranges

The **Pacific Ocean** is the largest and deepest ocean on **Earth**.
Are there alligators in **Lake Michigan**?
The **Nile River** is the longest river in the world.
The **Sahara** is the world's most famous desert.
What countries are the **Alps** mountains in?

- names of places: schools, businesses

I go to the **Columbia University**
How can I go to **Seoul National University**?
I work for **Amazon**.
Why did Bill Gates create **Microsoft**?

1. I go to a university.
2. I go to the **University of Toronto**.

In the first sentence, the word "university" is used as a common noun. Therefore, it is not capitalized. However, in the second sentence, "university" is part of the name "University of Toronto." Therefore, it must be capitalized.

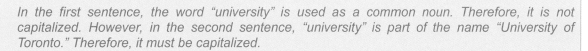

- names of places: streets, parks, and zoos

What is **Park Avenue** famous for?
He lives on **Broad Street**.
What hotels are near **Washington Square Park**?
Taronga Zoo located in **Sydney**, **New South Wales,** is **Australia**'s largest zoo.

1. They went to a park.
2. They went to **Central Park.**

In the first sentence, the word "park" is used as a common noun. Therefore, it is not capitalized. However, in the second sentence, "park" is part of the name "Central Park." Therefore, it must be capitalized.

- names of buildings, monuments, bridges, harbors, and tunnels

e.g.	The White House	Empire State Building	Eiffel Tower
	Statue of Liberty	Golden Gate Bridge	Lincoln Tunnel

The **Statue of Liberty** is a colossal neoclassical sculpture on **Liberty Island** in **New York Harbor** within **New York City**, in the **United States**.

- names of festivals, holidays, days of the week, and months of the year

e.g.	Mother's Day	Memorial Day	April Fool's Day	Thanksgiving Day
	St. Patrick's Day	New Year's Day	Boxing Day	Independence Day
	Halloween	Easter	Christmas	Valentine's Day
	Sunday	Wednesday	February	September

Wednesday is the day of the week before **Tuesday** and after **Thursday**.
Thanksgiving Day in the **United States** is a holiday that falls on the fourth **Thursday** of **November**.

> ⚠ ➢ **seasons**: spring, summer, fall/autumn and winter
> *The four seasons are not capitalized.*

- names of languages and nationalities

e.g.	I am from **South Korea**. I am **South Korean**. I speak **Korean**	I am from the **USA**. I am from **America**. I am **American**. I speak **English**.	I am from **Australia**. I am **Australian**. I speak **English**.

- names of religions

e.g.	Christianity	Islam	Hinduism	Buddhism	Judaism

- titles of books, movies, magazines, newspapers, articles, songs and plays

e.g.	*A Tale of Two Cities*	*Howl's Moving Castle*
	The Washington Post	*The New York Times*
	Les Misérables	*The Barber of Seville*

A *punctuation mark* is a special symbol that we use in a sentence, like the *comma* ("**,**"), the *period* ("**.**"), and the *question mark* ("**?**"). Each one holds a particular meaning and several functions. Sometimes, a *punctuation mark* is part of an established grammatical expression, for example the *comma* and the *apostrophe* ("**'**"). In such cases, it'd be absolutely incorrect to omit them. In other *punctuation* news, you can sometimes express complicated ideas with just a *punctuation mark*. The *semicolon* ("**;**") and the *em dash* "**—**" are often used for that purpose. The *semicolon* and the *em dash* both allow you to, among other things, combine two sentences into one.

In this chapter, I've only listed the major functions of each *punctuation mark*. Some hold many additional functions.

Full stop/ Period (.)	used at the end of declarative and imperative sentences	
	e.g.	This book is very interesting. They all enjoyed playing baseball. Please don't be late. Read a lot to improve your writing skills.
	used to mark abbreviations	
	e.g.	Let's find an A.T.M. so I can withdraw some cash. Dr. Smith will tell us about dental health care.
Comma (,)	used to join items in a list	
	e.g.	I bought two apples, three oranges, and some grapes. He enjoys tennis, badminton, skating, and football. At school we study English, math, science, history, and geography.
	used to join coordinate adjectives (see *Chapter 14*)	
	e.g.	A giraffe is a tall, long-necked, long-legged animal. He is a tall, handsome, smart, and ambitious young man.
	used to set off "yes" and "no," the name of a person you are speaking to, and sometimes "please"	
	e.g.	No, it has stopped. Good morning, sir! Can you tell me what time it is, please? Yes, it's a quarter past three, George. Hey, Lily, how are you.
Exclamation Point (!)	used after a command, an interjection; used to express strong emotions (e.g., surprise, anger)	
	e.g.	What a surprise! You are fired! I told you not to do that! I can't believe I got into law school!

Question Mark **(?)**	used at the end of a question
	e.g. How many stamps do you have? Who took my pen? Can you lend me your bicycle? Do you know the answer to this problem?
Apostrophe **(')**	used to show possession: - ('s) added after singular nouns or names - for plural nouns that end in -s, put the apostrophe after the -s - for plural nouns that do not end in -s, ('s) is added to the word just like with singular nouns
	e.g. John's dog is very friendly. Jane is wearing her mother's shoes. There is a bird's nest in that tree.
	Birds' beaks come in all different shapes and sizes. Henry goes to a boys' school. Dr. Kim parked his car in the doctors' parking lot at the hospital. My brothers' bedrooms are always messy.
	There are slides, swings, and seesaws in the children's playground. The bookstore sells newspapers, comics, and women's magazines.
	used to show that one or more letters in a contraction have been left out

e.g.	I have – I've	I have not – I haven't
	We will – We'll	We will not – We won't
	He does not → he doesn't	They are not – They aren't

*The **contractions** table is located below, in **Section 23.4**.*

Quotation **Marks** **(" ")**	used before and after direct speech and quoted text
	e.g. "I've been exercising lately," he said. "That's why I might look tired." "My dad told me he'd return soon," said Gabriel. "Why do you give us so much homework?" I asked my teacher.
Colon **(:)**	used to introduce the information that follows it *It signals the reader that something is coming*
	e.g. I've narrowed my choices down to two: Spaghetti Bolognese or Chicken Alfredo. The suspect had already committed three criminal acts in the past: child abuse, domestic violence, and drug possession. Here's the thing: he's honest even when he shouldn't be.
Semicolon **(;)**	used to separate two main clauses that are closely related
	e.g. Herbert Hoover was the 31st U.S. president; he led the country during the Great Depression. We made too many mistakes; we lost the game. We should go to the library; it's the only place where I can concentrate.

Slash (/)	used to show an alternative instead of using the word "or"	
	e.g.	Each contestant may begin when he/she is ready. If this flight is cancelled, you'll get a refund and/or new tickets for the next available one.
Hyphen (-)	used to join two or more words or affixes (i.e., prefixes, suffixes, and other root words) to form a compound word	
	e.g.	Do you have any caffeine-free coffee? His old-fashioned suit makes him appear older than he actually is. Stop second-guessing yourself; believe in your skills.
Dash (—)	**En dash** (i.e., short dash) used to express a numerical ranges, such as with sports scores, voting results, or connections between related people or things.	
	e.g.	I'll be in the office 8:00 AM–4:00 PM this Friday. The board voted 5–4 to accept the proposal. We will begin boarding the Denver–Chicago flight shortly.
	Em dash (i.e., long dash) used to introduce additional information about a certain part of the sentence... acts similarly to commas or parentheses "()" to set off removable clauses	
	e.g.	There are many fundamental aspects of living on one's own—cooking, cleaning, doing laundry—that many young adults are completely unprepared for. The committee—which I helped set up—will investigate spending irregularities by CEOs of charities and other not-for-profit groups.

When using English, in many situations you can shorten certain expressions. In other words, you can use the **apostrophe** ("'") to indicate omitted letters and combine the **subject** and the **verb** of the sentence into a single word. Shortening the **subject** and the **verb** in this way is referred to as **contracting**, and the resulting shortened expression is called a **contraction**.

As you'll see, most of these involve **auxiliary verbs**. In *Chapter 4*, we saw that there is only a small set of **auxiliary verbs** and that they usually don't really mean anything. Rather, they're used to express the correct **tense** or to fit other grammatical forms (e.g., **passive voice**, **conditionals**). In other words, **auxiliary verbs** aren't really that important in sentences. Hence, we tend to shorten expressions involving **auxiliary verbs** so that we can quickly move on to the more important part of the sentence. Again, to shorten an expression is to **contract** it, and we call the shortened version the **contraction**.

There are three things you must remember with regards to **contractions**.

1. **Some of them hold the same forms:**

   - **Example: "I had" → "I'd" & "I would" → "I'd"**

   - Unless the context is clear, your reader may have a hard time figuring out which original form was involved. Hence, it's better not to use these when it could cause confusion.

2. **Some of them sound the same as other words with different meaning:**

   - **Example: "You're" sounds like "Your" & "They're" sounds like "Their" and "There"**

   - Again, if you think using a **contraction** could cause confusion, you should avoid using it. Also, be careful to not use the wrong version of words like the above that sound alike.

3. **You can't use *contractions* everywhere:**

   - ***Contractions*** are mostly reserved for spoken English. Whenever you write something you probably shouldn't use **contractions**. It's okay to use **contractions** in informal writings, like when you're texting with a friend, but whenever you're sending an email to your professor, you need to avoid them.

That said, you might have noticed that I have used contractions throughout this book. I did this to mirror the semi-formal, conversational style you often encounter in a classroom. Many books handling English grammar tend to adhere to a formal tone—indeed, their goal is to teach their readers the rules of the English language, which should never be treated lightly. Still, I find that too stiff and dreary. Studying grammar is tedious in itself—dry explanations only make it worse. That's why I decided to use semi-formal language and include contractions in this book. I wanted to make my explanations at least a little enjoyable. As we near the end of our journey, I hope you appreciate my choice of semi-formal language throughout the book and feel that my explanations were palatable.

'be'-verb		will		would	
I am	I'm	I will	I'll	I would	I'd
you are	you're	you will	you'll	you would	you'd
he is	he's	he will	he'll	he would	he'd
she is	she's	she will	she'll	she would	she'd
it is	it's	it will	it'll	it would	it'd
we are	we're	we will	we'll	we would	we'd
they are	they're	they will	they'll	they would	they'd

have		negative			
I have	I've	is not	isn't	will not	won't
you have	you've	are not	aren't	would not	wouldn't
he has	he's	was not	wasn't	can not	can't
she has	she's	were not	weren't	could not	couldn't
it has	it's	have not	haven't	do not	don't
we have	we've	has not	hasn't	does not	doesn't
they have	they've	had not	hadn't	did not	didn't

had					
		must not	mustn't	might not	mightn't
I had	I'd	should not	shouldn't	etc.	
you had	you'd	modal verb + have		who will	who'll
he had	he'd	could have	could've	that is	that's
she had	she'd	would have	would've	there is	there's
it had	it'd	should have	should've	what is	what's
we had	we'd	must have	must've	who is	who's
they had	they'd	might have	might've	where is	where's

As we worked our way through the *tenses*, we saw that to form *questions* we either take a statement and change the word order (usually the order of the *subject* and the *'be'-verb*) or use the *auxiliary verb* "do." Questions formed in this way are called *direct questions*; they always demand a clear answer from the person being questioned.

However, *direct questions* are not the only type of *questions* in English. At the other end of the spectrum, we have *indirect questions*. Indirect questions have the same word order as statements (i.e., non-questions), but *indirect questions* employ inquiring expressions to signal that they are *questions* rather than statements. Examples of inquiring expressions include: "**Tom is asking...**," "**I wonder...**," "**do you know...**," and "**do you think...**," and they often appear at the beginning of *indirect questions*. Depending on which expression you use, the *indirect question* can either end with a *question mark* ("**?**") or a *period* ("**.**"). Finally, answering *indirect questions* is the same as answering *direct questions*—you generally answer either "**yes**" or "**no**" in the absence of *question words* (i.e., where, who, when, etc.) that solicit specific information; whereas if the *question* includes a *question word*, you answer according to it.

In real life, we use *indirect questions* more commonly than *direct questions* because they are more polite and formal. *Direct questions* demand answers from listeners, while *indirect questions* do not. Correspondingly, it's easier to avoid answering *indirect questions*; you can answer an *indirect question* with "**I don't know**," or "**I'd rather not say**." While you can do the same when asked a *direct question*, it often proves more difficult to do so.

Compare the following examples.

Direct Questions	Indirect Questions
Is this seat available?	He is asking if this seat is available.
Is she married?	I wonder if she is married.
Do they wish to purchase it?	Do you know whether they wish to purchase it?
Will he come?	I wonder if he will come.
Could I use your bathroom?	Do you think I could use your bathroom?
Where is the nearest subway station?	Could you tell me where the nearest subway station is?
What did she enjoy the most?	Do you know what she enjoyed the most?
Where did they go?	Have you any idea where they went?
Where did you find it?	Do you remember where you found it?
Why did you make that choice?	Could you tell me why you made that choice?
When does the restaurant close?	Can you tell me when the restaurant closes?
How much is this?	I'd like to know how much this is.
How long has she been in the bathroom?	Do you know how long she has been in the bathroom?
Why did your mom call my mom yesterday?	Can you tell me why your mom called my mom yesterday?

23.6 Question Tags

Another interesting *question* technique involves attaching a *question tag* to the end of a non-question statement. *Question tags* are frequently used in spoken English when we think we know the answer but want someone to confirm this. Again, the word order is equal to non-question sentences; we're just adding something to the end of a statement to transform the statement into a question.

In short, a *question tag* repeats the *verb* and the *subject* of the statement. The *question tag* always appears after a *comma* ("*,*"), and every sentence with a *question tag* ends with a *question mark* ("**?**"). However, an important aspect of this is as follows—the statement and the *question tag* hold opposite tones. In other words, we use a *negative tag* with a *positive sentence* and a *positive tag* with a *negative sentence*. We adjust the tone of the *question tag* by either including or not including "**not**" after the *verb*.

Consider the following examples.

Positive sentences, with negative tags	
Present simple 'be'	She's from the UK, **isn't she**?
Present simple, other verbs	They live in Sydney, **don't they**?
Present continuous	We're leaving next week, **aren't we**?
Present perfect	They've been to Paris, **haven't they**?
Present perfect continuous	She's been sleeping a lot recently, **hasn't she**?
Past simple 'be'	It was freezing yesterday, **wasn't it**?
Past simple, other verbs	He went to the concert last night, **didn't he**?
Past continuous	We were waiting in the parking lot, **weren't we**?
Past perfect	He had lost his wallet, **hadn't he**?
Past perfect continuous	We'd been working for three hours, **hadn't we**?
Future simple	She'll arrive by eight, **won't she**?
Future continuous	They'll be leaving soon, **won't they**?
Future perfect	You'll have gone home by nine, **won't you have**?
Future perfect continuous	She'll have been cleaning all day, **won't she have**?
Modal verbs	He can be excused, **can't he**?
	Kiara must stay, **mustn't she**?

Negative sentences, with positive tags	
Present simple 'be'	We aren't too early, **are we**?
Present simple, other verbs	She doesn't have any nephews, **does she**?
Present continuous	The bus isn't coming any soon, **is it**?
Present perfect	She hasn't eaten all the cookies, **has she**?
Present perfect continuous	He hasn't been running in the rain, **has he**?
Past simple 'be'	She wasn't at home last night, **was she**?
Past simple, other verbs	They didn't go out last weekend, **did they**?
Past continuous	You weren't paying attention, **were you**?
Past perfect	We hadn't been to Japan before, **had we**?
Past perfect continuous	You hadn't been getting enough rest, **had you**?
Future simple	They won't be annoyed, **will they**?
Future continuous	He won't be leaving the house tonight, **will he**?
Future perfect	She won't have left school before four, **will she have**?
Future perfect continuous	He won't have been cooking all day, **will he have**?
Modal verbs	She can't speak Chinese, **can she**?
	They mustn't come late, **must they**?

23.7 Reported (Indirect) Quotation

As you use English, you might come across a situation where you'd like to borrow someone else's words (i.e., repeat exactly what someone else said). The formal way to do this is by setting off their exact words with *quotation marks* (" "). For example, let's say that you want to quote the famous line from Thomas Edison: "**Genius is 1% inspiration, 99% perspiration**." You can use a form similar to the following.

- **Thomas Edison said, "Genius is 1% inspiration, 99% perspiration."**

We refer to the above as the *direct quotation* method. While a great way to borrow someone's words, the *direct quotation* method has a major drawback. You can't explicitly use *quotation marks* in spoken English— therefore, your audience may be confused about where exactly the quote starts and where it ends.

A better way to present someone else's words in spoken English is to use what's referred to as the *indirect* or *reported quotation*. With *indirect* or *reported quotations* you do not include *quotation marks*. Rather, you present your reflections on someone else's words, i.e., you present them from your own perspective. The basic idea is to place "**that**" before the *indirect* or *reported quotation* without *quotation marks*. However, now that you're presenting someone else's words from your own perspective, you need to adjust the quote by changing one or more of the following elements from the original quote.

A. <u>Pronouns</u>

B. <u>Verb tenses & forms</u>

C. <u>Time and place expressions</u>

Let's consider an example. You called Mark and he told you, "**I am playing tennis right now.**" With the *direct quotation* method, you'd say the following.

1. **Mark said, "I am playing tennis right now."**

On the other hand, with the *reported quotation* method, you'd say something more like this.

2. **Mark said that he was playing tennis at the time.**

As you can see, lots of things have changed from #1. First, as I said, the quote is now free of *quotation marks*, and we placed "**that**" in front of the material attributed to Mark. "**That**" indicates precisely where the quote starts. As such, in a <u>spoken English</u> setting, #2 would make it easier to understand what was said by Mark, compared to #1.

Next, we changed the *pronoun* "**I**" to the *pronoun* "**he.**" Since you're now delivering the quote from your perspective, Mark is no longer "**I.**" In #2, Mark is neither narrator nor audience and he is one male person—accordingly, we use the *3rd person singular masculine subject pronoun* "**he.**"

Next, we changed the *verb tense*—"**am playing**" in the *present tense* became "**was playing**" in the *past tense*. The reason for this is simple: <u>when you're describing someone's speech, the original speech is a thing of the *past*</u>. Mark's statement, "**I am playing tennis right now,**" was told in the *past*. As such, we'd usually refer to the quote in the *past tense*. As a side-note, we also changed the form of the *'be'-verb* (from "**am**" to "**is**"), but hopefully that's self-explanatory, as we changed the *pronoun* from "**I**" to "**he.**"

Finally, the *time expression* changed from "**right now**" to "**at the time** (i.e., when I talked to him)." Again, Mark telling you something is a thing of the *past*. "**Right now**" in #1 refers to what Mark was doing at the exact time you talked to him, <u>which is now in the *past*</u>. Therefore, it'd be wrong to say "**right now**" in #2, because we're no longer talking about the *present*. Instead, we need an expression that points to the *past*. In this case, "**at the time**" fits perfectly in #2. But you can also use expressions like "**back then,**" "**at the moment,**" and "**right then**" in other situations.

Do you now understand why we have to change so many things when we use the *reported quotation* method? Despite such complications, <u>the *reported quotation* method prevails in spoken English</u>—it is more popular than the *direct quotation* method as *reported quotations* are often easier to comprehend. However, do remember that <u>the *direct quotation* method is preferred in formal written English</u>.

As a final note, you can omit "**that**" when using the *reported quotation* method, but it's usually a good idea to include it unless it makes the statement too wordy.

Now, let's consider the specific rules.

A. <u>Pronoun Changes</u>

  ■ *Pronouns* must be adjusted in a *reported quotation* to preserve the meaning of the *direct quotation*.

  ■ <u>Examples:</u>

    I. "<u>We</u> are the best mechanics," he said.
       → He said that <u>they</u> were the best mechanics.

    II. "Brie called <u>us</u>," he said.
        → He said that Brie had called <u>them</u>.

    III. "<u>I</u> like your coat," she said.
         → She said that <u>she</u> liked my coat.

IV. **"I can rent you <u>my</u> attic," he said.**
   → **He said that <u>he</u> could rent me <u>his</u> attic.**

■ Sometimes, it is better to use a *noun* instead of a *pronoun* to avoid confusion.

I. **"<u>He</u> killed them," Ben said.**
   → **Ben said that <u>the man</u> had killed them.**
   (※ *Ben said that he had killed them. = Ben killed them. = Incorrect*)

■ "**This**" and "**these**" are usually replaced with "**the**," "**a/an**," or "**that**." "**This**" and "**these**" are from the perspective of the original speaker, not from yours; they no longer hold the same meaning.

I. **"They will complete it <u>this month</u>," he said.**
   → **He said that they would have completed it <u>that month</u>.**

II. **"I brought you <u>this necklace</u>," she said.**
   → **She said that she had brought me <u>a necklace</u>.**

III. **"We want <u>these toys</u>," they said.**
   → **They said that they wanted <u>the toys</u>.**

B. <u>Verb tenses & forms</u>

■ A *tense* <u>one step back in the *past*</u> should be used.

■ *Present simple/continuous → past simple/continuous*

I. **"I rarely <u>understand</u> you," she told me.**
   → **She told me that she rarely <u>understood</u> me.**

II. **"We <u>are jogging</u>," he explained.**
   → **He explained that they <u>were jogging</u>.**

■ *Present perfect → past perfect*

I. **"I <u>have broken</u> the flower pot," he admitted.**
   → **He admitted that he <u>had broken</u> the flower pot.**

II. **"I <u>have been driving</u> since the morning," he complained.**
   → **He complained that he <u>had been driving</u> since the morning.**

■ *Past → past perfect*
   (※ *The **past perfect** refers to a <u>further</u> **past** than the **past tense**.*)

I. **"She <u>went</u> to London," I thought.**
   → **I thought that she <u>had gone</u> to London.**

II. **"He <u>was thinking</u> of buying a new mobile phone," she said.**
   → **She said that he <u>had been thinking</u> of buying a new mobile phone.**

■ *Will → would*
   (※ *"**Would**" can stand in for the **past tense** of "**will**".*)

I. **"I <u>will come</u> back on Friday," he reminded me.**
   → **He reminded me that he <u>would come</u> back on Friday.**

II. **"She <u>will appreciate</u> it," he said.**
   → **He said that she <u>would appreciate</u> it.**

■ <u>Exceptions</u>:

I. <u>When you talk about facts, you don't change the *tense*</u>,

e.g., Denver said, "Asia <u>is</u> the biggest continent."
→ Denver said that Asia <u>is</u> the biggest continent.

II. <u>When the statement is still true in the *present*, you don't change the *tense*</u>,
e.g., Thomas said, "I <u>am</u> thirsty."
→ Thomas said that he <u>is</u> thirsty.

III. <u>When there is a *modal verb*, we don't change the *tense*</u>,
e.g., Bridget said, "He <u>ought to stay</u> in bed."
→ Bridget said that he <u>ought to stay</u> in bed.

C. <u>Time and place expressions</u>

■ <u>Time and place expressions</u> must be adjusted in the *reported quotation* to preserve the meaning of the *direct quotation*.

■ <u>Examples</u>:

I. Helen said, "Paul came <u>yesterday</u>."
→ Helen said that Paul had come <u>the day before</u>.

II. Chris said, "She will leave <u>tomorrow</u>."
→ Chris said that she would leave <u>the next day</u>.

III. Gary said, "I will always be right <u>here</u> for you."
→ Gary said that he would always be right <u>there</u> for me.

IV. Thomas said, "I'll be <u>here</u> at 2 o'clock."
→ Thomas said that he would be <u>there</u> at 2 o'clock.

■ The following couples/sets describe some of the <u>changes</u> that we make to <u>common time and place expressions</u> when we use the *reported quotation* method. For each match, the expression on the <u>left</u> indicates the <u>original expression</u> (i.e., <u>the expression the original narrator used</u>) while the expression on the <u>right</u> indicates <u>how it must be adjusted</u> in the *reported quotation*.

■ *Time expressions*:

● today - that day, tomorrow - the next day/the following day, the day after tomorrow - in two days' time, yesterday - the day before, the day before yesterday - two days before, next week/month – the following week/month, last week/month - the previous week/month, a year ago - a year before/the previous year

■ *Place expressions*:

● here - there, here - [specific place name]

Glossary

Abstract noun

A noun that stands for an idea, event, concept, feeling, or quality that does not have a physical form; something we cannot see or touch, *e.g., courage, pride, happiness*. *See also: **concrete noun***

Action verb (Dynamic verb)

A verb that describes an action, *e.g., run, sit, read, cook*. *See also: **state verb***

Active and Passive voice

The voice of a sentence refers to the relationship between the verb and the subject. More specifically, we distinguish different voices based on whether the subject is performing the action or is receiving the action.

Active voice: A way of writing a sentence in which the subject is <u>performing the action</u>.

Passive voice: A way of writing a sentence in which the subject is <u>receiving the action</u>.

*e.g., The dog bit him. (**Active**)*
   *→ He was bitten by the dog. (**Passive**)*

Adjective

A word that describes and gives more information about a noun or pronoun, *e.g., tall, beautiful, happy, old*.

   ✓ Gradable and non-gradable adjectives

Gradable adjectives: Can be modified by adverbs to adjust the strength of the base adjective.

Non-gradable adjectives: Cannot usually be modified. There are three types of non-gradable adjectives: extreme, absolute, and classifying.

   A. Extreme adjectives: Extreme versions of gradable adjectives. *e.g., bad → **awful**, funny → **hilarious**, good → **fantastic**, scary → **terrifying***
   B. Absolute adjectives: Describe fixed qualities or states; cannot be graded, *e.g., unique, perfect, impossible*
   C. Classifying adjectives: Used to say that something is of a specific type or class, *e.g., American, nuclear, medical*.
*See also: **comparative, superlative***

Adverb

A word or expression that modifies a verb, an adjective, another adverb, or a sentence,
*e.g., **quickly, soon, now, then**.*
   *I **really** enjoyed the party. (adverb + verb)*
   *She's **really** nice. (adverb + adjective)*
   *He works **really** slowly. (adverb + adverb)*
   ***Really**, he should do better. (adverb + sentence)*

Apostrophe (')

A punctuation mark used to show possession and indicate omitted letters in contractions, *e.g., there's, she's, it's, Jack's*.

Article

A word that indicates whether a noun is being used in a general or in a specific sense. Articles are a sub-category of determiners.
   the → specific or definite
   a → general or indefinite; for nouns that begin with a consonant sound
   an → general or indefinite; for nouns that begin with a vowel sound
*See also: **determiner***

Auxiliary verb (Helping verb)

A verb used with main verbs to modify their meanings. Often used to form different tenses. Common auxiliary verbs include "be," "have," and "do." *See also: **main verb, tense***

Capital letter

   ✓ Uppercase and lowercase letter

Every letter in the English language has two cases: the **uppercase (or the capital letter)** and the **lowercase (or the small letter)**. While most letters are written in their lowercase form, we must use the capital letter in certain situations. The act of starting a word with a capital letter is called "capitalization." *See also: **proper noun***

Cardinal and Ordinal numbers

   ✓ Cardinal and ordinal number

Cardinal Number: Numbers used to count. Does not include fractions or decimals, only whole, positive numbers, *e.g., one, two, three*.

Ordinal Number: Numbers used to describe the order or position of items in a list, *e.g., 1st, 2nd, 3rd, 4th, 5th*.

Clause

A group of words that contains a subject and a verb. A building block of sentences.

 ✓ Main and subordinate clause

Main clause (independent clause): Makes sense on its own (= a sentence). All sentences must include at least one main clause.

Subordinate clause (dependent clause): Does not make sense on its own; needs to be attached to a main clause to form a sentence,
e.g., It was raining (one clause);
It was raining and we were cold
(two main clauses joined by 'and');
It was raining when we went out
(main clause containing a subordinate clause).

Embedded clause: A type of subordinate clause. Used in the middle of a sentence. Contains information related to the sentence topic to give the reader more information and enhance the sentence. Usually set off by commas. If you remove the embedded clause, the remaining part would stand alone as a complete sentence,
*e.g., My bike, **which is very old**, is broken;*
*The witch, **who has green eyes**, is very spooky.*

Colon (:)

A punctuation mark used to introduce a list or to separate two independent, but linked clauses,
e.g., I love the following sports: tennis, football, basketball, and hockey.

Comma (,)

A punctuation mark that separates items in a list and marks divisions within sentences. You use commas between clauses, in lists, and between some adjectives,
e.g., We finished our food, and then we went home;
I'm going to invite Sam, Anna, and Toby;
We found an old, ugly chest.

Command

A speech act that orders someone to do something. A command can be expressed in various ways but is often associated with the **imperative sentence**. A command frequently begins with an **imperative verb**,
*e.g., **Sit** down! **Do** your homework. **Clean** your room! **Come** here. **Leave** me alone. **Be** quiet. See also:*
imperative, sentence

Common noun

A noun that refers to a general class of people, places, or things (i.e., not a particular person, place, or thing), *e.g., car, friend, dog, animal, planet. See also: **proper noun***

Comparative

The form of an adjective (or an adverb) that is used to compare the quantities or the qualities of two things. Often formed by adding the suffix "-er," *e.g., taller, faster, smaller, warmer. See also: **superlative***

Complement

A word or phrase that follows a verb and adds more information about the subject or the object.

 ✓ Subject and object complements

Subject complement: A complement that follows a verb (usually a linking verb) and adds more information about the subject,
*e.g., Kate is **a nurse**;*
*Both brothers became **doctors**.*

Object complement: A complement that follows and adds more information about the object,
*e.g., He makes me **very angry**;*
*Playing the guitar always makes me **happy**.*
*See also: **linking verb***

Complex preposition

A preposition that contains two or more words yet acts as a single unit, *e.g., next to, because of, on account of. See also: **preposition***

Complex sentence

A sentence that contains one or more subordinate clause. Each subordinate clause is added to the independent clause via either a conjunction or a relative pronoun.
Form: main clause + connective + subordinate clause,
e.g., I burned dinner when I was on the phone.
*See also: **conjunction, relative clause***

Compound sentence

A sentence that contains two or more independent clauses. Each pair is linked by a coordinating conjunction.
Form: main clause + connective + main clause,
*e.g., He went to meet her at the airport, but the plane was delayed. See also: **conjunction***

Compound word

A word created by joining two or more words, which has an entirely new meaning

✓ Types of Compound Words

Compound words: Are written as a single word, *e.g., haircut, newspaper, grandmother, doorknob, football, broomstick.*

Open Compounds words: Are written as separate words, *e.g., high school, living room, school bus, ice cream.*

Hyphenated Compounds words: Use a hyphen in between two separate words, *e.g., well-known, second-rate, merry-go-round, mother-in-law.*

Concrete noun

A noun referring to something you can see or touch, such as a person, an animal, a place or a thing, *e.g., man, cat, shop, bottle. See also: **abstract noun***

Conditional (sentence/clause)

A type of sentence used to present a condition and state its result. More specifically, we use conditionals to make guesses, discuss hopes, express regrets, and so on. Conditionals often begin with "if."

The zero conditional: A conditional that states facts, truths, and habits,

e.g., If you heat water to 100℃, it boils.

The first conditional: A conditional that describes a possible future situation that depends on a situation in the present,

e.g., If it rains, I'll stay here.

The second conditional: A conditional that describes an imaginary future situation based on an impossible/difficult present situation,

e.g., If I were you, I'd take an umbrella.

The third conditional: A conditional that describes an alternate past situation and its unreal result in a more recent past,

e.g., If I had studied harder, I would have passed the exam.

The mixed conditional: A conditional that describes an alternate past situation and a result that is untrue result in the present,

e.g., If you had saved enough money, you would own a car now.

Conjunction

A word that connects other words, phrases, or clauses. Placed between the two things being linked.

✓ Coordinating and Subordinating conjunctions

Coordinating conjunction: A conjunction that joins two things of equal importance/grammatical rank (i.e., two words, two phrases, or two independent clauses). Includes: *and, but, or, so,*
*e.g., It was raining **but** it wasn't cold;*
*Do you want to go now **or** shall we wait a bit longer?*

Subordinating conjunction: A conjunction that joins two clauses of unequal importance/grammatical rank (i.e., an independent clause and a subordinate clause). Appears at the beginning of the subordinate clause. Includes: *when, while, before, after, since, until, if, because, although, that,*
*e.g., We were hungry **because** we hadn't eaten all day.*
*We were hungry **when** we got home.*
*We won't go out **if** the weather is bad.*

Consonants and Vowels

The letters a, e, i, o, and u are **vowels**. All other letters in the alphabet are **consonants**.

Continuous (= progressive)

The form of a verb that shows that an action or activity is in progress. Used in continuous tenses.
Form: be + present participle,
*e.g., I'm writing. See also: **participle***

Contraction

A shortened expression made by combining two words using an apostrophe. In the contraction form, one or more letters from the two original words are dropped and replaced with an apostrophe, *e.g., I'm (I am), it's (it is), isn't (is not), would've (would have), he'd (he had), I'll (I will). See also: **apostrophe***

Countable and Uncountable nouns

Nouns can be either countable or uncountable. *See also: **noun***

✓ Countable and uncountable nouns

Countable noun: A noun that can be individually counted. We can use "a," "an," "some," or numbers with countable nouns, *e.g., an apple, four eggs.*

Uncountable noun: A noun that cannot be individually counted. We cannot use numbers with uncountable nouns, *e.g., sugar, water, cereal.*

Determiner

A word that introduces a noun and identifies it in detail. Usually appears in front of a noun. Includes:
Articles: *a/an, the*
Demonstratives: *this/that, these/those*
Possessives: *my/your/his/her/its/our/their*
Quantifiers: *some, any, no, many, much, few, little*
Numbers: *three, fifty, three thousand*

Direct and Indirect object

Direct object: The person or thing that is directly affected by the action of a verb in a sentence,
e.g., She fed <u>the cat.</u>

Indirect object: The person or thing that receives something as the result of an action of a verb in a sentence (i.e., they benefit from the action),
e.g., She gave <u>me</u> the book.

Direct and Indirect quotations

Direct quotation: A style of speech or writing used to report someone's exact words. Rarely used in spoken English,
e.g., Helen said, "I'm going home," / "What do you want?" I asked.
*See also: **quotation marks***

Indirect quotation (reported quotation): The style of speech or writing used for reporting someone words, without using quotation marks or exactly repeating the original words,
e.g., Helen said (that) she was going home. / I asked them what they wanted.

Exclamation point (!)

A punctuation mark used at the end of a sentence or after a word of exclamation (i.e., which expresses surprise, excitement, or anger). *See also: exclamatory sentence*

Exclamatory sentence

A type of sentence that includes an exclamation. An exclamation is a forceful statement that expresses a high level of emotion or excitement. Usually begins with "how" or "what." Usually takes an exclamation point (!) at the end,
e.g., How amazing! What a strange animal!
    What a beautiful day! How stupid (he is)!
*See also: **exclamation point***

Formal and Informal language

Formal language: A style of writing/speech used in official or formal situations. Also used to communicate with someone you don't know well. Exudes politeness.

Informal language: A style of writing/speech used to communicate with someone who you know well. More simple and relaxed than formal language but also less polite.

Full stop (.) (= Period)

A punctuation mark used at the end of a statement (i.e., not used with questions or exclamations).
*See also: **statement***

Future continuous

The tense of a verb that expresses that an action will be in progress at a certain point in the future.
Form: **will be + present participle,**
e.g., I <u>will be playing</u> for an hour.

Future perfect

The tense of a verb that expresses that an action will be completed at a certain point in the future.
Form: **will have + past participle,**
e.g., By September, Jenny <u>will have taken</u> over that role.

Future perfect continuous

The tense of a verb that expresses that an ongoing action will be completed at a certain point in the future.
Form: **will have been + present participle,**
e.g., If it rains again tomorrow, it <u>will have been raining</u> for three days.

Future simple

The tense of a verb that shows that an action or state will happen or exist at a later time (i.e., in the future). Often expressed by placing the auxiliary verb "will" before the main verb in its base form,
e.g., I <u>will</u> go to school tomorrow.
    We<u>'re going to</u> build a sandcastle.

Gerund

A noun formed from a verb. Takes the same form as the verb's present participle. Grammatically equivalent to the "'to'-infinitive,"
e.g., No <u>smoking</u>. He enjoys <u>reading</u>.
*See also: **infinitive***

Imperative

A type of sentence used to give commands or to make requests. Can also be used to give warnings or directions. Usually begins with a verb in its base form. Can consist of a single verb,
e.g., Stop! Wait there. Have a good time.
See also: **command, sentence**

Infinitive

The simplest form of a verb (i.e., the "base form" or the "bare infinitive"). The infinitive of a verb can be combined with "to" to form a noun. The resulting noun is called the "'to'-infinitive." The "'to'-infinitive" is grammatically equivalent to the gerund.
See also: **gerund**

Interjection

A word or phrase used to exclaim (i.e., to express surprise, shock, pain, etc.),
*e.g., **Wow! Hooray! Oh**, it was wonderful!*
See also: **exclamatory sentence**

Intransitive and Transitive verb

Intransitive verb: An action verb that does not take a direct object; it refers to an action that has no direct receiver, *e.g., cry, grow, leave, smile, talk, work.* See also: **direct and indirect objects**

Transitive verb: An action verb that takes a direct object; it refers to an action that has a direct receiver, *e.g., buy, catch, grab, receive, send, take, draw.* See also: **direct and indirect objects**

Irregular verb

A verb that does not follow the established rule in its past simple or its past participle form,
e.g., begin-began-begun, break-broke-broken, bring-brought-brought, drink-drank-drunk, forget-forgot-forgotten.
See also: **participle**

Linking verb

A verb that connects the subject of a sentence to a word or phrase that describes it (i.e., that links a subject to its complement), *e.g., be, seem, become, look, fell.*

Main verb

The verb in a verb phrase that expresses the action, state, or relation. A verb phrase usually has a single main verb; the rest are all auxiliary verbs,
*e.g., We are **going**. Lucy has **arrived**. Can you **play**?*
In these sentences, going, arrived and play are the main verbs. Are, has, and can are auxiliary verbs.
See also: **auxiliary verb**

Modal verb

A verb used with another verb to change its meaning. Used to show level of possibility, indicate ability, show obligation, or give permission. Modal verbs are a subset of auxiliary verbs, *e.g., can, could, may, might, shall, should, will, would, must, ought to.* See also: **auxiliary verb**

Negative and Positive

Negative: A sentence, clause, or phrase that contains a negative word such as not, no, never, or nothing.

Positive: A sentence, clause, or phrase that does not contain a negative word.

Noun

A word that refers to a person, place, thing, event, substance, or quality, *e.g., ball, apple, dog, horse, brother.*

Paragraph

A group of several sentences that start on a new line and deal with a single main event, description, idea, etc.

Participle

An adjective formed from a verb. Ends in either "-ed" or "-ing." Also a very commonly used part of different verb tenses.

  ✓ Past and Present participle

Past participle: The participle form of a verb that is used to form perfect tenses and to speak in the passive voice. Usually formed by adding "-ed" to the end of a verb, *e.g., walked, cooked, played, done, eaten.*

Present participle: The participle form of a verb that is used to form continuous tenses. Usually formed by adding "-ing" to the end of a verb., *e.g., walking, doing, fleeing, wearing.*

Past continuous

The tense of a verb that expresses an action that was in progress at a certain time in the past.
Form: **was/were + present participle,**
*e.g., I **was walking**. I **was singing**.*
*I **was falling** asleep when the phone rang.*
*We **were playing** tennis when it started to rain.*

Past perfect

The tense of a verb that describes a completed action in the far past that happened before and affected another action or state in the nearer past.
Form: **had + past participle,**
*e.g., Matilda **had baked** a cake before you arrived.*
*The train **had left** before we arrived at the station.*

Past perfect continuous

The tense of a verb that expresses an ongoing action in the far past that happened before and affected another action or state in the nearer past.
Form: **had been + participle,**
*e.g., I **had been playing** the game since I was ten until the developers shut down their servers.*
*She **had been studying** English for three years before she went to Australia.*

Past simple

The tense of a verb that expresses a completed action in the past,
*e.g., I **studied** French at school.*
*She **worked** in the market last year.*

Phrasal verb

A phrase that consists of a verb along with a preposition, an adverb, or both. Has a completely different meaning than its separate parts, *e.g., get up, run away, work out, calm down. See also: **phrase***

Phrase

A small group of words that does not contain both a subject and a verb (may contain either one), *e.g., a sunny day, in the garage, last week.*

Adjective phrase: A phrase headed by an adjective that describes a noun or a pronoun.

Adverbial phrase: A phrase wherein an adverb is the main word, *e.g., after a while, as fast as possible.*

Noun phrase: A phrase that functions as a single noun, *e.g., the blue house, an old man, a black dog with white paws*

Prepositional phrase: A phrase that contains a preposition, *e.g., on the mat, in the morning, under the chair, during the film.*

Preposition

A word or a phrase placed before a noun, pronoun, or gerund to express a place, time, direction, etc., *e.g., in, at, on, of, for.*

Preposition of place: A preposition that states where something is, *e.g., **in** the box, **under** the table.*

Preposition of time: A preposition that states when something happens, *e.g., **on** Monday, **in** the summer, **at** six o'clock.*

Present continuous

The tense of a verb that expresses an ongoing action in the present.
Form: **am/is/are + present participle(verb-ing),**
*e.g., Joe **is baking** a cake.*
*They **are painting** the fence.*

Present perfect

The tense of a verb that expresses an action that started in the past and is still continuing or that happened in the past but has a result in the present.
Form: **has/have + past participle,**
*e.g., I**'ve lost** my phone.*
*He**'s cut** his knee.*

Present perfect continuous

The tense of a verb that expresses an ongoing action that started in the past and is still continuing in the present.
Form: **has been/have been + present participle,**
*e.g., I **have been playing** for a year.*
*My grandfather **has been living** in this house for 50 years.*

Present simple

The tense of a verb that expresses a general truth about the present. Form: **base form/base form + s,**
*e.g., I **like** chocolate. He **plays** chess*

Pronoun

A word that is used instead of a noun or noun phrase, *e.g., he, she, it, they.* We use pronouns to avoid repeating the nouns,
*e.g., We took **the car** to the garage because **it** needed fixing.*

Personal pronoun: A pronoun used to represent a person or a thing that has already been mentioned. Primarily used to avoid repetition, *e.g., I, you, he, she, it, we, they.*

Reflexive pronoun: A pronoun used to refer back to the subject of a sentence or a clause, in order to emphasize the subject, *e.g., myself, yourself, herself, himself, itself, ourselves.*

Possessive pronoun: A pronoun that expresses ownership, *e.g., mine, yours, his, its, ours, theirs*

Indefinite pronoun: A pronoun that refers to an unspecific person or thing, *e.g., anyone, anything, everybody, everything, nobody, none, somebody, someone.*

Interrogative pronoun: A pronoun used to ask questions that demand specific answers, (i.e., not yes/no questions), *e.g., what, which, who, whom, whose.*

Relative pronoun: A pronoun used to connect a relative clause to a main clause, *e.g., who, that, which, whom, whose.*

Proper noun

A noun that is the name of a particular person, place, or thing. Always capitalized (i.e., the first letter of the word is written in the upper case), regardless of where it falls in a sentence. *See also: common noun, capital letter*

Punctuation

Special symbols used in writing that tell the reader when to pause, or that indicate a question, or that indicate an exclamation, etc. *See also: apostrophe, colon, comma, exclamation mark, full stop, question mark, quotation marks, semicolon*

Quantifier

A word that is usually placed before a noun to express its quantity or amount. Quantifiers are a subset of determiners, *e.g., several, few, many, much. See also: determiner*

Question

A sentence used to request information. Usually ends with a question mark. *See also: question mark*

✓ Closed and open question

Closed question: A question that can be answered with either "yes" or "no," *e.g., Are you Korean?*

Open question: A question that requests specific answers (i.e., that cannot be answered with "yes" or "no"). Starts with a question word, such as *what, where, who, why, wow, when. See also: question word*

✓ Direct and Indirect question

Direct question: A question that follows the established grammatical rule for forming questions. Can sound assertive and/or rude at times. Mostly only used with people you know well. Always ends with a question mark.
e.g. Where is the station? What time is it?

Indirect question: A modified version of a direct question that sounds more polite and sincere. More common in formal spoken English, especially when talking to someone you don't know well. Often used when asking for information. May not end with a question mark,
e.g., Where is the station? → *Do you know where the station is?*
What time is it? → *Can you tell me what time it is?*

Question mark (?)

A punctuation mark used at the end of a sentence to show that it is a question.

Question tag

In spoken English, brief questions are often added to the ends of statements. These are called question tags, and they are most often used to invite someone's agreement,
e.g., It's hot today, __isn't it?__
    The music is very loud, __isn't it?__
    The radio isn't too loud, __is it?__

Question word

A word that is used at the beginning of a question to request a specific answer (i.e., not "yes" or "no"). Includes interrogative pronouns, but some are formed by combining an interrogative pronoun with another word,
e.g., who, which, what, where, how, how much, how often, how long, which kind.
See also: pronoun

Quotation marks (" ")

A set of marks used to set off direct quotations (i.e., someone's exact words). Used in the direct quotation method, *e.g., "I'm sorry," he said. See also: direct and indirect quotations.*

Relative clause

A clause that starts with a relative pronoun such as *who, that, or which.* Gives additional information about something in the main clause, *e.g., This is the video __that I wanted to show you.__ See also: pronoun*

Semicolon (;)

A punctuation mark used to separate two independent (main) clauses that are closely related,
e.g., The party was great; we all enjoyed it.

Sentence

A group of written or spoken words that has a subject and a verb and expresses a complete thought or asks a question. A sentence always begins with a capital letter and ends with either a full stop, a question mark, or an exclamation point. There are four main types of sentences: declarative, interrogative, imperative, and exclamatory.

Declarative sentence: A statement, suggestion, etc., *e.g., The class yelled in triumph. Maybe we could eat afterwards.*

Interrogative sentence: A question, request, etc., *e.g., Is your sister here? Could you show me how?*

Imperative sentence: A command, instruction, etc., *e.g., Hold this! Take the second left.*

Exclamatory sentence: An exclamation, *e.g., How peaceful she looks! What a pity!*

Singular and Plural Nouns

Singular noun: A noun that represents exactly one person or thing.

Plural noun: A noun that represents more than one person or thing. *See also: **countable and uncountable nouns***

State verb

A type of verb that describes situations, thoughts, or feelings. A state verb refers to the state of something rather than to an action something takes, *e.g., seem, think, belong, know. See also: **action verb***

Statement

A sentence that expresses a fact, idea, or opinion; the most common type of sentence. *See also: **sentence***

Subject and Object

The **subject** of a sentence is the thing or person who performs the action denoted by the main verb or is described by the main verb.

The **object** of a sentence is the thing or person that is involved in an action but does not carry it out. The **object** either directly receives or benefits from the action.

Every sentence contains a **subject** and a verb, but it doesn't have to contain an **object**,
e.g., The man ate a cream cake.
      S   V   O
*See also: **direct and indirect objects, intransitive and transitive verbs***

Suffix and Prefix

Suffix: A unit of meaning added to the end of a word, to change or add to its meaning, *e.g., "-able" in acceptable, "-ness" in weakness.*

Prefix: A unit of meaning added to the beginning of a word to change or add to its meaning, *e.g., "dis-" in disappear, "im-" in impossible.*

Superlative

The form of an adjective (or an adverb) that indicates the highest or the lowest position on a certain scale of quality or quantity. The superlative is usually formed by adding the suffix "-est," *e.g., biggest, funniest, saddest, lightest. See also: **comparative***

Syllable

Each part of a word that contains a single vowel sound. All words are made up of one or more syllables, *e.g., teach (one syllable), teacher (two syllables).*

Synonym and Antonym

Synonym: A word that has exactly or nearly the same meaning as another word, *e.g., sad – unhappy, small – little, ask – inquire*

Antonym: A word that means the opposite of another word, *e.g., good – bad, wise – foolish, long – short.*

Tense

The tense of a verb tells us the time an action took place—i.e., in the past, the present or the future.

Verb

A word that expresses an action or a state of being. Every sentence must contain at least one verb.

Abbreviations and Shorthand Notations

> *Sentence components*

S	subject
V	verb
v.t.	transitive verb
v.i.	intransitive verb
O	object
IO	indirect object
DO	direct object
C	complement
OC	objective complement
SC	subjective complement

> *Parts of speech*

n.	noun
v.	verb
pron.	pronoun
adj.	adjective
adv.	adverb
prep.	preposition
conj.	conjunction
int.	interjection

Abbreviations for some common expressions

aux.	auxiliary verb
cf.	confer
cl.	clause
comp.	comparative
e.g.	for example
etc.	and so on
i.e.	that is
modal	modal verb
neg.	negative
No.	number
opp.	opposite
p.	past
p.p.	past participle
pass.	passive
phr.	phrase
pl.	plural
pref.	prefix
ref.	reference
sb.	somebody
sing.	singular
sth.	something
suf.	suffix
superl.	superlative
vs.	against

Answer Keys

Chapter 2

Parts of Speech Exercise 01

✓ **Identify each bold word as one of the 9 parts of speech:**

Answer

1) They **attended** the concert last weekend. → *Verb*
2) Several cats ran **into** Bob's garage. → *Preposition*
3) The truck driver delivered the packages **quickly**. → *Adverb*
4) **Fast** runners won all the awards at the track meet. → *Adjective*
5) My friends and I walked home **after** school. → *Preposition*
6) I wanted a peanut butter **and** jelly sandwich for lunch yesterday. → *Conjunction*
7) **She** was counting the ballots during social studies class. → *Pronoun*
8) **Hey**! That's my seat! → *Interjection*
9) Will **they** finish the test on time? → *Pronoun*
10) The **diagram** was pretty complicated for us. → *Noun*

Parts of Speech Exercise 02

✓ **Sort the words in the following paragraph by which part of speech they belong to:**

Answer

The world is very different now. For man holds in his mortal hands the power to abolish all forms of human poverty and all forms of human life. And yet the same revolutionary beliefs for which our forebears fought are still at issue around the globe—the belief that the rights of man come not from the generosity of the state, but from the hand of God.
(Taken from John F. Kennedy's famous "Presidential Inauguration Address.")

Nouns: world, man, hands, power, forms, human, poverty, life, belief(s), forebears, issue, globe, rights, generosity, state, God
Pronouns: his, which, our, that
Adjective: different, mortal, same, revolutionary
Verbs: is, holds, abolish, fought, are, come
Adverbs: very, now, still, not
Prepositions: in, to, of, for, at, around, from
Conjunctions: for, and, yet, but
Determiners: the, all

Chapter 3

Phrases, Clauses, and Sentences Exercise 01

✓ Write "C" if it's a clause. Write "P" if it's a phrase

Answer
1) __P___ feeling good about it
2) __C___ it went up the mountain
3) __P___ killed all the rats
4) __C___ they were here
5) __C___ we met some important people
6) __P___ traversing through the river
7) __P___ through difficult times
8) __P___ clever and intelligent dog
9) __C___ the girl had a dream
10) __C___ there is little hope

Phrases, Clauses, and Sentences Exercise 02

✓ The following sentences are formed by a combination of one independent clause and one dependent clause. Underline the independent clause.

Answer
1) Because he ran, <u>he was able to get on the train</u>.
2) Until the sun rises, <u>I will stay with you.</u>
3) As the lights dim, <u>we say good-bye.</u>
4) Wherever he should go, <u>I will follow him.</u>
5) As long as it's possible, <u>I will be waiting for you.</u>
6) Before the food gets cold, <u>you should eat it.</u>

Phrases, Clauses, and Sentences Exercise 03

✓ Read each sentence and add the correct punctuation mark (".", "?" or "!").
Then, label it imperative, declarative, interrogative, or exclamatory

Answer
1) How was school today _?__(Interrogative)
2) Do your assignments on time _.__(Imperative)
3) I'm so ecstatic I aced the test __!__(Exclamatory)
4) Crossing that road is so dangerous__!__ (Exclamatory)
5) Who will be on the stage tonight __?__ (Interrogative)
6) You need to read up on the rules _.__(Declarative)
7) He is the leader of the group ___.__(Declarative)
8) What is your favorite song _?__(Interrogative)
9) Congratulations on winning the prize __!__(Exclamatory)
10) That was a difficult game _!___(Exclamatory)

Chapter 4

Action Verbs & Linking Verbs Exercises 01

✓ **Identify each of the underlined verbs as either an action verb or a linking verb.**

Answer

1) One day, I <u>want</u> to be famous. → Linking
2) We <u>play</u> soccer after school. → Action
3) I <u>like</u> your new blouse, Katie. → Linking
4) Liam <u>goes</u> home at 4:30 pm. → Action
5) Fay <u>cooks</u> wonderful meals. → Action
6) Rob <u>takes</u> the bus to work. → Action
7) This cheese <u>tastes</u> a bit strange. → Linking
8) The sommelier <u>tastes</u> the newly arrived wine. → Action

Action Verbs & Linking Verbs Exercises 02

✓ **Identify each of the underlined verbs as transitive or intransitive.**

Answer

1) She <u>was crying</u> all day long. → Intransitive
2) We <u>showed</u> her the photo album. → Transitive
3) The doctor <u>advised</u> me to exercise regularly. → Transitive
4) It was <u>raining</u> at that time. → Intransitive
5) She <u>laughed</u> at the joke. → Intransitive
6) She <u>gave</u> a cookie to the child. → Transitive
7) They <u>slept</u> in the street. → Intransitive
8) I <u>ate</u> the cherries. → Transitive
9) My father <u>doesn't drink</u> coffee. → Transitive

Auxiliary Verbs Exercises

✓ **In each sentence, circle the helping verb and underline the main verb.**

Answer

1) I (am) <u>reading</u> about the Junior Olympics
2) She (was) <u>racing</u> in a wheelchair race.
3) Sarah (had) <u>joined</u> the Wheelchair Athlete Club.
4) The racers (were) <u>using</u> special racing wheelchairs.
5) They (are) <u>training</u> several times a week.
6) They (have) <u>lifted</u> weights too.
7) Sarah (has) <u>raced</u> for several years.
8) She (will) <u>race</u> many more times.
9) She (is) <u>practicing</u> for next year's Olympics.

Modal Verbs Exercises

✓ **Pick the most appropriate modal verb out of the three options for each sentence.**

Answer

1) You (*must* / *should* / *shouldn't*) be 18 before you can drive in Spain.
2) You (*don't have to* / *mustn't* / *shouldn't*) go to bed so late. It's not good for you.
3) You (*don't have to* / *mustn't* / *shouldn't*) wear a school uniform in most Spanish state schools.
4) You (*must* / *mustn't* / *needn't*) come. I can do it without you.
5) (*Should* / *Could* / *Must*) you help me open this can, please?
6) I (*could* / *would* / *should*) like to have a better house.
7) We (*may* / *can* / *would*) go to Portugal this November.
8) He was afraid he (*mustn't* / *shouldn't* / *wouldn't*) arrive on time.

Chapter 6

The Present Simple Exercises

✓ **Fill in the gaps by putting the verbs in the present simple.**

Answer

1) I work at a bank.
2) She lives with her parents.
3) Cows feed on grass.
4) He earns a handsome salary.
5) Janet wants to be a singer.
6) Emily is a great cook.
7) Arti and her husband are both Singaporeans.
8) I am addicted to card games.
9) You are a great writer.

The Present Simple Negative Exercises

✓ **Fill in the gaps by using the present simple negative forms of the verbs.**

Answer

1) He does not work at a bank.
2) I do not live with my parents.
3) Birds do not feed on grass.
4) Tay does not earn a handsome salary.
5) They do not want to be singers.
6) Christian is not a great cook.
7) Kate and her husband are not both British; only Kate is.
8) Sam is not addicted to card games.
9) You are not someone to be ignored with.

Present Simple Questions Exercises

✓ **Turn the following sentences into present simple questions.**

Answer

1) Mark is Korean. → Is Mark Korean?
2) Thomas is Ralph's brother. → Is Thomas Ralph's brother?
3) You are a great singer. → Are you a great singer?
4) She knows Tom Hanks. → Does she know Tom Hanks?
5) You go to the gym every day. → Do you go to the gym every day?
6) They visit their grandparents every week. → Do they visit their grandparents every week?
7) Dolphins have high intelligence. → Do dolphins have high intelligence?
8) Harry wants to have Chinese food tonight. → Does Harry want to have Chinese food tonight?

The Present Continuous Exercises

✓ **Complete the sentences using the present continuous forms of the provided verbs.**

Answer

1) He is painting the house.
2) She is running to her work.
3) I am eating breakfast.
4) They are racing their toy cars.
5) Who is she chatting to now?
6) What are you doing at the moment?
7) I am not cooking right now.
8) Helen **is** not wearing her wedding ring today.

Chapter 7

The Past Simple Exercises

✓ **Complete the following sentences using the past simple forms of the verbs given in brackets.**

Answer

1) I accidently arrived at school late yesterday.
2) The play tonight was excellent.
3) The last time Taylor and I played with each other was already a week ago.
4) After he got his test results, Doug became very pleased.
5) You were at home when I called you yesterday so you can't be the criminal.
6) As it turns out, the dinner Gary bought us yesterday cost him over $300!
7) We were in such a hurry that we almost forgot to bring our child!

The Past Simple Negative Exercises

✓ Complete the following sentences using the past simple negative forms of the verbs given in brackets.

Answer

1) I did not go out last night because I felt sick.
2) You did not come to the party last week. Where were you?
3) He did not feel well after watching the slasher movie.
4) David and I did not do a good job in our presentations yesterday.
5) The book was not very fun; I did not enjoy it much.
6) The comedians on stage last night were not entertaining at all.
7) I did not buy chocolates today because you need to start staying away from them.

Past Simple Questions Exercises

✓ Complete the following questions using the correct past forms of the verbs and the subjects given in brackets

Answer

1) Did you buy a new dress?
2) Why didn't you come to the party last week?
3) When did he leave work yesterday?
4) Was he always this tall?
5) Were you in the gym anytime during the last week?
6) Did you eat the cookies that were left here?
7) Weren't they over 40 years-old already?

The Past Continuous Exercises

✓ Complete each of the following sentences using the past continuous form of one verb and the past simple form of the other verb given in brackets.

Answer

1) I was walking to the bus stop when it suddenly started to rain.
2) She was trying really hard to fix it already before you arrived.
3) I heard the postman knocking on the front door while I was talking on the phone yesterday.
4) They stopped by the grocery store while they were driving home yesterday to buy some onions.
5) Students were whispering to each other until the principal told them to be quiet.

The Present Perfect Simple Exercises 01

   ✓   **Complete the following sentences using the present perfect simple tense of the verbs given in brackets.**

Answer
1) Today's the due day and he still hasn't done his homework.
2) I have visited the nurse's office several times during last week because of the flu.
3) My parents have not been on a plane before so they're feeling quite anxious now.
4) She has received an eviction notice from her landlord recently; that's why she's so stressed out.
5) He has known David for years; they're very close friends.
6) We have been here for two weeks already!
7) Ray hasn't met my new sister yet.

The Present Perfect Simple Exercises 02

   ✓   **Complete the following questions in the present perfect simple tense.**

Answer
1) Have you cleaned your room yet?
2) Haven't you seen the notice yet? They're renovating the gym!
3) Have you been sick lately? I haven't seen you in class recently.
4) Have you received any news from David recently? I haven't heard him in ages.

   ✓   **Choose the correct word for each sentence.**

Answer
1) I've (gone/been) to New York only once in my life.
2) She's (gone/been) to the hospital because she hurt herself badly while cooking.
3) They've (gone/been) to Paris to meet their business partners.
4) I've (gone/been) to the principal's office twice this week because I got into a fight with my classmate.

The Present Perfect Simple Exercises 03

   ✓   **Use either the past simple tense or the present perfect simple tense to complete the sentences**

Answer
1) He has visited the principal's office five times already this week. He went there yesterday too! I swear he's such a troublemaker!
2) I have been to China many times. In fact, I was in China this very moment last week!
3) Jack got out of the hospital two days ago. He has been in there over the last two weeks.
4) Michael has been to prison a couple of times in the past, but he wasn't in prison in March 2021.

The Present Perfect Continuous Exercises

✓ **Use either the present perfect simple or the present perfect continuous to complete the following paragraph.**

Answer

Hello, my name is Sam. I have been playing for Leeds United for three years now. I have dreamt of becoming a professional football player ever since I was a kid. To achieve that goal, I started training as early as when I was nine years-old. When I turned 15, I was accepted into the Leeds United academy. Ever since then, I have been training for over six hours every day, even after being accepted into the professional team. All the training definitely has paid off, as I have scored 26 goals for my team already in my 34 appearances. Especially, in the recent matches, I have been scoring almost every match! But, as you'd agree, I have worked hard to achieve this form. And I will continue to work hard to keep my performance up.

The Past Perfect Simple Exercises 01

✓ **Complete the following sentences using the past perfect simple or the past simple**

Answer
1) Before I came here, I had spoken to Jack. I can confirm that he is not responsible for this case.
2) I had watched the movie three times already by the time Jenny saw it for the first time. In fact, I'm the one who recommended her to watch it in the first place.
3) I had gone over the topic five times yesterday, so I didn't find the test difficult at all, unlike some others.
4) If I had read the book earlier, I would have been able to have a deeper conversation about it with you. It's a shame I haven't.

The Past Perfect Simple Exercises 02

✓ **Complete the following sentences using either the past perfect simple or the present perfect simple.**

Answer
1) You have changed your style recently. Did something happen to you?
2) I had noticed that my car was struggling by then, but it was too late to turn around.
3) There has been a change to the company policies. You should read up on them as soon as possible.
4) Have you seen my car keys? I swear I left them on the dinner table yesterday.
5) Emily had stayed in her house for a whole week already when her friend Jane realized that she's under quarantine.

The Past Perfect Continuous Exercises

✓ **Complete the following sentences using either the past perfect continuous or the present perfect continuous.**

Answer

1) Ryan has been studying about space ever since he was a kid. That's why he took the astrophysics major.
2) They have been constructing new buildings left and right around here recently. I bet this town is destined for a redevelopment.
3) Since 1929, America's economy had been falling continuously until the recession in 1937, which is when Roosevelt's New Deal Policies started to show positive results.
4) By the time Ray finally answered the phone, his parents had been trying to reach him for hours already.

Used to vs. Would Exercises 01

✓ **If it's possible, make a sentence with 'would'. If it's not possible, use 'used to'.**

Answer

1) She used to love playing tennis before she hurt her wrist.
2) He would walk along the beach every morning before breakfast.
3) We used to live in Sydney.
4) My family would often go to the zoo for the weekend when I was young.
5) She used to have long hair when she was a teenager.
6) We would go to the same cafeteria for lunch every day when I was a student.

Used to vs. Would Exercises 02

✓ **Find sentences with mistakes and fix them (some sentences may not have any mistakes).**

Answer

1) Yes, I remember the time when we would play in the woods every day. → OK!
2) We used to live in LA before moving to New York City. That's why we're so unaccustomed to the coldness around here during winter. → OK!
3) Based on my looks now, maybe you'd be surprise to hear that I ~~would~~ used to be extremely overweight up until just a few months ago.
4) I would visit my uncle almost every month when I was young. Unfortunately, now, we're not that close anymore. → OK!
5) I ~~would~~ used to love watching reality TV shows when I was a kid, but, these days, none of the shows are funny to me anymore.

Chapter 8

The "Will" Exercises

✓ **Use "will" to complete the following sentences in the future tense.**

Answer
1) I'm feeling too tired right now. Maybe I will exercise later.
2) I get a feeling that it will rain tomorrow.
3) We bought a lot of stuff today. Maybe I will carry the bags.
4) I'm excited to meet you tomorrow. You will be surprised at how much I've changed.
5) Something just came up. I will look at that later.
6) If we keep going this slow, we won't make it to the party in time.
7) There seems to be another thunderstorm on the way. We won't leave the house tonight.
8) Will you go to the party tonight?

The "Going to" Exercises

✓ **Use "going to" to complete the following sentences in the future tense.**

Answer
1) I bet she is going to get a perfect score on this test.
2) The train is going to arrive at 7:00 PM. We should get going now to pick her up in time.
3) The weather forecast says it is going to rain tomorrow.
4) According to the scientists, it is not going to be possible to develop a cure for this disease in the next few years.
5) Within the next decade, newspapers are not going to be printed anymore.
6) Are you going to come to the meeting tomorrow?
7) Is she going to tell him about what happened to his car?
8) Are they going to be promoted today?

The "Will" vs. "Going to" Exercises

✓ **Use either "will" or "going to" to complete the following sentences in the future tense. Choose carefully.**

Answer
1) I just realized that I haven't visited my grandparents in a while. I guess I will visit them this weekend.
2) I am going to visit my grandparents this weekend because this Saturday's my grandfather's birthday.
3) Are you going to attend the meeting this weekend?
4) I baked these cookies. I'm sure you will love them!
5) You seem pretty occupied. I will take out the garbage.
6) I'm genuinely excited for this concert. My favorite singer is going to be on stage tonight.
7) Jack is going to leave school a little early today because he has a dentist's appointment in the afternoon.

The Present for Future Events Exercises

✓ **Rewrite each sentence using <u>both</u> the present simple and the present continuous to express the future**

Answer
1) We are going to have a party tomorrow.
   → We have a party tomorrow. / We are having a party tomorrow.
2) A storm will come to Korea this week.
   → A storm comes to Korea this week. / A storm is coming to Korea this week.
3) The train will arrive soon.
   → The train arrives soon. / The train is arriving soon.
4) The movie is going to start now.
   → The movie starts now. / The movie is starting now.

Future Continuous Exercises

✓ **Complete the following sentences in the future continuous form.**

Answer
1) I will be starting a business in November.
2) This time tomorrow, she is going to be visiting her parents.
3) At three o'clock tomorrow, they are going to be evacuating the building due to a pre-scheduled disinfection job.
4) I can finish the report by 11:00 PM, but I guess you will be sleeping by then.
5) Our guests are going to be arriving at two o'clock tomorrow. Be ready to greet them politely.
6) I won't be playing golf this afternoon. I just got an urgent business that I need to take care of.
7) They will be having a good time in Spain by the end of this week.

The Future Perfect Exercises

✓ **Complete the sentences using the future perfect simple tense**

Answer
1) Hopefully, by this time tomorrow, I will have completed my homework.
2) By next year, they will have redeveloped this town. Everything will be different.
3) I will have lost some weight by then, because I need to attend my sister's wedding.
4) You will have received your test scores by this Sunday.

✓ **Complete the sentences using the future perfect continuous tense.**

Answer
1) By next month, they will have been working on that skyscraper for already a year.
2) In just a few weeks, this restaurant will have been running for 40 years.
3) In three years, Lionel Messi will have been playing professional soccer for 20 years.
4) If it rains tomorrow as well, it will have been raining for a week straight

The Future for Past Predictions Exercises

✓   **Use the future tense to complete the following past predictions.**

Answer
1) The ceremony was going to take place today, but it was delayed due to the rain.
2) Jake was going to leave for Paris yesterday, but he had some urgent business to take care of. He's leaving this afternoon.
3) I went home early yesterday because I was going to clean the house. But by the time I got home, I was too tired that I ended up not doing it.
4) They were going to close the school during the holidays, but they decided not to after realizing that many students were planning to stay on campus.

(You can use the other expressions (i.e., "would" or the past continuous) as well.)

Chapter 10

Countable and Uncountable Nouns Exercises

✓   **Write "C" in front of countable nouns and "UC" in front of uncountable nouns**

Answer

1) __C___ Car	5) _UC__ Music	9) __UC_ Homework
2) __UC__ Oil	6) _C_ Newspaper	10) __UC_ Equipment
3) __C___ House	7) __UC_ Internet	11) _UC_ Information
4) __UC___ Time	8) ___C__ Year	12) __C_ Hat

The Plural Form Exercises

✓   **Write the plural forms of the given nouns.**

Answer

1) Cat → cats	10) Stair → stairs
2) Desk → desks	11) Dish → dishes
3) Trip → trips	12) Stone → stones
4) Lock → locks	13) Store → stores
5) Thought → thoughts	14) Bay → bays
6) Try → tries	15) Hoof → hooves
7) Day → days	16) Domino → dominos
8) Fox → foxes	17) French fry → French fries
9) Wish → wishes	18) Ice cream → ice creams

Countable and Uncountable Nouns in Sentences Exercises 01

✓ **Fix the errors in the following sentences (some sentences may not have any errors).**

Answer
1) There are some ~~egg~~ eggs in the fridge.
2) I'd like to order two ~~cup~~ cups of black ~~coffees~~ coffee.
3) Here, have some rice. → OK!
4) This recipe calls for two cups of milk. → OK!
5) Can we place an order for two ~~spaghettis~~ plates of spaghetti?
6) There ~~is a~~ are three sandwiches in my lunch bag.
7) I've had some thoughts about your suggestion. → OK!
8) Two different opinions were raised in today's meeting. → OK!

Countable and Uncountable Nouns in Sentences Exercises 02

✓ **Make the following uncountable nouns countable by using appropriate units.**

Answer
1) Rice → bag of, bowl of, grain of …
2) Water → bottle of, cup of …
3) Music → sheet of, piece of …
4) Time → period of …

Countable and Uncountable Nouns in Sentences Exercises 03

✓ **Turn the following sentences into negative forms.**

Answer
1) There is no / isn't any cereal left in the cupboard.
2) There is no / isn't any water in the Sahara Desert.
3) There are no / aren't any children playing in the playground.
4) There is no / isn't a guest bed in my house.
5) There are no / aren't any people in the cafeteria.
6) There is no / isn't a smoking lounge in this hotel.
7) There is no / isn't any music playing in the café.
8) There are no / aren't any pets in my house.
9) There is no / isn't any news you need to hear.

Countable and Uncountable Nouns in Sentences Exercises 04

✓ **Turn the following sentences into simple questions (i.e., no quantities).**

Answer
1) There is some sugar left in the bag. → Is there any sugar left in the bag?
2) There is a plane leaving for New York today. → Is there a plane leaving for New York today?
3) There are some fishes in this lake. → Are there any fishes in this lake?
4) There is water on Mars. → Is there any water on Mars?

Countable and Uncountable Nouns in Sentences Exercises 05

✓ **Turn the following sentences into questions asking for quantities.**

Answer
1) There are some oranges in the fridge. → How many oranges are there in the fridge?
2) There is some time before the ceremony. → How much time is there before the ceremony?
3) There is some coffee left in the cup. → How much coffee is left in the cup?
4) There are some guests in the house tonight. → How many guests are there in the house tonight?

Subject-Verb Agreement Exercises 01

✓ **Choose the correct verb from the bracket for each sentence.**

Answer
1) Paris (is / are / was) often referred to as the "city of love".
2) This coffee (is / has / was) a very bitter flavor.
3) The United States (are / is / was) officially founded in 1776.
4) Jack and Emily (have / are / was) great friends for each other.
5) My team (has / is / have) reached the semi-finals in this tournament.
6) The workers' union (were / was / is) formed two years ago after the mistreatment of one of the workers by the company.
7) The Harvard University (is / has / was) currently one of the most respected universities in the world.

Abstract and Concrete Nouns Exercises 01

✓ **Identify the nouns in bold as either abstract ("A") or concrete ("C").**

Answer
1) ___A__ You need high **intelligence** to tackle this problem.
2) ___C__ This **picture** is breathtakingly beautiful.
3) ___A__ I respect your high **confidence**.
4) ___A__ It took a while for me to earn the **trust** of this street cat.
5) ___C__ One of my front **teeth** fell out today.
6) ___A__ I am going to visit my grandparents this **summer**.
7) ___C__ I took a math **exam** today.
8) ___C__ I went outside to take in some fresh **air**.
9) ___A__ The **air** around the house felt different today.

Compound Nouns Exercises 01

✓ **Form the plural forms of the following compound nouns.**

Answer
1) Bedroom → bedrooms
2) Motorcycle → motorcycles
3) Washing machine → washing machines
4) Driver's license → driver's licenses
5) Rainfall → rainfalls *(even when the compound noun doesn't end with a noun, if it's a single word, just add –s at the very end, not to the noun.)*
6) Haircut → haircuts

7) Policeman → policemen
8) Swimming pool → swimming pools
9) Greenhouse → greenhouses

Chapter 11

Verb Patterns Exercises

✓ **Use either the infinitive or the gerund to complete the following sentences.**

Answer
1) I hope to run my own restaurant in the near future.
2) I enjoy riding my bicycle to work.
3) She's kept quiet for long enough. She deserves a chance to speak now.
4) I love to eat / eating sweets whenever I feel down.
5) This appears to be a serious problem.
6) I usually avoid going to sleep too late, but sometimes, I can't help it.
7) I intend to lose / losing at least 10 kilos before my brother's wedding arrives.
8) I prefer to watch / watching movies at home rather than going to the theaters
(Don't be stressed that you didn't get some of these correct. You can't learn infinitives and gerunds. It just means that you don't have enough experience with them yet.)

Verb Patterns with Objects Exercises

✓ **Complete each sentence using the given noun as the object and the given verb as either the to-infinite or the gerund form.**

Answer
1) My mother wants me to study law but I really don't want to.
2) On my way home, I remembered my father asking me to buy some flowers. So, I stopped by at the florist store.
3) My friend always reminds me to clean my bathroom. Without her, it'd normally be much dirtier than it is now.
4) While driving by the tennis court yesterday, I saw Tom playing tennis with his girlfriend, Taylor.
(Again, don't stress yourself too much over not getting the infinitives/gerunds correct.)

Verb Patterns with Prepositions Exercises

✓ **Use the preposition and the verb given in the bracket to complete the sentences. If there's a noun in the bracket, use it as an object.**

Answer
1) He didn't give up in spite of failing many times.
2) After finishing her studies, she moved to the big city.
3) Check facts before reposting news or stories from shady websites.
4) What was the President's reaction on learning about this issue?
5) They won the award by working hard as a team.
6) After his teacher pointed it out, Jack apologized for telling a lie.
(Only the gerund form is correct in this question.)

Chapter 12

Personal Pronouns Exercises 01

✓ **Put appropriate subject pronouns in the blanks to complete the sentences.**

Answer
1) My name is Sue. I am 24 years-old.
2) My mom's name is Angie. She is from Germany.
3) Bob is my dad. He works as a chiropractor.
4) I still have two friends back in my hometown. They are both in the police force.
5) My favorite activity is running. It makes me feel energetic.
6) To all of the students in the class, have you ever been to Greenland?
7) Today is Jack's 70th birthday. He used to be my high school teacher.
8) Isabelle is my dog. She is a girl.
9) I have 13 colleagues at work. We all love playing tennis; that's why everyone's in the tennis group.

Personal Pronouns Exercises 02

✓ **Put appropriate object pronouns in the blanks to complete the sentences.**

Answer

1) My sister Jane loves books. This novel is for her.
2) My children like Disney films. The video is for them.
3) My brother Matt collects picture postcards. These postcards are for him.
4) We had to bring one dish each to the party. I brought casseroles for us.
5) I like watches. This new watch is for me.
6) Here is another souvenir. I don't know what to do with it.
7) I bought these flowers for you to celebrate your graduation.
8) My dream is to become a police officer. I enrolled into a police school for it.
9) Since you told me you wanted to watch a sad movie, I borrowed this one for us/you tonight.

Reflexive Pronouns Exercises 01

Use reflexive pronouns to complete the sentences. For some sentences, you should not use one.

Answer
1) He decided to fix the fence himself.
2) Calm yourself down. You shouldn't be so loud in an airplane.
3) I didn't believe in him until I saw the UFO myself.
4) Sally looked at herself in the mirror.
5) He went to bed (don't need) at 10 PM yesterday.
6) You should do your homework yourself.
7) Boys, can you make your beds yourselves?
8) We can move the table ourselves.
9) What does a cat think when it sees itself in the mirror?

Reflexive Pronouns Exercises 02

  ✓ **Pick the correct location to put the reflexive pronoun.**

Answer

A-2, B-1, C-1, D-2

Reflexive Pronouns Exercises 03

  ✓ **Complete the sentences by putting in a reflexive pronoun, "each other", or nothing.**

Answer
1) John hurt himself while climbing the tree.
2) Peter and Sue helped each other with the homework.
3) My parents helped themselves to some soup first at the buffet.
4) The wild monkey looked at itself in the mirror.
5) I feel (don't need) much better today.
6) Bridget and Billy smiled at each other.
7) I don't remember (don't need) where we spent our holiday last year.
8) Did you make that yourself?

Possession Exercises 01

  ✓ **Use possessive determiners to complete the sentences.**

Answer
1) Here's a postcard that I received from my friend, Peggy.
2) She lives in Australia, but the rest of her family lives in Japan.
3) Mark works at a fashion company. His company is located in Sydney.
4) Meg and Mohammed live in Newcastle. Their children both go to a school 15 minutes away from their house.
5) We decided to sell our car because we moved closer to our workplace.
6) Yesterday, I lost my purse in the metro. Thankfully, I picked it up today at Bryant Park station.
7) We mowed our lawn last weekend but it already looks like it needs another mowing.

Possession Exercises 02

  ✓ **Use possessive pronouns to complete the sentences.**

Answer
1) I bought this book for you. The book is all yours.
2) This games console is ours. We take turns using it.
3) We met Paul and Jane last night. That house across the street is theirs.
4) Mr. Smith has requested us to hold his luggage for him until he leaves tonight. These bags are all his.
5) I just bought this car yesterday. I still can't believe that it's mine!
6) There's a bird in our garden. That nest is its.
7) I just finished processing Mrs. Bellini's photos. Those ones on my desk are all hers.
8) This was not my fault. It was yours, so you should fix it.

Possession Exercises 03

✓ **Use the "apostrophe + s" ("-'s") to express possessions.**

Answer
1) Lizzie's cat
2) Thomas's car
3) Our parents' house
4) Men's rooms
5) America's favorite singer
6) My father's tools

Possession Exercises 04

✓ **Use appropriate expressions of possessions to fill in the blanks.**

Answer

It's so nice to be visiting my hometown. That house across the street used to be mine. I've lived there for nine years, right until I left this town. My parents also grew up in this town. I don't remember their house though. I have a friend who still lives in this town – Mark; that house over there is his. We went to the same elementary school, and we used to use the playground like it was ours. That's not Mark's car though – I know his car. It must be his wife's car. That pool is theirs too – I heard he installed it just last year.

Possession Exercises 05

✓ **Find what's wrong with the following sentences and correct the mistakes. Some sentences may not have any mistakes.**

Answer

1) Wait, that's Sarah's dog! I know ~~its her~~ it's hers! Why is it by itself?
2) Up until the late ~~2000's~~ 2000s, men usually wore ~~his~~ their ties long, but now, they usually wear them short.
3) Hey, that's ~~Tom's~~ Tom and Sarah's house! They moved in together after they got married.
4) That's his new car. I know it's his because I've seen it on Thanksgiving Day. → OK!
5) That's their ~~childrens'~~ children's toy. They get really mad if you touch it.
6) Happy birthday Gary! What's ~~you're~~ your first thought of entering your ~~30's~~ 30s?
7) Wait, isn't that Chris's watch? Why is it on my desk? → OK!

Indefinite Pronouns Exercises 01

✓ **Put indefinite pronouns in the blanks to complete the sentences.**

Answer
1) She wants to live somewhere by the sea one day.
2) She put everything in the box; literally all that she had.
3) Does anyone/anybody have a phone charger?
4) We went nowhere this weekend. We stayed at home.
5) You didn't bring anything! You knew it was Britany's birthday party today, right?
6) Is there someone/somebody in this bathroom stall?
7) Q: What's wrong? / A: Nothing, I'm fine.
8) Would you like to go someplace this weekend? We've stayed in the house for the entire week.
9) Everybody was really friendly, including all the managers and even the CEO.

Indefinite Pronouns Exercises 02

✓ **Find what's wrong with the following sentences and correct the errors. Some may not have any mistakes.**

Answer
1) You can have anything you want! → OK!
2) There is ~~anybody~~ somebody/nobody here. *OR* There ~~is~~ isn't anybody here.
3) Everybody ~~are~~ is here for Christmas – even my grandparents!
4) There really ~~isn't~~ is nothing you can do under his surveillance.
   OR There really isn't ~~nothing~~ anything you can do under his surveillance.
5) Does anybody need help? → OK!
6) Why is ~~anybody~~ somebody/nobody here? *OR* Why ~~is~~ isn't anybody here?
   (The meanings of above the questions are different!)
7) Can someone teach me how to play this game? → OK!

Chapter 13

Articles Exercises 01

✓ **Put "a", "an", or nothing in the blanks to complete the sentences**

Answer
1) This is a book.
2) I bought an interesting book yesterday.
3) I like to read (nothing) books.
4) He is an engineer at a small company.
5) Do you have a computer at home?
6) Do you like (nothing) chocolates?
7) Could you give me a pen, please?
8) People need (nothing) food.
9) He will arrive here in an hour.
10) She teaches (nothing) mathematics.

Articles Exercises 02

✓ **Put "a", "an", or "the" in the blanks to complete the sentences.**

Answer
1) Does Tom have a car?
2) He was not very successful as an actor.
3) I went to the supermarket to buy some bread.
4) The story that he told me was interesting.
5) There is an old man at the door.
6) Would you like a sandwich?
7) Madrid is the capital of Spain.
8) My son is at the airport now.
9) It's going to rain. Take an umbrella.
10) Maria is wearing a nice gray suit today.

Articles Exercises 03

✓ **Put "the" or nothing in the blanks to complete the sentences.**

Answer
1) Welcome to the United States!
2) I mostly use (nothing) Facebook to communicate with my friends.
3) Although Jack was born in (nothing) Canada, his mother language is (nothing) Russian.
4) The FBI headquarters is located in (nothing) Washington, D.C.
5) I heard that the University of Pennsylvania is collaborating with (nothing) Stanford University to find the cure to the disease.
6) The Pope delivered a speech about the gender minorities at the Vatican Palace.
7) The 1910s was an agonizing period for the Koreans as the country was under control by (nothing) Japan.
8) There's a huge hotel under construction on (nothing) Brighton Avenue.

Articles Exercises 04

✓ **Put "a", "an", "the", or nothing to complete the following paragraph.**

Answer
And so even though we face the difficulties of (nothing) today and (nothing) tomorrow, I still have a dream. It is a dream deeply rotted in the American dream. I have a dream that one day this nation will rise up and live out the true meanings of its creed: "We hold these truths to be self-evident, that all (nothing) men are created equal." I have a dream that one day on the red hills of Georgia, the sons of former slaves and the sons of former slave owners will be able to sit down together at the table of brotherhood. I have a dream that one day even the state of Mississippi, a state sweltering with the heat of (nothing) injustice, sweltering with the heat of (nothing) oppression, will be transformed into an oasis of (nothing) freedom and (nothing) justice. I have a dream that my four little children will one day live in a nation where they will not be judged by the color of their skin, but by the content of their character.
(Taken from Martin Luther King, Jr.'s famous speech, "I Have a Dream.")

Quantifiers Exercises 01

✓ **Put either "little" or "few" in the blanks.**

Answer
1) Julia ate little rice; she wasn't very hungry.
2) Mike ate few chips; he wasn't very hungry.
3) I have few cousins that speak French; the rest of them only speak English.
4) She found few cookies under her bed.
5) I need little water to feel better, that's all.
6) I want to save little money to buy a present for my mother.
7) Robert gave me few coins to buy a sweater; it is not enough!
8) Ashley needs little sugar for the cake!
9) My dad says that I should learn few words in German before leaving for Germany this weekend.

Quantifiers Exercises 02

✓ **Put either "much" or "many" in the blanks.**

Answer

1) There are many students who want to work in our school.
2) Claire has many brothers but only one sister.
3) I don't have much time; I can't wait for you.
4) Tom works many hours every day—that is why he is always tired.
5) Lisa doesn't drink much water when she eats.
6) They have many rooms in their house; it is very big.
7) How many apples did you buy?
8) How much money do you need to have to buy the TV?
9) People don't write many letters nowadays—they use the email instead.
10) I think it's too much salt for my taste.

Quantifiers Exercises 03

✓ **Put appropriate quantifiers in the blanks to describe yourself.**

Answer

The following are just examples. It's okay if yours look different.

1) I have a lot of friends at school.
2) I have only a few members in my family.
3) I get enough money for my weekly/monthly allowances.
4) I spend a large amount of time for my studies during the weekdays.
5) I spend much time to relax during the weekends.
6) I have many books in my house.
7) I have barely any toys in my house.
8) I eat almost no snacks between meals.
9) I drink lots of water during meals

Demonstratives Exercises

✓ **Put "this", "that", "these", or "those" in the blanks**

Answer

1) These books are mine. (close to you)
2) Those toys are broken. (far away from you)
3) This program was planned to boost your health.
4) It seems like that course didn't end up helping you much.
5) I went on a 4-hour hike yesterday. That was exhausting.
6) Thanks for inviting me to the party. This is so much more fun than I expected.
7) The books on this table are staying but those by the fireplace are going.
8) These are the cookies that I baked. Try them—they turned out great.

Numbers Exercises 01

- ✓ **Spell out the following expressions as how you'd *say* them.**

Answer
1) 294 → two hundred and ninety-four
2) 0.67 → (zero) point six seven
3) 1776 (year) → seventeen seventy-six
4) 7:30 PM → seven thirty PM
5) 22 (age) → twenty-two years-old
6) 1/5 → a/one fifth
7) 1500s (century) → the fifteen hundreds
8) '70s (decade) → the seventies
9) Jul 14 → July fourteenth
10) Sep 11, 2009 → September eleventh, two thousand (and) nine
11) 24360 (number) → twenty-four thousand, three hundred and sixty
12) 56% → fifty-six percent
13) 37th → the thirty-seventh
14) 5.282 → five point two eight two

Numbers Exercises 02

- ✓ **Convert the expressions in bold as numbers**

Answer

We welcome you to the 7th annual meeting of the Green Energy Society (GES)! It's being held on June 16, 2021 and our main focus this time is renewable energy. Over 1000 members have already expressed their will to attend this meeting, with roughly 1/5 of them being professors from all over the world! Regarding your stay, we regret to inform you that, due to the overflow of participants, we must allocate at least 30% of the attendees to a hotel that's not on the site. We hope you would understand the situation. Finally, don't forget to attend the dinner party on the day, which is held in the main hall at 6:30 PM! We're looking forward to meeting every single one of you!

Distributives Exercises

- ✓ **Put in appropriate distributives in the blanks.**

Answer
1) The train leaves every four hours.
2) There are two towels in the bathroom. You can take either of them. (only one)
3) I have two sisters. Both of them are teachers. (all of them)
4) Every child wants to win the prize but only one of them can win it.
5) Eva and Julie are both students.
6) I like neither of the films you've recommended. (none)
7) Both Susie and Eva are nice and friendly. I like them.
8) Everybody gets one meal during the flight. You can order either the beef or the chicken meal.
9) Neither the children nor the teachers found the principal's speech interesting.

Chapter 14

Using Adjectives Exercises 01

✓ **Rewrite** the sentences while using the adjective in the brackets to describe the noun in bold. Use the adjective <u>before</u> the noun.

Answer
1) He is a skillful **basketball player**. (skillful)
2) The intelligent **dog** returned to her owner with her toy. (intelligent)
3) The boring **presentation** took an hour to finish. (boring)
4) He is the fast **runner** who won the race. (fast)

Using Adjectives Exercises 02

✓ **Rewrite** the sentences while using the adjective in the brackets to describe the noun in bold. Use the adjective <u>after</u> the noun.

Answer
1) This train is long. (long)
2) This car is blue. (blue)
3) This chair is broken. (broken)
4) This tree is tall. (tall)

Using Adjectives Exercises 03

✓ **Rewrite** the sentences while using the adjectives in the brackets to describe the noun in bold. Be careful of the <u>order</u> in which you use the adjectives.

Answer
1) Look at that small brown **dog**. (brown, small)
2) A kind old **man** told me how to get to here. (kind, old)
3) He seems to really like that black leather **jacket**. (black, leather)
4) She just bought that big red American **truck**. (big, red, American)
5) He is an agile tall young **basketball player**. (young, agile, tall)
6) This is a comfortable new velvet **dress** I bought yesterday. (new, comfortable, velvet)
7) That's a lovely old ceramic **coffee mug**. (lovely, ceramic, old)
8) What a nice white cotton **skirt**! (white, nice, cotton)

Using Adjectives Exercises 04

✓ **Find what's wrong with the following sentences and fix them. Some sentences may not have anything wrong with them.**

Answer

1) The lightning and thunder really ~~frightening~~ frightened my dog last night.
2) The movie you recommended to me was very entertaining. → OK!
3) This song has very ~~interested~~ interesting lyrics.
4) I was really ~~boring~~ bored during the flight.
5) I was ~~alarming~~ alarmed by the loud sound.
6) The weather in UK is always so depressing! → OK!
7) John was really ~~embarrassing~~ embarrassed when he fell over in front of his friends.
8) Thanks for introducing me to this very ~~excited~~ exciting book.
9) I hate doing chores because it's exhausting. → OK!

Using Adjectives Exercises 05

✓ **Use the two adjectives in the brackets to describe the noun in bold. Think carefully about which sets are <u>coordinate</u> and which are not.**

Answer

I've added "and" between the coordinate adjectives here; you can also place a comma (",") instead

1) It's a happy and lively **puppy**. (happy, lively)
2) Who put this big red **sticker** here? (red, big)
3) What a gratifying and productive **day**. (gratifying, productive)
4) This is a thrilling and suspenseful **book**. (thrilling, suspenseful)
5) Thanks for this lovely little **gift**. (lovely, little)
6) His large brick **house** has three rooms. (large, brick)
7) Smart and funny, **Jamie** quickly advanced as a class leader. (smart, funny)
8) Your son is a nice and intelligent **boy**. (nice, intelligent)
9) Your daughter is an athletic young **girl**. (athletic, young)

Comparatives & As... As Exercises 01

✓ **<u>Combine</u> the two sentences into one by using an appropriate comparative to compare the two nouns in bold.**

Answer

1) Tom is shorter than Jack. / Jack is taller than Tom.
2) A cheetah is faster than a coyote. / A coyote is slower than a cheetah.
   (For the rest, only one version of the sentence is written.)
3) A Ragdoll cat weighs (is) heavier than an American Shorthair cat.
4) Fireworks are louder than car horns.
5) Coca Cola costs more (is more expensive) than Pepsi.
6) The sun rises earlier during (in) the summer than during (in) the winter.
7) *Wonder* is shorter than *The House of the Scorpions*.

Comparatives & As... As Exercises 02

✓   **Rewrite** the sentences using the **double comparative** expression.

Answer

(Be careful of the cause and result – the cause must come first!)

1) The harder you train, the stronger your body gets.
2) The harder you study, the more you learn.
3) The faster the car is, the more dangerous it is to drive.
4) The more you think about your problems, the less relaxed you feel.
5) The richer the person, the more privilege he enjoys.
6) The more you study for a test, the higher your score will be.
7) The crazier the idea, the more fun it is to try.
8) The more difficult the task is, the sweeter it is to succeed.

Comparatives & As... As Exercises 03

✓   **Express the following similarities and differences using the "as... as" expression.**

Answer

(You must include the entire specific adjective between "as... as".)

(In the case where two nouns have similar qualities, the positions of the nouns can be swapped.)

1) Ralph is as tall as Craig.
2) Domestic cats are not as slow as Galapagos tortoises. /
   Galapagos tortoises are not as fast as domestic cats.
3) Ragdoll cats weigh as much as (are as heavy as) Maine Coon cats.
4) Traffic is as loud as vacuum cleaners.
5) The sun rises not as late during the winter as during the summer. /
   The sun rises not as early during the summer as during the winter.
6) Sitting for too long is as bad for your health as smoking.
7) *Wonder* is not as long as *The House of the Scorpions*. /
   The House of the Scorpions is not as short as *Wonder*.

Superlatives Exercises 01

✓   **Use superlatives to write two sentences for each given group to express both extremes.**

Answer

1) Jake is the tallest (person in the group); Brooke is the shortest (person in the group).
2) KTX trains are the fastest; subway trains are the slowest.
3) Cheetahs are the lightest (animal in the group); tigers are the heaviest (animal in the group).
4) A whisper is the most quiet (sound in the group); a firework is the loudest (sound in the group).
5) *A Wrinkle in Time* is the shortest (book in the group); *The House of the Scorpions* is the longest (book in the group).

Complete the sentences using too or very.

Answer
1) The tea is very hot, but I can drink it.
2) The tea is too hot. I can't drink it.
3) I can't sleep. It's too noisy in the dorm at night.
4) You can't lift a car. A car is too heavy.
5) An elephant is big. A mouse is very small.
6) I lost your dictionary. I'm very sorry. I'll buy you a new one.
7) I can't put my dictionary in my pocket. My dictionary is too big.
8) Did you enjoy your dinner last night? / Yes. The food was very good!
9) Can you read that sign across the street? / No, I can't. It's too far away.
10) A sports car is very expensive, but Anita can buy one if she wants to.

Chapter 15

Adverbs of Manner Exercises 01

✓ **Add the adverb given in brackets into each sentence.**

Answer *(For some adverbs, you can use them elsewhere as well.)*
1) James coughed loudly to attract her attention.
2) He plays the flute beautifully.
3) We dress casually on Fridays.
4) She finished her dinner quickly.
5) He opened the door quietly.
6) It rained heavily through the entire night.
7) You should close the lid tightly.
8) The nurse picked up the baby gently.
9) You performed fantastically in the concert yesterday.
10) She opened the present hurriedly.

Adverbs of Manner Exercises 02

✓ **Fix the errors in the following sentences. Some may not have any errors.**

Answer *(For some adverbs, you can use them elsewhere as well.)*
1) I slept badly last night. → OK
2) You speak ~~fluently~~ English fluently.
3) He ~~hard~~ worked hard to get a promotion.
4) Try to do it carefully so we don't have to redo it. → OK
5) Julie tearfully said goodbye to her boyfriend. → OK
6) They happily ate ~~happily~~ the food.
7) The ball ~~fast~~ flew past them fast.
8) They unfortunately missed ~~unfortunately~~ the train.
9) The cat skillfully caught the mouse. → OK
10) The dog quickly ran after the ball. → OK

Adverbs of Manner Exercises 03

✓ Put **either** the adverb or the adjective in the blanks. Pay attention to the type of verb being used in the sentence.

Answer

1) Peter quickly walked toward the door.
2) The wine tastes fine.
3) Sarah felt terrible about shouting to her mother.
4) The sommelier tasted the wine carefully.
5) The food all went bad.
6) She slammed the door angrily.
7) He gently woke the sleeping woman.
8) Though she was scared stiff, she remained calm.
9) I knew that giving a good impression would become important later.

Adverbs of Manner Exercises 04

✓ You're combining the two sentences into one. Choose between A or B where to put the adverb in bold.

Answer

1) He told me that everyone in the house was asleep. So, he asked me to be quiet while leaving the house.
   → He asked me to leave the house quietly. (B)
2) Upon arrival, she soon realized that she didn't like the party. So, she decided to leave as soon as possible.
   → She quickly decided to leave the party. (A)
3) She had to leave the party, but she didn't want anyone to notice. So, she decided to act fast.
   → She decided to leave the party quickly. (B)
4) The children were being so loud. So, the teacher asked them to be quiet and finish their game.
   → The teacher asked the children to finish their game quietly. (B)
5) The children were taking too long finishing the game. So, the teacher gently asked them to finish it.
   → The teacher quietly asked the children to finish their game. (A)

Adverbs of Degree Exercises 01

✓ Add the adverb given in brackets into each sentence.

Answer

1) The water was extremely cold.
2) The movie is quite interesting.
3) She is running very fast.
4) You are walking too slowly.
5) You are running fast enough.
6) You seem absolutely exhausted.
7) I am totally starving.
8) This cake is absolutely wonderful.
9) The temperature was barely above freezing.
10) Our driveway is completely frozen.

Adverbs of Degree Exercises 02

✓ Add the appropriate word in the blank between the two given in brackets. Think about whether the adjective/adverb is gradable or non-gradable.

Answer

1) Let's stay in tonight; it's absolutely freezing outside. *(non-gradable)*
2) I was absolutely devastated when I heard the news. *(non-gradable)*
3) This work of art is totally unique. *(non-gradable)*
4) It's very important to have good friends. *(gradable)*
5) Peter is extremely angry with Sarah today. *(gradable)*
6) The documentary is extremely interesting. *(gradable)*
7) These photographs are very good. *(gradable)*
8) David's new house is absolutely enormous. *(non-gradable)*
9) I'm totally starving. What's for dinner? *(non-gradable)*

Adverbs of Time Exercises

✓ Add the adverb given in brackets into each sentence.

Answer

(Except for "just", "all day", and "now", you can use the adverb at the start too.)
1) Robin Hood swindled the Sheriff of Nottingham yesterday.
2) I'm sick of living in chaos, so I'm going to clean my house today.
3) She stayed at her grandmother's house all day.
4) My father was up with the heartburn for hours.
5) She was born in 1978.
6) They're tired because they've just arrived home.
7) There was a storm during the night.
8) They have lived here since 2004.
9) My mother lived in France for a year.
10) We should leave now.

Adverbs of Frequency Exercises

✓ Add the adverb given in brackets into each sentence.

Answer

1) I always remember to do my homework.
2) He normally gets good marks in exams.
3) They are never pleased to see me.
4) She isn't usually bad tempered.
5) She can sometimes beat me in a race.
6) I would hardly ever be unkind to someone.
7) They might never see each other again.
8) They could occasionally be heard laughing.
9) I normally walk to work.
10) I seldom put pepper on my food.

Adverbs of Place Exercises

✓ **Add the adverb given in brackets into each sentence.**

Answer *(You can use some adverbs in different positions.)*
1) You have to go upstairs for the men's bathroom.
2) I could find him nowhere.
3) She took the child outside.
4) I'm going back to school in September.
5) Maya looked upwards to the sky.
6) Don't go in. There's someone inside.
7) Oscar travelled onward to Los Angeles.
8) The parents searched far and near for their child.
9) The school is within walking distance of my house.
10) Tina dropped the ball, and it rolled down the hill.

Adverbs of Affirmation & Negation Exercises

✓ **Add the adverb given in brackets into each sentence.**

Answer
1) I would obviously feel awesome about your comment.
2) The family truly embraces the Western culture.
3) The soldier should certainly get an award for bravery.
4) Ryan exactly knows the right thing to do.
5) They are definitely leaving tomorrow.
6) Mark doubtlessly agrees on his side.
7) He is not very active.
8) Simon rarely visits his mom on weekends.
9) I never talk to him this way.
10) Narendra Modi is undoubtedly a great politician.

Chapter 16

Prepositions of Place Exercises 01

✓ **Put appropriate prepositions in the blanks.**

Answer
1) I'm currently in a cab right now; I'll be with you in a couple of minutes.
2) Have you seen my car keys? I swear I left them on the table yesterday.
3) Right by/next to/beside my house, there's a nice park. I go there for strolls every day.
4) It's so hot; I need some air conditioning. Let's go into that building.
5) I've just arrived at the train station. Where are you?
6) Walk 300 meters down this way; the building you're looking for should be on your right.
7) Sally's at the hospital right now. I'll have her call you back when she returns home.
8) Here's a present I brought for you all the way from my hometown.
9) I'm travelling to Switzerland next week for a family trip.
10) Whoa! A seagull just flew over my head!

✓   **Put appropriate prepositions in the blanks (cont'd).**

Answer

1) No, there isn't a monster **under** your bed. There's not enough space for one in the first place.
2) Be careful when you jump **across** that gap. Your foot might get stuck in there.
3) What's that loud sound? / There's a plane flying right **above** our house right now.
4) A butterfly just landed **on top of** the dog's nose! Look how still he's being not to disturb it!
5) Come sit **by** me. I purposefully left this seat empty for you.
6) Oh, it's raining! Quickly, let's go **under** that awning.
7) There's a convenience store **between** my house and my school. I always visit it after school.
8) I know you're hiding **behind** that tree; I can see your hair sticking out!
9) The police arrested the person who parked **in front of** the fire station, blocking the garage.
10) There's no department store **near** my home! I have to take the bus every time I need food.

Prepositions of Time Exercises 01

✓   **Put appropriate prepositions in the blanks.**

Answer

1) This place has been under renovation **since** last year. I have no idea when they'll finish.
2) Smith has been working here **for** ten years already! Today's party is to honor him!
3) I need to get a haircut **before** this Saturday. I have to attend a wedding then.
4) Wow, I had no idea that "naïve" came from French **until** you just told me now.
5) Jack worked in this school **between (from)** Jan 2019 **and (to)** Dec 2020.
6) **During** last year alone, Peter has lost fifty pounds!
7) You must arrive **by** half **past** seven (7:30), or you won't be allowed to enter the show.
8) It's currently quarter **to** nine (8:45), and I still haven't had my dinner!
9) **By** next Sunday, the winner of the contest will have been decided.

Prepositions of Time Exercises 02

✓   **Put either "on", "in", or "at" in the blanks.**

Answer

1) He always jogs **in** the morning; I meet him every day while I'm going to work.
2) I have a doctor's appointment **on** Monday, so I won't be able to pick you up from school.
3) It never gets cold in Los Angeles – even **in** the winter!
4) **At** lunchtime today, a fire started in the cafeteria, so the teachers ordered lunch in for us.
5) Back **in** the '70s, Daejeon was nothing but farms.
6) My father and I always go hiking **on** the weekends.
7) We left our house an hour ago. We'll be there **in** half an hour.
8) There was a robbery here **at** 7 o'clock yesterday.
9) In the Gangwon province, it sometimes snows even **in** March.

Other Prepositions Exercises

✓ Put appropriate prepositions in the blanks.

Answer
1) This book is a present **from** Yvonne. It's written **by** my favorite author, Charles Dickens.
2) The suspect escaped the scene **on** foot.
3) I just got **off** the train. I'll be there in twenty minutes.
4) Sean Connery passed away **at** the age of 90, **in** 2020.
5) I got **out of** my car **without** my umbrella, and I got soaked.
6) It only takes six minutes to get there **by** car; we can probably walk.
7) Come join us! We were just about to have a discussion **about** the book *The Giver*.
8) I arrived at her birthday party **with** just minutes to spare.

Dependent Prepositions Exercises

✓ Put appropriate prepositions in the blanks.

Answer

The police have just announced that they have apprehended the criminal **responsible for** the jewelry shop theft last week. **According to** the spokesperson, the investigators noticed that the burglary was very **similar to** the one that happened in the neighboring town several weeks ago, following their inspection of the crime scene. From this, they theorized that the suspect could be particularly **interested in** diamond sellers. **Based on** their hypothesis, they **advised** nearby police departments to **keep their eyes out for** suspicious people **hovering around** diamond-bearing jewelry stores. Around 8 o'clock today, a policeman noticed a suspicious person in front of the Zales store on 5th Ave. He seemed to be **hooked on** a diamond necklace on display, **unaware of** the policeman approaching him. When he finally noticed the policeman, he tried to **escape from** him, but the policeman soon **caught up to** him. When questioned, the suspect **insisted on** his innocence for a long time, stating that he has never **heard of/about** the robbery. But he eventually **gave in** and **admitted to** his actions. Despite the criminal **begging for** mercy, the police **intend to sentence** him **to** at least five years in prison.

Chapter 17

Coordinating Conjunctions Exercises 01

✓ Put in the appropriate coordinating conjunction in each blank.

Answer
1) We were out of milk, **so** I went to the store to buy some.
2) The children ran **and** jumped all over the playground.
3) Would you like cereal **or** toast for breakfast? *(either one)*
4) The old castle seemed grand **yet** haunting.
5) Slowly **but** surely, the turtled finished the race.
6) This bowl of French onion soup is hot **and** delicious.
7) Rocky refuses to eat dry cat food, **nor** will he touch a can of tuna.
8) They next bus was scheduled too late, **so** I decided to take the taxi.
9) Juanita eats healthy, **for** she wants to stay in shape.
10) I really want a kitten, **yet** my mom says we have too many cats already.

Subordinating Conjunctions Exercises

✓ **Identify inappropriate subordinating conjunctions and fix them**

Answer
(These are the best options; others may work too.)
1) Although my mom told me to come home early, I stayed out late. → OK!
2) She didn't know she was a talented singer after she sang in the school concert. → until
3) You will not pass the exam unless you work harder. → OK!
4) Everyone looked at me when I came in the room. → OK!
5) Robin wasn't allowed in the car anymore so that he wouldn't wear a seatbelt. → because
6) As if his father got home, Jack took a secret ride in his father's car. → after
7) Since Fei refused to pay her electric bills, electricity was cut from her house. → OK!
8) Even though the semester is over, I can focus more on my health. → now that
9) I'll start working on Mr. Finch's homework while his class finishes. → as soon as
10) He took off for the traffic light as if someone was chasing after him. → OK!

Chapter 18

"It" Exercises

✓ **Rewrite the following sentences using the dummy subject, "it".**

Answer
1) It is important to be honest with each other in a relationship.
2) It is essential to know when to give up for a happy life.
3) It is helpful to read articles from respected news agencies to improve your vocabulary.
4) It is always fascinating to learn about your country's recent history from your parents because they've actually lived through that era.

"There" Exercises

✓ **Rewrite the following sentences using the dummy subject, "there".**

Answer
1) There was a big argument between my parents during dinner yesterday.
2) There are more than 3,000 deadly sick patients in this hospital right now because of the pandemic.
3) There is a construction taking place just two kilometers away from my house of what is to be the biggest mall in this city.
4) There are only two professional electricians in this town.

Chapter 19

Relative Pronouns & Their Uses Exercises

✓ **Put appropriate relative pronouns in the blanks.**

Answer
1) I need a television which/that works!
2) Her necklace, which she'd just bought, was stolen.
3) Jay, who(m) I used to live with, came to stay with us for a few days.
4) I'm looking for a job which/that I'll enjoy.
5) Do you know anyone who/that knows how to fix a bike?
6) He's the actor who/that we saw last week.
7) The suspect, who(m) we had been following for many days, was arrested.
8) The book which/that I just read is excellent.
9) We spoke to Linda, who had recently been mugged.
10) Our new house, which is by the beach, is beautiful.

Defining & Non-Defining Relative Clauses Exercises

✓ **Identify the relative clause in each sentence as either defining (D) or non-defining (ND).**

Answer
1) __D_ I'm writing about people who commit crimes.
2) __D_ I saw the car which the criminal stole.
3) _ND__ All the burglars were arrested, which was a great relief.
4) __D_ They live in a house whose roof is full of holes.
5) _ND__ We stopped at the museum, which we had never visited before.
6) _ND__ Yesterday I met a woman named Susan, whose husband works in London.
7) __D_ The dish that I ordered was delicious.
8) _ND__ Stratford-on-Avon, which many people have written about, is Shakespeare's birthplace.
9) __D_ There's something that you should know.

Relative Adverbs Exercises

✓ **Put in appropriate relative adverbs in the blanks.**

Answer
1) I've just come back from London, where John lives.
2) The reason why I came here today is not important.
3) Let's go to a country where the sun always shines.
4) I remember my twentieth birthday. It was the day when the tsunami hit.
5) Do you remember the place where we caught the train?
6) There's a new system whereby students submit their work online.
7) I still remember the day when I met him.
8) 1821 is the year when Napoleon Bonaparte died.
9) This is exactly the reason why they don't let you run in museums.

Shortening Relative Clauses Exercises

✓ **Shorten the following sentences, if possible.**

Answer

1) My grandmother, who is dead now, came from the North of England. → Impossible
2) He gave me the letter that was in a blue envelope. → Impossible
3) Everything (that) you say seems silly to me.
4) The doctor (whom) I was hoping to see wasn't on duty.
5) He sent me the email, which I read immediately. → Impossible
6) This is the best film (that) I've ever seen.
7) I'm sorry, but that is all that I saw. → Impossible
8) Ralph's father, who lives in Australia, has four grandchildren. → Impossible
9) Nothing (that) anyone does can make me happy right now.
10) Do you have anything that will help my throat? → Impossible

Common Mistakes Exercises 01

✓ **Identify what's wrong with the following sentences and fix the errors. Some sentences may not have any errors in them.**

Answer

1) I don't know the person **from that** I received this package. → WRONG!
   → I don't know the person that I received this package from.
   OR I don't know the person who(m) I received this package from.
   OR I don't know the person from who(m) I received this package.
2) My boss, **that** is very nice, lives in Manchester. → WRONG!
   → My boss, who is very nice, lives in Manchester.
3) Chris did awfully in his exams, which is quite a surprise.
   → OK!
4) Michael Faraday is the **man invented** the electric motor. → WRONG!
   → Michael Faraday is the man who/that invented the electric motor.

Common Mistakes Exercises 02

✓ **Identify what's wrong with the following sentences and fix the errors. Some sentences may not have any errors in them (cont'd).**

Answer

1) This is the fence that Tay painted **it**. → WRONG!
   → This the fence that Tay painted.
2) This is the textbook with which I studied math during my high school freshman year.
   → OK!
3) The woman my brother loves is from Mexico.
   → OK!
4) My sister, **that** I live with, knows a lot about computers. → WRONG!
   → My sister, who I live with, knows a lot about computers.

Chapter 20

How to Form the Passive Exercises

✓ **Rewrite the following sentences in the passive voice; include the subject**

1) "Hey Jude" <u>was written</u> by The Beatles.
2) This house <u>has been being built</u> by my father for two years.
3) Chester's fence <u>is being painted</u> by him. → *Watch out for your pronoun usage!*
4) The lion <u>had been killed</u> by the hunter already when he realized that it was off-season.

✓ **Rewrite the following sentences in the passive voice; drop the subject.**

1) Waste materials <u>are disposed of</u> in a variety of ways.
2) The windows <u>have been cleaned</u>.
3) Lunch <u>was being served</u>.
4) The doors <u>will be locked</u> at ten o'clock.

When to Use the Passive Exercises 01

✓ **Between the active (A) and passive (P) voice, pick the more natural one.**

Answer

1) ~~A: Someone broke into our house last night.~~
   P: Our house was broken into last night (by someone).
2) A: I am studying astrophysics.
   ~~P: Astrophysics is being studied (by me).~~
3) ~~A: The workers will have prepared the pamphlets by Sunday.~~
   P: The pamphlets will have been prepared (by the workers) by Sunday.
4) ~~A: They have now removed the roadblock on 5th Avenue.~~
   P: The roadblock on 5th Avenue has been removed (by them).
5) A: I met Jane, my old friend, at the mall yesterday.
   ~~P: Jane, my old friend, was met (by me) at the mall yesterday.~~

When to Use the Passive Exercises 02

✓ **The following sentences are all in the active voice. Rewrite the ones that you think the passive voice would fit better**

Answer

1) Passive: English is spoken by many people around the world.
   → *The focus is "English", not "many people".*
2) Passive: The criminal has been sentenced to six years in prison.
   → *The agent (the judge) is obvious; judges are always the ones who punish criminals.*
3) Active: The train had left before we arrived at the station. → OK! *("left" = intransitive)*
4) Passive: The rats were administered with small doses of the test drug.
   → *The agent (the scientists) is unimportant.*
5) Active: I bought this shirt yesterday at the thrift shop. → OK!
6) Passive: The building was engulfed by fire. → *The building is more important than fire.*

Chapter 21

Basic Conditionals Exercises
(Watch your tenses!)

✓ Convert each set of cause & result into a zero conditional sentence.

1) If you heat ice, it melts.
2) If I drink too much coffee, I can't sleep at night.
3) If it rains, the grass gets wet.
4) If babies are hungry, they cry.

✓ Convert each set of cause & result into a first conditional sentence.

1) If the train is delayed, she will be late.
2) If she doesn't leave soon, she will miss the bus.
3) If it doesn't rain tomorrow, we will go to the beach.
4) If I have enough money, I will buy some new clothes.

Basic Conditionals Exercises
(Watch your tenses!)

✓ Convert each set of cause & result into a second conditional sentence.

1) If she studied, she would pass the exam.
2) If I spoke Italian, I would be working in Italy.
3) If you went to bed early, you wouldn't be tired.
4) If I were you, I wouldn't worry.

✓ Convert each set of cause & result into a third conditional sentence.

1) If I hadn't eaten so much, I wouldn't have been sick.
2) If we had taken a taxi, we wouldn't have missed the plane.
3) If she had gone to a university, she would have become a teacher.
4) If he had left his house at nine, he would have been on time for the interview.

Basic Conditionals Exercises
(Watch your tenses!)

✓ Convert each set of cause & result into a mixed conditional sentence.

1) We look at the map. → We are not lost.
2) I work harder at school. → I have a better job now.
3) I don't get the job in Tokyo. → I am not with my current partner.
4) You decide to study. → You are a professor now.

✓ **Rewrite each conditional sentence by stating the result first.**

1) If you freeze water, ice forms.
2) If I go jogging, I will lose weight.
3) If I knew her number, I would call her.
4) If I had woken up on time, I would have done my hair.

Basic Conditionals Exercises

✓ **Identify the following conditionals into either zero ("0"), first ("1"), second ("2"), third ("3"), or mixed ("M").**

1) _0_ If you heat ice, it melts.
2) _M_ If you'd been born a month earlier, you would be a Virgo like me.
3) _3_ If you'd been wearing a coat, you might have stayed warm.
4) _2_ If I had more time, I could take up karate.
5) _2_ I'd call him if I had his number.
6) _0_ Oil floats when you pour it onto water.
7) _1_ If it snows, I'll go skiing.
8) _3_ I could have been a doctor if I'd studied harder.
9) _1_ If we go to Africa, we'll go on a safari.

English Grammar for Matriductive Learners

엄마표 영어로 인풋이 안정된 친구들을 위한 영문법

초판 1쇄 인쇄 2022년 6월 3일
초판 1쇄 발행 2022년 6월 17일

지은이 AJ(안재환)

대표 장선희 **총괄** 이영철
기획편집 이소정, 정시아, 한이슬, 현미나
디자인 김효숙, 최아영 **외주디자인** 이창욱
마케팅 최의범, 강주영, 김현진, 이동희
경영관리 문경국

펴낸곳 서사원 **출판등록** 제2021-000194호
주소 서울시 영등포구 당산로 54길 11 상가 301호
전화 02-898-8778 **팩스** 02-6008-1673
이메일 cr@seosawon.com
블로그 blog.naver.com/seosawon
페이스북 www.facebook.com/seosawon
인스타그램 www.instagram.com/seosawon

ⓒAJ(안재환), 2022

ISBN 979-11-6822-077-5 13740

• 이 책은 저작권법에 따라 보호를 받는 저작물이므로 무단 전재와 무단 복제를 금지합니다.
• 이 책 내용의 전부 또는 일부를 이용하려면 반드시 저작권자와 서사원 주식회사의 서면 동의를 받아야 합니다.
• 잘못된 책은 구입하신 서점에서 바꿔드립니다.
• 책값은 뒤표지에 있습니다.

서사원은 독자 여러분의 책에 관한 아이디어와 원고 투고를 설레는 마음으로 기다리고 있습니다. 책으로 엮기를 원하는 아이디어가 있는 분은 이메일 cr@seosawon.com으로 간단한 개요와 취지, 연락처 등을 보내주세요. 고민을 멈추고 실행해보세요. 꿈이 이루어집니다.